Child Care and Adoption L
A Practical Guide

Child Care and Adoption Law
A Practical Guide

The Hon Mr Justice McFarlane

Madeleine Reardon
Barrister, 1 King's Bench Walk, London

Published by
Jordan Publishing Limited
21 St Thomas Street
Bristol BS1 6JS

British Library Cataloguing-in-Publication Data

A catalogue record for this book is available from the British Library.

ISBN 0 85308 972 8

Typeset by Columns Design Ltd, Reading, Berkshire
Printed and bound in Great Britain by Antony Rowe Ltd, Chippenham, Wilts

FOREWORD

All professionals working with children, whether teachers, social workers, nurses or doctors have at times to grapple with legal matters. This book is a simple and accessible guide. It explains the jargon, whether this is the categories of persons with parental responsibility, a section 8 order, hearsay evidence, or inherent jurisdiction.

The book comprises eight main sections; an introduction to child protection and adoption, 'from 999 call to adoption' as the authors put it; parental responsibilities and disputes between parents; local authorities and the family; referrals, assessments and emergency intervention; care and supervision orders; adoption; secure accommodation; and wardship.

The contents comprise the legal nuts and bolts of all these topics. The authors have managed to turn a dry subject (the law) into an explanation that requires no legal or specialist knowledge on the part of the reader. The text is helpfully broken up into small numbered elements, with numerous sub-headings, making it simple to look up, and follow, any topic. The book also contains some useful worked examples of problems, such as a 16-year-old boy in care, who has moved to a new foster family following the breakdown of a previous placement. The new foster parents lock him in his bedroom when he becomes drunk and abusive. Was locking the door lawful? What should happen next? For the answers, and for many other useful problem scenarios, read the book!

Tim David

Professor of Child Health, University of Manchester
Honorary Consultant Paediatrician,
Booth Hall Children's Hospital, Manchester

August 2006

PREFACE

The aim of this book can be simply stated. It is to provide a comprehensive overview of the law relating to child protection and adoption for the use of those who do not need the specialist knowledge of a child care lawyer. We hope that this text will be of value to all those who need to know the landscape of child care law in order better to carry out their own specialist role; for example health professionals, teachers, non-child care specialist lawyers and others who work with children. In addition parents and prospective adopters, who may find themselves in court proceedings, may be assisted by the route map that we have attempted to provide.

Hitherto the law relating to child protection and the law relating to adoption, which had each developed separately, have found themselves sown together in a sometimes ill-matched patchwork. The Adoption and Children Act 2002 regulating adoption law, which came into force on 30 December 2005, has been drawn up to mirror and dovetail with its companion, the Children Act 1989, which governs the general law relating to children. For the first time these two core statutes, together with the Human Rights Act 1998, provide a seamless, legislative whole. It is thus timely to be writing one book that seeks to describe this unified scheme.

Jargons and acronyms appear only so that they may be explained. The text is not overburdened with references to case law; however we have explained the content of the key court decisions in their proper context. The aim throughout has been to present a description of the law in an uncomplicated and clear narrative. The law can only function effectively if it is readily understood by all who have to use it. Our hope is that this modest work will provide a plain-speaking guide for all those concerned with the protection of children, whatever their specialist role or interest.

This preface is being written on Lammas Day. Lammas was traditionally the day upon which the first bread was made with wheat from the new harvest; it is a time of new beginning. As our first collaborative effort 'comes out of the oven', this chance analogy does not seem wholly inappropriate!

Andrew McFarlane

Madeleine Reardon
One Kings Bench Walk
London

1 August 2006

CONTENTS

TABLE OF CASES

TABLE OF STATUTES

TABLE OF STATUTORY INSTRUMENTS

TABLE OF ABBREVIATIONS

AA 1976	Adoption Act 1976
AAR 2005	Adoption Agencies Regulations 2005
ACA 2002	Adoption and Children Act 2002
ACACRR 2005	Adopted Children and Adoption Contact Registers Regulations 2005
AIIS(PC)R 2005	Adoption Information and Intermediary Services (Pre-Commencement Adoptions) Regulations 2005
APC(G)R 1991	Arrangements for Placement of Children (General) Regulations 1991
C(AP)O 1991	Children (Allocation of Proceedings) Order 1991
C(LC)R 2001	Children (Leaving Care) (England) Regulations 2001
C(PAF)R 2005	Children (Private Arrangements for Fostering) Regulations 2005
C(SA)R 1991	Children (Secure Accommodation) Regulations 1991
C(SA)R(No 2)R 1991	Children (Secure Accommodation) (No 2) Regulations 1991
CA 1989	Children Act 1989
CAA 2006	Children and Adoption Act 2006
CAFCASS	Children and Family Advisory and Support Service
CDA 1998	Crime and Disorder Act 1998
CYPA 1969	Children and Young Persons Act 1969
ECHR	European Convention on Human Rights
ECtHR	European Court of Human Rights
FLRA 1987	Family Law Reform Act 1987
FP(A)R 2005	Family Procedure (Adoption) Rules 2005
FPC(CA1989)R 1991	Family Proceedings Court (Children Act 1989) Regulations 1991
FPR 1991	Family Proceedings Rules 1991
FSR 2002	Fostering Services Regulations 2002
HFEA 1990	Human Fertilisation and Embryology Act 1990
HRA 1998	Human Rights Act 1998
IRO	Independent Reviewing Officer

LAC Review	Looked After Child Review
LASSA 1970	Local Authority Social Services Act 1970
LASSC(E)R) 2006	Local Authority Social Services Complaints (England) Regulations
PCPR 1991	Placement of Children with Parents etc Regulations 1991
RCCR 1991	Review of Children's Cases Regulations 1991
SOA 2003	Sexual Offences Act 2003
SSCP(W)R) 2005	Social Services Complaints Procedure (Wales) Regulations
UNCRC	United Nations Convention on the Rights of the Child

1

CHILD PROTECTION AND ADOPTION: INTRODUCTION

Chapter Summary

- Introduction
- Children Act 1989 – structure and key principles
- The family courts
- Family Proceedings Rules 1991
- Adoption and Children Act 2002
- Human rights legislation and conventions
- Statutory rules and Government guidance
- Wardship and the inherent jurisdiction

1.1 The modern reformulation of the law relating to child protection and of the law relating to adoption took place some 13 years apart, but there are striking similarities to the gestation of each of these separate reforms. In each case proposals for reform had been developed over a period of years, but had failed to find a space in the government's legislative programme until a major scandal and ensuing public enquiry provided the political impetus for legislation. In the case of child protection the Review of Child Care Law began in 1984 and produced recommendations which the government adopted and produced as a White Paper, 'The Law on Child Care and Family Services' in 1987, but it was not until the Butler-Sloss Inquiry into child sexual abuse allegations in Cleveland[1] reported in July 1988 and recommended the 'urgent' implementation of these reforms that the issue was taken up as a government priority and led to the Children Act 1989. Similarly the government Adoption Law Review was announced in 1989 and resulted in a detailed blueprint for reform in 1992. There followed a White Paper in 1993 and a draft Adoption Bill in 1996, yet it was not until the

1 *Report of the Inquiry into Child Abuse in Cleveland 1987* (1988) Cm 412.

publication of the Waterhouse Inquiry into abuse in residential children's homes in Wales in 2000 that the Prime Minister announced a review of adoption law by the Performance and Innovation Unit of the Cabinet Office, which resulted in a further White Paper[2] in December 2000 and in due course the passing of the Adoption and Children Act 2002.

1.2 The Children Act 1989 and the Adoption and Children Act 2002 are each wide-ranging and radical reforms of the previous law. The coming into force of the latter Act in December 2005 completes the process of reform and, for the first time, adoption law is fully compatible with the new law relating to children under the 1989 Act that has been in force since 1991. The two sets of provisions complement each other and provide a unified code, from '999 call to adoption', for the protection of children from abuse. The purpose of this Practitioner's Guide is to describe this code of law in plain, non-legal, terms so that all practitioners engaged in work with children may gain a ready understanding of the new legal landscape and so that they may be better able to use the system to meet the needs of individual children.

1.3 The following chapters look at individual aspects of child protection and adoption law. In order to see these details in context, we will look first at the structure and themes of the legislation.

CHILDREN ACT 1989

Parental responsibility

1.4 The Children Act 1989 (CA 1989) covers both the private law (as between parents and family members) and public law (state involvement) relating to children. Central to both elements of the CA 1989 is the key concept of 'parental responsibility'.[3] Parental responsibility is the whole bundle of duties that a parent may have towards their child, together with the parallel powers and authority (previously 'parental rights') over him. A mother will have parental responsibility for her child from birth; a father will either have it automatically (for example because he is married to the mother) or may be able to acquire it by agreement or court order. In the context of child protection, a local authority will acquire parental responsibility, and the power to control the exercise of parental responsibility by anyone else, when a care order is made. If an adoption order is made, its principal effect will be that parental responsibility held by the natural parents will

---

2 *Adoption: a new approach.*

3 Parental responsibility is more fully considered in Chapter 2.

be extinguished and parental responsibility will be acquired by the adopters. Much of the private law relating to children is concerned with the exercise, or control, of parental responsibility in circumstances where those who hold it may be in dispute with each other.[4]

Welfare is paramount

1.5 A second key concept in the CA 1989, and one that is again common to both private and public law, is that the child's welfare must be the court's paramount consideration when determining any question with respect to the upbringing of a child.[5] This principle is fleshed out in a 'welfare checklist' which lists seven generic sets of circumstances which, to a greater or lesser extent, will be important in determining the 'welfare issue' in each case. The paramountcy principle and the welfare checklist apply when a court is considering whether to make, vary or discharge a public law order under CA 1989, Part IV or a private law order under Part II.[6]

Child protection

1.6 Moving away from principles which are common to both private and public law, the CA 1989 deals with issues of child protection in the following Parts (groups of sections):

- Part III Local authority support for children and families (ss 17–30)
- Part IV Care and Supervision (ss 31–42)
- Part V Protection of Children (ss 43–52).

Subsequent parts of CA 1989 make provision for many of the services provided for children (for example, children's homes, child minding and private fostering).

1.7 The structure of Parts III to V is set upon the premise that local authorities have a statutory duty to provide services for 'children in need' and their families.[7] The expectation within the legislation is that where a child is in need, the local authority for the area in which he lives will, without the need for court proceedings, make the necessary provision of services to meet his needs. In the process it is anticipated

---

4 A detailed consideration of the private law relating to children is beyond the scope of this book. Readers are referred to the companion title Mitchell *Children Act Private Law Proceedings: A Handbook* (Family Law, 2006).

5 CA 1989, s 1(1).

6 For the welfare principle in care proceedings, see Chapter 5. For private law proceedings, see Chapter 2.

7 CA 1989, s 17; see **3.10**.

that those who have parental responsibility for the child will work in partnership with the local authority. A clear example of this process occurs where the parents and social services are agreed that the child should live away from home and be 'provided with accommodation' by the local authority.[8] To the lay observer the child will be being 'put into care', but the process is not one that involves court proceedings or a care order and is accomplished entirely upon a voluntary basis.

1.8 In many cases where a child is in need, which might include the need to be protected from abuse, the whole process of child protection may be accomplished by agreement without resort to a court. However, where a local authority perceives the need to intervene in a family's care of a child in a way that is resisted (or is likely to be resisted) by those with parental responsibility, the case will move out of CA 1989, Part III and into the territory of Part IV with the local authority seeking public law orders (care order or supervision order) from the court in order to protect the child.

Care order and supervision order

1.9 The primary provision within Part IV is s 31 which provides that a court may only make a care order or supervision order with respect to a child if it is satisfied:

(a) that the child concerned is suffering, or is likely to suffer, significant harm; and
(b) that the harm, or likelihood of harm, is attributable to:
  (i) the care given to him, or likely to be given to him if the order were not made, not being what it would be reasonable to expect a parent to give to him; or
  (ii) the child's being beyond parental control.

The criteria in s 31 (known as the 'threshold criteria') are the minimum circumstances which must be found to exist before a court can even begin to contemplate whether the state should be enabled to intervene compulsorily in family life.

1.10 If the circumstances of the child are not found to be sufficient to satisfy s 31, the threshold is not crossed and the court does not have jurisdiction to consider whether the child's welfare requires that a care or supervision order be made. That this should be so can readily be understood by considering just how much power is given to a local authority if a care order is indeed made at the end of care proceedings. If a care order is granted a local authority is given parental responsibility for the child, together with the power to control the use of

---

8 CA 1989, s 20.

parental responsibility by any other person. Under a care order a local authority may, for example, keep a child in foster care for the remainder of her childhood. Further, the local authority may use its status under a care order to move the child forward towards adoption and the permanent severing of the child's link with her natural family.

1.11 If a care order is made, save for the jurisdiction of the court under s 34 to regulate the degree of contact that the child has with other people, the responsibility for maintaining a care plan for the child, and for delivering that care, will be that of the local authority and not that of the court.

1.12 A supervision order, which like a care order requires the court to be satisfied that the threshold criteria are made out, is a lower level of state intervention under which the local authority does not acquire parental responsibility for the child. Under a supervision order the local authority is required to advise, assist and befriend the named child for a finite period of time (initially no more than a year).

1.13 An application for a care order ('care proceedings') will typically take a number of months to process from the date of the application being made to the court's final determination. During that time evidence will be gathered and assessments made of the need to protect the child and of the plan that will best meet the child's needs. The question will therefore arise in each case as to the arrangements for the care of the child during the interim period. In some cases these arrangements will be agreed between the local authority and the parents without the need for a court order. In the event of a disagreement, or where there is a need for the local authority to have parental responsibility pending the final hearing, the court has the power to make an interim care order (or an interim supervision order).

Emergency powers

1.14 The final element in the structure of CA 1989 that directly relates to child protection is in Part V, which contains a range of provisions for the emergency, or short term, protection of a child. The two central facilities provided by Part V are the jurisdiction of the court to make an Emergency Protection Order (s 44) and the power of the police to accommodate a child in a case of emergency (s 46). Where there are no pending court care proceedings, and no interim care order, the use of an emergency protection order will often be the first resort available to the court in a child protection case which has suddenly developed into a perceived emergency need to provide short term and immediate protection for a child. The making of the an EPO will frequently be followed by the issue of a full blown application for a care order and, within that, an application for an interim care order once the initial EPO expires.

THE FAMILY COURTS

1.15 There is at present no unified 'Family Court'. Three levels of the court structure may hear a public law case under CA 1989 or an adoption case under the Adoption and Children Act 2002 (ACA 2002): a Family Proceedings Court (ie a magistrates court), a care centre (or adoption centre) county court or the Family Division of the High Court. There is provision for the transfer of cases between the various levels of court. The unified courts' structure established by the Courts Act 2003 has brought all three levels of court within the same establishment (Her Majesty's Courts Service) and, so far as family courts are concerned, the President of the Family Division of the High Court is the administrative head of the family justice system. Each of the six circuits (or regions) in England and Wales is headed by a Family Division Liaison Judge (in the South East the role is shared by three judges) who act as the President's lieutenants in the regions. Each county court care centre is presided over by a Designated Family Judge and each FPC has a panel of justices authorised to hear family cases with a chair at its head.

1.16 From time to time the President of the Family Division will issue Practice Directions designed to establish a unified practice in relation to the delivery of family justice in all three levels of court across the jurisdiction of England and Wales. Northern Ireland and Scotland are separate jurisdictions; the statute law in Northern Ireland is similar to that in England and Wales, but the system in Scotland is very different.

FAMILY PROCEEDINGS RULES 1991

1.17 The court's jurisdiction under CA 1989 is accessed and delivered by means of detailed procedural rules (Family Proceedings Rules 1991). At present a separate set of rules (Family Proceedings Court (Children Act 1989) Rules 1991) govern procedure in the magistrates' court. The Family Procedure Rules Committee aims to produce one set of rules governing all courts by 2007.

1.18 Most public law cases are required to start in the local Family Proceedings Court, but there is provision for cases to be transferred to the appropriate level of court depending upon factors such as complexity and length of hearing.

1.19 The parties to care proceedings will be the applicant local authority, the parents and the child. Other parties may be added by the court. The child, no matter how young, will be represented by a children's guardian and a solicitor. The children's guardian will be a professional social worker employed by the Children and Family Court Advisory and Support Service (CAFCASS). The need for a voice for the child, which is separate and independent from the social services and the parents, was identified in a number of public inquiries in the 1980's,[9] and the resulting 'tandem model' of representation (guardian and solicitor) is valued by the courts.

1.20 Care proceedings are normally heard in private and there are restrictions within the rules upon the disclosure of any material that is put before the court to most outsiders. Often where serious abuse is alleged, there will be a parallel police investigation and a consequent need to consider and control the flow of material evidence between the care proceedings and the police.

1.21 In care proceedings the court has to consider two basic issues:

(i) are the threshold criteria (significant harm) in CA 1989, s 31 met in respect of the child;

if so the court has jurisdiction to make a care or supervision order and must ask:

(ii) taking the child's welfare as the paramount consideration, is any CA 1989 order required and, if so, which order is the most appropriate.

The principle that the child's welfare is paramount only applies to stage (ii). It is not uncommon for the court to conduct a 'split hearing' whereby the 'threshold' question and any necessary fact-finding are conducted at stage one, and the final 'welfare' stage is conducted at a later date after further time for consideration and assessment.

1.22 An aggrieved party may seek permission to appeal against a decision.

ADOPTION AND CHILDREN ACT 2002

1.23 The law relating to adoption in England and Wales is entirely regulated by statute. Prior to 2006 the applicable law had last been fundamentally reformed nearly 30 years earlier, had become out of line

---

9 Jasmine Beckford (1985); Tyra Henry (1987); Kimberley Carlile (1989) and Doreen Aston (1989).

with the modern approach to adoption work and did not dovetail easily in places with the CA 1989. Following a series of extensive reviews of adoption law, the ACA 2002 was passed and was brought into force on 30 December 2005. The ACA 2002, and the vast body of statutory instruments that underpin it, regulate all aspects of the adoption process and are described in Chapter 6.

1.24 In essence 'adoption' in English law is the process by which a child becomes regarded in law as the child of the adopter(s) and of no other person. Any parental responsibility that any person previously had for the child is extinguished by the adoption order and the child is regarded as if he had been born to the adopter(s). This state of affairs remains the case not just for the remainder of the child's childhood, but for life. Whilst the legal effect of adoption can thus be simply stated, the emotional and social consequence of such a fundamental dislocation of family relationships cannot be over-stated.

1.25 An adoption order may only be made if at one or more key stages in the process each parent with parental responsibility for the child has either agreed to the child being adopted or has had their agreement to adoption dispensed with. The only grounds for dispensing with consent are either (a) that the parent is incapable of consenting or cannot be found or (b) that the child's welfare requires that consent to be dispensed with. The child's welfare is the court's paramount consideration and a specially tailored adoption 'welfare checklist' must be applied.

1.26 One innovation introduced by ACA 2002 is to raise the step of 'placing a child for adoption' to that of a key stage in the process. A local authority, or adoption agency, may not place a child for adoption with prospective adopters unless they either have the consent of each parent with parental responsibility to do so, or they have obtained a 'placement order' from the court. This process replaces the previous scheme for obtaining an order 'freeing' the child for adoption.

RELATIONSHIP BETWEEN CARE PROCEEDINGS AND THE ADOPTION PROCESS

1.27 Whilst the legislation and procedure governing public law proceedings under CA 1989 and that governing proceedings under ACA 2002 are different and potentially free-standing, the reality in many cases is that there will be overlap between the two processes. Where during the currency of care proceedings a local authority forms the opinion that the child should be adopted rather than rehabilitated back to her family, it may (and in some circumstances must) issue an application for a placement order which can then be consolidated with the care proceedings. Thus the court will have the power at the conclusion of the consolidated proceedings not only to grant a care order approving a care plan for adoption, but to go further and make a placement order. The effect of a placement order is substantial and may well limit the parents' ability to oppose any subsequent adoption application. The consolidated proceedings in such a case may therefore be the main and only full hearing of the issues not only about care but also about adoption and parental consent.

WHO CAN ADOPT?

1.28 The paradigm image of adopters is of a mixed gender couple who are selected by an adoption agency to be substitute parents to a child who is in care. Many adoptions, however, involve members of the child's family, with the most obvious example being adoption by a step-parent in order to regularise relationships within a step-family. ACA 2002 widened the pool of potential adopters so that children may be adopted by 'couples' who may be of the same or different genders. A 'couple' will be a married couple, or civil partners or two people who are partners in an enduring family relationship. In addition, an adoption order may be made in favour of a single person.

INTER-COUNTRY ADOPTION

1.29 The need to regulate and control the adoption of children brought to the UK from another country achieved a national profile with the case of the 'internet twins' who were procured for adoption by Mr and Mrs Kilshaw in 2000. The responsibility of local authorities, central government, adoption agencies and the courts is now comprehensively established under ACA 2002 and the relevant statutory regulations.

FAMILY PROCEDURE (ADOPTION) RULES 2005

1.30 The procedure governing the court process in adoption proceedings is regulated at all three levels of family court by the Family Procedure (Adoption) Rules 2005 and associated Practice Directions.

HUMAN RIGHTS ACT 1998

1.31 The Human Rights Act 1998 (HRA 1998) requires a court in England and Wales and any official body to act in a manner that is compatible with the European Convention on Human Rights (ECHR). In addition, where any aspect of English law falls to be interpreted, such interpretation must be compatible with the ECHR unless that goal is impossible to achieve (in which case a court may make a 'declaration of incompatibility' which triggers a referral of the incompatible provision before Parliament with the potential for repeal or reform).

1.32 The HRA 1998 and the ECHR are considered in detail in Chapter 9. The impact of the ECHR affects all aspects of the state's intervention in the life of a child and family by care or adoption proceedings. Both the CA 1989 and the ACA 2002 were drawn up with the aim of compatibility with the ECHR. The key ECHR provision that is applicable to this field is Art 8 which requires respect for rights to family and private life. Put shortly, any step by the state (for example in the form of the social services or the court) to intervene in the life of a family will be in breach of Art 8, unless it can be shown that:

(a) the intervention is in accordance with the law;
(b) the intervention is to meet a legitimate need (for example the protection of the child);
(c) the intervention is necessary (in the sense of there being a pressing social need for it); and
(d) the level of proposed intervention is in proportion to the need to intervene.

Of these the latter two are the most influential and will dictate that the level of intervention justified to protect a child must be the least intrusive into the family's life with the child and for the shortest time that is necessary. Thus for example, where a supervision order is sufficient, that order, rather than the more intrusive care order, must be made. Another example is that, even where there is a care order, the aim should be for the child to be rehabilitated back to the family unless it is necessary to rule that option out and look for a long-term placement elsewhere.

1.33 The other ECHR article that is of particular relevance in this context is Art 6 which protects the right to a fair trial. Article 6 not only affects the trial process before the court, but a combination of Arts 6 and 8 mean that a family and child will have 'procedural rights' with respect to the manner in which the authorities involve them in any internal decision-making process before, during or after any court proceedings.

1.34 The family court is expected to conduct its proceedings in a manner that is compatible with the ECHR. Any specific points relating to the impact of the ECHR should be raised within those proceedings, and will not normally be subject to a separate, free-standing application under the HRA 1998.

THE UN CONVENTION ON THE RIGHTS OF THE CHILD

1.35 The United Nations Convention on the Rights of the Child (UNCRC) was adopted in 1989 and has been consented to by every state in the world save for Somalia, Timor-Leste and the USA. It is a wide-ranging statement of children's human rights encompassing the following four key principles:

- the right of children to participate in decisions affecting them (article 12);
- the right of children to protection and to prevention from harm (articles 2, 3, 8, 11, 16, 19, 22 and 32–38);
- the right of children to provision of basic needs (articles 17, 24, 26–28 and 31);
- the right of children for their best interests to be given priority.

Unlike the ECHR, the UNCRC is not incorporated into UK domestic law. The principles of the UNCRC are, however, at times referred to in court proceedings and have persuasive effect. Further, the UNCRC may be used as a tool to clarify and interpret the ECHR (which does have a direct effect upon domestic law).

STATUTORY RULES AND GOVERNMENT GUIDANCE

1.36 In addition to the main blocks of legislation contained within the CA 1989 and the ACA 2002, the law relating to child protection and adoption is regulated by a large body of statutory rules and regulations and government guidance. The statutory material makes detailed provision for various disparate topics from child minding to running a secure residential unit. Much of the engine room of the statutory scheme is in the rules and regulations.

1.37 In addition to the statutory material there is an additional layer of 'guidance' from central government. This 'guidance' is in fact binding upon local authorities by virtue of the Local Authority Social Services Act 1970, s 7. The guidance may take the form of substantial glossily published volumes (for example those accompanying the implementation of the CA 1989 and the ACA 2002) or more modestly presented circulars issued by the relevant government department (currently the Department for Education and Skills). Much of the guidance in force is available from the DFES website: www.dfes.gov.uk.

WALES

1.38 Social services functions within Wales are devolved to the Welsh Assembly, consequently separate statutory rules and regulations and guidance are issued for Wales. The substance of the Welsh provisions is very broadly identical to those for England; however, there are some minor differences. Regard should also be had to the fact that the implementation date for apparently similar provisions may differ as between the two parts of the jurisdiction.

FAMILY JUSTICE COUNCIL

1.39 The primary role of the Family Justice Council is to promote an inter-disciplinary approach to the needs of family justice, and through consultation and research, to monitor the effectiveness of the system and advise upon reforms necessary for continuous improvement. The FJC is chaired by the President of the Family Division and contains within its membership representatives from all levels of the judiciary, local authorities, the medical profession, CAFCASS, barristers and solicitors. The work of the FJC is undertaken both at national level and at local level with each care centre having its own local FJC. The FJC's website contains further information.[10]

WARDSHIP AND THE INHERENT JURISDICTION OF THE HIGH COURT

1.40 This description of the law and procedure relating to child protection and adoption has thus far been largely based upon 'black letter law' set out in Acts of Parliament, regulations or statutory guidance. There is however a parallel jurisdiction relating to children which is available to the High Court in cases which call for judicial intervention, yet fall outside the statutory system. This jurisdiction, known as the 'inherent jurisdiction', derives from the ancient right and duty of the Crown as *parens patriae* (parent of the state) to take care of those who are not able to take care of themselves.[11] The High Court's jurisdiction to do right in respect of the affairs of children or vulnerable adults is, in theory, unlimited and unrestricted; however, CA 1989 marks a clear boundary between the High Court's inherent jurisdiction and the statutory scheme for placing a child in care: a child may not be subject to both jurisdictions at the same time and the High Court may not place a child in care other than under the CA 1989 scheme.

1.41 Prior to the CA 1989 the inherent jurisdiction with respect to children was typically invoked through wardship proceedings, under

10 www.family-justice-council.org.uk
11 *Re L (An Infant)* [1968] 1 All ER 20.

which the child was made a 'ward of court'. The principal effects of being a ward of court are that the court itself has parental responsibility for the child and no important step in the child's life may be taken without the prior permission of the High Court. Whilst wardship remains available, and is still used in some cases, the inherent jurisdiction is now more frequently invoked without resort to wardship by way of a specific application based upon one aspect of parental responsibility.

1.42 Examples of the type of issue that might justify the use of the inherent jurisdiction are where there is dispute about the medical treatment of a child, or where an injunction is sought to control press publicity. The jurisdiction is flexible and constantly adapting to modern needs. In recent times, for example, there have been a number of orders made under the inherent jurisdiction to protect young people who may be subject to forced arranged marriages.

2

PARENTAL RESPONSIBILITY AND DISPUTES BETWEEN PARENTS

Chapter summary

- Introduction
- What is a parent?
- Parental responsibility
- Guardians and special guardians
- Section 8 orders
- Removing a child from the jurisdiction
- Section 8 orders: procedure
  - the application
  - respondents
  - welfare reports
  - the child as a party

INTRODUCTION

2.1 The law distinguishes between 'private' and 'public' disputes. 'Private law' concerns disputes between private individuals or bodies; 'public law' relates to the actions of the state in its various forms. In the context of child law, the interaction between local authorities and the family is at the heart of 'public law' proceedings. The bulk of this area of law consists of applications for care orders and other orders permitting state intervention in a family's life. It may also involve adoptions, which often include a high degree of local authority involvement, although the application for an adoption order itself is brought by the prospective adopters and not by the state.

2.2 'Private law' proceedings concern disputes between parents or other individuals with an interest in the child. A detailed consideration of private children law is outside the scope of this work.[1] It is, however, necessary for social workers and others who deal almost exclusively with public law cases to have an understanding of the framework of the private law. Many public law cases start as a private dispute between the child's parents; during the course of the proceedings it becomes evident that there is a need for a social services referral and the local authority becomes involved. The question of parental responsibility for a child – who has it, how it is gained and what it means – may also become significant when a local authority is seeking to take a child into care and in its subsequent interactions with the family.

2.3 The central statutory provisions governing private law children disputes are contained in the Children Act 1989 (CA 1989), Parts I and II.

WHAT IS A PARENT?

2.4 Under English common law, a woman who gives birth to a child is that child's mother. She automatically has parental responsibility for the child and will retain it throughout the child's minority unless the child is adopted.[2]

2.5 The position of the child's father is more complex. Where the child is born following a sexual relationship between a man and a woman, the man is the child's father for the purposes of the law.

2.6 Where a couple have together been involved in a course of assisted reproduction, the man will be treated as the father of any child conceived and born, regardless of whether or not he is the child's biological father.[3] The man has the right to withdraw from the treatment at any time until an embryo is implanted, and if he does so he will not be treated in law as the child's father. Children who are born by donor insemination, or following the withdrawal of consent to treatment by the woman's partner, are treated in law as having no father.

---

1 See Mitchell, *Children Act Private Law Proceedings: A Handbook* (2nd edn, Family Law, 2006).

2 Or unless a parental order is made under the HFEA 1990, s 30 transferring parental responsibility following a surrogacy agreement. For a detailed discussion of surrogacy, see Children Law and Practice, Hershman and McFarlane, Family Law A[174].

3 Human Fertilisation and Embryology Act 1990, s 23(3).

2.7 Upon the making of an adoption order, the child's adoptive parents become his parents and his birth parents are known as 'former parents'. They have no legal status with regard to the child and are legal strangers to him.[4]

DNA testing

2.8 Where the issue of a child's paternity arises during proceedings it is very likely that the court will wish it to be determined with the highest possible degree of certainty. In most cases this will mean by DNA testing. Section 20 of the Family Law Reform Act 1969 gives the court power in civil proceedings to direct that bodily tests should be carried out to establish whether or not a person is excluded from being a child's father. A sample cannot be taken from an adult without that person's consent, but the court may direct that a sample should be taken from a child if it considers that this would be in the child's best interests. The sample is generally one of saliva taken from a mouth swab, and any distress to the child is minimal.

2.9 In cases where paternity is in issue, it is very rare that a court will refuse to order DNA testing. In *Re H and A (Paternity: Blood Tests)*[5] Thorpe LJ said that there were two points of principle to be drawn from the authorities on paternity testing. The first is that 'the interests of justice are best served by the ascertainment of truth'. The second is that 'the court should be furnished with the best available science and not confined to such unsatisfactory alternatives as presumptions and inferences'.

2.10 An adult has the right to withhold consent to the taking of a bodily sample and therefore a direction under s 20 of the Family Law Reform Act 1987 should be phrased as a direction and not as an order. If he or she does refuse to submit to the sample, the court may draw inferences against him or her. This can cause problems when it is not entirely clear in which direction the inference should be drawn, and, in practice, if adults will not cooperate with testing, the child's paternity may remain unclear.

PARENTAL RESPONSIBILITY

What is it?

2.11 Parental responsibility was introduced as a new concept by the Children Act 1989. It is defined as 'all the rights, duties, powers,

---

4 Save for the purposes of Sch 1 to the Marriage Act 1949 and ss 10 and 11 of the Sexual Offences Act 1956 (incest and prohibited degrees of relationship). For these purposes the adopted child retains his links to the natural family.

5 [2002] 1 FLR 1145.

responsibilities and authority which by law a parent of a child has in relation to the child and his property'.[6]

2.12 Parental responsibility is a flexible concept. In most cases two parents, both with parental responsibility, will have an equal say in the child's upbringing and an equal right to make important decisions in his life, even if only one of them lives with the child.[7] However, the extent to which any person may exercise his parental responsibility may be shaped or restricted by order of the court, by the child's special guardian, or by a local authority holding a care order or a placement order in respect of the child.

2.13 Whether or not a person has parental responsibility does not affect his liability to maintain the child, or any rights which he may have to property inherited on the child's death.[8] An application to the Child Support Agency may be made against any parent, whether he has parental responsibility or not.

Who has it?

2.14 Since the Adoption and Children Act 2002 came into force the categories of persons with parental responsibility have been widened. The table below sets out the various persons or bodies who may have parental responsibility for a child, either for the duration of the child's minority or for a more limited period.

Relationship to child	Circumstances in which PR held	Relevant law
(Birth) mother	all circumstances, unless removed by adoption or by s 30 of the HFEA 1990	CA 1989, s 2(1), (2)(a)
Father	married to mother at child's birth or subsequently	CA 1989, s 2(1), (3)
Father	registered (or re-registered) as father on child's birth certificate after 1 December 2003	CA 1989, s 4(1)(a)
Father	who has entered into a PR agreement with mother	CA 1989, s 4(1)(b)
Father	who has been granted PR by the court	CA 1989, s 4(1)(c)

6 CA 1989, s 3(1).

7 This seems to be the import of CA 1989, s 2(7). The law on parental rights and decision-making is not clear: for a discussion of the arguments in the context of the decision whether or not to circumcise a child see *Re J* [2000] 1 FLR 571; and generally under 'specific issue orders' below.

8 CA 1989, s 3(4).

Father	with a residence order (separate PR order must be made so that the father retains PR even if the residence order is discharged)	CA 1989, s 12(1)
Other residence-order holder	for the duration of the residence order	CA 1989, s 12(2)
Guardian	For duration of appointment as guardian	CA 1989, s 5
Step-parent	who is married to or a civil partner of the child's parent and has entered into a PR agreement with all parents with PR or been granted PR by court order	CA 1989, s 4A(1)
Special guardian	for duration of special guardianship order	CA 1989, s 14C(1)(a)
Prospective adopter	when child is placed with him/her for adoption	ACA 2002, s 25(3)
Adoptive parents	on making of an adoption order	ACA 2002, s 67
Local authority	holding a care order, or authorised to place the child for adoption	CA 1989, s 33(3)(a), ACA 2002, s 25

2.15 The ACA 2002 made it possible for the first time for a step-parent to be granted parental responsibility for a child. A step-parent may have parental responsibility by agreement with all other persons with parental responsibility, or by a court order. This means that where a father has not acquired parental responsibility, a mother may enter into a parental responsibility agreement with her new husband at any time, whether or not the child's father agrees.

2.16 A 'step-parent' for the purposes of CA 1989, s 4A(1) means the spouse or civil partner of the child's parent. Unmarried partners cannot have parental responsibility for their partner's child (unless a residence order, which carries with it parental responsibility, is made in their favour). Now that unmarried couples can adopt a child together,[9] and 40% of 'cohabitant' families contain one or more stepchildren,[10] this is perhaps a surprising omission.

Parental responsibility and the child: Gillick competency

2.17 It has long been recognised that a parent's influence over a child (whether or not it is given the formal title of parental responsibility) changes radically over the span of the child's minority. Well before CA

---

9 ACA 2002, s 50 and s 144(4).

10 Compared to 8% of families where the parents are married: National Statistics (formerly the Office of National Statistics), www.statistics.gov.uk

1989 introduced the concept of parental responsibility, Lord Denning observed that the parental 'right' to the custody of a child is 'a dwindling right which the courts will hesitate to enforce against the wishes of the child, and the more so the older he is. It starts with the right of control and ends with little more than advice'.[11]

2.18 In 1985 the House of Lords ruled by a majority of three to two against Victoria Gillick, a mother of four young girls who had sought to prevent her area health authority from providing them with contraceptive or abortion advice without her knowledge and consent. It was held that children under the age of 16 had the capacity to consent, or to refuse to consent, to medical treatment once they reached an age 'of sufficient discretion to enable [them] to exercise a wise choice in [their] own interests.' The age at which a particular child will be capable of making a mature and considered decision will vary. Therefore, although the CA 1989 specifies that a parental responsibility order or agreement will last until the child is 18, unless brought to an end earlier,[12] in reality the 'rights' element at least of a parent's parental responsibility will carry decreasing weight as the child grows older.

2.19 The age at which the courts will consider that a child's views are determinative of the issue in question will vary according to the maturity of the child and, importantly, the nature of the decision that he or she is seeking to make. Where, for example, contact is regularly taking place and the only issue relates to the detail of the contact arrangements, most courts will give considerable weight to the views of relatively young children. Where the issue concerns serious medical treatment the age at which the child is to be treated as being capable of making his own decision will be much higher.[13] An 11-year-old boy has recently been refused permission, in a case where contact had broken down, to discharge his guardian and oppose a proposed plan for contact and therapy.[14] Coleridge J said that the essential question was not whether the child was capable of articulating instructions but whether he was of sufficient understanding to participate as a party, in the sense of being able to cope with all the ramifications of the proceedings and give considered instructions of sufficient objectivity.

GUARDIANS AND SPECIAL GUARDIANS

2.20 Many adults are caring on a permanent basis for a child who is not their own. In most circumstances it will be appropriate for these

11 *Hewer v Bryant* [1970] QB 357.

12 CA 1989, s 91(7) and (8).

13 The child's psychological condition will also be very relevant. A 16-year-old girl with anorexia nervosa has been compelled to undergo medical treatment against her wishes: *Re C* [1997] 2 FLR 180.

14 *Re N* [2003] 1 FLR 652.

persons to have parental responsibility for the children they are bringing up, in order that they may make (or assist in making) arrangements and decisions for them over the course of their childhoods. Foster parents are the exception: while they are acting as foster parents they may not have parental responsibility for the child, and decisions regarding the child are made by the local authority, in consultation with the child's parent(s).

2.21 In some cases, a residence order, which automatically confers parental responsibility on the child's carer, will be sufficient to ensure the child's stability and to enable the carer to take decisions regarding his upbringing. This will be particularly appropriate where the child's parents are not living with him but play an ongoing role in his life. However, there are always cases where a child's parents play little or no part in his upbringing, because they have died or cannot be found, or because their particular situation means that their involvement with the child needs to be limited. In these cases it may be appropriate for the child's carer to have sole or 'overriding'[15] parental responsibility for the child.

2.22 There are of course any number of wider family members, unmarried fathers and others who care for children for whom they do not have parental responsibility, whether because they are unaware of its availability or because they do not feel the need to acquire it. Section 3(5) of CA 1989 therefore provides that:

> 'A person who—
>
> (a) does not have parental responsibility for a particular child; but
> (b) has care of the child
>
> may (subject to the provisions of this Act) do what is reasonable in all the circumstances of the case for the purpose of safeguarding or promoting the child's welfare.'

Guardians

2.23 A parent with parental responsibility may appoint one or more persons as a guardian to care for his or her children in the event of the parent's death.[16] The appointment must be in writing, dated and signed. The appointment will take effect on the death of the appointing parent if:

---

15 A special guardianship order permits the special guardian to exercise parental responsibility to the exclusion of all other persons with parental responsibility (see below and Chapter 5).

16 The statutory provisions covering the appointment of guardians are set out in CA 1989, s 5.

- the child then has no parent who has parental responsibility for him; or
- immediately before the appointing parent's death, there was a residence order in that parent's favour and not in favour of the other surviving parent.

2.24 Guardianship may be disclaimed by the appointed guardian, revoked (by the appointing parent or guardian, or in certain specified circumstances[17]) or terminated by court order. An application to terminate the appointment of a guardian may only be made by the child (with leave) or a person with parental responsibility. This means that a father without parental responsibility who finds that the mother has appointed another person as guardian cannot challenge this appointment unless he applies for and gains parental responsibility himself.

2.25 The court may appoint a person as guardian of a child on that person's application, or in any family proceedings, if the court considers that the appointment should be made. It may do so only if:

- the child has no parent or special guardian with parental responsibility for him; or
- a parent with a residence order has died while the order was in force, and any surviving parent did not also hold a residence order.

2.26 Once a person becomes a child's guardian, he or she has (in addition to parental responsibility) the same rights as a parent to consent or withhold consent to the child's adoption. If the child is made the subject of a care order, the guardian shares parental responsibility with the local authority in the same way as a parent and the local authority has the same duty to afford the guardian reasonable contact with the child.

Special guardianship

2.27 To meet the needs of those children who need a permanent parental figure, but who are not to be fostered or adopted, the ACA 2002 introduced the concept of special guardianship. Any person, other than the child's parent, may be a special guardian. A prospective special guardian must undergo a local authority assessment (very similar in structure to an assessment of prospective adopters) before the order can be made by the court. Once granted, a special guardianship order enables the special guardian to exercise parental responsibility for the

17 Chiefly divorce or dissolution of a civil partnership: CA 1989, s 6.

child 'to the exclusion of any other person with parental responsibility for the child (apart from another special guardian)'.[18]

2.28 Special guardianship is discussed fully in Chapter 5.

SECTION 8 ORDERS

2.29 Section 8 is at the heart of the Children Act's private law scheme. It gives the court power to determine a wide variety of issues that may arise in a child's life, from where and with whom he lives to the name by which he is called and where he goes to school. 'Section 8 orders' fall into four categories, defined in the legislation, which between them cover the vast majority of issues which may arise between a child's parents. The four orders and their statutory definitions are set out below.

Order	**Section 8 definition**	**Other key sections**
Contact order	an order requiring the person with whom a child lives, or is to live, to allow the child to visit or stay with the person named in the order, or for that person and the child otherwise to have contact with each other	CA 1989, s 9: restrictions on making s 8 orders CA 1989, s 10: the court's power to make s 8 orders – those who are entitled to make the application and those who need the court's leave
Residence order	an order settling the arrangements to be made as to the person with whom a child is to live	CA 1989, s 12: residence orders and parental responsibility CA 1989, s 13: restrictions on removing a child from the jurisdiction or changing her name while a residence order is in force CA 1989, ss 9 and 10 as above

18 CA 1989, s 14C(1)(b).

Order	Section 8 definition	Other key sections
Specific issue order	an order giving directions for the purposes of determining a specific question which has arisen, or may arise, in connection with any aspect of parental responsibility for a child	CA 1989, s 9 as above and particularly s 9(5): the court must not use its power to make a specific issue order or prohibited steps order with a view to achieving a result which could be achieved by making a residence or contact order; or in any way which is denied to the High Court exercising its inherent jurisdiction. CA 1989, s 10 as above
Prohibited steps order	an order that no step which could be taken by a parent in meeting his parental responsibility for a child, and which is of a kind specified in the order, shall be taken by any person without the consent of the court	CA 1989, ss 9 and 10 as above

2.30 Section 8 orders may not, other than in exceptional circumstances, be made in respect of a child who has reached the age of 16. A residence order may be made to last until a child is 18; other section 8 orders may only be made to last beyond 16 only in exceptional circumstances.[19]

2.31 A section 8 order may have conditions attached which must be complied with by any person in whose favour the order is made, who is a parent of the child or has parental responsibility for her, or with whom the child is living.[20] It is fairly common for conditions to be attached to a contact order, and the Children and Adoption Act 2006 (see **2.42** below) makes provision for the increased use of conditions to ensure that contact orders are complied with. Conditions attached to residence orders are rarer, but the courts have in a couple of recent cases been prepared to impose conditions on where within England and Wales the resident parent may live, where it has been felt that absent such a condition the child's relationship with the other parent may be jeopardised.[21]

Contact orders

2.32 A contact order is directed to the person with whom the child lives and is a mandatory order requiring that person to permit the child

19 CA 1989, s 9(6) and (7).

20 Ibid, s 11(7).

21 *B v B (Residence: Condition Limiting Geographic Area)* [2004] 2 FLR 979; *Re S (Residence Order: Condition)* [2003] 1 FCR 138.

to have contact with another named person. Contact orders may be expressed in such a way that will permit the person in whose favour they are made to enforce them against the other party.

2.33 Strictly speaking, there is no legal presumption that contact with the non-resident parent is in a child's interests. However, the courts are increasingly aware of the benefits to a child of maintaining a relationship with the non-resident parent and most judges and CAFCASS officers will be looking to see if there are any good reasons why contact should *not* take place, assuming that absent such reasons contact should be promoted and encouraged.

2.34 Since the implementation of the Human Rights Act 1998 there has been considerable judicial discussion of the implications of Article 8 of the ECHR for contact disputes. The European Court of Human Rights has confirmed that where there is a conflict between a child's rights and those of a parent, the child's rights will take priority. However, there is increasing recognition of the non-resident parent's right to a swift and fair determination of his application for contact, and in tandem with that increased emphasis on the court's obligation to do what it can to promote the relationship of (in Munby J's words) the 'wholly deserving father' with his child.[22] The courts are becoming more imaginative in the use of external resources to support fragile contact arrangements. In *A v A*[23] a National Youth Advisory Service worker was commended for her tireless efforts to assist a family where the parents' mutual hostility meant that contact was hanging by a thread and the children's emotional welfare was at risk.

2.35 In difficult cases, where contact has broken down due to the hostility of one parent towards the other, the court should be ready to seek expert evidence on the reasons for the breakdown and any steps that might be taken to restore contact. The court must not 'give up' on the case until it is clear that to pursue it further will cause harm to the child.[24]

Contact orders and domestic violence

2.36 In 2000 the Court of Appeal considered four cases where violence that had taken place within the family had been put forward as a reason for restricting or refusing the violent parent's contact with the children.[25] The court was assisted by a report prepared by Drs Claire

22 *Re D* [2004] 1 FLR 1226.
23 [2004] 1 FLR 1195.
24 *Re S* [2004] 1 FLR 1279.
25 *Re L; Re V; Re M; Re H* [2000] 2 FLR 334.

Sturge and Danya Glaser, two consultant child psychiatrists, which set out research findings on the effects on children of domestic violence.

2.37 The Sturge/Glaser report highlighted the fact that violence in the family, even if not directed at the children, inevitably impacts on the children's emotional wellbeing. The experts felt that there needed to be greater awareness of the effect on children not only of being involved in violence but of being exposed to it. Children often had an awareness of their carer's fear of the violent parent and this might lead them to suffer post-traumatic anxieties and symptoms or influence their own attitudes towards violence in the future.

2.38 The Court of Appeal rejected the Sturge/Glaser report's recommendations that there should be a presumption against contact in cases where violence was proved to have taken place. However, the court emphasised the need to consider the risks to the child of contact and said that the court's priority must be to secure the safety and wellbeing of the child and the primary carer. Butler-Sloss P said that violence involves 'a significant failure in parenting – failure to protect the child's carer and failure to protect the child emotionally'. Violence was not restricted to physical violence but included situations of threats and psychological abuse.

2.39 The Court of Appeal laid down guidelines for the investigation and determination of allegations of domestic violence in contact cases. Where the court feels that any allegation is of such a nature that if found proved it would be likely to affect the court's decision on contact, the allegation must be heard and adjudicated on at an early stage. In some cases it may be appropriate to have a 'split hearing', as in care proceedings,[26] so that once the court has made findings on the allegations of violence it may order a risk assessment or any other evidence that may be necessary before coming to a conclusion on what contact, if any, is appropriate.

2.40 In recognition of the accepted view that violence between the parents is as relevant to the child's welfare as violence directed towards the child, the definition of 'harm' in the Children Act has been amended to include 'impairment suffered from seeing or hearing the ill-treatment of another'.[27]

Interim orders

2.41 Interim orders, particularly in cases where there is a significant dispute of fact, pose real problems. On the one hand the court must be

---

26 See Chapter 5.

27 CA 1989, s 31(9), amended by ACA 2002, s 120.

wary of imposing an interim order that could prove to be entirely inappropriate, or to have put the child at risk, once the evidence has been heard and findings made. On the other, as Munby J observed in *Re D*,[28] too often cases drift from review to review, suffering long delays whilst CAFCASS or expert reports are ordered and awaited, and in the meantime the child's relationship with the absent parent is weakened. The answer in Munby J's view is to 'grasp the nettle' in any case where there are factual disputes that might affect the outcome. In some cases the courts should take a robust view of allegations made:

> 'Judges must resist the temptation to delay the evil day in the hope that perhaps the problem will go away. Judges must also resist the temptation to put contact "on hold", or to direct that it is supervised, pending investigation of the allegations. And allegations which could have been made at an earlier stage should be viewed with appropriate scepticism.'

The tension between these comments and the need to take a cautious attitude to risk, emphasised in *Re L* (see **2.36**) and elsewhere, indicate the difficulty of the task facing judges on a daily basis.

The Children and Adoption Act 2006

2.42 There has been high public awareness over recent years of the difficulties some non-resident parents (usually fathers) have had in securing regular and meaningful contact with their children. Campaigns by groups such as Fathers for Justice and Families Need Fathers have fuelled public concern at the problems faced by fathers in maintaining relationships with their children after separation. On the other hand, women's groups have emphasised that in some cases where the relationship has broken down following violence within the home, the resumption of contact may be harmful to the child.

2.43 The catalyst for reform was provided by the report in 2001 of the Children Act 1989 Advisory Committee (chaired by Wall J), entitled *Making Contact Work*. This was followed in 2004 by the Green Paper *Parental Separation: Children's Needs and Parental Responsibilities: Next Steps*. The Paper contained an explicit agenda for promoting contact between the child and the non-resident parent following separation. It also considered the problem faced by non-resident parents seeking to enforce a contact order. At present the options available to the court dealing with an intransigent resident parent who refuses to comply with a contact order are limited: on committal for breach of an order the court may fine a parent or impose a prison sentence, both of which options are likely to impact adversely on the child.

28 [2004] 1 FLR 1226.

2.44 The Children and Adoption Act 2006 introduces new enforcement and enabling measures to improve compliance with contact orders. These include:

- enforcement orders imposing an unpaid work requirement, which may be imposed on a person who fails without reasonable excuse to comply with a contact order;[29]
- 'contact activity' directions and conditions: counselling and other programmes designed to assist either parent to support or facilitate contact
- monitoring of contact orders by a CAFCASS officer for a period of up to 12 months following the making of the order, with provision for swift referrals back to court if orders are not complied with.

The Act will come into force on a day to be appointed.

Residence orders

2.45 A residence order is an order that determines with whom a child is to live. Its implementation in place of the former orders of 'custody' and 'care and control' was designed to effect a change in the courts' approach to parenting disputes. The more neutral residence order is meant to establish only the child's living arrangements, with parental responsibility conferring on parents and others the right to have an input into other decisions that are made on behalf of the child.

2.46 A residence order carries with it parental responsibility. If the order is made in favour of the child's father and he does not already have parental responsibility, the court must also make a parental responsibility order under s 4 of CA 1989, which will last until the child is 18 or parental responsibility is removed by the court. If a residence order is made in favour of a non-parent, he or she will have parental responsibility only while the residence order is in force.

2.47 A residence order discharges a care order, and vice versa. A non-parent who held the residence order immediately before the care order was made does not retain parental responsibility. However, the local authority must consider the views of the former residence order-holder when taking certain decisions, particularly in relation to contact.

---

29 An unpaid work requirement may not however be imposed unless the court is satisfied beyond reasonable doubt that the person in question has failed to comply with the order: CA 1989, s 11J as inserted by CAA 2006, s 4.

Shared residence: the new contact?

2.48 The concept of shared residence is flagged up explicitly in CA 1989, s 11(4), which provides that 'where a residence order is made in favour of two or more persons who do not themselves all live together, the order may specify the periods during which the child is to live in the different households concerned'. However, in the years immediately following the Act's implementation the courts were reluctant to make shared residence orders[30] other than in 'exceptional circumstances'. It was said in a number of cases that the benefit to the child of having a settled home outweighed any benefit of spending more time with the other parent, and that having two competing homes would be likely in most circumstances to cause 'confusion and stress'.[31]

2.49 The 'exceptional circumstances' test applied until *D v D*[32] in 2001. In this case, a Court of Appeal comprising Hale LJ and Butler-Sloss P held that all that is required for a shared residence order is that the making of the order should be in the child's interests, following the welfare checklist in CA 1989, s 1(3). The 'exceptional circumstances' test was no longer to be applied and it was probably no longer necessary to show that there should be a 'positive benefit' to the child in the making of the order.

2.50 A shared residence order need not provide for a 50/50 split of the child's time between both parents. As the popularity of the orders has risen, the variety of arrangements which may amount to a shared residence order has increased. It is now not at all unusual for a shared residence order to be made in the common situation where the child spends alternate weekends and perhaps some time during the week with one parent, and equal time with each parent during the holidays.

2.51 In *D v D* the court referred for the first time to the psychological benefits, *from the parents' point of view*, of a shared residence order. Over the last few years there have been more examples of shared residence orders being made to address a real or perceived power imbalance between the parents.[33] It seems that although the CA 1989 concept of parental responsibility was intended to put parents on a level playing field, many still prefer the sense of equality that a shared residence order is thought to bring with it, as between the parents and also in the eyes of the schools, doctors and other agencies with whom the family is concerned.

---

30 'Shared residence' is the preferred term where the parties do not live together, 'joint residence' being used to describe couples who live together and jointly care for the child.

31 See for example *Re H* [1994] 1 FLR 717.

32 [2001] 1 FLR 495.

33 See for example *A v A* [2004] 1 FLR 1195.

Specific issue and prohibited steps orders

2.52 Where one or more persons share parental responsibility for a child (or where a father who does not have parental responsibility plays a significant role in the child's life), disputes may sometimes arise concerning the decisions that must be made about the child's education, medical care and other aspects of her upbringing. The law is silent on who, in such circumstances, should have the final say in the decision-making process. This means that where there is a dispute one or other parent will have to make an application to the court.

2.53 Section 8 gives the court two options for controlling either parent's exercise of his or her parental responsibility. Specific issue orders provide a general scheme for determining any issue that may arise in connection with the child's upbringing. Issues that have been determined by the use of a specific issue order include:

- schooling
- change of name
- serious medical treatment
- removing the child from the jurisdiction (see **2.57**).

2.54 A prohibited steps order is a more focused order designed to prevent a person from taking a specified step. Again prohibited steps orders are linked to parental responsibility, in that the step that might be taken must be one that could be taken by a parent 'in meeting his parental responsibility for a child'. However, prohibited steps orders may be made against any person, whether or not he or she is a parent of the child or in fact has parental responsibility, and whether or not he or she has notice of the proceedings or is present in court.[34] However, such an order cannot be enforced by way of committal proceedings unless it has been personally served prior to the breach.[35]

2.55 Complications arise when one parent acts unilaterally without obtaining the other parent's consent or an appropriate court order. The only statutory restriction on such actions is set out in CA 1989, s 13. Section 13 provides that:

> '(1) Where a residence order is in force with respect to a child, no person may—
>
> (a) cause the child to be known by a new surname; or
> (b) remove him from the United Kingdom
>
> without the consent of every person who has parental responsibility for the child or the leave of the court.

---

34 *Re H* [1995] 1 FLR 638.

35 *Lewis v Lewis* [1991] 2 FLR 43.

(2) Subsection 1(b) does not prevent the removal of a child, for a period of less than one month, by the person in whose favour the residence order is made.'

This does not mean that where there is no residence order, either parent may change the child's name or take her out of the jurisdiction at will. There has been strong judicial encouragement of parental cooperation in decision-making with regards to children,[36] and a mother who takes a serious unilateral step without the agreement of the child's father, whether or not he has parental responsibility, will find herself severely criticised and risk her decision being reversed, where this is still possible. As a rule of thumb, the more serious the decision, the more appropriate it is that both parents should be consulted and, if they do not agree, one should make an application to the court.

2.56 In *A v A*[37] Wall J approved a schedule of issues drawn up and agreed by the parents and setting out which decisions each could take alone and which should only be taken in consultation with the other parent and/or with that parent's consent. This schedule is set out in Appendix 7.

REMOVING A CHILD FROM THE JURISDICTION

2.57 Applications to remove a child permanently from the jurisdiction may be made under s 8 as a specific issue order application, or under s 13 if a residence order is in force. The court's approach to the application will almost always be the same in either case.

2.58 The leading case on applications to remove a child from the jurisdiction is *Payne v Payne*.[38] In this case the Court of Appeal was asked to approve the trial judge's decision to allow a mother's application to take a 4-year-old child to live permanently in New Zealand. The mother herself was from New Zealand and following the breakdown of her relationship with the child's father wished to return there to be close to her family. The child had regular contact with her father, spending 23 nights with him in every 56.

2.59 The Court of Appeal held that the trial judge was right to permit the mother to take the child to live in New Zealand. In leave to remove cases, the court must balance the loss to the child (usually a diminution in contact with the remaining parent) with the impact on the child of

---

36 See for example *Re J (Specific Issue Order: Religious Upbringing and Circumcision)* [2000] 1 FLR 571.

37 [2004] 1 FLR 1195.

38 [2001] 1 FLR 1052.

the psychological harm caused to the resident parent by a refusal. The court said that in many cases, the most crucial finding for the judge would be the 'effect of a refusal on the mother's psychological and emotional stability'.

2.60 The courts' approach to leave to remove cases is one of the most controversial areas of private children law. Arguably, recent cases have shown an increasing reluctance amongst trial judges to permit removal where this will have a damaging effect on the child's relationship with the non-resident parent. In *R v R*[39] Baron J accepted the psychiatric evidence that the mother would be 'devastated' by a refusal but took a robust view of her assertion of her emotional need to live in France: 'the grass is never greener on the other side'. In *Re Y*[40] an application to remove a half-Welsh and bilingual child to Texas was refused despite the mother's likely 'frustration and distress' if she were forced to remain in Wales.

2.61 However, the Court of Appeal has cautioned against imposing 'too high a test' on applicants for leave.[41] It has recently been said that it is not necessary to establish that 'psychiatric harm' would flow from the refusal, simply that the resident parent would suffer emotional distress and that this would have an effect on the child.

SECTION 8 ORDERS: PROCEDURE

The application

2.62 A section 8 order may be made on application or of the court's own motion within existing family proceedings. A local authority may not apply for a residence or contact order and no court may make such an order in favour of a local authority.

2.63 Section 9 of the Children Act distinguishes between those who are entitled to apply for an order under CA 1989, s 8, and those who need the court's leave to apply. The restrictions in s 9 vary according to the order sought. Section 10 contains added restrictions on applications for section 8 orders. The provisions of ss 9 and 10 are summarised in the table below.

39 [2005] 1 FLR 687.
40 [2004] 2 FLR 330.
41 *Re G* [2005] 2 FLR 166.

A. Order	B. Entitled to apply	C. May apply with leave	D. Prevented from applying
Residence or contact order	parent, guardian or special guardian any person with a residence order with respect to the child party to a marriage or civil partnership (whether or not subsisting) where the child is a child of the family person with whom the child has lived for at least 3 years person applying to vary or discharge an order made on his application or, in the case of a contact order, a person named in the order	local authority foster parent who has the consent of the LA, is a relative of the child or has had the child living with him for at least 1 year the child, if the court is satisfied he has sufficient understanding to make the application any other person not excluded in column D	local authority foster parents who do not meet one of the requirements in column C
Specific issue order or prohibited steps order	parent, guardian or special guardian any person with a residence order with respect to the child person applying to vary or discharge an order made on his application or, in the case of a contact order, a person named in the order	local authority foster parent who has the consent of the LA, is a relative of the child or has had the child living with him for at least 1 year the child, if the court is satisfied he has sufficient understanding to make the application any other person not excluded in column D	local authority foster parents who do not meet one of the requirements in column C

2.64 When considering an application for leave to apply for a section 8 order, where the proposed applicant is not the child concerned, the court must apply the checklist in CA 1989, s 10(9). The factors that will be relevant to the application for leave include:

- the nature of the proposed application;
- the applicant's connection with the child;
- any risk there might be of the proposed application disrupting the child's life to such an extent that he would be harmed by it; and

- where the child is being looked after by a local authority:
  - the authority's plans for the child's future, and
  - the wishes and feelings of the child's parents.

The risk of disruption must be considered only in the context of the leave application. The court should not go on at the leave stage to consider whether the order sought would itself be likely to cause disruption to the child.

The respondents

2.65 The respondents to a section 8 application are set out in Appendix 3 to the Family Proceedings Rules 1991. In general, the respondents to a section 8 application will be all persons with parental responsibility. Although the rules do not specifically provide for fathers without parental responsibility to be respondents or even to be given notice of a section 8 application, in practice where an order is sought against, or affecting, a father without parental responsibility he will be made a respondent to the proceedings.

Welfare reports

2.66 Sections 7 and 37 of CA 1989 give the court power to direct in appropriate cases that an investigation should be carried out into welfare issues relating to the child, and that a report should be prepared, either by an officer of CAFCASS or by a local authority social worker. Reports ordered under s 37, in cases where a serious child protection issue has arisen, are dealt with in Chapter 4.

2.67 A report ordered under s 7 may be prepared either by a CAFCASS officer or by social services. In most cases a CAFCASS report will be more appropriate. However, in cases where there has been some social services involvement with the family, albeit that the situation is not so serious as to warrant a full child protection investigation, a report from a social worker may be required.

2.68 The s 7 reporter has been described as the judge's 'eyes and ears'. He or she has a duty to visit the child and, where appropriate, to ascertain as far as possible her views regarding the issues involved in the application. Although the recommendations of the reporter are by no means determinative of the issue before the court, the judge must be prepared to justify a departure from the recommendations contained in the report.[42]

---

42 *Re M* [2005] 1 FLR 656.

The child as a party: guardians ad litem in private law proceedings

2.69 In an appropriate case the child may himself be made a party to the proceedings. If this is done then it is highly likely that the court will invite CAFCASS or an alternative agency (often the National Youth Advisory Service) to appoint a guardian ad litem under the Family Proceedings Rules 1991, r 9.5. Cases which may be appropriate for the separate representation of children by a guardian include those where:

- the CAFCASS officer is of the opinion that the child should be made a party;
- the child has interests which are inconsistent with or incapable of being represented by any of the adult parties;
- there is an intractable dispute over residence or contact, including where all contact has ceased, or where there is irrational but implacable hostility to contact or where the child may be suffering harm associated with the contact dispute;
- an older child is opposing a proposed course of action;
- the issues are unusually complex or there are international complications;
- there are serious allegations of abuse;
- the proceedings concern more than one child and the children's welfare is in conflict;
- there is a contested issue about blood testing.[43]

2.70 Wall J has described 'implacable hostility' cases, where all contact has broken down, to be 'one of the prime categories for the tandem model of separate representation in private law proceedings'.[44]

2.71 Following Guidance issued by the President on 25 February 2005, until further notice the appointment of a Rule 9.5 Guardian in the county court should only be made by a Circuit Judge. Where a District Judge considers that a case may be appropriate for the appointment of a guardian he or she should adjourn it to be listed before a Circuit Judge.

---

43 President's Direction of 5 April 2004 [2004] 1 FLR 1188.

44 *Re M* [2003] 2 FLR 636.

3

LOCAL AUTHORITIES AND THE FAMILY

Chapter summary

- Local authorities, children and families: the structure
- The provision of services and financial assistance
- Children in need
- Looked after children
- Accommodating children (local authority)
- Accommodating children (non-local authority)
- Leaving care

LOCAL AUTHORITIES, CHILDREN AND FAMILIES: THE STRUCTURE

3.1 From the day they are born, children begin to access a variety of services provided by the state. They, like their parents, are entitled to free health care. If they are part of a family with limited financial resources, they may be housed by the state. Their education, whether they are at state school, private school or being educated at home, is the responsibility of the local education authority. Some of these services are provided at a national level; others are the responsibility of the local city or county council or, in London, borough council.

3.2 Social services, like housing and education, are provided at a local level. The provision of social services for the children in its area is one of the broadest functions that a local authority carries out. Services provided range from nurseries and toddler groups to therapeutic residential units and adoption services. With such a broad responsibility, the local authority's social services functions often overlap with those of other local or national agencies, and the appropriate source of funding for a particular service is not always obvious. Section 27 of the CA 1989 imposes a specific duty on local authorities to consider whether any other education, health, housing or other authority could assist it in carrying out its social services functions, and to request help if appropriate.

3.3 Within the local authority, responsibility for the provision of social services devolves onto the social services committee. Every local authority must establish one.[1] Each local authority must also appoint a director of social services, who must be a full time officer of the authority.[2] The powers and duties of the social services committee and the director of social services may be delegated to sub-committees or officers of the authority; in practice most decisions relating to individual children are taken by local authority social workers or their managers.

3.4 The Children Act 2004 brought together local authority social services for children, educational services and some aspects of health provision for children under the broad umbrella of 'Children's Services'. A Director of Children's Services in each local authority oversees both social services and educational provision for children.[3]

3.5 In this chapter, as in the rest of the book, the term 'local authority' means a local authority acting as a provider of social services, unless the context indicates otherwise.

THE PROVISION OF SERVICES

3.6 The structure of local authority support services for children and families is set out in Part III of the CA 1989. The local authority has the power and in some circumstances a duty to provide services of a different nature to:

- all children
- children under the age of 5
- children in need.

3.7 Where a statute imposes a duty upon the local authority, the local authority must act in accordance with that duty. Where a statute gives the local authority the power to provide a service, the local authority must exercise its discretion in deciding whether or not to exercise that

---

1 Local Authority Social Services Act 1970 (LASSA 1970), s 2.
2 Ibid, s 6.
3 This role was created by the Children Act 2004, s 18, largely in response to the failings in the child protection system identified by Lord Laming in the report of the Victoria Climbie inquiry: www.victoria-climbie-inquiry.org.uk

power. If it exercises its discretion unreasonably, whether by acting or failing to act, it may be possible to challenge the decision by way of judicial review.

Services provided to all children

3.8 There are a number of different services that the local authority must or may ensure are available to all children and families in its area. The local authority may delegate the provision of these services to other agencies, including voluntary groups, but the responsibility remains with the local authority.

3.9 Each local authority has a duty under the CA 1989 to provide family centres for the use of families and children in its area.[4] Family centres vary in their nature and the kinds of services that they provide. The most basic simply provide a meeting place for families with children, with play and recreational facilities and some limited activities. Others may be staffed by trained workers who are available to provide counselling and other forms of therapeutic support for parents and families in crisis. Many family centres are set up and controlled by charities or local voluntary groups.

3.10 Local authorities may also provide a wide range of services including leisure facilities and after school and holiday care and activities.

CHILDREN IN NEED

3.11 A child in need is defined as a child:

- who is unlikely to achieve or maintain a reasonable standard of health or development without the provision of support services by the local authority;
- whose health or development is likely to be significantly impaired without the provision of such services; or
- who is disabled.[5]

Disabled children

3.12 A child is 'disabled' for the purposes of the legislation if he is blind, deaf or dumb, suffers from any mental disorder or is substantially and permanently handicapped by illness, injury or congenital deformity.

---

4 CA 1989, Sch 2, para 9.
5 Ibid, s 17.

The local authority must keep a register of all disabled children in its area, and has a specific duty to provide services that will enable all such children to live as normal a life as possible.[6]

3.13 When a person with parental responsibility caring for a disabled child asks the local authority to carry out an assessment of his ability to meet the child's needs, the local authority must do so. Once it has assessed the child's needs and the parent's ability to meet them it may either put in place the necessary support or, in certain circumstances, make payments to the carer to enable him to meet the child's needs himself.[7]

Services for children in need

3.14 The local authority must provide certain services to all children in its area who are in need and their families. 'Family' includes all persons with parental responsibility, and any person with whom the child is or has been living.

3.15 The local authority has a general duty to safeguard and promote such a child's welfare, and, so far as is possible, to promote her upbringing by her family. This should be read in conjunction with the duty, imposed on the local authority by Sch 2 to the CA 1989,[8] to take reasonable steps to reduce the need to bring proceedings for care or supervision orders with respect to children within its area. The aim of Part III of the Children Act is to encourage cooperation between parents and local authorities, so that the needs of the majority of children can be met by low-impact support services rather than by invoking the powers of the court.

3.16 The specific services that a local authority must or may provide to children in need are set out in Sch 2 the CA 1989. The obligatory services are:

- advice, guidance and counselling;
- occupational, social, cultural or recreational activities;
- day care (for children under 5);
- home help (which may include laundry facilities);
- facilities for, or assistance with, travelling to and from home for the purpose of taking advantage of any other service provided under the Children Act or of any similar service;
- assistance to enable the child and his family to have a holiday;
- where the child is living apart from his family, but not looked after

6 CA 1989, Sch 2, paras 2 and 6.
7 Carers and Disabled Children Act 2000, s 6, and CA 1989, s 17A.
8 CA 1989, Sch 2, para 7(a)(i).

by the local authority, support to enable him to live with his family or to promote contact with them.

3.17 The local authority must make what it considers to be 'appropriate' provision to ensure that these services are available to children in need.

3.18 In addition the local authority *may* provide:

- accommodation for the family;[9] and
- (in exceptional circumstances) cash.

This section opens the door to the provision by a local authority via its social services budget of accommodation not just for a child but for a whole family. The question of when the responsibility for housing a family should be that of the social services department rather than the housing department is a vexed one and outside the scope of this book.

3.19 The local authority may charge for its services, but must have regard to the family's means and may only charge what it perceives to be a 'reasonable sum'.[10]

LOOKED AFTER CHILDREN

3.20 The purpose of Part III of the Children Act is to enable children in need to live at home and be cared for by their families wherever possible. Where this cannot be achieved the local authority must take responsibility for accommodating the child. The term 'looked after children' includes children who are living in local authority accommodation with their parents' consent, or because there is no person with parental responsibility for them. The term also includes children who have been placed in the care of the local authority by a court order. These children may in some circumstances remain living at home; but the local authority has parental responsibility for them and any placement at home will be closely monitored.

3.21 There are about 60,000 children looked after by local authorities at any one time. Of these 65% are subject to care orders. 31% are accommodated with parental consent and the rest are remanded to local authority accommodation by a criminal court, subject to short-term emergency protective measures[11] or freed for adoption.[12]

---

9 CA 1989, s 17(6).

10 Ibid, s 29.

11 See Chapter 4.

12 www.dfes.gov.uk/rsgateway

3.22 The local authority has a general duty to safeguard and promote the welfare of every child it is looking after, and to make reasonable use of the services that are available in the area to children who are being cared for by their parents.[13] When a local authority makes any decision in relation to a child it is looking after it must, as far as reasonably practicable, consult the child, his parents, any other person with parental responsibility and any other person whose views the local authority considers relevant.[14] It must give due consideration to the wishes and feelings of these persons, and to the child's religious persuasion and racial, cultural and linguistic background.

3.23 A local authority that is looking after a child, whether with the parents' consent or under a care order, has an obligation to ensure, so far as it is reasonably practicable and consistent with the child's welfare, that any accommodation they provide is near his home and that the child is accommodated together with any siblings.[15] In some situations it may be possible for the child to live with members of the extended family or a family friend; and the local authority must consider such a placement and facilitate it unless this is not reasonably practicable or consistent with the child's welfare.[16]

Looked After Child ('LAC') Reviews

3.24 The local authority has a duty to review the case of every looked after child, initially within four weeks of her first becoming looked after, and then three months after the initial review and every six months thereafter.[17]

3.25 Before the first review the local authority is required to formulate a plan for the child's care, taking into account the views of the child and significant members of her family and carrying out such assessments of her needs as may be appropriate.[18] This plan forms the basis of the ongoing review process, which exists to monitor the plan for the child and ensure that decisions made are implemented.

3.26 The local authority must, where reasonably practicable, seek the views of, and in most cases invite to all LAC reviews, the following persons:

- the child's parents;

---

13 CA 1989, s 22(3).
14 Ibid, s 22(4).
15 Ibid, s 23(7).
16 Ibid, s 23(6).
17 Review of Children's Cases Regulations (RCCR) 1991 (SI 1991/895).
18 CA 1989 Guidance and Regulations, Volume 4, paras 2.43–2.72.

- any other person with parental responsibility;
- any other person whose views it considers to be relevant; and
- (where appropriate) the child himself.[19]

The local authority must also invite to any LAC review meetings the child's Independent Reviewing Officer, who has an obligation to attend meetings wherever possible and will ordinarily act as chair. The role of the Independent Reviewing Officer is discussed at **3.39**.

3.27 The local authority must record the minutes of all LAC reviews and ensure that any information obtained relating to the review and any decision made is recorded in writing.[20]

CHILDREN ACCOMMODATED BY THE LOCAL AUTHORITY

3.28 Children are accommodated by the local authority if they are provided with accommodation for a period in excess of 24 hours. The CA 1989 does not distinguish between short-term ('respite') accommodation and long-term accommodation.

3.29 For the most part, children who are accommodated by the local authority without a care order are provided with local authority accommodation because their parents are unable to care for them and consent to their accommodation by the local authority. The exceptions are:

- children for whom no person has parental responsibility;
- children who have been lost or abandoned;
- children subject to an emergency protection order;
- children placed (or freed) for adoption; and
- children remanded to local authority accommodation or detained in connection with criminal proceedings.

Accommodation where the child has no parent or the parents consent: CA 1989, s 20

3.30 A local authority must provide accommodation for children in its area where there is no person with parental responsibility for them, they are lost or abandoned or their parents are unable to provide them with suitable accommodation or care. It may not keep such a child in local authority accommodation if any person with parental responsibility,

19 RCCR 1991, reg 7(1).
20 Ibid, reg 10.

who is able to provide the child with accommodation, objects. A person with parental responsibility may remove the child from local authority accommodation at any time, unless:

- the child is over 16 and wishes to be accommodated; or
- any person in whose favour a residence order is in force[21] consents to the child being accommodated.

EXAMPLE

A 14-year-old girl lives with her mother under a residence order and has contact with her father, who has parental responsibility for her. Her mother has been suffering from severe depression and is unable to care for the child. She has asked the local authority social services department for help. The local authority offers a short-term placement in foster care and the mother accepts. The child moves to live with local authority foster parents for 3 months. When her father finds out he objects to this and wants to know why the child cannot come to live with him. The mother is adamant that she should remain in foster care.

While the mother, who is the residence order holder, consents to the child remaining in local authority accommodation the father cannot remove her. His only remedy is to apply to a court for a residence order in his own favour.

When the child is over 16 the local authority must provide accommodation if her welfare would be seriously prejudiced if it did not do so. It may continue to provide accommodation for young people up to the age of 21 (see **3.81**).

CHILDREN IN CARE

3.31 In the CA 1989, the term 'child in the care of a local authority' is used only in relation to those children in respect of whom a court has made a care order under s 31.[22] It does not include other looked after children. Informally the term 'in care' is often used to signify any child accommodated by the local authority. To avoid confusion, this book follows the CA 1989 definition.

3.32 When a court makes a care order under CA 1989, s 31 (or an interim care order under s 38) parental responsibility for the child is shared between the local authority and any other person with parental responsibility, whether a parent, guardian or special guardian. The local

21 Or a person with care of the child under an order made in the exercise of the inherent jurisdiction of the High Court.

22 CA 1989, s 105(1); see Chapter 5 for care and supervision orders.

authority may determine the extent to which the child's parents and any other persons may exercise parental responsibility for the child. This means in effect that the parents cannot take any significant decisions in relation to the child without the local authority's agreement, and the local authority has ultimate responsibility for securing the child's welfare. Care orders are considered in detail in Chapter 5.

3.33 Children 'in care' may sometimes live at home with a parent or parents under a care order. The local authority has the same obligations towards these children as it does to other children who are subject to care orders but live away from home. The circumstances in which it may be appropriate to place a child in care at home are considered below.

Care plans and reviews

3.34 A court cannot make a final care order in relation to a child without considering the local authority's plans for the child and the arrangements proposed for her accommodation, education and contact with family members and friends.[23] These arrangements are set out in a 'care plan' prepared by the local authority. While the statute only requires a care plan where the court is asked to make a final care order, the guidance[24] and the Protocol[25] require local authorities to prepare a plan detailing the interim arrangements for the child within a few weeks of issuing proceedings.

3.35 Care plans, particularly final care plans, are not binding on the local authority. It is accepted that without a crystal ball the local authority cannot be expected to foresee all the possible developments that may occur during the course of a child's journey through care, and the local authority must be entitled to respond to each eventuality as best it can given the child's needs and its own resources. However, there has been disquiet in recent years at the lack of monitoring of local authority actions after the court has made a final care order, and a sense that children have in some cases simply vanished into the care system without sufficient attention being paid to the plans that were put before the court when the care order was made.

3.36 The court's powers to scrutinise and oversee the implementation of the care plan after a final order has been made have been discussed in several cases. An important principle of the CA 1989 is that there should be a line drawn between the responsibilities of the local

23 CA 1989, s 31(3A).

24 LAC(99) 29.

25 *Protocol for Judicial Case Management in Public Law Children Act Cases* [2003] 2 FLR 719.

authority and of the court. While the care plan is an important factor in the court's decision whether or not to make a final care order, once the order is made, responsibility for the child passes to the local authority and the court has no jurisdiction to monitor the implementation of the care plan.

3.37 Unsurprisingly, this was challenged when a local authority facing a financial crisis and cuts to its social services budget failed to implement a care plan that envisaged an attempt at rehabilitating two children with their mother.[26] While the mother in that case could apply to the court for a judicial review of the local authority's decision not to implement the care plan, the obvious difficulty for the future was that in cases where the parents were no longer involved in the child's life, there was no one to make such an application on behalf of the child, the Children's Guardian having been discharged at the conclusion of the final hearing.

3.38 The Court of Appeal's remedy was to propose a mechanism for 'starring' the key elements of a care plan and bringing the case back to court if any of these starred features were not implemented. This proposal went to the House of Lords, which acknowledged that the discharge by local authorities of their responsibilities to children in their care sometimes falls short of an acceptable standard. However, Lord Nicholls said that the CA 1989 did not give the courts power to control local authorities to the extent proposed by the Court of Appeal. He did not agree that this meant that the CA 1989 was incompatible with the European Convention on Human Rights, but felt that it might indicate a 'lacuna' in the law.

3.39 This lacuna has been addressed – to some extent – by the government in the Adoption and Children Act 2002 and its ancillary regulations. Local authorities are now obliged to appoint an Independent Reviewing Officer ('IRO') for all looked-after children. The IRO is independent of the day-to-day management of the child's case, but not of the local authority. He or she will chair review meetings relating to the child, monitor the local authority's implementation of the care plan and, if appropriate, refer the case to CAFCASS and/or assist the child in obtaining his own legal advice. Referral of the case outside the local authority is intended to be a last resort: the IRO is expected to resolve any problems within the local authority where possible. There has as yet been no review of the effectiveness of the new system.

---

26 *Re S* [2002] 1 FLR 815.

ACCOMMODATING CHILDREN (LOCAL AUTHORITY)

3.40 The majority of looked after children live in foster placements (68%). 13% live in children's homes and 10% are placed with their parents under care orders.[27] The younger the child, the more likely it is that a foster placement will be available rather than a placement in a children's home: over 90% of looked after children under the age of 10 (other than those placed with their parents) are in foster placements.

3.41 The local authority's duty to accommodate and maintain looked after children is set out in CA 1989, s 23.

Foster care

3.42 Children in foster care may be placed with:

- a local authority foster parent;
- a foster parent identified and approved by a private fostering agency; or
- a member of the extended family or a friend, who has been assessed and approved by the local authority as a foster carer.

In each of these cases, the foster parent(s) provide a home for the child. They do not acquire parental responsibility. If the child is in care parental responsibility is shared between the parents (and/or any other person with parental responsibility) and the local authority. If he is voluntarily accommodated his parent(s) exercise parental responsibility alone. The effect of this is that a foster parent may only take such steps as are necessary to meet the child's needs on a day-to-day basis. Any significant decision affecting the child must be made by a parent, the local authority or both.

Relatives and friends

3.43 When the local authority wishes to place a looked after child with a relative or friend who does not have parental responsibility, that person must be approved as a foster parent and the fostering regulations apply.[28] However, a child may be placed with a relative or friend for a period of up to six weeks without being approved as a foster parent provided that:

27 www.dfes.gov.uk

28 This can lead to the unexpected situation where the local authority wishes to endorse a wider family placement but cannot approve the proposed carers as foster parents. See *Re W and X* [2004] 1 FLR 415 for a creative solution.

- the local authority is satisfied that this is the most suitable way of discharging its duty to safeguard and promote the child's welfare;
- the local authority has interviewed the carer, inspected the accommodation and obtained basic information about others living in the household; and
- the carer has entered into a written agreement with the local authority.[29]

Regulation

3.44 The provision of fostering services by a local authority or private agency is regulated by:

- the Care Standards Act 2000;
- the Fostering Services Regulations 2002 (FSR 2002);
- the Arrangements for Placement of Children (General) Regulations 1991 (APC(G)R 1991);[30]
- the National Minimum Standards for Fostering Services, issued by the Department of Health; and
- the Children Act Guidance and Regulations Volumes 3 and 6.

3.45 The actions of the local authority in relation to the discharge of its fostering functions are under the supervision of the National Care Standards Commission. If the local authority fails to satisfy the Minimum Standards it will be reported to the Department of Health.

3.46 The following is intended as a guide to the overall structure of the regulation of fostering services. For further information detailed reference should be made to the relevant regulations and guidance.

Local authority foster parents

3.47 Any person with whom a local authority proposes to place a looked after child must be an approved and registered foster parent. The only exceptions are prospective adopters and persons who fall within the Placement of Children with Parents etc Regulations 1991.[31]

3.48 The approval process is detailed and involves a series of interviews, checks and references. At the conclusion of the process the local authority prepares a report which is presented to its fostering panel. The panel consists of a mixture of local authority employees and independent members, including at least one current or recent foster

29 Fostering Services Regulations 2002 (SI 2002/57), reg 38.

30 SI 1991/890.

31 SI 1991/893.

parent. The panel will make a recommendation which the local authority fostering service must take into account.

3.49 If the local authority decides to approve the prospective foster parent it must set out in writing the terms of the approval, including any limitations on the number or age of children who may be fostered and the duration of any placement.[32] There is a limit of 3 foster children in any one placement at any one time, unless a specific exemption is granted or the children are all siblings.[33]

3.50 The local authority then enters into a written agreement with the foster parent. This agreement is known as the 'foster care agreement' and covers arrangements for support and training; review; the procedures for placement of children; and notification of changes in circumstances. The foster parent must agree to care for the child as if he were a member of the foster parent's own family. Corporal punishment is not permitted in a foster placement and the foster parent must formally agree not to administer corporal punishment to any foster child.

3.51 A person who is informed that the local authority proposes not to approve him as a foster parent may submit written representations within 28 days of notification of the decision. The application goes back to the fostering panel, which may make a fresh recommendation. If, following this, the local authority's decision is unchanged it must give the applicant written reasons for the decision not to approve him.

3.52 A person must not be approved as a foster parent if he has been convicted of or cautioned for a 'specified offence'. The list includes serious sexual offences and offences against children.[34]

3.53 The local authority must review its foster parents on at least a yearly basis. The review process is less detailed than the initial approval process but the local authority must prepare a written report on the occasion of each review.

---

32 FSR 2002, reg 28.

33 CA 1989, Sch 7.

34 FSR 2002, reg 27(7).

Approval of foster parents: the process

- Assessment: matters to be covered
  - health
  - marital status
  - other adult members of the household
  - other children in the family
  - accommodation
  - religion, race, cultural and linguistic background
  - employment, activities and interests
  - experience and skills relevant to child care abilities
  - outcome of previous applications to foster/adopt etc
  - previous convictions and cautions for each adult in the household
- Interview of 2 referees
- Presentation of written report to the fostering panel, including
  - assessment of applicant's suitability
  - proposals for any terms and conditions to attach to approval
- Decision to approve
  - including any terms and conditions
- Foster care agreement between foster parent and local authority

Agency foster parents

3.54 Private fostering agencies are regulated in the same way as local authorities which provide a fostering service, and must comply with the same provisions regarding the approval process. They must also establish a fostering panel, although this may be done jointly with up to two other fostering service providers.

3.55 A significant difference between the local authority as a fostering service provider and a private (or voluntary) fostering agency is that the private agency does not have parental responsibility for the children placed with its foster carers. A local authority will often make use of private fostering agencies in its area to provide foster placements. If the local authority places a child in its care with private foster carers, the local authority retains parental responsibility for the child.

3.56 A person may only be approved as a foster parent by one fostering service provider (whether local authority or private) at any one time.

Emergency placements

3.57 Ordinarily the local authority must carry out checks before placing a child with foster parents to ensure that the proposed placement is the most suitable way of meeting the child's needs, including medical and educational needs and any cultural or other characteristics of the child.[35] It must also provide the foster parent(s) with information about the children and enter into a written foster placement agreement with them.[36] However, in an emergency a local authority may place a child for up to 24 hours with any person who has been approved by any foster service provider, as long as the foster parent has agreed in writing to carry out basic fostering duties.[37] If the local authority wishes to keep the child in foster care after the 24-hour period is up it must ensure that it has completed the necessary pre-placement checks.

Rights and duties of foster parents

3.58 The relationship between the local authority and the foster parent is shaped by two important documents: the foster care agreement, signed by the foster parent at the time of approval, and the foster placement agreement, signed at the beginning of each placement. These should set out the arrangements for managing the practical aspects of each placement, including the financial support to be provided by the local authority and the plans for reviewing and terminating the placement.

3.59 Foster parents must be made aware of the difference in legal status between a child who is subject to a care order and one who has voluntarily been placed in care by his parents. A child who is voluntarily accommodated in foster care may be removed at any time by his parent or any other person with parental responsibility, unless any person with a residence order objects, or the child is over 16 and wishes to remain in foster care.[38]

3.60 A child who is the subject of a care order may be removed at any time by the local authority, subject to the local authority's duty to

35 CA 1989, ss 22–23.

36 FSR 2002, reg 34(3).

37 Ibid, reg 38.

38 CA 1989, s 20.

obtain the views of parents and other relevant persons, and any arrangements for termination of a placement set out in the foster care agreement or foster placement agreement. It is the local authority's duty immediately to remove a child from a foster placement if it believes that the placement is no longer the most suitable way of promoting and safeguarding the child's welfare.[39]

3.61 Foster parents who disagree with a local authority's decision to terminate a placement, or with any other decision relating to them as foster parents, have only a limited number of options available to them. If the local authority's review and complaints procedures do not result in a change of heart the foster parent's most likely remedies will be to make an application for a residence order, or for judicial review of the local authority's decision.

3.62 Foster parents who wish to remain in contact with children they have fostered may, if the matter cannot be arranged by agreement between themselves and the parents and/or local authority, apply with the leave of the court for a contact order under s 8 (if the child is not in care) or s 34 (if the child is in care).

3.63 Foster parents have a right to be given information regarding the children placed with them, and the local authority owes a duty of care to its foster carers and their own children: see *W v Essex County Council*.[40]

Funding

3.64 Every local authority will make arrangements for the financial support of children in foster care. The amounts paid to foster parents vary according to the age of the child, any special needs he has and (more controversially) the individual policies of the different local authorities. It is not permissible for a local authority to pay less to an extended family foster parent than it would to one of its own foster parents.[41] As this book goes to press, the government is seeking responses to a consultation paper on *National Minimum Allowances for Foster Carers*, available via the DFES website.

Children's homes

3.65 A foster parent may offer a home to a maximum of three children unless one of the exceptions (see **3.49**) applies. Any establishment

---

39 FSR 2002, reg 36(1).

40 [2001] 2 AC 592.

41 *R v Manchester City Council, ex parte L* [2002] 1 FLR 43.

providing a home for more than three children is a children's home. The operation of a children's home is regulated by the Children's Homes Regulations 2001.[42]

Placement with parents

3.66 The local authority may decide to place a child who is the subject of a care order with:

- his parent(s);
- any person with parental responsibility; or
- a person in whose favour a residence order was in force immediately before the care order was made.[43]

3.67 The local authority has a specific duty to consider such a placement, or a placement with another relative or friend of the child, and must facilitate such a placement unless to do so would not be reasonably practicable or consistent with the child's welfare.[44]

3.68 These placements are subject to the Placement of Children with Parents etc Regulations 1991 (PCPR 1991).[45] The requirements of the Regulations are modified when the child is over 16.

3.69 The decision to place a child in care with a parent or holder of parental responsibility is a significant one. In many cases, the parent with whom it is proposed that the child should be placed is the same parent whose care of the child has been so inadequate that the threshold criteria for a care order have been met.[46] For this reason, the decision to place a child with a parent may only be made by the local authority's director of social services or a local authority officer nominated in writing for that purpose.[47]

3.70 A local authority that is proposing to place a child (or allow her to remain placed) with one of the people listed above must in most cases carry out an assessment before making the placement decision. However, that does *not* mean that a child already living with her parents must be removed while the assessment is carried out.[48] Further, the local authority may make an immediate placement if it considers that to be

---

42 SI 2001/3967.
43 CA 1989, s 23(4).
44 Ibid, s 23(6).
45 See also the Children Act 1989 Guidance and Regulations, Volume 3, Family Placements (HMSO).
46 See Chapter 5.
47 PCPR 1991, reg 5(2).
48 Ibid, reg 2(4).

necessary in order to safeguard and promote the child's welfare. In such circumstances it need not carry out the full assessment before the placement, but must interview the person with whom the child is to be placed. During that interview it must in particular ascertain as much relevant information about any adult members of the household as possible. The full assessment should then be carried out as soon as practicable after the placement.[49]

3.71 This power to make an immediate placement can be contrasted with the position where it is proposed that a child should be placed with a member of the extended family who does not have parental responsibility and did not hold a residence order before the child was taken into care. In such a case the relative must be approved as a foster parent and there is no power to make an immediate placement while the necessary assessments are carried out. It is no answer to make a residence order in favour of the relative as this will have the effect of discharging the care order.[50]

Placement with parents: assessment checklist

The assessment should encompass the following:

- the health of the child;
- the suitability of the person with whom it is proposed that the child should be placed;
- the suitability of the proposed accommodation, including the proposed sleeping arrangements;
- the educational and social needs of the child; and
- the suitability of all other members aged 16 and over of the household in which it is proposed that the child will live.

3.72 A non-exhaustive list of the factors to be taken into account when assessing suitability (of the proposed carer and his or her household) is set out in Sch 1 to the PCPR 1991. Many of these (such as the person's age, health and experience of looking after children) are a matter of common sense. In addition to these matters the local authority must also take into account in respect of any member of the household over the age of 16:

- the result of any application to have a child placed with him or to adopt a child or any application for registration (for child minding or day care) and details of any prohibition on his acting as a

49 PCPR 1991, reg 6.
50 CA 1989, s 91(1).

child-minder, providing day care, or caring for foster children privately or children in a voluntary or registered children's home; and
- details of any criminal offences of which he has been convicted or for which he has been cautioned.

3.73 The local authority must seek to reach a written agreement with the parent or other person with whom the child is placed. The areas covered by the agreement must include (amongst others) the following key matters:

- arrangements for the local authority to visit the child;
- circumstances in which the child will be removed from the placement;
- arrangements for notifying the local authority of significant changes in the family circumstances;
- arrangements for providing for the child's health and educational needs.

3.74 If the local authority is of the view that the continuation of the placement no longer safeguards or promotes the child's welfare, or that the child's safety is prejudiced, it must immediately terminate the placement and remove the child. It must, as far as is reasonably practicable, give notice in writing of the proposed termination to the child (if appropriate), the person with whom she is placed and any other person whose wishes and feelings are relevant.[51]

3.75 The local authority must support and review the placement. It must arrange for the child to be visited at least every 6 weeks during the first year of the placement, and at least every 3 months thereafter for as long as the care order is in force. On each visit the social worker must (if practicable) arrange to see the child alone. A written report must be prepared after each visit.[52]

ACCOMMODATING CHILDREN (NON-LOCAL AUTHORITY)

3.76 A small minority of children are neither cared for by their parents (or by someone with parental responsibility[53]), nor by the local authority. These children may be:

---

51 PCPR 1991, reg 12.

52 Ibid, reg 9.

53 Note that a residence order has the effect of giving parental responsibility to the holder of the residence order for the duration of the order: CA 1989, s 12(2).

- fostered under a private fostering arrangement;
- accommodated by a voluntary organisation;
- accommodated (generally by a health authority) in a nursing home, mental nursing home or residential care home;
- living with a person under an informal, private arrangement that does not fall within the definition of private fostering.

Most of these arrangements are subject to regulation. Private fostering is governed by the Children (Private Arrangements for Fostering) Regulations 2005 (C(PAF)R 2005).[54] Voluntary organisations are covered in the Children Act, Part VII. Accommodation by a health authority is also covered in the CA 1989, ss 85–86, but responsibility for children in this position is that of the appropriate health authority and the placement is regulated by the Children's Homes Regulations 2001.[55]

3.77 The local authority's overall duty to children in its area extends to a duty to monitor private fostering arrangements[56] and the arrangements made by voluntary organisations to accommodate children.[57] Where a health authority is responsible for accommodating a child, it must inform the appropriate local authority and the two authorities must consult.[58]

Private fostering

3.78 Private fostering is defined in s 66 of the CA 1989. A privately fostered child is a child under the age of 16 who is living with and being cared for, for a period of more than 28 days, by a person who is not a parent or relative or a person with parental responsibility.

3.79 Parents who intend to enter into a private fostering arrangement have an obligation to notify their local authority of their intentions, and any person who proposes to foster a child privately must also notify the local authority and cooperate with its investigations. The local authority has a duty to visit children who are being privately fostered and satisfy itself of their welfare, and may prohibit a person from acting as a private foster carer or impose restrictions on him.[59] Persons who have been convicted of certain specified offences are disqualified from acting as private foster carers.[60]

---

54 SI 2005/1533.
55 SI 2001/3967.
56 C(PAF)R 2005, regs 7 and 8.
57 CA 1989, s 62.
58 APC(G)R 1991, reg 12.
59 CA 1989, s 67.
60 Ibid, s 68.

Private fostering arrangements – duties of the local authority checklist

The local authority must satisfy itself of the suitability of the fostering arrangement in relation to the following key factors:[61]

- the purpose and intended duration of the fostering arrangement
- the child's wishes and feelings about the arrangement
- the child's development and arrangements to meet his needs
- financial arrangements
- the carer's capacity to look after the child
- the suitability of other members of the household
- arrangements for the child's health care and accommodation
- arrangements for contact with the child's family

Accommodation by voluntary organisations

3.80 When a voluntary organisation is providing accommodation for a child, it is the 'responsible authority' for the purposes of the regulations[62] and much of the responsibility for safeguarding and promoting the child's welfare devolves upon the organisation. However, the local authority has a continuing duty to satisfy itself that the voluntary organisation is carrying out its duties in a satisfactory manner. In particular it must arrange for children who are accommodated by a voluntary organisation to be visited on a regular basis.[63] It has the power at any reasonable time to enter and inspect the accommodation and to examine any child there, and to inspect the records kept by the organisation.[64]

3.81 If the local authority is concerned that a child's welfare is not being satisfactorily safeguarded or promoted by a voluntary organisation it must consider whether it would be in his interests to be accommodated by a parent or other relative and, if not, consider whether the local authority itself should intervene.[65]

Other informal arrangements

3.82 An unascertained number of children live with a relative who is not a parent and who does not have parental responsibility for them.

61 C(PAF)R 2005, Sch 3.
62 APC(G)R 1991 and FSR 2002.
63 CA 1989, s 62(1).
64 Ibid, s 62(6).
65 Ibid, s 62(5).

These extended family arrangements, often involving a grandparent, fall outside the private fostering legislation and there is no formal structure in place to monitor the security of the placement or the child's wellbeing.

3.83 Research indicates that these children are more likely to be children in need and their family units often suffer financial and other hardship.[66] Extended family carers may receive one-off support under the children in need legislation, but are unlikely to be eligible for regular assistance. These carers often face difficulties securing the state benefits that parents are entitled to, and unless they have a residence order giving them parental responsibility may have problems dealing with schools and health professionals. They may not be eligible for public funding to apply for a residence order, and unless the child has lived with them for a year may not apply for one without the leave of the court.[67]

LEAVING CARE

3.84 For the purposes of the CA 1989 children cease to be children on their eighteenth birthdays. On this date the effect of any care order comes to an end and a child who is being provided with accommodation is no longer a 'looked after child'. The local authority's duties towards the young person, as a child in its area, are concluded. However it retains limited responsibility for 18- to 21-year-olds who have been looked after as children, and must take reasonable steps to monitor their welfare as young adults. In the period leading up to the child's eighteenth birthday the local authority must help him to plan for independence.

3.85 The need for support and assistance for these often vulnerable young people is obvious. In 2003 only 43% of care leavers had at least one GSCE or NVQ (compared to a figure of 95% in the general population). Local authorities were still in touch with 80% of care leavers by their nineteenth birthdays, and of this group just under half were in some sort of education, training or employment; compared with 86% of all 19-year-olds.[68]

3.86 The local authority has specific obligations towards children leaving care. These were introduced by the Children (Leaving Care) Act 2000 and apply to 16- and 17-year-olds who are or have been looked

---

66 Joan Hunt, *Family and Friends Carers*, Department of Health, March 2003.

67 CA 1989, s 10(5)(b).

68 *Children Looked After by Local Authorities, year ending 31 March 2003*, available for download from www.dfes.gov.uk

after by the local authority. They are designed to ease the transition from care to independent living. A distinction is drawn between 'eligible children' and 'relevant children'. The definitions are technical; broadly speaking, eligible children are those who are still being looked after by the local authority; relevant children are those who have recently been looked after.

Eligible children

3.87 An eligible child is a child who:

(a) is aged 16 or 17,
(b) is looked after by the local authority, and
(c) has been looked after by the local authority for a total period of at least 13 weeks that began after he reached the age of 14 and ended after he reached the age of 16. The 13-week total does not include any short 'respite care' period of less than 4 weeks following which the child returned to the care of a person with parental responsibility.[69]

Relevant children

3.88 A relevant child is a child who:

(a) is aged 16 or 17, and
(b) is not looked after by the local authority, but
(c) was, before he ceased to be looked after, an eligible child, or
(d) on his sixteenth birthday was in hospital or detained in a young offenders' or other similar institution, but was a looked after child immediately prior to his detention of hospital admission and, were it not for that, would have become an eligible child on his sixteenth birthday.[70]

A relevant child who returns to live with his family for a period of 6 months ceases to be a relevant child; but will become one again if the placement breaks down.[71]

Responsibilities towards eligible and relevant children

3.89 Many of the local authority's responsibilities towards eligible and relevant children are focused on planning and preparatory work for the transition period between adolescence and adulthood. It is important to

69 Children (Leaving Care) (England) Regulations 2001 (SI 2001/2874) (C(LC)R 2001), reg 3.
70 C(LC)R 2001, reg 4.
71 Ibid.

recognise that in addition to the duties set out below the local authority must carry out for eligible children all the duties it owes to looked after children. If the eligible child is subject to a care order the local authority must continue to exercise parental responsibility for the child until she reaches the age of 18.

3.90 Some of the local authority's obligations are common to both eligible and relevant children. In all cases the local authority must:

- prepare a written statement with details of how the child's needs will be assessed, including the timetable for the assessment and the person(s) responsible for carrying it out;
- carry out an assessment of the child's needs, taking into account the child's views and those of his parents and/or carers, school and any other interested person;
- develop a 'pathway plan' setting out, with dates, the manner in which the local authority proposes to meet the child's needs, and keep it under regular review; and
- appoint a personal adviser for the child.

3.91 The role of the personal adviser is to provide practical advice and support, to liaise with the local authority in implementing the pathway plan and to keep in touch with the child. He or she must keep a written record of contacts with the child and must ensure that he remains informed about the child's progress and wellbeing. The personal advisor should participate in the preparation and review of the child's pathway plan.

3.92 The pathway plan must be reviewed when the child or his personal adviser requests it, and in any event not less than every 6 months.

3.93 Because 'relevant children' are no longer being accommodated by the local authority the local authority has the following main obligations with respect to them in addition to those set out above:

- to keep in touch with the child and re-establish contact if it loses touch with her; and
- to safeguard and promote her welfare and, unless satisfied that her welfare does not require it, to support her by:
  - maintaining her;
  - providing her with suitable accommodation, and

  providing her with assistance to meet her educational, training or employment needs.

3.94 Although the local authority has an obligation, if her welfare requires it, to provide accommodation for a relevant child, this will not be a placement in foster care or other local authority accommodation (a child so placed is a 'looked after child'). The accommodation provided for a relevant child, who is *not* 'looked after', will often be housing authority accommodation, a privately-rented flat or a 'half-way house'. The local authority's duty is to provide financial support and to check that the proposed accommodation is suitable for the child.

4

REFERRALS, ASSESSMENTS AND EMERGENCY INTERVENTION

Chapter summary

- The initial referral
- Section 47 investigations
- Section 37 investigations
- The Child Protection Register
- Police protection
- Emergency protection orders
- Child assessment orders
- Recovery orders
- Child safety orders and parenting orders

INTRODUCTION

4.1 The previous chapter considered the local authority's general responsibility for children in its area, and the assistance that local authorities are under a duty to provide for families and children with varying levels of need.

4.2 This chapter sets out to track the routes taken by the more serious cases where the balance shifts from the provision of support services to child protection. In the short term an order of the court may be required to ensure a child's safety or to grant the local authority access to him. In the longer term, if the child protection issues remain live and cannot be resolved by the family working voluntarily with the local authority, these cases may result in the child being placed in the care or under the supervision of the local authority. Care and supervision orders are discussed in Chapter 5.

THE INITIAL REFERRAL

4.3 There are a number of ways in which a child at risk may come to social services' attention. In emergency cases, where there is an obvious and urgent child protection issue, children may have been taken into police protection or made the subject of an emergency protection order by a court. In these cases the local authority must immediately initiate a full child protection investigation under CA 1989, s 47.

4.4 In other, generally less urgent, cases the initial referral may be made by a professional involved with the child: commonly a health visitor, GP, police officer, hospital doctor or teacher. Referrals are sometimes made by family members, friends or neighbours, anonymously or otherwise, directly or via other agencies such as Childline or the NSPCC.

The local authority's response

4.5 The local authority must decide within one working day of a referral whether any response is required. Unless the decision is to take no action, the local authority must then carry out an initial assessment within 7 days. The aim of the initial assessment is to collate information about the child held by other agencies, interview relevant family members and see the child. At the end of this process social services must decide whether or not the child is a child in need, and whether or not there are grounds to suspect he is suffering or likely to suffer significant harm. A decision that the child is 'in need'[1] means that the local authority must draw up a plan setting out the services to be provided for him (see Chapter 3 for the different services available.) A decision that the child is at risk of significant harm triggers the more comprehensive child protection investigation under CA 1989, s 47 (see **4.8**).

4.6 The timescales for the investigation and assessment process are set out in the *Social Services Assessment and Care Planning Aide-Memoire*, published by HMSO available at www.opsi.gov.uk.

4.7 The following flow-chart illustrates the routes that typical cases will take from the initial referral, via one or more assessments, to an application for a care order or alternative supportive action.

---

1 See **3.10**.

THE CHILD PROTECTION INVESTIGATION: SECTION 47

4.8 Section 47 of the CA 1989 sets out the local authority's duty in certain circumstances to carry out a comprehensive child protection investigation. The provisions of s 47 are triggered when the local authority:

- has reasonable cause to suspect that a child within its area is suffering, or is likely to suffer, significant harm; or
- is informed that a child within its area:
  - is subject to an emergency protection order; or
  - has been taken into police protection.

4.9 The local authority's investigation is designed to establish whether or not the local authority should be taking further steps to protect the child. In many cases the s 47 investigation is the preliminary to an application for a care or supervision order. It is a fairly detailed child protection assessment.

4.10 The structure of the assessment is prescribed by the *Framework for the Assessment of Children in Need and their Families*,[2] guidance published by the Department of Health and available to be downloaded from the Department of Health website (www.dh.gov.uk/publicationsandstatistics). The assessment will focus on three main areas: the child's developmental needs; relevant family and environmental factors; and the parenting capacity of those with primary responsibility for his care. The framework is designed to cover all assessments of children in need, not just those who are thought to be at risk of significant harm and in need of urgent intervention. The investigation is likely to move more quickly when carried out under s 47, ie when the child is thought to be at significant risk, but the overall structure of each assessment should be broadly the same.

4.11 The timescales for a section 47 investigation will vary widely. When the trigger for the assessment process is a child in police protection or subject to an emergency protection order, things will have to move quite quickly. Children can remain in police protection for only 72 hours, and subject to an emergency protection order for a maximum of 15 days, so by the end of that period the local authority must be in possession of the information it needs in order to decide on any further action that must be taken.

4.12 If a local authority carrying out a section 47 investigation is denied access to the child, or is not given information about his

---

2 (HMSO, April 2000).

whereabouts, it has a specific duty to consider whether an application to the court is necessary (s 47(6)). It must apply for an order (emergency protection order, child assessment order, or care or supervision order) unless satisfied that the child's welfare can be adequately safeguarded without court intervention.[3]

A COURT 'REFERRAL': SECTION 37

4.13 When private law proceedings are under way between parents, or between others concerned with a child, it is not uncommon that allegations are made on one or both sides that raise issues regarding the child's safety or welfare. Alternatively if a CAFCASS officer has been instructed to report on the family (see Chapter 2) his or her report may highlight areas of concern. As most family proceedings are heard in private the local authority will not automatically become aware of any risk to the children that comes to light. Section 37 of the CA 1989 gives power to the court itself, in any family proceedings in which a question arises with respect to the welfare of a child and it seems to the court that an application for a care or supervision order may be appropriate, to direct the appropriate local authority to investigate the child's circumstances.

4.14 It is important to note that the court may only make such a direction when it appears that it may be appropriate for the local authority to make an application for a care or supervision order. The court must not use the procedure to require the local authority to investigate where the concerns are of a relatively minor nature and it is unlikely that the threshold criteria for a care or supervision order (likelihood or incidence of significant harm) are met, or where even if the threshold criteria are met it is unlikely that a care or supervision order will be necessary. The appropriate course for the court to take where it feels that there may be a role for social services but a care or supervision order is unlikely to be appropriate is to request a report from the local authority under CA 1989, s 7. When preparing such a report the social worker is carrying out the same task as an officer of CAFCASS, albeit from a social services perspective.

4.15 When a direction is made under s 37 the local authority must carry out an investigation to consider whether or not there is a need to make an application for a care or supervision order (see Chapter 5) or whether any other protective or supportive measures are necessary.

---

3 CA 1989, s 47(6).

4.16 A local authority that is subject to a s 37 direction must within 24 hours allocate a social services team manager who will be responsible for the preparation of the report. Under the Protocol[4] the report should be filed with the court within 35 days. It should focus on the issue of whether or not it would be appropriate to apply for a care or supervision order, and is not a general welfare report; although inevitably this issue will require questions of the child's general welfare to be considered. Whilst a s 37 direction requires a local authority to consider applying for a care or supervision order, the court has no power to direct the local authority to make such an application.

Interim care or supervision orders

4.17 When the court makes a direction under s 37, it may at the same time make an interim care order or interim supervision order to cover the period of the local authority's investigation. The court's interim order must not extend beyond the hearing date by which the local authority is due to file its report. The court will fix a date for the next hearing and direct the local authority to file its report in writing shortly before this date. The local authority will be given time to carry out its investigations and if, following those investigations, it decides not to issue proceedings itself, it must give its reasons and specify any other action it proposes to take in respect of the child.

4.18 The s 37 procedure illustrates the delicate balance of responsibility between the courts and the local authority. Although the court can flag up concerns about a child and prompt the initial local authority involvement, ultimately the decision to apply for a care order is the local authority's alone.

EXAMPLE

A 17-year-old girl, who has left home, makes an application for contact with her 12-year-old sister. The girls' mother has an erratic lifestyle and the younger child is often left alone at home for up to a week at a time. She has not been in school for almost a year. The judge who hears the case at the first directions hearing is so concerned about her welfare that he makes a section 37 direction requiring the local authority to report back to the court in 8 weeks, and makes an interim care order until the reporting date. In the meantime the local authority carries out an investigation and decides that in fact the mother is prepared to modify her own lifestyle. It does not believe that there is a need for an order and does not make an application. The interim care order lapses

---

4 The Protocol for Judicial Case Management in Public Law Children Act Cases is available from www.courtservice.gov.uk. The 'route map' is reproduced at Appendix 5.

and, unless it has plans to provide support or assistance of any kind, the local authority has no further involvement with the case.

Appointment of a Children's Guardian

4.19 When the court has made a section 37 direction and has made, or is considering whether to make, an interim care order, the proceedings become 'specified' for the purposes of CA 1989, s 41. This means that the court must appoint an officer of CAFCASS to act as a Children's Guardian,[5] unless satisfied that it is not necessary to do so in order to safeguard his interests. It has been pointed out that in a case where the local authority is requested to carry out an urgent and intensive investigation, there may not be time for a guardian to play any meaningful role during the assessment process.[6]

4.20 If the local authority subsequently decides *not* to apply for a care or supervision order, the proceedings cease to be 'specified proceedings'. The role of any guardian appointed under s 41 therefore cannot continue. In an appropriate case, where the court feels that there are still issues that warrant separate representation for the child, the guardian may be 'reappointed' under the Family Proceedings Rules, r 9.5 as a 'guardian ad litem'.[7]

THE CHILD PROTECTION REGISTER

4.21 The Child Protection Register is one of the most important mechanisms used by the local authority to manage information about children in its area who are thought to be at some risk, but whose circumstances do not warrant immediate or emergency intervention. The operation of the Child Protection Register and the case conference system is prescribed by the Secretary of State through the *Working Together* guidance.[8] Children are registered under one or more of four categories:

- physical abuse;
- emotional abuse;
- sexual abuse; and
- neglect.

4.22 Local authorities' use of the Child Protection Register may be regulated by the courts via the process of judicial review. The local

---

5 For 'Children's Guardian', see **5.91**.
6 *Re CE* [1995] 1 FLR 26.
7 For 'guardian ad litem' see **2.69**.
8 *Working Together* (HMSO, 1999).

authority's duty to protect children in its area must be set against the necessary invasion of a family's private life that the registration process involves.

4.23 The operation of the registration process is monitored by the appropriate Local Safeguarding Children Board. This is a multi-agency group set up with the intention of facilitating communication and the sharing of information between the various agencies working within the area of child protection.

4.24 Decisions concerning registration and de-registration are taken at a child protection conference. Responsibility for convening conferences rests with the local authority but if the conference is to have before it a full picture of the child's circumstances it is important that a wide variety of professionals and those with an interest in the child should participate. When the decision is taken to convene an initial case conference the local authority must decide who should be invited to attend. The following should generally be included:

- the child's parents and, if appropriate, wider family members
- social services staff
- the child's GP and/or practice nurse
- the child's health visitor
- the form tutor and/or head teacher of the child's school
- a representative from the police
- professionals involved with the parents.

4.25 Parents should be invited to attend case conferences unless there is a good reason why this would put the child or another person at risk: for example, where there is a history of violence perpetrated by one parent against the other. If a parent is excluded from a conference meeting he or she should be invited to meet with the chair in advance of the meeting and given the opportunity to put forward his views.

The initial child protection conference

4.26 It is the social worker's responsibility to ensure that the conference has available to it as full a picture as possible of the child's circumstances, the areas of concern, and the family's views. The social worker should provide the conference with a written report including a chronology of significant events and information on the child's health, safety and development and the parenting capacity of the parents and other relevant family members. This report will generally be based on the initial section 47 assessment. It should be made available to the parents prior to the conference.

4.27 The main purpose of the initial child protection conference is to establish whether the child should be placed on the Child Protection

Register and, if so, under what category or categories. A vote is generally taken. The conference will also make recommendations for a child protection plan.

The initial child protection conference: key functions

- Should the child be placed on the CP Register?
- Outline the child protection plan and set a date for production of the full plan
- Appoint a key worker from social services
- Identify the members of the core group and timescales for core group meetings
- Establish how the family are to be involved in the planning process
- Identify what further core and specialist assessments are required
- Consider the need for a contingency plan
- Clarify the purpose of the initial child protection conference, core group and review conference(s)
- Fix a timetable for review conferences

The core group

4.28 A 'core group' is frequently set up. This group will meet more frequently than the full case conference, and on a less formal basis. The core group consists of the parents, foster carers and wider family if appropriate, and key professionals who have regular direct contact with the family: the key worker and, where relevant, the health visitor and any family support or youth workers.

4.29 The identity of the core group should be established at the initial child protection conference and the first core group meeting should take place within 10 working days. The core group is responsible for developing the child protection plan and according to the guidance should provide a report for the conference. Core group meetings tend to be much more informal than the child protection conference. Where the parents are working with social services, meetings will often take place in the home.

Review conferences

4.30 The first child protection review case conference should take place within 3 months of the initial conference. Thereafter reviews should take place at least every 6 months.

Ongoing legal proceedings

4.31 If there are ongoing legal proceedings concerning the family, it is good practice to invite the parents' and the child's legal representatives to the case conferences. In most circumstances the local authority should also invite the Child's Guardian. Where the guardian feels that his attendance might cause the parents to doubt his independence from the local authority he need not attend but should nevertheless be provided with a copy of the conference minutes.

4.32 If the local authority solicitor attends a case conference he or she should take care to participate only as an observer and adviser should a legal point arise.

POLICE PROTECTION: SECTION 46

4.33

Police protection: key features

- No court order necessary
- Officer must have reasonable cause to believe child is likely to suffer significant harm
- Maximum duration 72 hours
- Child must be provided with suitable accommodation (refuge or local authority accommodation)
- Officer does not acquire parental responsibility
- Local authority must be informed as soon as reasonably practicable that the child has been taken into police protection

4.34 In an emergency situation police officers have the power to take a child into their protection, without a court order, for a maximum period of 72 hours. The test is whether the officer has reasonable cause to believe that the child would be likely to suffer significant harm if protective measures were not taken.[9] The police officer may remove the child to suitable accommodation and keep him there, or take reasonable steps to ensure that he is not removed from any place where he is being accommodated.

Duties of the officer taking the child into police protection

4.35 A police officer who takes a child into police protection must, as soon as reasonably practicable:

- inform the local authority where the child was found, and the local authority where he ordinarily lives (if different), of the steps that have been taken and the location of the child;
- speak to the child (if possible) to let him know what steps have been taken and the reasons for them, and to ascertain his wishes and feelings;
- find suitable accommodation for the child, either in a refuge or in local authority accommodation; and
- inform a designated (child protection) officer.

The police officer must also take whatever steps are practicable to inform the child's parents, any person with parental responsibility and any person with whom he was living of the action that has been taken, the reasons for it, and the plans for the child while he remains in police protection.

Duties of the designated officer

4.36 Once the designated child protection officer has been informed of the situation he or she must make enquiries to ensure that the test for keeping the child in police protection continues to be met: ie that there is still reasonable cause for believing that the child is at risk of significant harm. If that appears no longer to be the case the child must be released from police protection. The designated officer must also:

- consider whether he or she should apply on behalf of the appropriate local authority for an emergency protection order;
- allow the child's parents, and any other appropriate person,[10] such contact with him as the designated officer feels is in the child's best interests. If the child has been placed in local authority accommodation, this responsibility passes to the local authority.

---

9 CA 1989, s 46(1).

10 Persons with parental responsibility; any person with whom the child was living; any person in whose favour a contact order has been made under s 8 or s 34; and anyone acting on behalf of any of these persons: s 46(10).

4.37 The limitation on the length of time a child may spend in police protection means that the police have the power to act on behalf of the local authority in some limited respects during the period when the child remains in their care, in particular where there is a need to safeguard the child's welfare. The police officer does not, however, acquire parental responsibility for the child and as soon as the local authority is in a position to do so it will take over the child's care from the police.

4.38 When the local authority is informed that a child has been taken into police protection it must:

- initiate an investigation into the child's circumstances under s 47; and
- consider whether there is a need to apply for an emergency protection order.

EMERGENCY PROTECTION ORDERS: SECTION 44

4.39

Emergency protection orders: key features

- For emergency situations where immediate risk of harm
- Applicant may be any person; normally a local authority
- Initial order for 8 days; may be extended once only for up to 7 days
- Authorises the applicant to remove a child from where he is being accommodated or prevent his removal
- Applicant has parental responsibility, but this is limited to taking necessary steps to secure the child's short-term welfare

4.40 An application for an emergency protection order may be made by any person where there is an urgent need to remove, or prevent the removal of, a child at risk of significant harm. Most professionals facing an emergency situation in relation to a child should be able to enlist the help of social services or, failing that, the police. In extreme situations where for any reason such assistance is not available, any person may make the application, by telephone if necessary. If the application has been made by a person other than the local authority, the local authority will be notified and must consider whether it ought itself to take over the application.[11]

4.41 It is unlikely that a parent would need to make an application for an emergency protection order, as he or she would almost certainly be in a position to apply, if necessary without notice, for one of the section 8 orders (most likely a residence order or specific issue order). In practice the application is generally made by a local authority or a person, such as a police officer, acting on its behalf; and in this section references to 'the local authority' include other applicants unless it is clear from the context that this is not the case.

4.42 An emergency protection order gives the applicant parental responsibility for the child. Those persons who already have parental responsibility retain it, but take second place to the local authority (or other applicant) for the period of the order. It is a short-term order with two objectives: to remove an immediate risk of harm and to enable the local authority to carry out any assessments necessary to decide what, if any, longer-term measures are needed to protect the child.

Procedure

4.43 The application is made to the Family Proceedings Court, unless it is made as a result of a court-directed investigation or within pending court proceedings, in which case the application is to the court where those proceedings are ongoing. The respondents are all those persons the applicant believes to have parental responsibility, or to have had it immediately prior to the care order if the child is in care; and the child himself. They must be served with the application at least one day in advance of the hearing date. Notice of the proceedings must also be given to parents without parental responsibility; any local authority providing accommodation for the child; any person with whom the child is living; and any person providing refuge accommodation for the child. These people are not automatic respondents but may attend court and apply to become parties.

4.44 In cases where giving notice to the child's parents or to others may put him at risk, or there is some other compelling reason why

11 Emergency Protection Orders (Transfer of Responsibilities) Regulations 1991 (SI 1991/1414).

giving notice is not possible or appropriate,[12] the application may be made without notice. The permission of the justices' clerk is required. The application may be made by telephone, in which case the written application must be filed with the court within 24 hours, or as directed by the justices' clerk. The respondents must be served with the application (and order, if granted) within 48 hours.[13] If the court feels that there were insufficient grounds for making the application without notice it may fix a date for a hearing on notice to all parties.

4.45 An initial emergency protection order lasts for a maximum of 8 days; if the eighth day is a public holiday, it will expire at noon on the first day thereafter that is not a public holiday. Public holidays are defined as Christmas Day, Boxing Day, Good Friday, bank holidays and Sundays. The order may be extended on application for up to a further 7 days.[14]

4.46 The urgent nature of applications for emergency protection orders, and their limited duration, means that a full investigation of evidence by the court is unlikely to be possible or appropriate. It is rare that such an application will be adjourned for more than a couple of days. The application cannot be transferred from the Family Proceedings Court to the county court (although it may be transferred to another Family Proceedings Court if, for example, there is no magistrate available to hear the application). The strict rules of evidence do not apply and the court may take account of any oral or written evidence it considers relevant.

4.47 Applications for emergency protection orders are 'specified proceedings' for the purposes of CA 1989, s 41, and so a Children's Guardian must be appointed for the child unless the court is satisfied that this is not necessary. Given the limited duration of emergency protection orders it may not be possible for a guardian to be appointed in time to participate in the proceedings, in which case the court should appoint a solicitor to represent the child.

4.48 An emergency protection order should name the child where possible; if the child's name is not known the order should describe him or her in as much detail as possible.

---

12 Orders should be made without notice only where the child's welfare or some other important factor demands it. If an application is made without notice the applicant is under a duty to make full disclosure of all relevant information to the court, and subsequently to disclose to the other parties all evidence put before the court. See *Re S* [2001] 1 FLR 308.

13 FPC(CA1989)R 1991, r 4(4)(i).

14 CA 1989, s 45(5).

4.49 An emergency protection order may be made in respect of a child who is in care. In such a case the emergency protection order will take priority and for its duration the care order will take effect subject to the emergency protection order.[15]

Application for EPO: checklist

- Application in Form C1 with Supplement C11
- What are the plans for (a) the child's accommodation and (b) contact with parents/others?
- Is there a need for a direction regarding any medical or other assessment?
- Identify all respondents (those with parental responsibility; the child)
- Serve respondents with the application at least 1 day prior to hearing
- Child to be served via solicitor or Guardian (appointed by court upon issue of proceedings)
- Give notice of the proceedings (date, time and place of hearing, but not copies of the application) to:
  - parents without parental responsibility;
  - any local authority providing accommodation;
  - any person or refuge providing accommodation.

If application made without notice:

- Seek permission of the justices' clerk [on C11]
- Keep a note of what is said to the court in support of the application and serve it on respondents on request
- Serve respondents with the application and order as soon as possible (or as directed by the court) and give required notice to others

If application made by telephone:

- Issue the application at court within 24 hours, or as directed by the court
- Serve respondents and give required notice to others within 48 hours

---

15 CA 1989, s 91(6).

Grounds

4.50 There are two alternative grounds for an emergency protection order. They are that:

- there are reasonable grounds to believe that the child is likely to suffer significant harm if he is not removed to accommodation provided by the applicant, or kept in the accommodation where he is; or
- (provided that the applicant is a local authority or authorised person[16]):
  - the local authority is carrying out an investigation of the child's circumstances under s 47 (see **4.8**), or the authorised person is making enquiries with respect to the child's welfare;
  - the enquiries are being frustrated because access to the child is being denied; and
  - the local authority (or authorised person) has reasonable cause to believe that access is required as a matter of urgency.

4.51 Provided that one of the alternative grounds is established, the child's welfare is the paramount consideration when the court is deciding whether or not to grant an emergency protection order, and the 'no order' principle applies: the court may only make the order if satisfied that to do so would be better for the child than making no order at all. The detailed welfare checklist does not apply,[17] although many of the factors on the welfare checklist may well be of relevance.

4.52 It has been emphasised that emergency protection orders are designed for situations where there is an immediate risk of harm. They are not to be used when the risk is longer-term and the more appropriate course is the detailed court-directed investigation that would result from an application for a care or supervision order.[18]

4.53 Applications for emergency protection orders are not 'family proceedings' and therefore the court does not have the wide jurisdiction to consider alternative remedies: it may only make or refuse to make the emergency protection order.[19] Similarly, once the order has expired the local authority must decide whether or not to apply for any other order; the court cannot make further orders of its own motion.

---

16 An 'authorised person' means any person authorised by the Secretary of State under CA 1989, s 31(9) to bring care proceedings. At present the only 'authorised person' is the NSPCC.

17 CA 1989, s 1(4).

18 *Re C and B (Care Order: Future Harm)* [2001] 1 FLR 611.

19 The only exception is a child assessment order: see **4.71**.

4.54 Where the grounds for an order are that the child is living with a particular person who is said to pose a risk, the local authority should explore the possibility of that person leaving the home so that the child can remain living where he is. The local authority may assist the alleged abuser to find alternative accommodation and may assist with funding.[20] Alternatively it may encourage the child's main carer to exclude the alleged abuser from the home via one of the remedies under the Family Law Act 1996. These options should be explored before the local authority applies for an order excluding the alleged abuser from the home (see **4.63**).

Effect of the order

4.55 An emergency protection order:

- gives the applicant parental responsibility for the child;
- authorises the applicant to remove the child to accommodation provided by him, or to prevent the child's removal from a place where he is being accommodated; and
- requires any person who is in a position to do so to produce the child to the applicant on request.[21]

4.56 The local authority (or other applicant) may only exercise parental responsibility to the extent that is reasonably required in order to safeguard the child's welfare, bearing in mind the duration of the order.[22] The local authority may therefore take action to meet the child's immediate needs by, for example, providing food and accommodation and arranging for any urgent medical treatment to be carried out; but it must not interfere with any longer-term arrangements, for instance by changing the child's school.

4.57 The court may attach supplementary provisions to the order. The available directions fall into four categories:

- provisions to assist the local authority to locate or remove the child;
- regulation of the child's contact with his parents or others;
- the exclusion of a named person from the place where the child lives; and
- directions permitting, or preventing, any medical or psychiatric examination of the child.

---

20 CA 1989, Sch 2, para 5.
21 Ibid, s 44(4).
22 Ibid, s 44(5).

Locating and removing the child

4.58 Where the local authority does not have enough information about a child's whereabouts to locate him, the court may direct any named (or identified) person or persons who appear to have such information to disclose it to the local authority on request.[23]

4.59 An emergency protection order does not of itself authorise the local authority to enter premises without the occupant's permission. Where it is thought that a parent or other occupant is likely to refuse to cooperate with the local authority's social worker, or that a child may be alone in the premises, the court may give permission to the local authority to enter without the occupant's permission and search the premises for the child.[24] The local authority, however, has no means of enforcing such an order and if access to the child continues to be refused, or if it is likely from the outset that an order permitting entry will not be sufficient, the court may issue a warrant authorising a police officer to enter and search the premises, using reasonable force if necessary.[25] Note that without a warrant, a police officer may only enter and search private premises for limited purposes, including 'to save life and limb'.

4.60 The court may direct that a doctor, nurse or health visitor should accompany the social worker and/or police officer.[26]

Contact

4.61 The court is given power under s 44(6) to make directions regarding the contact the child is to have with any person during the period of the order, and may impose conditions on that contact. If no specific direction is made the local authority must allow the child to have 'reasonable contact' with his parents and any person with parental responsibility. It must also allow anyone with whom the child was living before the order, anyone in whose favour a contact order under s 8 or s 34 is in force, and any person acting on behalf of such a person to have reasonable contact with the child.

4.62 The local authority is not required to draw up detailed care plans in relation to children under emergency protection orders. It is important therefore that thought is given at an early stage to the contact that will be offered; that practical arrangements are put in place and that the parents are notified of these arrangements. If it is proposed that

23 CA 1989, s 48(1).
24 Ibid, s 48(3).
25 Ibid, s 48(12).
26 Ibid, s 48(11).

no contact should take place between the child and her family for the duration of the order, or that contact should be very limited, the local authority must seek a direction of the court to this effect when the application is made.

Exclusion requirement: section 44A

4.63 Where it is possible to identify a particular person who poses a risk to the child, an emergency protection order may include a requirement that that person be excluded from the place where the child lives. The alleged abuser may be prevented from living in the child's home, entering the home or coming within a defined area in which the home is situated. The exclusion requirement will generally last for the same period as the emergency protection order, although it may last for a shorter period. If it is breached the local authority may make an application to enforce it.

4.64 The court may only include an exclusion requirement in an emergency protection order if there is someone else living in the home who is willing and able to care for the child, and who consents to the exclusion requirement being imposed.

4.65 A power of arrest may be attached to the exclusion requirement. The effect of this is to give the police the power to arrest without a warrant any person who they have reasonable cause to believe is in breach of the exclusion requirement.

4.66 In place of an order, the court may accept an undertaking from the person whom the local authority seeks to exclude. The undertaking is enforceable in the same way as an exclusion requirement that is part of the order. The only difference is that a power of arrest cannot be attached to an undertaking. If a breach is anticipated and it is likely that the assistance of the police will be needed, an undertaking is unlikely to be acceptable and the court should make an order together with a power of arrest.

4.67 If during the period of the exclusion requirement the child is removed from the home to other accommodation for a period in excess of 24 hours, the local authority must inform the person excluded and the exclusion requirement will cease to have effect.

Medical examinations and assessments

4.68 As part of its exercise of parental responsibility, the local authority may and should arrange for the child to have any medical treatment that becomes necessary during the period of the emergency protection order. Bearing in mind the duration of an emergency protection order, and the limitations on its exercise of parental responsibility, the local authority would be wise not to arrange any non-essential medical examination during the period of the order without the court's permission. The court may give any directions it deems appropriate regarding a medical or psychiatric examination or assessment, and may direct that no such assessment should be carried out.[27] If a medical or psychiatric assessment is proposed this should be raised with the court as soon as possible and a direction sought.

4.69 As in all situations where the local authority shares parental responsibility, the child's parents should be consulted where possible in relation to all proposed medical treatment. A child who is *Gillick*-competent[28] may refuse to submit to an examination or treatment.

Challenging an emergency protection order

4.70 The routes by which an emergency protection order may be challenged are restricted. There is no right of appeal. A party may attend the initial hearing and oppose the making of an emergency protection order; but if he is not successful he cannot then apply for it to be discharged. An application for discharge of the emergency protection order can only be made by a person who did *not* attend the initial hearing. The application can be made as soon as the emergency protection order is made, but cannot be heard until a period of 72 hours has elapsed.[29]

EXAMPLE: POLICE PROTECTION TO AN EMERGENCY PROTECTION ORDER

On Christmas Eve (a Friday) at 9pm, two police officers are called to a fight in a house. They attend and find a woman badly injured, her drunk partner, who readily admits to having beaten her up, and their 3-year-old son. Having called an ambulance and arrested the partner it is plain that there is no one available to care for the boy. The officers tell the parents they are taking the child into police protection and inform them that they will be told as soon as possible of the address where he will be accommodated and that arrangements will be made for them to see him. The officers take the child to the police station and telephone social services' out-of-hours number. Early on Christmas morning a duty social worker finally manages to arrange an emergency foster placement and arrives to pick up the child. Although the child remains in police protection, he is now staying in accommodation

27 CA 1989, s 44(6) and (8).

28 See **2.18**.

29 CA 1989, s 45(9).

provided by the local authority and therefore social services are responsible for making decisions about his contact with his parents.

The designated officer is informed in the early hours of Christmas Day. He speaks to the officers in the case and is of the view that the boy would be at risk of significant harm if he were to return home. The officer is aware that the 72-hour period will expire at 9pm on Monday 27 December, also a bank holiday, and that it is unlikely that the local authority will be able to apply for an emergency protection order before then. Therefore on Sunday 26 December the designated officer telephones the local Family Proceedings Court's emergency number. A justices' clerk is located and gives the officer permission to make the application.[30] *A District Judge is located and the application is made and granted by telephone. The order is made for a period of 4 days.*

The District Judge orders that the parents should be notified immediately of the order and that the formal application should be issued. He lists the matter at court on Wednesday afternoon. On Tuesday 28 December the designated officer manages to contact a local authority solicitor who takes over the case. He prepares the application and issues it on Tuesday afternoon. At the hearing on Wednesday afternoon the emergency protection order is extended for a period of 7 days.

CHILD ASSESSMENT ORDERS: SECTION 43

Child assessment orders: key features

- For non-emergency situations where attempts to carry out an assessment are being frustrated
- Applicant is the local authority or authorised person
- Maximum duration 7 days; no extension
- The applicant does not acquire parental responsibility

4.71 Child assessment orders, made under CA 1989, s 43, have close connections to emergency protection orders. They are designed to facilitate access to a child where it is suspected that he is at risk but the local authority is having difficulties in carrying out an assessment to establish whether or not this is the case. They do not have the force of emergency protection orders or orders under Part IV of the Act (care and supervision orders): the local authority does not acquire parental

30 FPC(CA 1989)R 1991, r 4(4)(i).

responsibility and therefore is powerless if the family does not comply with the order. If there is a failure to cooperate once the order is made, the local authority's only option is to apply for an emergency protection order or, if it is in a position to do so, an interim care order.

4.72 This means that if there is an immediate risk to the child, and his parents have not responded to previous efforts to engage them, an emergency protection order rather than a child assessment order may be necessary. If the court feels it is appropriate, it may treat an application for a child assessment order as an application for an emergency protection order. Once it has decided to do so, it cannot then 'go back' and make the child assessment order but may only make or refuse the emergency protection order.

4.73 The order lasts for a maximum of 7 days, and there is no permitted extension.[31]

Procedure

4.74 While any person may apply for an emergency protection order, the applicant for a child assessment order must be the local authority or an authorised person (currently only officers of the NSPCC). The respondents are:

- the child;
- any person with parental responsibility; and
- (where relevant) any person who had parental responsibility before a care order was made.

4.75 The application, like the application for an emergency protection order, is made in the family proceedings court unless it arises out of a court-directed investigation or is made within pending proceedings. Unlike an application for an emergency protection order, it must be made on notice to all the parties.

4.76 Applications for child assessment orders, like applications for emergency protection orders, are 'specified proceedings' and a Children's Guardian must be appointed unless the child's interests may otherwise be safeguarded. The observations above concerning the short duration of emergency protection orders and the fact that any involvement of a guardian will necessarily be limited are equally relevant to child assessment orders.

4.77 The court may:

---

31 CA 1989, s 43(5).

- make the child assessment order;
- refuse to make the order;
- treat the application as an application for an emergency protection order and, if appropriate, make that order.

4.78 As is the case in proceedings for an emergency protection order, the proceedings are not 'family proceedings' and the wide discretion to make other orders is not available to the court.

Grounds for the order

4.79 The grounds for a child assessment order are that:

- the applicant has reasonable cause to suspect that the child is suffering or is likely to suffer significant harm;
- an assessment of the child's health or development, or the way in which he has been treated, is necessary to enable the applicant to establish whether or not he is at risk of significant harm; and
- it is unlikely that such an assessment will be carried out satisfactorily without an order.

4.80 The child's welfare is paramount and the 'no order' principle applies. The welfare checklist does not apply, but many of its factors may be relevant.

4.81 The local authority will have to satisfy the court that the proposed assessment is a necessary one. It will need to inform the court of the steps that have already been taken in an attempt to carry out the assessment. If the parents have refused to cooperate with the proposed assessment the court will need to be satisfied that they are frustrating the local authority's enquiries. It will not be enough to show that there is a dispute about how or by whom an assessment should be carried out.

Effect of the order

4.82 A child assessment order does not give the local authority parental responsibility. It authorises the local authority to carry out the assessment specified in the order. The order may, if necessary, make directions regarding the person who is to carry out the assessment and the place and time where the child is to be produced for the assessment. Because the scope of the order is limited to a specified assessment it is important that what is proposed is set out clearly both in the application and in the order.

RECOVERY ORDERS: SECTION 50

4.83 A recovery order may be made when a child who is in the care of the local authority, in police protection, or subject to an emergency protection order has been abducted, run away or gone missing. Abduction of a child from care is a criminal offence.[32]

4.84 The court's powers to make recovery orders should be considered in tandem with its powers to make directions for the location and recovery of a child in conjunction with an emergency protection order. Where the grounds for an emergency protection order exist, this may well be the preferred option.

Procedure

4.85 The applicant for a recovery order must be the person who has parental responsibility by virtue of the original order (ie the local authority) or, if the child is in police protection, the designated officer. The application may be made without notice, with permission of the justices' clerk, and may be made by telephone. In general the procedure is very similar to that on an application for an emergency protection order.

4.86 The respondents are:

- the child;
- any person with parental responsibility;
- any person with parental responsibility prior to any existing care order;
- the person who is said to have abducted or to be keeping the child.

4.87 Notice must be given to:

- any local authority providing accommodation for the child;
- any person (for example a foster carer) with whom the child was living;
- any person providing an authorised refuge where it is said that the child is staying.

4.88 The application is made in the family proceedings court, unless connected to ongoing proceedings elsewhere.

Effect of the order

4.89 A recovery order authorises the person with parental responsibility to remove the child from wherever he is being kept. It also

32 CA 1989, s 49.

operates as a direction to any person who is in a position to do so to produce the child on request, or to disclose any information he possesses about the child's whereabouts to a police officer or an officer of the court. The order may specify premises that a police officer is authorised to enter, by force if necessary, to search for the child.

4.90 The person with parental responsibility (usually the local authority) must authorise one of its officers to exercise its powers under the recovery order. Normally an officer of the local authority will attend the property where it is thought the child is being kept together with one or more police officers.

4.91 Under the CA 1989 it is an offence to obstruct an authorised person implementing a recovery order.[33] The maximum sentence for this offence is a fine. However, a person who resists a police officer acting in the execution of his duty may be arrested without a warrant and sentenced on conviction to a month's imprisonment.

EXAMPLE

A local authority applies for a care order in respect of a child. At the first hearing in the family proceedings court the parents (who have been served with the application) do not attend. The court makes an interim care order on the local authority's care plan for immediate removal. Social workers immediately attend the child's home, but the parents refuse to let them in. The local authority returns to court the same day with an application (without notice) for a recovery order. This is granted and the social worker returns to the home with two police officers. The officers force entry to the house. The child's mother will not give the child up to the officers. When it becomes clear that she cannot be persuaded, she is arrested for obstructing a constable in the execution of his duty and the officer, as he is entitled to do, uses reasonable force to effect the arrest. The child is then recovered.

Older children

4.92 A care order lasts until a child is 18, unless it is previously discharged. This means that, in theory, a child aged 16 or 17 who decides to leave 'home', may be made the subject of a recovery order. If the child refuses to return it is unclear whether or not she can be forced to do so. It is difficult to see how. A local authority facing this situation should think carefully about whether it ought to be making an application under s 50 or whether there is some other way of protecting the child.

---

33 CA 1989, s 50(9).

4.93 While a person who assists or provides a refuge to a child who has run away from care is guilty of a criminal offence,[34] an exception is made for those who provide registered accommodation in a refuge for children at risk. This means that charities and other groups who provide 'safe houses' for runaway children are not liable to prosecution.[35]

CHILD SAFETY ORDERS AND PARENTING ORDERS

4.94 The Crime and Disorder Act (CDA) 1998, which introduced the anti-social behaviour legislation ('ASBO's) also gave local authorities the power to apply for orders to assist them in managing the behaviour of children and young people in their areas.

4.95 A Child Safety Order can be made in respect of a child under the age of 10 who has committed an offence, is likely to commit an offence, has contravened a curfew or has acted in a manner that caused or is likely to cause harassment, alarm or distress. The order places the child under the supervision of a named 'responsible officer' (either a social worker or a member of a youth offending team).[36]

4.96 The application is made to a magistrates' court and the court is required to obtain information about the child's family circumstances before making the order. The power of a magistrates' court to make a care order following a child's failure to comply with a requirement of the order has been removed by the Children Act 2004.[37]

4.97 A parenting order may be made in proceedings in any court where:

- a child safety order is made;
- an anti-social behaviour order is made in respect of a child;
- a child is convicted of an offence; or
- a parent is convicted of an offence relating to a failure to secure a child's attendance at school.[38]

4.98 A parenting order may be made in such a case provided that the court considers it would be desirable in the interests of addressing the child's anti-social or offending behaviour, or the problems with her school attendance. The order may require the child's parent to attend a specified counselling or guidance programme or to comply with any other requirements contained in the order.

---

34 CA 1989, s 49(1)(b) and (c).
35 Ibid, s 51.
36 CDA 1998, s 11.
37 CA 2004, s 60.
38 CDA 1998, s 8.

4.99 The maximum duration of a parenting order or a child safety order is 12 months.

5

CARE AND SUPERVISION ORDERS

Chapter summary

- The orders
- The threshold criteria
- The welfare checklist
- Care proceedings: application and procedure
- Representing the child
- Evidence
- The role of the expert witness
- Parental contact with children in care
- Special guardianship
- Further issues

THE ORDERS AVAILABLE

5.1 Part IV of the CA 1989 deals with care and supervision orders. These two orders are designed for the more serious cases where there is a risk of significant harm to a child. They enable the court to sanction the kind of long-term local authority intervention and monitoring that cannot be provided via any of the supportive services described in Part III of the Act (see Chapter 3).

Care orders

5.2 A care order gives the local authority designated in the order[1] parental responsibility for the child. Parental responsibility is shared with the parents, but the local authority is in the driving seat and may restrict the parents' exercise of their parental responsibility. In practical terms, this means that the local authority may if necessary take over responsibility for meeting the child's needs. There are some limitations on the local authority's power to exercise parental responsibility: it cannot change the child's religion or consent to his adoption, or change his surname without the permission of the court. Children subject to a care order may be placed with their parents, with other relatives, in a children's home or in foster care.[2]

5.3 A care order may not be made once the child has reached the age of 17. If it is made before this time it will last until the child is 18, unless it is discharged by the court.

5.4 A child who is the subject of a care order may continue to live at home with her parents. However, the parental responsibility given to the local authority by the order will allow it to remove the child and place her in local authority accommodation at any time. In an emergency this may be done without notice to the parents.

5.5 The making of a care order automatically discharges any current section 8 order (see Chapter 2) and any supervision order or interim care or supervision order made in respect of the child.

5.6 A child who is the subject of a care order is a 'looked after child' for the purposes of the CA 1989 (see Chapter 3).

Supervision orders

5.7 A supervision order does not give the local authority parental responsibility. It imposes a duty on the local authority to 'advise, assist and befriend' the supervised child. The parents must allow the local authority reasonable contact with the child.[3] However, there are no sanctions for breach of a supervision order; if the local authority has concerns about the parents' lack of cooperation it will have to convince

---

1 The designated local authority is the authority in which the child ordinarily resides: CA 1989, s 31(8). Disputes may arise where it is not clear which of two local authorities is the 'designated authority' for the purposes of a care order. For guidance see *C v Plymouth City Council* [2000] 1 FLR 875 and **5.53**.

2 See Chapter 3 for the local authority's duties concerning the provision of accommodation.

3 CA 1989, Sch 3, para 8(2)(b).

the court that there is a need for the more draconian care order. An initial supervision order lasts for a maximum of 1 year;[4] it may be extended to a maximum of 3 years in total but will terminate once the child is 18.

5.8 Proceedings arising out of applications for care and supervision orders are known as 'care proceedings'. On an application for a care order the court may make a supervision order, and vice versa.

THE THRESHOLD CRITERIA

5.9 When a local authority applies for a care or supervision order it must satisfy the court that two initial conditions for state intervention are met. These conditions are:

(1) The child must be suffering, or likely to suffer, significant harm.
(2) The harm or likelihood of harm must be attributable to one of the following:
   - the care given to the child, or likely to be given if the order were not made, not being what it would be reasonable to expect a parent to give, or
   - the child's being beyond parental control.[5]

Unless both these conditions are met the court cannot sanction state intervention in the form of a care or supervision order. The conditions are known as the 'threshold criteria'. If the local authority can prove on the balance of probabilities that the threshold criteria have been established, the court must then go on to decide, applying the welfare checklist,[6] whether it is in the child's interests that a care or supervision order should be made.

Significant harm

5.10 The CA 1989 gives guidance on what is meant by 'harm', although the line between harm and 'significant' harm is not defined. 'Harm' is defined broadly, and can include ill-treatment or the impairment of health (physical or mental) or development. All aspects of a child's development are relevant. Ill-treatment includes sexual abuse and need not be physical ill-treatment.

5.11 The court should have in mind, when considering the significance of the harm suffered in terms of impaired development, what could

4 CA 1989, Sch 3, para 6(1), (3).
5 Ibid, s 31(2).
6 Ibid, s 1(3) – see **5.23**.

reasonably be expected of a similar child.[7] Frequently it will have access to information that places the child on the spectrum of children of a similar age. If the child is not meeting his developmental milestones, or has fallen from his normal position on the percentile chart for his height or weight, it will be necessary to find out why this is and whether it is attributable to the quality of parental care. It is likely that prolonged unauthorised absences from school will give rise to significant harm.

5.12 It is important to be alert to the risk or presence of emotional harm to the child. An abandoned baby is not just at risk of physical injury but is also likely to suffer significant emotional harm as a result of having no knowledge of his parents or background.[8] Witnessing violence is a common cause of emotional harm, even when the child is not directly involved. This has long been acknowledged by professionals and the courts, and is now given statutory endorsement by the Adoption and Children Act 2002, which has extended the definition of harm in s 31 of the CA 1989 to include 'impairment suffered by hearing or seeing the ill-treatment of another'.

5.13 Whether or not the harm alleged is 'significant' is something for the court to decide. Significant should be given its ordinary meaning ('considerable, noteworthy or important') and the child's particular characteristics should be taken into account: a two-year-old left alone with a pan of boiling water within reach is likely to suffer significant harm, but a thirteen-year-old is not. Similarly, the harm caused to a diabetic child by being fed a bag of sweets is significant; another child will suffer nothing worse than an upset stomach and toothache.

'Likely to suffer'

5.14 The phrase 'likely to suffer' in s 31(1) does *not* mean 'is more likely than not to suffer' or 'has a greater than 50% chance of suffering'. 'Likelihood' in this context means a real, substantial risk. The court must ask itself whether the risk of harm is or was such that it could not sensibly be ignored.

5.15 However, where the likelihood of harm occurring in the future is based on disputed past events, the court must first decide, on the balance of probabilities, where the truth lies.

EXAMPLE

A toddler is brought to hospital suffering from serious head injuries. The doctors operate but the child dies. The parents say that the child fell

---

7 CA 1989, s 31(10).
8 *Re M* [1996] 2 FLR 84.

down the stairs: the safety gate was faulty. The doctors are suspicious – the injuries suggest a blow rather than a fall – and contact social services and the police. An initial criminal investigation results in no further action being taken. Two years later the parents have another child. Social services are very worried and apply for a care order based on the likelihood of future harm to the new baby.

At first glance it would seem that the court could well decide that the threshold criteria are made out. If there is a real possibility that the first child's death was non-accidental, there must be a real possibility – or 'likelihood' – that the second child will also suffer significant harm. It might be thought that this amounts to a risk that cannot sensibly be ignored.

5.16 However the House of Lords[9] has held that where there is a disputed past event the court must not treat this as grounding a future risk without making a finding of fact about its truth. Therefore the court must first decide what happened in the past. On the balance of probabilities, was the first child's death an accident or the result of deliberate injury? If the court cannot find that it is more probable than not that the first death was non-accidental, there is no past event on which to base future risk, and the threshold criteria are not met.

The relevant date

5.17 The date for determining the occurrence or likelihood of significant harm is the date when the hearing takes place, or, if earlier, the date when the local authority first took steps to protect the child (eg made an application for an order, or placed the child with his parents' consent in foster care), provided that whatever arrangements the local authority made have been in place continuously up until the date of the hearing.

5.18 The court may take into account evidence that comes to light *after* the local authority has put in place protective measures, if it throws light on the situation at the relevant time. So if a child living in foster care under an interim order describes to his foster carer an occasion when he was beaten by his father, this evidence may be used to substantiate the threshold criteria. However, this will only be the case if the beating took place *before* the local authority took steps to protect the child by placing him in foster care. If the beating happened after the placement, perhaps during a contact visit, it cannot form part of the

---

9 *Re H* [1993] 1 FLR 643. This case (which resulted in a split House of Lords) illustrates the difficulty of striking a balance between the two aims of protecting the child and preserving the autonomy of the family.

'threshold' evidence. It will come to be considered if the court finds the threshold criteria made out and moves on to consider the welfare checklist, below.

'Attributable to parental care'

5.19 The harm that the child has suffered or is likely to suffer must be attributable to the care that is given to him being below the standard reasonably expected of a parent. This means that there must be a causal link between the care given to the child and the incidence or likelihood of him suffering significant harm. The child's own characteristics will be relevant: a child with complex medical needs may have suffered significant harm, but whether or not this is attributable to the care he has received may be a very difficult question to answer. The person whose care for the child may present a risk need not actually be the child's parent: the unsatisfactory care provided by a grandparent, step-parent or even childminder may fall within the scope of s 31(2).

The standard expected of a 'reasonable' parent

5.20 Parents often feel, once care proceedings are under way and the spotlight is on them and their family, that nothing less than Mary Poppins-style perfection will do. From a social worker's point of view it can be difficult to know what is outside the bracket of 'reasonable' parenting. Physical chastisement of children falls into this grey area. Terms such as 'acceptable' and 'appropriate' tend to creep in, but can be subjective and need to be used with care.

5.21 Of course there are times when it is plain that a child has been neglected or hurt or abused, and that his parent is responsible. The threshold criteria are very likely to be met in these cases, and the real question for the court will be whether, perhaps with support from social services or other agencies, the parent(s) can be helped to provide what has come to be known as 'good enough' parenting.

5.22 Parents who are themselves vulnerable, perhaps because they are very young or have some degree of learning disability or physical impairment that affects their ability to care for their child, may argue that it is not 'unreasonable' of them to provide a lower standard of care than the average parent. But the test is an objective one and the issue is whether the harm is attributable to the care that it would be reasonable to expect *a* parent – not *this* parent – to give. In practice, courts are prepared to brand the inadequate care caused by a parent's youth, drug addiction or even mental illness 'unreasonable'; but it would be a harsh court that found the threshold criteria made out on the basis of a parent's physical disability alone. When the parent is himself vulnerable the levels of support provided by the local authority, and the parent's willingness to accept this support, will be highly relevant to the court's assessment of the plan for the child's future care.

The child beyond parental control

5.23 A child who is putting himself at risk through no fault of his parents may be the subject of care proceedings, provided that the harm or likelihood of significant harm exists. It is important to remember that not every child who is beyond parental control will have suffered or be at risk of significant harm. Indicators of harm may include persistent truancy, absconding and drug or alcohol abuse.

5.24 Where a child in local authority accommodation is putting himself or others at risk of injury, or regularly absconds and is likely thereby to suffer significant harm, he may be placed in secure accommodation: see Chapter 7.

THE WELFARE CHECKLIST

5.25 If, and only if, the court finds the threshold criteria have been made out it will go on to decide whether or not to make an order. The 'no order' principle and the welfare principle will apply (see Chapter 1). The task for the court is to decide what order, if any, the child's needs and interests require, and the welfare checklist is a tool designed to highlight particular aspects of the child's situation that will be relevant to this decision.

5.26 The matters in the welfare checklist are as follows:

(a) the ascertainable wishes and feelings of the child concerned (considered in the light of his age and understanding);
(b) his physical, emotional and educational needs;
(c) the likely effect on him of any change in his circumstances;
(d) his age, sex, background and any characteristics of his which the court considers relevant;
(e) any harm which he has suffered or is at risk of suffering;
(f) how capable each of his parents, and any other person in relation to whom the court considers the question to be relevant, is of meeting his needs;
(g) the range of powers available to the court under this Act in the proceedings in question.

5.27 Many of the factors listed in the welfare checklist will be taken into account as a matter of common sense. There are a number of situations commonly considered by the courts where one or more of the factors in the welfare checklist are likely to be relevant.

The birth family

5.28 It has been emphasised several times that local authorities must not lose sight of the importance of the child's natural family, and must work towards reunification of the family where that is possible. The Human Rights Act 1998 brought into domestic law the European concept of proportionality: any interference with a person's right to a private and family life must be justified, and no more than is necessary in order to protect the child. Where a child's rights conflict with an adult's the child's interests will take priority; but the child too has a right to family life, and a right to know and be brought up by his natural parents wherever possible.

5.29 If the child cannot live with a member of her natural family, the court must not forget the importance to her of maintaining a relationship with them. This may be through ongoing direct contact or, at the very least, an exchange of letters and photographs. Even when a child is to be adopted, the adoption agency will collect information about the birth family to help the child ultimately to have some understanding of her birth identity and parentage.

5.30 The Adoption and Children Act 2002 requires the local authority and the court to consider an adoption-specific welfare checklist when coming to a decision relating to the adoption of a child (and presumably when considering a care plan that provides for the child to be adopted).[10] The following extracts from the checklist illustrate the focus on the birth family:

> '(c) the likely effect on the child (throughout his life) of having ceased to be a member of the original family and become an adopted person …
>
> (f) the relationship which the child has with relatives, and with any other person in relation to whom the court or agency considers the relationship to be relevant, including
>
> (i) the likelihood of any relationship continuing and the value to the child of its doing so,
>
> (ii) the ability and willingness of any of the child's relatives, or of any such person, to provide the child with a secure environment in which the child can develop, and otherwise meet the child's needs,
>
> (iii) the wishes and feelings of any of the child's relatives, or of any such person, regarding the child.'

---

10 For a detailed discussion of the ACA 2002 and the 'adoption' welfare checklist, see **6.27** ff.

Splitting siblings

5.31 When a parent cannot manage to look after all of his or her children, but may be able to care for one of them, the court must balance the benefits of keeping siblings together against the advantage of being brought up by a natural parent. This is a difficult decision and the court must look at each case individually. Much will depend on the strength of the sibling relationship. In one case where the plan was that contact between the siblings should continue in any event, the court held that the benefit of keeping one child with his father outweighed the disadvantages of splitting the siblings.[11]

Babies and young children

5.32 A local authority seeking to remove a child at or shortly after birth must be prepared to justify this 'draconian' action, even on an interim basis, and make proper arrangements for contact including arrangements for breast-feeding if the mother wishes. Contact should generally take place most days of the week for lengthy periods of time.[12]

5.33 If a final care order is to be made, however, the younger the child the more likely it is that the court will be prepared to endorse a care plan that provides for the child to be adopted out of its natural family. There are two reasons for this: first, the stability that adoption offers in comparison to a childhood spent moving around different foster homes and care homes; and secondly, the fact that the younger the child is, the greater the chances are of a successful adoption.

5.34 Note that although the local authority may make plans for issuing legal proceedings before the birth of a child, no application for any order may be made until the child is born. If there is an urgent need to protect the child the local authority must have the application ready for issue upon the child's birth. If this has not been possible and the grounds for emergency intervention exist, an emergency protection order may be sought following the child's birth, or the child may be taken into police protection (see Chapter 4).

Older children

5.35 The older the child, the more likely it is that his wishes and feelings will be given serious consideration. Since the case of *Gillick v*

11 *Re D* [1999] 1 FLR 134.

12 *Re M* [2003] 2 FLR 171. But the local authority's available resources are also a relevant factor.

West Norfolk and Wisbech Area Health Authority[13] in 1986 the courts have had to pay careful attention to the views of a child whose level of maturity and understanding means that she is competent to make many decisions for herself.

5.36 The age at which children's views are nearly determinative of the issue will vary according to the nature and seriousness of the matter in question as well as the maturity of the child. In private law proceedings children tend to achieve this level of competence younger than in care proceedings: it is not uncommon that the views of a child as young as 10 will tip the balance in a residence or contact application. In care proceedings, however, the stakes tend to be higher and the child may not have the ability to appreciate, for example, any risk of emotional harm. Although children aged (say) 10 to 13 may have clearly-expressed views, they may not have the maturity to make an informed judgment in the context of their welfare needs in the long term.

5.37 In practice a child's age and sense of independence may make it almost impossible for the local authority to effect a care plan that is contrary to his wishes, notwithstanding that it may be in his long-term interests. The local authority may find itself forced to compromise by providing a package of support to the child at home, if the alternative is a foster placement that carries a high risk of breaking down.

Teenage parents

5.38 It is the welfare of the child who is the subject of the proceedings that is paramount, even when one or both of the parents is also a child. Where the mother is very young, the proceedings should be transferred to the High Court and a separate guardian ad litem appointed for the mother. It is not inevitable that babies of very young mothers should be adopted: where there is family or other support for the mother this may well not be the case. However, where the mother's own background or vulnerability makes it likely that the local authority will seek a care order with a plan for adoption, the local authority should begin planning for both mother and baby at an early stage, well before the birth.[14]

Special needs

5.39 A child's special needs may in the end be the factor that determines whether or not his parents can provide him with adequate care. However, it is important to bear in mind the services that a local

13 [1986] 1 FLR 224.

14 *Re R* [2000] 2 FLR 660.

authority must provide to children in need, a category that includes disabled children (see Chapter 3). Local authorities should be prepared to explain what support services have been or may be provided to the family of a disabled child, and why his parents are nevertheless unable to care for him, before seeking a care order.

5.40 Similar considerations may apply, with similar caveats, to particularly gifted children. A parent with learning disabilities may struggle to meet the needs of a very bright child. Again, however, the local authority should proceed with caution: the aim of the court is not to provide the child with a designer family, and the benefits to a child of making a care order must be clear and compelling if they are to outweigh the advantages of being brought up by a natural parent.

The care plan

5.41 The variety of situations which may lead to an application for a care or supervision order illustrates the need for local authorities to place the child's particular needs and circumstances at the heart of their planning for the child. These needs must inform not only the placement that is to be offered to the child but the educational, therapeutic and other services that will be provided to her and the contact she will have with her birth family. The court will measure the local authority's care plan against the pointers contained in the welfare checklist and will be concerned to see that the child's needs, as indicated by the welfare checklist, will be met. The content and structure of the local authority's care plan is discussed more fully below at **5.75**.

CARE PROCEEDINGS: APPLICATION AND PROCEDURE

The parties

5.42 The applicant for a care or supervision order is almost always the local authority. The only other body at present authorised to bring care proceedings is the NSPCC; in practice, it is far more likely that the NSPCC will refer the case to the local authority.[15] Regardless of who made the application, any care or supervision order will place the child in the care or under the supervision of a local authority.

---

15 The NSPCC has a duty before making an application to consult with the local authority in whose area the child is ordinarily resident: s 31(6).

5.43 The 'automatic' respondents to an application for a care or supervision order are the child, and any person who has parental responsibility for him.[16] In addition the local authority is obliged to give notice of the proceedings to:

- any person with whom the child is living;
- any local authority providing accommodation for the child;
- any person providing a refuge for the child;
- any party to pending relevant court proceedings relating to the child; and
- any parent (ie father) without parental responsibility.[17]

5.44 These persons will be informed of the date and place of the first hearing but will not be served with the application or any papers that have been filed. They may attend the hearing and apply to be joined as parties to the proceedings. The old test for joinder (whether the respondent's position disclosed an arguable case) has been refined in the light of the Human Rights Act and the Article 8 rights of extended family members as well as parents to a private and family life.[18] However, where a person's position or point of view is identical to that of an existing party, it is unlikely that he or she will also be joined to the proceedings.[19]

5.45 A father without parental responsibility is in a stronger position. Although he is not automatically a party and will require the court's permission to take part in the proceedings, this permission will be granted unless there is a good reason for refusing it.[20]

5.46 Once a person has been joined as a party to the proceedings his or her Article 6 right (to a fair trial) is engaged. This does not always extend to the right to see all of the papers filed in the proceedings: in rare cases where disclosure of all the papers would be an unacceptable infringement of another party's right to a private and family life the court may order limited confidentiality.[21]

5.47 Where the factors that led to a person being joined as a party cease to apply, the court may order that party's removal from the proceedings.

---

16 FPR 1991, r.4.7.
17 Ibid, r 4.4.
18 *Re J* [2004] 1 FLR 114.
19 *Re W* [2005] 2 FLR 468.
20 *Re B* [1999] 2 FLR 408.
21 *Re C* [1996] 1 FLR 797.

Intervenors

5.48 Where allegations are made within proceedings against a person who is not a party, or where a non-party's interests may be affected by the proceedings, the court may direct that that person may participate in the proceedings to a limited extent, without becoming a full party. He or she may have legal representation but is unlikely to see all the papers in the proceedings or attend for the entirety of the hearing. The judge must determine the extent of the intervenor's participation and the way in which the relevant evidence will be presented. A prime example of a person who may be permitted to intervene is a person against whom serious allegations of abuse have been made, but who is not otherwise a party to the proceedings.

Transfer of proceedings

5.49 Unless made as a result of a section 37 direction[22] or in pending proceedings, the application for a care or supervision order must be made in the family proceedings court. At the first hearing the court must consider whether the case should be transferred up to the county court on the grounds of gravity, complexity or importance or for any other reason. The county court may subsequently transfer the case to the High Court. Although some cases are plainly inappropriate for hearing in the family proceedings court or indeed county court, in a borderline case the court must consider whether the transfer would give rise to any delay in the proceedings.[23]

5.50 It has been said that cases with a time estimate of more than 2–3 days are unlikely to be appropriate for determination in the family proceedings court.[24] However, the courts are becoming increasingly reluctant, no doubt because of the delays and shortage of judges at county court level and above, to transfer cases upwards. Many family proceedings courts now have an informal 'cut-off' point of five days. If an application for transfer is refused by the justices or the justices' clerk any party may apply to a district judge of the county court to transfer the proceedings. Note that this is a fresh application and not an appeal.

5.51 The family proceedings court and the county court may transfer the proceedings 'sideways' – ie to another court at the same level – if there is a good reason for doing so, for example that there is a likelihood that the matter will be heard more quickly if it is transferred.

---

22 See Chapter 4.

23 Children (Allocation of Proceedings) Order 1991 (SI 1991/1677).

24 *Re H* [1993] 1 FLR 440.

5.52 Where during the proceedings it becomes apparent that the grounds for transfer no longer subsist the county court or High Court may transfer the case back to the lower court.

Grounds for transfer: FPC to county court (C(AP)O 1991, reg 7)

- The proceedings are exceptionally grave, important or complex, in particular:
  - because of complicated or conflicting evidence about the risks involved to the child's physical or moral wellbeing or about other matters relating to the welfare of the child;
  - because of the number of parties;
  - because of a conflict with the law of another jurisdiction;
  - because of some novel and difficult point of law; or
  - because of some question of general public interest.
- It would be appropriate for the proceedings to be heard together with other family proceedings pending in another court.
- Transfer is necessary to avoid significant delay that would seriously prejudice the child's welfare.

Grounds for transfer: county court to High Court (C(AP)O 1991, reg 12)

- The proceedings are appropriate for determination in the High Court, and
- Such determination would be in the interests of the child.

The designated local authority

5.53 Any local authority may initiate care proceedings, but if an order is made the local authority named in the order must be that where the child is ordinarily resident or, if the child is not ordinarily resident in any local authority, the authority where the circumstances arose that led to the making of the order.[25]

5.54 In most cases the designated local authority is the same as the authority that brings the proceedings. On occasion it is necessary to determine which is the designated authority. The courts have consistently shown their disapproval of lengthy litigation over what

25 CA 1989, s 31(8).

should be a practical and administrative matter.[26] The underlying issue, particularly in a long or complex case, is almost always one of resources.

5.55 Because children will sometimes be placed in foster care outside their 'home' authority, a child's ordinary residence is to be determined by reference to where the child was living before being accommodated. Any period in local authority accommodation does not count for the purposes of determining ordinary residence.

5.56 Where the designated local authority is not the authority bringing the proceedings the two authorities should liaise as soon as possible and, depending on the stage that has been reached, the designated local authority may take over the proceedings.

The role of the court

5.57 The court cannot make a care or supervision order except on an application by the local authority or other authorised person. It may make a care order on an application for a supervision order, and vice versa. The only exception to the general rule is that the court may make an interim care or supervision order if it has made a section 37 direction requiring the local authority to investigate the child's circumstances (see Chapter 4).

5.58 The court's power under the Crime and Disorder Act 1998 to make a care order on non-compliance with a child safety order was removed by the Children Act 2004 as from 1 March 2005. See Chapter 4 for child safety orders and parenting orders under the 1998 Act.

5.59 The court's role is investigative. Even where the parties have all come to an agreement it is the duty of the judge to scrutinise that agreement and ensure that the threshold criteria have been made out, the proposed order is necessary, proportionate and in the child's interests, and the care plan will best meet his needs.

The Protocol

5.60 The court must follow the Protocol for Judicial Case Management. Since 2003 courts have been managing all care cases in accordance with the Protocol timetable, which was designed with the aim of completing proceedings within 40 weeks of the application being issued. A key Protocol principle is judicial continuity: it is expected that wherever possible the same judge will deal with all hearings in the case to ensure effective case management throughout the proceedings.

---

26 See for example *Northamptonshire County Council v Islington Borough Council* [1999] 2 FLR 881.

5.61 The Protocol is available at http://www.hmcourts-service.gov.uk/docs/protocol-complete.pdf and summarised at Appendix 5.

Interim orders

5.62 It can be several months from the application to the final hearing of care proceedings. The court must decide whether there is a need for the local authority to share parental responsibility for the child during this interim period by means of an interim care order; whether there should be an interim supervision order; or whether the child will be sufficiently protected without an order until the matter is heard.

5.63 The grounds for an interim order differ from those for a final order in that it is not necessary to prove that the threshold criteria are made out, but only that there are reasonable grounds for believing that this is the case.[27] The reason for this is that at an interim stage it is unlikely that the court will have sufficient evidence before it to make findings of fact on the threshold criteria. At a disputed hearing concerning an interim care or supervision order the court should hear oral evidence;[28] but this evidence is likely to be limited and the court should take care not to make a premature determination of issues that are likely to be in dispute at the final hearing.

5.64 An initial interim care or supervision order may be made for a maximum of 8 weeks; further interim orders last for up to 4 weeks. This means that if the court decides or the parties agree that the child should remain under an interim order until the final hearing, there will be a series of interim orders renewed every 4 weeks. Renewal of the order at the conclusion of each 4-week period is not an automatic process. It may take place without a hearing, but only if all parties consent in writing to its renewal. The parties may sign a consent form that allows for rolling renewal of the interim order, and provided that no party withdraws his or her consent in writing the order will be renewed on paper.[29]

---

27 CA 1989, s 38(2). The only exception to this is that if the court makes a residence order at an interim stage, it must also make an interim supervision order, without considering the threshold criteria, unless satisfied that the child's welfare would be adequately protected without it: s 38(3).

28 *S v London Borough of Merton* [1994] 1 FCR 186.

29 This process varies from court to court. See FPC(CA 1989)R 1991, r 28 and FPR 1991, r 4.14(3)(c) for the rules; within these rules local practice will vary. At the PRFD, if written consents are not filed with the court by 12 noon on the day before the interim order expires, a representative of the local authority must attend before the District Judge of the day at 2pm on the expiry date to make an oral application for renewal.

5.65 If a parent (or other party) refuses to consent to ongoing renewal of an interim care order, the matter should be considered afresh every 4 weeks. Initially the courts emphasised this principle and it was said by Waite LJ[30] that 'at the expiration of every interim care order the granting of any further adjournment (and consequently of any further interim care order) must be considered independently on its merits when judged in the light of the circumstances existing at the time'. More recently, however, it has been said that the court may limit its consideration to any significant change in circumstances since the last hearing.[31] If there is no consent it must list the matter for hearing, but unless something significant has changed this hearing will be little more than a formality.

5.66 An interim order maintains a 'holding position'. It should not be determinative of the ultimate outcome of the proceedings. Even if the 'interim threshold criteria' are made out, the court must apply the welfare checklist to the question of an interim order. This approach should be informed by an understanding of the child's and parent's Art 6 and Art 8 rights under the ECHR. The court may only sanction such interference with the family's Art 8 rights as is necessary to ensure the child's immediate safety or wellbeing. Where this was not demonstrably the case, and the interim order was effectively determinative of the outcome of the final hearing, the interference with the parents' Art 6 rights to a fair trial was unjustified.[32]

Exclusion requirements

5.67 When making an interim care order the court may impose an exclusion requirement if the removal of a person who is alleged to pose a risk to the child will enable the child to remain living at home. The grounds for an exclusion requirement under s 38A are that:

- there is reasonable cause to believe that if a relevant person is excluded from the place where the child lives, the child will cease to suffer, or be likely to suffer, significant harm; and
- there is someone else living in the home who is able to care for the child and consents to the imposition of an exclusion requirement.

An exclusion requirement may incorporate a power of arrest. It will cease to operate if the child is removed from the house by the local authority to alternative accommodation for a period of 24 hours.

---

30 *Re P* [1993] 2 FLR 749.
31 *Re B* [2001] 2 FLR 1217.
32 *Re H* [2003] 1 FCR 350.

5.68 Note the local authority's power generally to assist an alleged abuser with finding alternative accommodation if this would enable a child at risk to remain at home.[33]

Split hearings

5.69 Where there is a significant dispute of fact between the local authority and the parents, it is often necessary to resolve this at an early stage. These hearings are sometimes referred to as 'threshold' hearings, because it is often inevitable that a finding of fact (serious sexual abuse, for example) will mean that the threshold criteria are made out. However, in some cases the disputed fact, while important, will not necessarily establish the threshold criteria, but an early resolution of the disputed issue is nevertheless needed to enable a psychiatrist or other expert to carry out an assessment. In a third category of case there may be no dispute that the threshold criteria will be satisfied on the basis of either of two possible factual bases, but there is a need to establish which is correct.

EXAMPLE

(a) *A child tells his teacher that he has been sexually abused by his father. He is taken to the doctor and there is some medical evidence to support the allegation. The father denies it.*

If the court finds on the balance of probabilities that the abuse took place, the threshold criteria will be satisfied. If it does not make such a finding, the threshold is not crossed and the proceedings will come to an immediate end.

(b) *Social workers are told by a grandmother that several years ago her son-in-law used to beat up her daughter. The couple have children who appear happy and well cared-for and have never shown signs of witnessing violence. Both parents deny the allegations.*

The court is asked to make a finding on whether the domestic violence occurred. If the court finds that it did not, the proceedings will come to an end. But even if the court finds that there was violence in the relationship, albeit many years ago, it will not automatically find the threshold criteria made out and may require some further evidence, probably from a child psychologist, as to any harm or likelihood of harm to the children.

(c) *A mother has over a period of 12 months attended A & E on several occasions, sometimes with her children, complaining that their father has hit her. The hospital records indicate that the mother appeared to be in pain, but do not disclose any visible injuries. The mother tells a social worker that on several occasions the children have witnessed*

33 CA 1989, Sch 2, para 5.

violence and verbal abuse and have been terrified. When spoken to, the children say that 'daddy always hits mummy', but are unable to give any further details of what they have seen. Two days before the hearing the mother tells her GP that she made up all the allegations.

If the court finds that violence has occurred and that the children have been involved and frightened by it, the threshold criteria will be made out. However, even if the court finds that no abuse of the mother has taken place, it is likely that the involvement of the children by the mother in her fabricated allegations against their father has caused them significant emotional harm and the court may find the threshold criteria made out on this basis.

5.70 For the difficult situation where it is impossible for the court to determine which of two or more people has caused the harm to the child, see below under 'Further Issues' at **5.164**.

5.71 It is important that if at all possible the same judge should hear both parts of a split hearing. Formally, the fact-finding process constitutes the first stage of the final hearing, even though it may be some months between the first stage and the second.

Assessments

5.72 Section 38(6) of the CA 1989 gives the court power, on making an interim care or supervision order, to direct a 'medical or psychiatric examination or other assessment of the child'. This subsection is used fairly widely to order a variety of assessments, from those focusing on the child's specific medical or educational needs to broad multi-disciplinary assessments of the family dynamics and the parenting capacity of the adults. Where there is a dispute about whether an assessment is appropriate or necessary the court should consider primarily whether the proposed assessment will provide it with the information (or some of the information) necessary to make its decision at the conclusion of the case.

5.73 The parties should at an early stage put their minds to the consideration of what assessments if any are necessary. Unnecessary duplication of assessments should be avoided and the court may specifically direct that a proposed assessment is *not* to take place. See also the discussion of expert evidence at **5.124**.

5.74 Any proposed expert assessment will involve some consideration of the available resources. The cost of assessing a large family at a flagship multi-disciplinary unit can run into the tens of thousands. A residential mother and baby assessment is likely to cost over £1,000 per week. Until recently it was difficult for local authorities to object to extensive assessment programmes either on 'resources' grounds or on the basis that the proposed programme was geared towards treatment for the adults rather than assessment of the child. However, the House of Lords[34] has now restricted the assessments that the court may order to those programmes that focus on the child, and provide the information the court needs to make its decision. An assessment under s 38(6) should not last longer than 2–3 months. 'Resources' arguments are relevant and the local authority should not be expected (as had become the practice) to call its financial officer to justify a refusal to fund an assessment. A significant element of parent-focused therapy in a proposed assessment programme is likely to place it outside the bounds of s 38(6). The 'human rights' arguments of the parents were robustly dismissed by Scott LJ: 'there is no Article 8 right to be made a better parent at public expense'.

The local authority's care plan

5.75 The local authority must inform the court and the other parties, at both interim and final stages, of its plans for the child.[35] The care plan is a key document in care proceedings: it is only by reference to its plans for the child that a local authority can satisfy the court that a care or supervision order will be better for the child than making no order at all.

5.76 Guidance on the content and format of care plans is set out in the local authority circular LAC(99)29. It suggests that care plans should be divided into five sections as follows:

- Overall aims (and timetable)
- Child's needs (including child's wishes and feelings) and the arrangements for meeting those needs, including contact arrangements
- Views of others (parents and anyone else with a sufficient interest in the child)
- Placement details and timetable
- Management and support by the local authority: implementation, reviews and contingency plan.

5.77 Interim care plans should be prepared at the latest by the case management conference, and final care plans should be filed together with the local authority's final evidence in advance of the final hearing so that the other parties may set out in their own evidence their views on the local authority's proposals.

---

34 *Kent County Council v G and others* [2005] UKHL 68.

35 See the Protocol for details of the plans to be filed at each stage.

5.78 The local authority's implementation of its care plan following a final order, and the court's limited powers to continue to monitor and oversee the care plan, are discussed at **3.34**.

Twin-track planning

5.79 The period from application to final hearing – up to 40 weeks, assuming compliance with the Protocol timetable – will often be a long one and it is important that while the court process is underway time does not stand still as far as long-term planning for the child's future is concerned. Often the issue to be determined in the proceedings will be whether the child's long-term future lies with his parents or other family members, or outside the family. With younger children this will often mean an adoptive family; for older children the only alternative to a placement at home may be long-term local authority accommodation.

5.80 To ensure that once the final hearing is concluded there is the minimum of extra delay before permanent plans for the child are put into place, local authorities are encouraged to pursue a policy of twin-track or 'parallel' planning. The plans for rehabilitation to the birth family will run in parallel with plans for a placement elsewhere. Ideally, once the final hearing has concluded, the local authority will be in a position immediately to implement its long-term plans. This may mean that the child's case has already been presented to the Adoption and Fostering panel and some enquiries regarding the availability of alternative carers have been carried out. For details of the family-finding process, in both fostering and adoption contexts, see Chapters 3 and 6[36] respectively.

Concurrent planning

5.81 Concurrent planning is a specific form of twin-track planning (above). In rare cases the local authority may place a child with foster parents who are prepared to adopt her if at the end of the proceedings she cannot be rehabilitated to the birth family. For obvious reasons the foster parents must be carefully prepared and trained and this approach should not be taken without thorough consideration.

Final order or interim order?

5.82 When should the court make a final order and (subject to the review mechanisms) let go of the case? There is always some uncertainty in the plans for a child's future, especially if the child is very young, and

36 At **6.95** ff.

if a final care order is to be made the court must be prepared to leave the resolution of issues that may arise in the future to the local authority. However, if the central features of a care plan cannot be finalised because important information is still outstanding (for example, the result of an assessment that may recommend either adoption or long-term foster care) the court should not make a final care order, even when it is not disputed that this will be the final outcome whatever the care plan. In such a case the judge should make an interim care order until the outstanding information is available.

5.83 If the court disagrees with a local authority's final care plan, but considers that a care order is necessary, it may make an interim order and invite the local authority to reconsider its plan for the child. In rare cases it may refuse to make the care order. The court does not have the power to impose conditions on a care order, or to dictate to the local authority where the child should be placed.[37]

Withdrawing the application

5.84 An application for a care order may only be withdrawn with the leave of the court. Where the court considers that the child's welfare demands that the proceedings should continue, and the local authority's contrary view means that the case is not presented as fully as the court feels necessary, the court may use its power to call witnesses itself.[38]

Discharging the order

5.85 An application to discharge a care or supervision order may be made by:

- the child
- the local authority
- any person with parental responsibility.

5.86 If a previous application has failed no person may make a further application without the leave of the court until 6 months have elapsed.[39]

5.87 The procedure is similar to that followed on an application for a care or supervision order. The application is made to the court which made the original order, and the automatic respondents are, in addition to the usual respondents to an application for a care or supervision

---

37 *Re T* [1994] 2 FLR 423.
38 *Re N* [2000] 1 FLR 134.
39 CA 1989, s 91(15).

order, the parties to the original application. Where the child is under a supervision order, his supervisor is also a respondent. Any person may be removed or joined as a party.

5.88 When a child is in care the local authority is obliged to consider at each Looked After Child Review[40] whether an application should be made to discharge the care order.

5.89 The court may substitute a supervision order for a care order. It need not consider the threshold criteria afresh.[41] Upon discharging an order the court may make no order in respect of the child, or any section 8 order.

REPRESENTING THE CHILD

The role of the Children's Guardian

5.90 The child is automatically a respondent to care proceedings. However, the extent to which he will actively participate in those proceedings will vary according to his age and understanding. The court must appoint an officer of CAFCASS[42] to represent the child's interests in care proceedings[43] unless satisfied that it is not necessary to do so in order to safeguard his interests. When acting in this capacity the officer is known as the Children's Guardian. He or she acts independently of the local authority and the other parties.

5.91 The Guardian will meet the child or children and ascertain their views, and has a duty also to support the child and give advice. He or she will prepare at least one report for the court which should set out the Guardian's recommendations and contain an analysis of the child's needs, based on the welfare checklist, and any comments on the local authority's care plan. The Guardian's role as an officer of the court is to represent the child's interests, and not to represent the child directly. There will frequently be cases where the recommendation of the Guardian is at odds with the children's wishes. If the children are very young and their wishes are plainly at odds with their interests the court is likely to give their wishes little weight. However, when an older child disagrees with her Guardian about what is in her interests the child's solicitor should consider whether she has sufficient understanding to give direct instructions.

---

40 See Chapter 3.

41 Ibid, s 39(4).

42 See Chapter 1.

43 And other specified proceedings: CA 1989, s 41(6).

5.92 Where the court is asked to make findings of fact, particularly regarding issues of harm, the role of the Guardian is not to come down firmly on one side or the other but to assist the court. This may mean flagging up relevant evidence that the other parties have for whatever reason not sought to put before the court. The Guardian should be wary of expressing a view on factual issues that are likely to be in dispute (such as the truth or otherwise of a child's allegations of abuse); the role of adjudicating on factual disputes is for the judge alone.

5.93 The child will not normally attend court: the court should only allow his attendance if satisfied that this would be in his interests. It is rare that it will be in a child's interests to hear the evidence presented and discussed, or to see his parents cross-examined. If an older child is keen to come to court to ensure her views are taken into account, the judge may invite her to attend at some point during the hearing to visit the courtroom and meet the people involved in her case. A judge should not, except in the most exceptional circumstances, see a child alone in chambers and anything said by the child to the judge should be communicated to the other parties.

The role of the solicitor for the child

5.94 The solicitor for the child is appointed by the Children's Guardian, or by the court if no Guardian has been appointed. His or her role is to represent the child. If the child is too young to give instructions the solicitor takes instructions from the Guardian. It is not unusual for there to be a delay of some weeks in the appointment of a Guardian and so until a Guardian is appointed the solicitor must act in furtherance of the child's interests.

5.95 When a solicitor is appointed for an older child who, in the solicitor's opinion, has sufficient understanding to give instructions, he or she must take instructions directly from the child. Where there is a conflict between the child's views and the Guardian's, the solicitor must act as an advocate for the child. In such a case the Guardian must inform the court of the conflict as soon as possible. It is likely that the Guardian will remain a party to the proceedings and will be permitted to instruct a new solicitor, and the original solicitor will continue as the child's advocate. The advantage of retaining the Guardian is that the court continues to have access to the investigations and recommendations of a neutral party.

5.96 The question of when a child becomes able to instruct a solicitor in his own right is a difficult one. The cases on this issue suggest an older 'threshold' age than might be expected. It has been pointed out that what matters, for the purposes of a child being able to instruct his own solicitor, is not so much his chronological age or even his intellectual ability, but whether or not he has the emotional and other resources to analyse the evidence and understand its implications. A 15-year-old, who in two years' time will be too old for the court to make a care order, will nevertheless not always have sufficient understanding to give instructions. The complexity of the issues at stake will be a factor: there will be some cases where it is very unlikely that even a bright teenager will have the necessary maturity and experience to participate directly in the proceedings.

5.97 The decision is initially one for the child's solicitor. However, he or she would be well advised, particularly in cases where it seems that the child may be psychologically or emotionally disturbed, to seek an expert opinion on the child's level of understanding. If there is uncertainty the court can decide the issue.

EVIDENCE

Fundamental principles

5.98 As a general principle, all relevant evidence is admissible. This is a principle that applies, subject to exceptions, in all areas of the law. In criminal proceedings, for example, the general principle is limited by fairly detailed and stringent rules that restrict, among other matters, the admissibility of hearsay evidence and evidence concerning a defendant's previous criminal history.

5.99 In proceedings relating to children there are only a few exceptions to the general rule that if evidence is relevant, it should be admitted. The main reason for this is that children cases, particularly in public law, are non-adversarial. The court's primary role is not to adjudicate between the parties to the proceedings but to determine and promote the interests of the child. It is important therefore that the court has as full a picture as possible. For example, hearsay evidence that is extremely damaging to one of the adult parties, and would perhaps be inadmissible against that party in criminal proceedings, is likely to be admissible in care proceedings.

5.100 One general rule of evidence that is applicable to CA 1989 proceedings, and should be borne in mind, is the rule against opinion evidence. In general, a witness may only give evidence of his opinion (as opposed to evidence of what he saw or heard or did) if the court accepts that he is appropriately qualified to do so, ie that he is an expert in the particular field. The court should be careful to prevent non-experts giving evidence of their opinion on issues that are solely a matter for the court.

5.101 Notwithstanding any statute or other rule of evidence, the court may take into account any statement contained in the Guardian's report, and any evidence given in connection with matters referred to in the report, in so far as it is relevant to any question the court is considering.[44] Similarly, any document from the local authority records copied by the Guardian is admissible as evidence of any matter referred to by him.[45]

5.102 The standard of proof in all civil proceedings, including family proceedings, is the balance of probabilities. The party seeking a finding from the court – in care proceedings, usually the local authority – must satisfy the court that it is more probable than not that the allegation he makes is true. In cases where the allegation is serious the court must approach the evidence with particular care: see below under 'Further Issues' at **5.158**. However, the standard to be applied to the evidence remains the same.

Hearsay evidence

5.103 The original rule against hearsay evidence has been almost completely eroded in civil and family proceedings. It remains in criminal proceedings, although weakened by the Criminal Justice Act 2003. It is worth having an understanding of the original rule in order to appreciate the approach the court will take to hearsay evidence.

5.104 Hearsay evidence is evidence of something said by a person who is not himself giving evidence in the proceedings, when it is put before the court in order to establish the truth of what was said.

EXAMPLE

(a) *Social worker: 'I went to the house and knocked on the door. A neighbour told me that the family had gone away.'*
This is hearsay evidence if, as seems likely, it is put before the court to establish the truth of what was said, namely that the family had gone away.

(b) *Social worker: 'I went to the house and knocked on the door. A neighbour shouted out, "Go away you meddling old busybody!" '*
This is not hearsay evidence: it is not put before the court to establish the truth of what was said. It is simply direct evidence that the neighbour said it.

5.105 The Children (Admissibility of Hearsay Evidence) Order 1993[46] provides that in family proceedings evidence given in connection with

---

44 CA 1989, s 41(11).
45 Ibid, s 42(2).
46 SI 1993/621.

the upbringing, maintenance or welfare of a child will be admissible, notwithstanding that it is hearsay. In practice this is construed widely and includes most evidence that a party is likely to want to put before the court in care proceedings, including evidence of criminal or dangerous behaviour on the part of the adults in so far as it is relevant to the child's welfare.

5.106 If hearsay evidence does not relate to the upbringing, maintenance or welfare of a child it can be admitted under the Civil Evidence Act 1995, s 1(1) of which provides that in civil proceedings (including family proceedings) evidence shall not be excluded on the ground that it is hearsay. By s 2 the party seeking to rely on hearsay evidence must give notice of this to the other side, but failure to do so does not render the evidence inadmissible and this rule is honoured more in the breach than the observance.

5.107 It is difficult to think of a relevant hearsay statement that would not be admissible in care proceedings, whether by means of its inclusion in the Guardian's report or under the Civil Evidence Act 1995 or the Children (Admissibility of Hearsay Evidence) Order 1993. However, whether or not a statement is hearsay is important when the court comes to consider how much weight should be given to it. Second hand or remoter hearsay ('the neighbour told me that her sister heard from her daughter's policeman boyfriend that Bob was a known paedophile') will carry much less weight than direct evidence. In cases where a serious allegation is made and adult witnesses are potentially available to give direct evidence, the court will generally expect the local authority to call them to give evidence rather than to rely on hearsay evidence of what they have said.

Interviewing children

5.108 Statements made by children may sometimes form the central part of a local authority's or other party's evidence. Where children have spoken to a social worker, their Guardian, or indeed a parent, about their wishes and feelings about their family or their future, this evidence can often simply be reported directly to the court: indeed, this is one of the important functions of the Children's Guardian.

5.109 Occasionally, however, children will disclose to a party or other person something that, if it is true, will have extremely serious consequences for the child and/or any other person. Often this will be an allegation of serious physical and/or sexual abuse. If this is the case the local authority must take care to ensure that the evidence is put before the court in a careful and responsible way. The *Report of the Inquiry into*

Child Abuse in Cleveland 1987[47] stands as a warning as to what may happen when an investigation into allegations of sexual abuse is not undertaken in the proper manner.

5.110 When an allegation is made that is likely to lead to a criminal investigation, the police and social services may jointly conduct an interview with the child. The guidance for such interviews is set out in *Achieving Best Evidence in Criminal Proceedings*,[48] and the court's approach is set out in the annex to Section 4 of the *Handbook of Best Practice in Children Act Cases*. Although this document is primarily designed for interviews that take place within the context of a criminal investigation, the guidance should be followed by any agency conducting an interview of a child who has made serious allegations that are likely to be considered in court proceedings. It covers not only the interview itself but the preparation process. The aim is to ensure that the evidence given by the child in interview is as reliable and uncontaminated as possible.

5.111 The interview should be conducted by a trained and experienced interviewer. Usually there will be a 'lead' interviewer and a second interviewer; the guidance recommends that if possible one interviewer should be a police officer and the other a social worker. It is important that the interview process should not be forced and that if a child is reluctant to answer questions the interviewer should take care not to coerce him.

Interviewing children: key checklist

- Preparation
  - Should any medical or other examination be carried out prior to or after the interview?
  - What inter-agency cooperation has already taken place? Has there been or should there be a strategy discussion between the police, social services and any other agencies? (See *Working Together*, paragraph 5.2.8)
  - Does or should the interviewing team have access to material such as core assessments in order to gather information about the child and plan for the interview?
  - Who should carry out the interview?
  - If the child is very young or very traumatised is an intermediary necessary?
  - Consider maximum length of the interview and breaks
  - Is video-recording appropriate?

47 Available at www.opsi.gov.uk
48 www.cps.gov.uk/publications/prosecution/bestevidencevol1.html

- Discussion with the child regarding the purpose and process of the interview

- The interview
  - Establish rapport with the child
  - Does the child understand the difference between truth and lies?
  - Give an opportunity for free narrative recall
  - Questions from the interviewer (minimise leading questions)
  - Closure phase, including an explanation to the child of the next stage in the investigative process

Disclosure

5.112 The local authority has a duty to disclose all relevant information in its possession that might assist a parent or any other person against whom an allegation has been made in rebutting the allegation. The courts are likely to interpret this duty widely; it extends to the disclosure of assessments carried out by the local authority that may not support its case. Local authorities that withhold disclosure of such material are likely to be severely criticised.

5.113 The Children's Guardian is entitled to, and should, examine and take copies of documents and records held by the local authority that are relevant to the child.[49] These may then be filed as evidence in the proceedings.

Public interest immunity

5.114 The local authority's duty to disclose relevant information is subject only to material that is protected by public interest immunity. Public interest immunity ('PII') applies where the content of a document may be protected from disclosure because of one or more aspects of public policy. The local authority should not disclose information where it appears that this may be the case. Examples of material in respect of which public interest immunity *may* arise are medical records, NSPCC records and information held by the police. Where the local authority seeks to resist disclosure of such information on public interest grounds it is for the court to strike a balance between the need for a fair and open trial and the importance of maintaining the confidentiality of certain records. Initially the local authority should write to the parties indicating the existence of such material; it is then

---

49 CA 1989, s 42(1).

for any party to make an application to the court for disclosure. There is probably no one category of material in respect of which the blanket protection of public interest immunity arises; the question must be determined in relation to each individual document or part thereof.[50]

5.115 Where the police or Crown Prosecution Service have provided the local authority with information, either under a court order or upon the understanding that such information will not be further disclosed, the local authority must not disseminate the information any further without leave of the court. This does not apply to disclosure to the Guardian, who has the right to inspect any of the local authority's records; but it does apply to the other parties, who must make an application for disclosure to the court. If the application is resisted the police and/or CPS should be given the opportunity to make representations.

5.116 In very rare cases the court may order that material should be disclosed in the proceedings, but *not* disclosed to a particular party. This will only happen where there are very powerful arguments against disclosure based on the interests of a child, party, witness or victim.[51]

Confidentiality and disclosure outside the proceedings

5.117 The documents filed in all proceedings relating to children are confidential. Since October 2005, however, the restrictions on disclosure of these documents to those who are not involved in the proceedings have been relaxed. The new rules supplement the existing rules, which permit disclosure to legal representatives, experts and the Legal Services Commission. Additionally it is now permissible for parties to the proceedings to disclose documentation as follows:

---

50 *R v Chief Constable of West Midlands Police, ex parte Wiley* [1995] 1 AC 274.
51 *Re C* [1996] 1 FLR 797.

Documentation	Disclosable to whom	For what purpose
Any information or document	A lay adviser (CAB or McKenzie friend)	Seeking advice in connection with the case
	Spouse, cohabitant or close family member	Having confidential discussions about the case
	Health care or counselling professional	Seeking health care or advice or counselling
	Children's Commissioner	Referral of a case
	A person carrying out an approved research project	Carrying out the research project
	Mediator	Mediation
	Person responsible for investigating complaints against legal representatives	Investigating complaints
Text or summary of all or part of a judgment	MP or MEP (NB not local councillor)	Advice/raising complaints
	General Medical Council	Making a complaint
	Police officer	Investigating a crime
	Crown Prosecution Service	Enabling it to carry out its legal functions

5.118 Of these perhaps the most radical change from the old law is that it is now permissible, without an order of the court, to disclose any court document or information to a close family member. Note that the trial judge retains the power to restrict or permit disclosure notwithstanding the new rules and in a particularly sensitive case it may be appropriate to seek a direction that certain information should not be disclosed.

5.119 Where the new rules do not apply it will be necessary for the trial judge to authorise disclosure. For instance, at the end of (or during) care proceedings, the police may seek disclosure of documents with a view to their use in criminal proceedings. This application should be made to the care proceedings trial judge. Again the balance that must be struck is that between the public interest in protecting the confidentiality of proceedings relating to children, and the public interest in making available to the police documentation that may assist them in carrying out their duties. The Court of Appeal has ordered that, even where criminal proceedings have not been commenced, transcripts of evidence given in care proceedings relating to the death of a child should be disclosed to the police to help them decide how to proceed with their investigation.[52]

---

52 *Re EC* [1996] 2 FLR 275.

5.120 It seems that disclosure will be ordered more readily when a defendant seeks the information: Munby J has said that it would be an exceptional case where a family court would deny a defendant access to material that might help him defend himself against a serious criminal charge.[53]

5.121 There may be other occasions when it is in the public interest for information filed or findings made within the care proceedings to be disclosed to a third party. It is fairly common for the local authority to be given leave where a final order has been made to disclose limited documentation to the child's future adoptive parents, in order that they may have some understanding of the child's circumstances. Typically the Guardian's report and any relevant expert reports will be disclosed, edited to remove any material that the prospective adopters do not need to know.

5.122 Otherwise the occasions when disclosure is ordered outside the proceedings will be rare. Factors weighing against disclosure are, chiefly, the risk of harm to the child and the public interest in ensuring that parents, professionals and witnesses are able to speak freely and frankly. In support of this principle, CA 1989, s 98(2) provides that an admission made by a party in children proceedings shall not be evidence against him in any criminal proceedings, other than on a charge of perjury. Disclosure outside the proceedings tends to be ordered only where there is a compelling reason to do so, such as the risk of harm to others; but even in such cases disclosure is not automatic and may be refused. The following matters have been the subject of an application to disclose:

- a finding in care proceedings that a doctor had sexually abused his daughter (disclosure to the General Medical Council authorised);[54]
- evidence in care proceedings that a party was seeking to deceive the immigration authorities (disclosure authorised);
- findings of sexual abuse of children (disclosure to the housing association where the abuser lived authorised, but general disclosure to any future housing association or landlord to whom the abuser might make an application for housing refused).[55]

5.123 The rules of confidentiality apply only to documents that are filed in the proceedings. They should not prevent the sharing of information between agencies, including social services and the police, that are concerned with child protection.

---

53 *Re Z* [2003] 1 FLR 1194.

54 *A County Council v W and Others* [1997] 1 FLR 574.

55 *Re C* [2002] 2 FLR 375.

THE ROLE OF THE EXPERT WITNESS

5.124 The courts rely heavily on the evidence of experts, particularly in contested public law children cases. This does not mean, however, that the expert usurps the role of the court in deciding the outcome of the case and the future for the child. The final decision is always that of the trial judge. An expert may only give his opinion on matters in which he has professional expertise. It is unlikely that expert evidence will assist in determining matters which are factually in dispute, and, in particular, issues that depend on the credibility of a witness are a matter for the judge alone.

5.125 The use of expert evidence should be strictly controlled by the court. No person may permit a child who is the subject of proceedings to be medically or psychiatrically examined or assessed in any way by an expert reporting to the court without the court's prior permission.[56] The proposed expert needs the court's express permission to examine the child; once a named expert has been instructed, he is entitled to see the papers filed in the proceedings and a separate direction to this effect is unnecessary.[57]

5.126 A medical practitioner involved in the treatment of the child is likely to be an important witness, both as to fact and as to the professional opinion upon the child's condition that informed the provision of treatment. Other medical experts, who were not involved in the child's treatment, may be instructed for the proceedings. The roles of the treating clinician and the court appointed expert are separate and distinct in the court process. It is unusual for a treating clinician to be sent all the court papers and instructed to give a comprehensive expert overview, nevertheless their contribution to the case (based upon first hand knowledge) is likely to be important both to the court appointed experts and to the ultimate decision.

5.127 An assessment of the child will in most cases be carried out by an expert instructed jointly by the parties. However, in complex cases where, for example, medical opinion is conflicting or unclear the interests of justice may demand that the parents should be permitted to instruct their own expert. A refusal to permit a party to call potentially relevant expert evidence may be a breach of the ECHR Art 6 right to a fair trial.

5.128 Experts should be instructed at an early stage and their availability both to prepare a report and to attend the final hearing should be confirmed. Once this is done the letter of instruction should

56 FPR 1991, r 4.18.
57 Ibid, r 4.23.

be sent out as soon as possible. Letters of instruction to an expert should be agreed between the instructing parties and should:

- set out the factual background to the case in as neutral a manner as possible, identifying issues where there is a dispute of fact;
- include an agreed chronology;
- list the documents which the expert is asked to read;
- inform the expert of any examination or assessment of the child permitted by the court; and
- remind the expert of his duty to the court, including his duty to discuss the case with any other expert instructed in his field and, where possible, prepare a schedule setting out areas of agreement and disagreement in advance of the final hearing.

5.129 An expert witness, whether jointly instructed or not, must approach the case in an impartial and objective manner and must assist the court. Once he has reported the party instructing him is under a duty to disclose the report to the court and the other parties, regardless of whether or not it supports that party's case. An expert may be called by any party, or by the court.

5.130 An expert who has been jointly instructed by two or more parties must take care to ensure that all communication between the expert and any one party is copied to the other parties; that a note is kept of any conversation between herself and any party; and that she does not attend any meeting or conference unless it is a joint one. Further guidance for expert witnesses and those who instruct them is set out in:

- the Protocol;
- the Handbook of Best Practice in Children Act cases; and
- the Expert Witness Group's Expert Witness Pack.

PARENTAL CONTACT WITH CHILDREN IN CARE

5.131 Before making a care order, including an interim order, the court must consider the proposed arrangements for contact and invite the parties to comment on them.[58] In the interim period, contact between the child and his parents, and others who have a significant relationship with him, should be maintained unless there are good reasons for restricting or suspending it.

5.132 The local authority has a duty under CA 1989, s 34(1), both in the interim period and following a final order, to allow the child to have reasonable contact with:

---

58 CA 1989, s 34(11).

- his parents;
- any guardian of his;
- any person in whose favour a residence order was in force immediately before the care order was made; and
- any person with care of the child, prior to the care order, under an order made in the exercise of the High Court's inherent jurisdiction.[59]

5.133 In addition, the local authority's duties under CA 1989, Sch 2, Part II (looked after children) apply to children subject to an interim or final care order. The local authority must, unless it is not reasonably practicable or consistent with the child's welfare, endeavour to promote contact between the child and any parent, person with parental responsibility, relative, friend or other person connected with him. Any such person who is not a party to the proceedings may apply for leave to make an application for contact.

5.134 The court may make orders specifying the contact that is to take place between the child and any named person and imposing any conditions it feels are appropriate. If it does not do so, the local authority has a discretion regarding the amount of contact it offers, and any conditions imposed on that contact, subject to its duties above.

5.135 The local authority may suspend or terminate contact between the child and any person who would otherwise be entitled to reasonable contact under s 34(1). It may suspend contact without a court order for a period of up to 7 days, provided that it is necessary to do so in order to safeguard or promote the child's welfare.[60] The remedy of the person affected is to apply to the court for a contact order.

5.136 If the local authority wishes to refuse contact for a period in excess of 7 days it must apply to the court for an order authorising it to do so. This is a permissive rather than a mandatory order and the local authority may use it as it sees fit. The application may be made at any time, but is commonly made in the run-up to a final hearing where the final care plan provides for the ultimate cessation of contact between the child and his parents. It will be considered by the judge after the decision on the final care order has been made. If granted, the s 34(4) order relieves the local authority of the duty to allow reasonable contact and permits it to phase out contact between child and parents in accordance with its care plan.

5.137 When an application for a contact order under s 34 has been made by any person (other than the local authority) and refused by the

---

59 CA 1989, s 34(1).
60 Ibid, s 34(6).

court, no further application may be made by the same person within a period of 6 months unless the court gives leave.[61] Note that this provision applies to interim as well as final orders, and so may have the effect of permitting only one application by any person within the course of the proceedings.

SPECIAL GUARDIANSHIP

5.138 Although not strictly speaking a public law order, in that it does not involve the ongoing involvement of the local authority, the new special guardianship order introduced by the Adoption and Children Act (ACA) 2002 is included in this chapter as it is intended primarily as an alternative to adoption or fostering and so will frequently be considered by the court during or at the conclusion of care proceedings. The concept of special guardianship is introduced by s 115 of the ACA 2002, which inserts the new sections 14A–14G into the CA 1989.

5.139 Special guardianship is intended to offer a new option for courts seeking to make a permanent plan for a child. It has been introduced to meet the needs of children for whom none of the previously available options (primarily adoption, long-term fostering or a residence order) is entirely suitable. It is intended to combine the advantages of a continued legal relationship with the birth family with the security of a long-term placement. One important aspect of special guardianship is that there are restrictions on its discharge or revocation. A special guardianship order is revocable, and so can never be as 'secure' as an adoption; but the legislation is plainly geared towards the child's long-term future and it is anticipated that the occasions when such an order is discharged will be rare.

5.140 In summary, the effect of a special guardianship order is to:

- secure the child's long-term placement;
- give the special guardian parental responsibility;
- maintain the child's links with his or her parent(s); BUT
- enable the special guardian to control on a day-to-day basis the parents' exercise of their parental responsibility.

5.141 Those who may apply for special guardianship include wider family members and foster carers. Parents are specifically excluded.

5.142 Section 14C of the CA 1989 sets out the effect of a special guardianship order. The order:

---

61 CA 1989, s 91(17).

- gives the special guardian parental responsibility for the child;
- subject to any other orders in force under the Children Act, enables the special guardian to exercise parental responsibility to the exclusion of any other person with parental responsibility (other than another special guardian);
- does not permit the special guardian to do anything which requires the consent of all those with parental responsibility: for example, consent to an adoption or placement for adoption, a change of name or a permanent removal from the jurisdiction.

5.143 A key feature of a special guardianship order, and that which is likely to make it most attractive to prospective carers in cases where there is a background of parental neglect or abuse, is that the special guardian may exercise parental responsibility to the exclusion of the child's parent(s).

Application and procedure

5.144 The most important feature of the application process is that notice must be given to the child's local authority, which must then prepare a report for the court. The applicant for a special guardianship order must give the relevant local authority[62] at least 3 months' notice of his intention to apply for a special guardianship order. The local authority must then investigate and prepare a report dealing with:

- the suitability of the applicant to be a special guardian; and
- any other matter it considers relevant.

5.145 The matters to be covered in a special guardianship report are set out in detail in the Schedule to the Special Guardianship Regulations 2005.[63]

5.146 The court may make a special guardianship order in family proceedings of its own motion and, to that end, may request the local authority to carry out an investigation and prepare a report. The court is not permitted to make a special guardianship order unless it has received a report dealing with the matters set out above.[64] This means that the issue of special guardianship must be considered at an early stage. If it appears that there is a possibility that the court may wish to make a special guardianship order (for example, in favour of grandparents in care proceedings) the time needed to prepare the report must be factored into the proceedings timetable.

---

62 If the child is being looked after by a local authority, that local authority; otherwise, the local authority in whose area the applicant lives.

63 SI 2005/1109.

64 CA 1989, s 14A(11).

Support services

5.147 The ACA 2002 also imposes on local authorities a duty to make arrangements for the provision within its area of special guardianship support services, and a complaints procedure for those dissatisfied with the support services provided. The services that must be made available include counselling, training, respite care and mediation (for example, in connection with contact arrangements), and services must be provided to special guardians, children and birth families. Details are set out in the Regulations.

5.148 The circumstances in which a local authority must provide financial support to special guardians (or prospective special guardians) are set out in the Regulations. In general, financial support is only payable to meet specific needs in the following circumstances:

- where the local authority considers such support necessary to ensure that the special guardian can look after the child;
- where the child needs special care because of his own special needs or past experiences;
- for legal costs in connection with the special guardianship application or other related applications; and
- where the local authority consider that a contribution to the costs of accommodating and maintaining the child is appropriate.

5.149 Former foster carers are in a different position. For these special guardians, financial support may include an element of remuneration, but only where the local authority considers it necessary, and the special guardian was previously paid an element of remuneration as a foster carer.

5.150 Where an element of remuneration is included in payments to a special guardian, this ceases to be payable after 2 years following the making of the order, unless there are exceptional circumstances. Although long-term foster carers were initially envisaged as being likely to form a significant category of applicants for special guardianship orders, the restrictions on their funding (in contrast to the funding they would continue to receive as foster carers) may counterbalance the attractions of the autonomy and freedom from local authority control that a special guardianship order would provide.

Interaction with other orders

5.151 The making of a special guardianship order does not of itself affect any section 8 order; indeed, the special guardian's ability to exercise parental responsibility is circumscribed by any existing Children Act orders. However, the court is expressly required to consider on making the special guardianship order whether any current section 8 order should be varied or discharged.[65]

5.152 The making of a section 8 order, including a residence order, does not affect a special guardianship order. There is no statutory bar to co-existing residence and special guardianship orders in favour of different people, although it is unlikely that this combination of orders will be common (except perhaps on an interim basis.)

5.153 A special guardianship order, like a residence order, discharges a care order.[66] However, a care order does not discharge a special guardianship order. The effect of this is that the status of a special guardian continues to be recognised, albeit in a diluted form, notwithstanding the care order. As with parents, the local authority with a care order can determine the extent to which special guardians exercise parental responsibility.[67] Similarly, the local authority's obligations towards the parents of children in care are, generally speaking, extended to special guardians: so, for example, s 34 of the CA 1989 is amended to include special guardians within the categories of persons to whom the local authority must afford reasonable contact with the child.

5.154 If a special guardianship order is in force, no application for a residence order with respect to the child may be made by any person without leave.[68] This important provision indicates the extent to which special guardianship orders are intended to be permanent. Similar restrictions operate in relation to their variation and discharge.

Variation and discharge

5.155 The court may vary or discharge a special guardianship order on its own motion, or on the application (as of right) of:

- the special guardian;
- any person with a (current) residence order;
- any person with parental responsibility *other than a parent or step-parent* (see below);
- a local authority designated in a care order with respect to the child;

and, with leave:

- the child;

65 CA 1989, s 14B(1).

66 Ibid, s 91(5A), inserted by ACA 2002, Sch 3, para 68.

67 CA 1989, s 33(1)(b).

68 Ibid, s 10(7A), inserted by ACA 2002, Sch 3, para 57.

- any parent or guardian;
- any step-parent with parental responsibility;
- any person who had parental responsibility prior to the making of the special guardianship order, but no longer has it.

5.156 Where the applicant for leave is a parent or guardian, step-parent or previous holder of parental responsibility, the court may not grant leave unless there has been a significant change in circumstances since the special guardianship order was made.[69] This places parents seeking to discharge a special guardianship order in a significantly worse position than those who are applying to discharge a care order. It is not yet clear what will constitute a 'significant change of circumstances', and what approach the courts will take to leave applications by parents who have made efforts to address their own difficulties and wish, perhaps several years down the line, to take over the care of their children from a special guardian.

FURTHER ISSUES

5.157 The following issues arise fairly frequently within care proceedings. They often raise questions that are not easily resolved. What follows is intended to flag up the sort of situations where these issues may arise and to point the way towards the most relevant authorities.

Serious allegations and the standard of proof

5.158 The standard of proof in child care proceedings is the same as in any other civil proceedings: the balance of probabilities. This means that if a court is satisfied that it is more probable than not that an allegation is correct, it will find it proved. This test is to be applied across the spectrum of care proceedings, from the most common cases of physical or emotional neglect to those involving serious sexual abuse, physical injury or death.

5.159 However, the House of Lords[70] has held that in cases where the allegations made are extremely serious, the judge must approach the evidence with an awareness of the inherent improbability of these allegations and the need for correspondingly stronger evidence before they can be found proved. This does not mean that the standard of proof in such cases is raised (although Lord Nicholls acknowledged that

---

69 CA 1989, s 14D(5).

70 *Re H and R* [1996] 1 FLR 80.

'the result is much the same'). It means that the evidence must be approached with great care and, broadly speaking, the more serious the allegation the stronger the evidence must be to support it.

5.160 The standard of proof in criminal cases is, of course, the 'beyond reasonable doubt' test. A criminal jury must be sure that the offence they are considering has been committed. This factor, together with the wider range of evidence that is admissible in a civil trial, means that it is not uncommon for a judge in care proceedings to come to a different result from a jury trying the same allegation in the course of a criminal trial.

EXAMPLE

A mother is charged with causing grievous bodily harm to her child through salt poisoning. At her criminal trial she calls expert evidence to the effect that the child may suffer from a rare condition that prevents his body from processing salt and that would account for the high salt levels found in his body. The jury finds her not guilty, presumably on the basis that there is a reasonable doubt about whether she was responsible for the child's condition. Six months later a judge in care proceedings holds a fact-finding hearing. The same expert gives evidence. At the conclusion of the hearing the judge finds on the balance of probabilities, applying the principles laid down by the House of Lords, that the mother poisoned the child. The judge comments that she has heard a far wider range of evidence than the jury in the criminal trial and has been particularly influenced by the evidence of the social worker concerning the mother's behaviour towards the child over the past few years.[71]

5.161 It is also possible (although necessarily much rarer) for a judge in care proceedings to find an allegation not proved, notwithstanding that a criminal jury has convicted on the basis of the same allegation.

Human rights and the threshold criteria

5.162 The court will commonly find that the threshold criteria are satisfied on the basis of the quality of care provided by only one of the parents. Particularly where the parents are separated and have little to do with each other, this may mean that the other parent plays a very minor role in the threshold stage of the proceedings, and is powerless to resist a determination that the threshold criteria are made out. Bearing in mind that the function of the section 31 threshold requirement is to

---

71 Judges have recently been reminded of the need in care proceedings to consider any expert medical evidence in the context of the case and the evidence as a whole: see *A County Council v K, D and L* [2005] 1 FLR 851.

protect families from intervention unless it is necessary to protect the child, does this infringe the 'innocent' parent's ECHR Art 8 rights to an unacceptable extent?

EXAMPLE

A young child's parents are separated and he lives with his mother who has a heroin addiction. His father has made several unsuccessful attempts to intervene and protect him. Ultimately the local authority issues care proceedings and the court finds, perhaps with all parties' agreement, that the threshold criteria are met on the basis of the mother's care. The father wishes to resist a care order; he hopes to care for the child himself, although he is struggling to cope with the breakdown of a relationship and is also looking after an older teenager who has been in trouble a few times with the police.

If the child had been living with the father when the local authority became involved, it is unlikely that the threshold criteria would have been met. As it is he starts 'several lengths down', with the threshold for state intervention having already been reached through no fault of his own; and his own circumstances mean that at the welfare stage, there is a real chance that the court may feel the child's needs will be better met elsewhere.

5.163 Similarly, there is no requirement that the threshold criteria should still be satisfied at the time when the order is made. The threshold criteria apply to the situation at the time when the local authority initiates protective measures. So an initial interim care order may be made when parents are in the middle of a particularly acrimonious split and are unable to prioritise the children's needs over their own. Several months later this may no longer be the case, and the problems that drew the family to the local authority's attention may have been resolved. Nevertheless, the threshold has been crossed and the court process engaged. The court has no power to 'revisit' the threshold criteria in the light of the circumstances prevailing at the later time.

Uncertain perpetrators

5.164 Cases where it is apparent that a person has caused harm to a child, but it is not clear which of two (or more) persons is responsible, pose a particular difficulty. In the equivalent criminal case, where it is not clear which of two co-defendants is guilty of the offence, although it is obvious that one of them must be, the jury's duty is to acquit both.

5.165 Such an approach would give a very unsatisfactory result in a situation where, for example, the two potential perpetrators are both the child's parents. The court's paramount aim of protecting the child means that it cannot decline to intervene because, although the child is at risk from at least one of her parents, it cannot tell which one.

5.166 In such circumstances the court's duty is first to establish on the balance of probabilities whether there must be one or more people responsible for the harm caused to the child (ie to exclude any accidental cause). If this is the case, the threshold criteria will be met. There must of course be a nexus linking the harm done to the child to the parental care: a random and unforeseeable attack on the child by a stranger will not establish the threshold criteria; sexual abuse within the family, of which the parent(s) should have been aware even if not perpetrators themselves, will.

5.167 The court must then identify all possible perpetrators of the harm, asking itself the question whether there is 'a likelihood or a real possibility that one or more of a number of people with access to the child was the perpetrator or a perpetrator of the inflicted injuries'.[72] If the answer to that question is yes, the threshold criteria will be met on that basis, notwithstanding that the court cannot apportion responsibility for the harm between the potential perpetrators. The judge will then do what she can to assist professionals at the subsequent 'welfare' stage, who must proceed on the basis that any one of the identified persons is a possible perpetrator of the harm. This may result in very difficult situations for the court and for the family and child.

EXAMPLE

A child is brought to hospital by her parents with serious head injuries. Both parents admit being at home with the child when the injuries occurred. The doctors suspect non-accidental injury and the police and social services are informed. Both parents are charged with causing grievous bodily harm and at a subsequent trial, because the prosecution cannot prove beyond reasonable doubt that either was responsible, both are acquitted. Following the fact-finding hearing in the care proceedings the judge finds that:

(a) the child's injuries were non-accidental;
(b) one or other, or both, of the parents was responsible for causing the injuries by hitting the child against a hard surface; and
(c) he cannot make a finding regarding which parent was responsible: it is possible that one may be entirely blameless and the other responsible, or that both share responsibility.

At the subsequent disposal hearing the parents have separated. Each seeks care of the child (and blames the other for his injuries). The local authority's position is that because neither parent can be exonerated

72 *North Yorkshire County Council v SA* [2003] 2 FLR 849.

from blame for the child's injuries, the risk of placement with either parent is too high. The care plan is for adoption. Although he recognises the potential injustice to an innocent parent, the judge has no option but to prioritise the child's safety and the care order is made.

Care or supervision order?

5.168 In some cases, the proceedings may conclude with it being clear that the child should remain at home with his parents, but an element of future risk to him remains. In these circumstances the court must consider whether the risk is such that the child can only adequately be protected by a care order, or whether a supervision order would suffice.

5.169 Factors which have pointed towards a care order have included the following:

- Previous violence towards the child: despite a period of calm, the local authority needed to share parental responsibility to enable it to remove the child quickly if the situation deteriorated. Imposing a care order was preferable to relying on the local authority's power to apply for an emergency protection order in the future: *Re S.*[73]
- Inability to attach conditions to a supervision order: a care order would ensure that the child remained at a school suitable for his special needs. A condition to that effect, attached to a supervision order, would not be capable of enforcement: *Re V.*[74]

5.170 On the other hand, a supervision order may be more appropriate when the risk to the child is low. If the court makes a residence order within care proceedings, it must also make an interim supervision order unless satisfied that his welfare will be satisfactorily safeguarded without such an order being made.[75] Where the threshold is satisfied on a final basis, it will usually be appropriate to impose a supervision order, whether or not in conjunction with a residence order, as a minimum protective measure and to ensure ongoing local authority involvement.[76]

---

73 [1993] 2 FLR 919.
74 [1996] 1 FLR 776.
75 CA 1989, s 38(3).
76 *Re DH* [1994] 1 FLR 679.

6

ADOPTION

Chapter summary

- What is adoption?
- Who can be adopted
- Who can adopt a child
- The welfare of the child
- Parental consent
- Adoption services
- Access to adoption information
- Placing a child for adoption
- Care proceedings and a plan for adoption
- Care proceedings: how does a plan for adoption develop?
- Contact on placement and after adoption
- Illegal placements
- Applying for an adoption order
- Consequences of an adoption order
- Adoptions with an international element

WHAT IS ADOPTION?

6.1 Societies across the world have developed arrangements whereby adults, who are not the natural parents of a child, may act as his parents in their place. In many countries such arrangements may be informal, or arranged within the extended family; in others a formal legal process of 'adoption' may be required. However, even where there is a legal adoption, the resulting status will vary from country to country from a 'full adoption', under which there is a complete and irrevocable severance of all legal ties between the child and his natural family, to 'simple adoption', which is less severe in one or more respects.

6.2 Adoption in England and Wales is entirely regulated by statute law. Until the passing in 1926 of the Adoption of Children Act, while permanent but informal arrangements were made for children, legal adoption was not available in the UK. There is still no procedure for adoption under the common law.

6.3 A UK adoption order is a 'full adoption' and sets out to bring about security and stability for the child by irrevocably[1] altering the rights and duties of the adults involved in order to consolidate the child in his new adoptive family. As from 30 December 2005 the applicable legislation is that contained in the Adoption and Children Act 2002 (ACA 2002) and a large body of related subordinate legislation and guidance.

6.4 On the making of an adoption order parental responsibility for a child is given to the adopters. At the same time, the order operates to extinguish permanently the parental responsibility which any person had for the child immediately before the making of the order. An adoption order is irrevocable, save in the very restricted circumstances of ACA 2002, s 55 (revocation upon subsequent legitimation).

6.5 An adopted child is deemed to be the adopter's legitimate child, as if he had been born to either the adoptive couple, or to the single adopter (irrespective of gender). If adopted by a couple,[2] or a single adopter who is the partner of a parent of the child, the child is to be treated as the child of the relationship of the couple in question.[3]

6.6 Adoptive parents are thus treated in law as the child's parents, save that an adoptive parent cannot be guilty of an offence under the Sexual Offences Act 2003 (SOA 2003), ss 64 or 65 (sex with an adult relative),[4] and an adoption order does not of itself confer citizenship or a right to remain in the UK.

6.7 Adoption is the legal process by which a child becomes a permanent and full member of a new family. Long-term foster care has disadvantages which may arise from the possible change of carers, of social workers, or of plans for the child, all of which may erode the child's sense of stability and security. Consequently, in the 1970s and 80s, long-term fostering fell from favour as the preferred social work

---

1 Save for revocation upon subsequent legitimation: see ACA 2002, s 55.
2 For a wide definition of 'couple', see ibid, s 144(4).
3 Ibid, s 67(2).
4 Ibid, s 74 (as amended).

option for most children in long-term care.[5] Adoption has become the goal which is sought for most children, especially younger children, who require a permanent family placement away from their natural parents. The move towards adoption has been given impetus by the Prime Minister's review of adoption law[6] and the consequent introduction of government adoption 'targets'. The government's focus in recent years has been on the need to find a permanent family for those children who wait in care. But adoption orders may also be made in favour of a natural parent of the child, either alone or, more commonly, together with his or her partner.[7]

6.8 In *Re H (Adoption: Parental Agreement)*,[8] Ormrod LJ answered the question: 'What do the adoptive parents gain by an adoption order over and above what they have already got on a long-term fostering basis?' He said:

> 'To that the answer is always the same – and it is always a good one – adoption gives us total security and makes the child part of our family and places us in parental control of the child; long-term fostering leaves us exposed to changes of view of the local authority, it leaves us exposed to applications, and so on by the natural parent. That is a perfectly sensible and reasonable approach; it is far from being only an emotive one.'

INTERCOUNTRY ADOPTION

6.9 The term 'intercountry adoption' is a non-legal term used to describe an adoption order in which the applicant resides in a different country from the child. An intercountry adoption may involve a child who is habitually resident in the UK going abroad for adoption, but, more commonly, the arrangement will be that a non UK resident child will be brought here for adoption by UK resident adopters. Strict legal requirements apply whether the child is going out of the UK or being brought in, and whether there has been some form of adoption process in the foreign jurisdiction or none. An international convention (the 1993 Hague Convention on Protection of Children and Co-operation in respect of Intercountry Adoption) regulates the process as between

5 See the seminal work by Rowe and Lambert, *Children Who Wait* (Association of British Adoption Agencies, 1974).

6 Prime Minister's Review of Adoption, published 7 July 2000, available from www.dfes.gov.uk/adoption

7 For an informative general introduction to the history and uses of adoption, see Cretney, *Family Law in the 20th Century* (Oxford University Press, 2003), Chapter 17 and Bridge and Swindells, *Adoption: The Modern Law* (Family Law, 2003), Chapters 1 to 5.

8 [1981] 3 FLR 386; quoted with approval by House of Lords in *Re C (A Minor) (Adoption Order: Conditions)* [1988] 2 FLR 159 at 168G.

fellow Convention States.[9] In general, subject to the additional requirements and limitations concerning bringing a child into the country, the ordinary domestic adoption law will apply in full to an intercountry adoption.[10]

WHO CAN BE ADOPTED

6.10 An adoption application may only be made in respect of a person who is under the age of 18 years, but an adoption order may be made after that age if the person is still under 19 years old.[11] Most adoptions relate to younger children, but, given the need to look to the child's welfare throughout his lifetime, an adoption order for a late teenager may sometimes be appropriate.

6.11 An adoption order may be made in respect of a previously adopted child, but not in relation to one who is, or has been, married or in a civil partnership.[12] The child must either be habitually resident in England and Wales, or physically present here, when the adoption application is made. Where the child is habitually resident abroad, the requirements of the Adoptions with a Foreign Element Regulations 2005, Chapter 2[13] must be met before the child can be brought into the UK for adoption.

WHO CAN ADOPT A CHILD?

6.12 A child can be adopted either by a single person or by a couple (whether married or in a civil partnership or not and whether of different gender or the same gender).[14] In each case there are specific requirements that must be satisfied before an adoption order can be made.

Adoption by a couple

6.13 An adoption order may be made in favour of two applicants if they are a married couple, a couple who have entered into a civil

9 The Hague Convention is ratified and implemented in England and Wales as from June 2003 by the Adoption (International Aspects) Act 1999.

10 Further discussion of intercountry adoption is at **6.194**.

11 ACA 2002, s 49.

12 Ibid, ss 46(5), 47(8), (8A).

13 SI 2005/392.

14 ACA 2002, ss 50, 51 and 144(4).

partnership or 'two people (whether of different sexes or the same sex) living as partners in an enduring family relationship'.[15] There is no room for discrimination on the grounds of sexual orientation, or against a couple who have chosen not to formalise their relationship through a marriage or civil partnership. It is important to recognise however that adoption agencies and courts will be anxious to ensure for the sake of the child's stability that the couple's relationship is committed and likely to endure. A couple wishing to adopt must be living 'as partners'. Two close relatives (for example parent and child, or sister and brother) are not a 'couple' for the purposes of the Act and cannot jointly adopt a child.[16]

6.14 Each of the applicant couple must have attained the age of 21 years,[17] except where one is the mother or father of the child (in which case the parent must be over 18 years). While there is no legal upper age limit for an adoptive parent, adoption agencies will not usually place a child with adopters where the age gap between the child and the adopters is more than 45 years unless the child has special needs.[18]

6.15 An application for an adoption order may only be made if one of the following two conditions is satisfied:[19]

(1) at least one of the couple must be domiciled in a part of the British Islands;[20] or

(2) both of the couple have been habitually resident in a part of the British Islands[21] for a period of not less than one year ending with the date of the application.

Different considerations apply in an international case if the application is for a Convention adoption order.[22]

6.16 Where the child has not been placed for adoption by an adoption agency there is an additional requirement that the child must have had his home with the adopters, or at least one of them, for a specified period (between 10 weeks and 3 years, depending on the adopters' connection with the child).[23]

---

15 ACA 2002, ss 50, 144(4).
16 Ibid, s 144(5), (6).
17 Ibid, s 50(1).
18 *Adopting a Child* (BAAF, 2006).
19 ACA 2002, s 49(2), (3).
20 Ibid.
21 Ie the UK, the Channel Islands or the Isle of Man (Interpretation Act 1978, Sch 1).
22 For Convention adoptions, see **6.199**.
23 ACA 2002, ss 42, 44.

6.17 There is no legal requirement concerning the race of the applicants. In placing a child for adoption, the adoption agency must however give due consideration to the child's religious persuasion, racial origin and cultural and linguistic background.[24] The White Paper preceding the ACA 2002 referred to the common perception that adoptions were being blocked by 'politically correct' social workers who would refuse to place a black child with a white couple (or vice versa). While trans-racial adoptions did and do take place, the new law acknowledges that potential adopters of a child from a different culture or race need to be sufficiently sensitive to assist her to understand and take pride in all the elements of her background.[25]

Parent as an adopter

6.18 A natural parent may make a joint application with her/his spouse or partner to adopt her/his own child. In such a case the age requirement[26] is relaxed so that an adoption order may be made provided that the mother or father has attained the age of 18 years and her/his spouse/partner has attained the age of 21 years.[27] Such an application is only likely to succeed where the identity of the child's other natural parent is unknown or he or she has played and wishes to play no role in the child's life.

6.19 In rare cases a parent may apply to adopt his or her own child alone. The main effect of such an adoption is to extinguish the parental responsibility of the other parent. If the desired result is to exclude a parent as completely as possible from the child's life (and assuming of course that there are good reasons for doing so), this can usually be achieved by a combination of orders under the CA 1989 and injunctions restricting the parent's involvement with the child. This route will usually be preferable to the drastic and irrevocable route of an adoption.

Step-parent adoption

6.20 As with any other applicant, a child's step-parent may make an application for an adoption order either on his own or as one of a married or unmarried couple. He must satisfy the basic requirements;[28] in particular, he and his spouse/partner must each have attained the age of 21 years, unless his spouse is a parent of the child.

---

24 ACA 2002, s 1(5).

25 *Re C (Adoption: Religious Observance)* [2002] 1 FLR 1119.

26 ACA 2002, s 50(1).

27 Ibid, s 50(2).

28 For joint applicants' requirements, see **6.13**.

6.21 Adoption by a step-parent together with a natural parent of the child has the artificial effect of changing the legal relationship between the parent and the child from a natural one to an adoptive one. ACA 2002, s 51(2) seeks to avoid this consequence by permitting a person who is the partner of the child's parent to make an application to adopt on their own. On adoption the child will be treated in law as being the child of the adopter (the non-parent partner) and the other one of the couple (the parent).[29]

6.22 The key consequence of a step-parent adoption is that the legal relationship between the child and the natural parent who is not the step-parent's partner will be extinguished. The courts have shown a reluctance to make step-parent adoption orders where the natural parent had formerly had an established relationship with the other parent and/or the child and is objecting to the adoption.[30] However, a step-parent adoption does not breach Art 8 of the ECHR where the absent parent has had very limited contact with the child, and strong family ties exist between the child and her step-parent.[31]

6.23 As an alternative to adoption a step-parent may now acquire parental responsibility by way of a parental responsibility agreement or court order under CA 1989, s 4A. This welcome amendment of the CA 1989 enables an involved and committed step-parent to become a 'third' parent of the child without the need to exclude the child's other natural parent.

Sole applicant

6.24 An adoption application (unless it is a Convention (international) application)[32] may only be made by a sole applicant if either:

(1) he is domiciled in the British Islands;[33] or
(2) he has been habitually resident in the British Islands for a period of not less than one year ending with the date of the application.[34]

6.25 An adoption order may be made on the application of one person, if:

(1) he has attained the age of 21 years;[35] and

---

29 ACA 2002, s 67(2), (3); for effects of adoption, see **6.4**.
30 *Re PJ (Adoption: Practice on Appeal)* [1998] 2 FLR 252.
31 *Soderbäck v Sweden* [1999] 1 FLR 250.
32 For Convention adoptions, see **6.199**.
33 ACA 2002, s 49(2).
34 Ibid, s 49(3).
35 Ibid, s 51(1).

(2) he is unmarried or, if married or in a civil partnership, the court is satisfied that:[36]
   (a) his spouse/civil partner cannot be found; or
   (b) he has permanently separated from his spouse/civil partner; or
   (c) his spouse's/civil partner's physical or mental health is such that they are incapable of making an application for an order;
(3) (unless the adoptive placement was made by an adoption agency) the child has his home with the applicant within England and Wales.[37]

Previous applicants

6.26 A court may not hear an application for an adoption order where a previous application for adoption made in the British Isles (and Channel Islands) in relation to the same child by the same persons was refused by any court, unless it appears to the court that, because of a change in circumstances or for any other reason, it is proper to hear the application.[38]

THE WELFARE OF THE CHILD

The paramountcy principle

6.27 Whenever a court or adoption agency is coming to a decision relating to the adoption of a child, the paramount consideration must be the child's welfare throughout his life.[39] This amounts to a significant shift in emphasis from the old law, which required the courts only to give 'first consideration' to the need to promote the child's welfare 'throughout his childhood'.[40] The circumstances in which the paramountcy principle applies include those where the issue is whether or not to dispense with parental consent to placement and/or adoption.[41]

6.28 The court or adoption agency must at all times bear in mind that, in general, any delay in coming to the decision is likely to prejudice the child's welfare.[42]

---

36 ACA 2000, s 51(3) and, s 51(3A) inserted by Civil Partnership Act 2004, s 79.
37 Ibid, ss 42, 44.
38 ACA 2002, s 48.
39 Ibid, s 1(1), (2).
40 Adoption Act 1976, s 6 (repealed).
41 ACA 2000, s 1(7).
42 Ibid, s 1(3).

6.29 The court or adoption agency must also have regard, among other factors, to the adoption 'welfare checklist':[43]

(1) the child's ascertainable wishes and feelings regarding the decision (considered in the light of the child's age and understanding);
(2) the child's particular needs;
(3) the likely effect on the child (throughout his life) of having ceased to be a member of the original family and become an adopted person;
(4) the child's age, sex, background and any of the child's characteristics which the court or agency considers relevant;
(5) any harm (within the meaning of the CA 1989) which the child has suffered or is at risk of suffering;
(6) the relationship which the child has with relatives and with any person in relation to whom the court or agency considers the question to be relevant including:
    (a) the likelihood of any such relationship continuing and the value to the child of its doing so;
    (b) the ability and willingness of any of the child's relatives, or of any such person, to provide the child with a secure environment in which the child can develop and otherwise to meet the child's needs;
    (c) the wishes and feelings of any of the child's relatives or of any such person regarding the child.

6.30 In placing a child for adoption, the agency must give due consideration to the child's religious persuasion, racial origin and cultural and linguistic background.[44]

6.31 Finally, the court or agency must always consider the whole range of powers available to it in the child's case; and the court must not make any order under ACA 2002 unless it considers that making an order would be better for the child than not doing so.[45]

6.32 The welfare provisions of ACA 2002, s 1, while in similar terms and format to CA 1989, s 1, are materially different: welfare of the child 'throughout his life', and a checklist that focuses on terminating and establishing legal relations, are prominent features of the adoption provisions. We would draw particular attention to:

- ceasing to be a member of the original family and becoming an adopted person;[46]

---

43 ACA 2002, s 1(4).
44 Ibid, s 1(5).
45 Ibid, s 1(6).
46 Ibid, s 1(4)(c).

- relationships which the child has with relatives.[47]

Ceasing to be a member of the original family and becoming an adopted person

6.33 ACA 2002, s 1(4)(c) requires the court or agency to project its consideration throughout the child's life. It has a twofold focus:

(1) ceasing to be a member of the original family; and
(2) becoming an adopted person.

6.34 On adoption the cessation of membership of the original family is total and intended to be so for all time. The original parents' parental responsibility is extinguished and there is a complete severing of all legal ties with the family. The cut-off from his family of origin may have a potentially damaging impact on the child's sense of identity and emotional wellbeing.

6.35 In considering the likely effect on the child of these changes, the court or adoption agency will be focusing upon the degree of interference with the child's ECHR Art 8 rights to family life that would be consequent upon an adoption. This will have to be balanced against the family life that the child is, or will be, enjoying with the adoptive family.

6.36 In *Re M (Adoption or Residence Orders)*[48] Ward LJ described the issues involved in considering adoption for a child:

> 'The legal nature and effect of an adoption order is … [that] … it changes status. The child is treated in law as if she had been born a child of the marriage of the applicants. She ceases in law to be a child of her mother and the sister of her siblings. The old family link is destroyed and new family ties are created. The psychological effect is that the child loses one identity and gains another. Adoption is inconsistent with being a member of both old and new family at the same time. Long-term fostering does enable the child to have the best of both worlds by feeling she belongs to both families though she must reside with … only one.
>
> The significant advantage of adoption is that it can promote much-needed security and stability, the younger the age of placement, the fuller the advantage. The disadvantage is that it is unlike any other decision made by adults during a child's minority because it is irrevocable. The child cannot at a later stage even in adulthood reverse the process. That is a salutary reminder of the seriousness of the decision. The advantage of the care/residence order is the converse – it can be adapted to meet changing

47 ACA 2002, s 1(4)(f).
48 [1998] 1 FLR 570 at 589.

needs, but therein lies its disadvantage – it does not provide absolute certainty and security. Children Act 1989, s 91(14) minimises, if not eliminates, the uncertainty.

In weighing up these considerations, the court must have an eye to the realities of the child's situation, bearing in mind the torture of adolescence through which the child must live, finding and then asserting the independence of growing adulthood. When times are bad – and it would be surprising if there were not such times – it will be the emotional attachment forged between the adopters and the child, not that piece of paper entitled "adoption order", which will prevent a disaffected child searching for a grass which will always seem so much greener in the pastures occupied by the old family.'

6.37 More recently there has been a growing awareness among childcare professionals of the possibility of a 'dual identity' for adopted children. The average age of an adopted child in the UK is 4 years and 5 months;[49] these children will always retain memories of their birth family and a sense of birth family identity that, however strong the adoptive relationship, will never be extinguished. The use of 'life story work' and, in appropriate cases, ongoing contact with the birth family after the adoption, have developed in response to this awareness. Both are discussed later in this chapter.

Relationship which the child has with relatives

6.38 ACA 2002, s 1(4)(f) requires a court or adoption agency to consider the child's existing family relationships to a degree and in a manner which is not expressly required by the companion welfare checklist in CA 1989, s 1(3).

6.39 The court or agency is required to consider 'the relationship which the child has with relatives and with any person in relation to whom the court or agency considers the question to be relevant'.[50] The pool of relationships is not confined to relatives, but will include any de facto relationships considered to be of importance; on the facts of a particular case this might include foster parents.

---

49 *Children Looked After by Local Authorities*, Year Ending 31 March 2004 – available at www.dfes.gov.uk/rsgateway

50 ACA 2002, s 1(4)(f). A 'relative' in relation to a child means a grandparent, brother, sister, uncle or aunt, whether of the full blood or half-blood or by marriage or civil partnership. For the purposes of ACA 2002, s 1, a 'relative' includes the child's mother and father.

6.40 The welfare checklist applies to any decision relating to adoption and so consideration of existing relationships (particularly between siblings) is likely to be very important in the context of any proposed contact arrangements.[51]

6.41 In the context of ACA 2002, s 1(4)(f) the court or adoption agency must consider:

(1) the likelihood of any such relationship continuing and the value to the child of its doing so;
(2) the ability and willingness of any of the child's relatives, or of any such person, to provide the child with a secure environment in which the child can develop and otherwise to meet the child's needs; and
(3) the wishes and feelings of any of the child's relatives or of any such person regarding the child.

6.42 These factors embrace consideration of:

- the value to the child of a continuing relationship with his relatives (and any other person who is important to the child); and
- the wishes and feelings of those relatives. Again, within the pool of possible relationships, particular importance is likely to be given to relationships between siblings.

6.43 ACA 2002, s 1(4)(f)(ii) contains a statutory requirement for an assessment by the adoption agency, and ultimately the court, of the capacity and willingness of relatives or others to provide a long-term home for the child. The type and degree of assessment required will no doubt vary from case to case.

Religion, race and culture

6.44 ACA 2002, s 1(5) provides that 'in placing a child for adoption, the adoption agency must give due consideration to the child's religious persuasion, racial origin and cultural and linguistic background'.

6.45 It is important that prospective adopters are aware of the child's background and able, as far as possible, to assist the child to form a sense of her cultural and racial heritage. Where a child's heritage is very mixed, it will rarely be possible for it all to be reflected in the make-up of the adoptive home.

6.46 Issues relating to religion are of importance, but the court must afford paramount consideration to the child's welfare and this may

---

51 For 'contact after adoption', see **6.163**.

require a placement which does not accord with the parent's religious wishes.[52] The issue demands awareness and sensitivity from practitioners: for a sad case where a mistake about the child's religious identity caused severe distress to both child and adopters some 30 years after the adoption took place, see *Re B (Adoption: Setting Aside)*.[53]

Whole range of powers and 'no order' principle

6.47 ACA 2002, s 1(6) provides that the court or adoption agency must always consider:

(1) the whole range of powers available to it in the child's case (whether under ACA 2002 or CA 1989); and
(2) the court must not make any order under ACA 2002 unless it considers that making the order would be better for the child than not doing so.

Whole range of powers available

6.48 The requirement in ACA 2002, s 1(6) is upon the court and the adoption agency and applies throughout the course of 'the child's case'. The requirement is dynamic and wide-ranging; it applies 'always' and to the 'whole range of powers available'. The relevant powers available may change from time to time during the life of the child's case.

6.49 The range of options in a particular case may include:

(1) rehabilitation with birth parents;
(2) placement with extended family members or friends;
(3) residence order (with or without a supervision order);
(4) orders coupled with a restriction on further applications under CA 1989, s 91(14);
(5) special guardianship orders: the new ss 14A–14G of CA 1989;
(6) fostering or other accommodation under a care order; and
(7) adoption:
    (a) twin-track planning, or concurrent planning;[54]
    (b) placement agreement or placement order.

6.50 It is essential to have regard to the nature and effect of each order and the advantages and disadvantages each brings to the safeguarding and promotion of the child's welfare.

---

52 *Re E (An Infant)* [1963] 3 All ER 874; *Re C (Adoption: Religious Observance)* [2002] 1 FLR 1119.

53 [1995] 1 FLR 1.

54 *Re D and K (Care Plan)* [1999] 2 FLR 872.

'No order' principle

6.51 ACA 2002, s 1(6) provides that 'the court must not make any order under this Act unless it considers that making the order would be better for the child than not doing so'. While using different phraseology to CA 1989, s 1(5), this statement of the 'no order' principle has a like effect and encapsulates the 'least interventionist' approach and the principle of proportionality under the ECHR.

PARENTAL CONSENT

Overview

6.52 The issue of parental consent must now be considered twice: first at the point of placement, or when the adoption agency becomes authorised to place the child (even if a placement does not immediately take place); and secondly when the court comes to consider whether or not to make a final adoption order. However, natural parents and their advisers must be aware that the 'second bite at the cherry' that the Act appears to offer, ie the opportunity to withhold consent first at the placement stage, and then, if that fails, at the final adoption hearing, is largely illusory.

6.53 At the final hearing the court must satisfy itself that the consent of all relevant persons to the adoption has been validly given (and not validly withdrawn) or dispensed with. However, if the parents have already consented to the child's placement, or if the local authority holds a placement order, the parents' participation in the final adoption hearing is severely restricted. This is illustrated by the following diagram which traces the court's approach to the issue of parental consent at the final adoption hearing.

6.54 In agency placement cases, or where a parent has given advance consent to the adoption, the parent may not oppose the making of an adoption order without the court's leave; and the court may not give leave unless there has been a change of circumstances since the consent was given or the placement order was made. It follows that where the child is placed for adoption (by consent or by order), or a parent has given advance consent to adoption, the parent may not then oppose the making of an adoption order at the final hearing unless there has been a change of circumstances. What will amount to a change of circumstances is yet to be established.

6.55 The following section deals with parental consent to adoption. It sets out the steps that the court must go through at the adoption hearing, in relation to parental consent. It must be read in the knowledge that, if the child has been placed for adoption by an agency authorised to do so, the opportunities for parental participation in the court's decision-making process are limited. The way in which the court (or adoption agency) must approach the issue of consent at the placement stage is considered below at **6.128**.

Consent to adoption

6.56 An adoption order may only be made if the court is satisfied in the case of each parent or guardian of the child:

(1) that the parent or guardian consents to the making of the adoption order:
- unconditionally; and
- with full understanding of what is involved;[55] or

(2) that the parent or guardian has given advance consent to adoption under ACA 2002, s 20 (and has not withdrawn that consent) and does not oppose the making of the adoption order;[56] or

(3) that the parent's or guardian's consent should be dispensed with under one of the two statutory grounds available.[57]

6.57 The provisions of ACA 2002, s 1, which require the court to give paramount consideration to the welfare of the child throughout his life, apply to a decision upon whether consent should be dispensed with.[58]

'Parent'

6.58 A 'parent' means 'a parent having parental responsibility for the child under the Children Act 1989'.[59] The following people are therefore included within the meaning of 'parent' for the purposes of the Act:

(1) the child's natural mother (unless parental responsibility has been removed by order of a foreign court or a previous adoption order);

(2) the child's natural father:
   (a) if he was married to the child's mother at the time of the child's birth;
   (b) if he subsequently married the child's mother;[60]
   (c) if after 1 December 2003 he is registered as the child's father on the birth certificate;[61]

---

55 ACA 2002, ss 47(2)(a), 52(5).
56 Ibid, s 47(2)(b).
57 Ibid, s 47(2)(c); for dispensing with consent to adoption, see **6.74**.
58 Ibid, s 1(7).
59 Ibid, s 52(6).
60 Legitimacy Act 1976, s 2 and FLRA 1987.
61 CA 1989, ss 4(1), 11(1).

(d) if he has obtained an order granting him parental responsibility with respect to the child;[62]

(e) if, before the commencement of CA 1989, he has obtained an order granting him parental rights and duties in respect of the child[63] as that order will be deemed to be an order under CA 1989, s 4 granting him parental responsibility for the child;[64]

(f) if he has acquired parental responsibility for the child under a parental responsibility agreement made with the mother;[65]

(2) the child's adoptive parent if he has been the subject of a previous adoption. (In those circumstances, the child's natural parents' consent would not be relevant.)

6.59 The consent of the father without parental responsibility is not required within adoption proceedings.[66] However, adoption agencies and local authorities must be careful to establish where possible the identity of the child's father and, unless there are good reasons not to do so, notify him of the adoption application. The father then has an opportunity to apply for parental responsibility within the proceedings. A failure by a local authority to take reasonable steps in this regard is likely to amount to a breach of the father's rights under Articles 6 and 8 of the ECHR.[67]

Guardian

6.60 A child's 'guardian', for the purpose of adoption proceedings, has the same meaning as in CA 1989, and includes a special guardian.[68]

In an international case, whether or not a 'guardian' (which may be an institution rather than a person) is a guardian under ACA 2002 must be determined under English law.[69]

Consent to placement for adoption

6.61 An adoption agency is only authorised to place a child for adoption 'with parental consent' under ACA 2002, s 19 if it is satisfied

---

62 CA 1989, s 4(1), 11(1).

63 FLRA 1987, s 4 (repealed by CA 1989, Sch 15, and converted by CA 1989, Sch 14, para 4).

64 Ibid.

65 CA 1989, s 4(1)(b).

66 ACA 2002, s 52(6); *Re C (A Minor) (Adoption: Parental Agreement: Contact)* [1993] 2 FLR 260.

67 See for example *Gorgulu v Germany* [2004] 1 FLR 894, *Keegan v Ireland* (No 16969/90) (1994) 18 EHRR 342, ECHR.

68 ACA 2002, s 144(1).

69 *Re AMR (Adoption: Procedure)* [1999] 2 FLR 807.

that each parent or guardian of a child has consented (and has not withdrawn the consent) to the child being placed for adoption with prospective adopters identified in the consent, or being placed for adoption with any prospective adopters who may be chosen by the agency.[70] Any consent given by a mother is ineffective if given less than six weeks after the child's birth.[71] ACA 2002, s 19 is subject to the general provisions regarding parental consent in s 52.[72] Consent therefore means consent that is given unconditionally and with full understanding of what is involved.[73]

6.62 Consent to a child being placed for adoption with prospective adopters identified in the consent may be combined with consent to the child subsequently being placed for adoption with any prospective adopters who may be chosen by the agency in circumstances where the child is removed from or returned by the identified adopters.[74]

6.63 Consent to placement for adoption may be withdrawn; however, any attempt to withdraw consent will be ineffective if it occurs after an adoption application has been made.[75]

Advance consent to adoption

6.64 A parent or guardian who consents to the child being placed for adoption by an adoption agency under ACA 2002, s 19 may, at the same or any subsequent time, consent to the making of a future adoption order.[76] A parent giving advance consent may consent to an adoption by named prospective adopters (if any) who are identified in the consent form, or to an adoption by any prospective adopters who may be chosen by the agency.[77]

6.65 Advance consent to adoption may be withdrawn,[78] but any purported withdrawal will be ineffective if it occurs after an adoption application has been made.[79]

---

70 ACA 2002, s 19(1).
71 Ibid, s 52(3).
72 Ibid, s 19(5).
73 Ibid, s 52(5).
74 Ibid, s 19(2).
75 Ibid, s 52(4).
76 Ibid, s 20(1).
77 Ibid, s 20(2).
78 Ibid, s 20(3).
79 Ibid, s 52(4).

6.66 Any consent given by a mother is ineffective if given less than six weeks after the child's birth.[80] ACA 2002, s 20 is subject to the general provisions regarding parental consent in s 52.[81]

Consent to making of adoption order

6.67 Before the consent of a parent or guardian can be accepted by the court, the court must be satisfied that the parent or guardian, with full understanding of what is involved, consents unconditionally to the making of an adoption order, whether or not he knows the identity of the applicants.[82]

6.68 In an adoption application, unless the parent has already given advance consent, the consent must be to the specific application that has been made (even if the parent is unaware of the identity of the adopter).[83] Any consent given by a mother is ineffective if given less than six weeks after the child's birth.[84] In a wholly exceptional case, an adoption order may be set aside on appeal on the ground that the parent's consent had been founded upon a basic mistake.[85]

6.69 The consent must be unconditional; however, if the parent or guardian (or other relative/significant person) expresses wishes and feelings about the upbringing of the child, the adoption agency must have regard to those matters when coming to any decision relating to the adoption of the child.[86]

Form and proof of consent

6.70 The parent's or guardian's consent to placement or to adoption (including advance consent) must be given in the form prescribed by the rules or a form to the like effect.[87] It must be appropriately witnessed, in England and Wales by a CAFCASS officer.

Intercountry adoptions: consent

6.71 The provisions set out above apply equally to non-Convention adoption applications relating to a child who has come from another

---

80 ACA 2002, s 52(3).
81 Ibid, s 20(6).
82 Ibid, s 52(5).
83 Ibid, ss 47(2)(a), 52(5); see also FP(A)R 2005, Form A104.
84 ACA 2002, s 52(3).
85 *Re M (Minors) (Adoption)* [1991] 1 FLR 458; *Re A (Adoption: Agreement: Procedure)* [2001] 2 FLR 455.
86 ACA 2002, s 1(1) and (4)(f)(iii).
87 Ibid, s 52(7); FP(A)R 2005, r 28(1) and (2).

country. (For Convention adoptions, see **6.199**.) The consent of his parent or guardian will either have to be proved or dispensed with before an adoption order may be made. Potential problems at the final hearing can be avoided if the evidence of consent has been obtained in accordance with the rules at the time of the original placement, which will normally have taken place abroad.

The effect of giving consent

Placement for adoption or advance consent to adoption

6.72 Where a child is placed for adoption with parental consent, the birth parents can validly withdraw their consent to placement and/or advance consent to adoption at any time before an application for an adoption order is made.[88] If consent to placement is withdrawn before an application has been issued, statutory provision is made for the removal and return of the child.[89]

6.73 Where consent to a placement, or advance consent to adoption, has not been withdrawn prior the issue of an adoption application, the birth parent may only oppose the making of an adoption order with the leave of the court, and the court may only give leave if there has been a change of circumstances.[90]

Dispensing with parental consent

Grounds for dispensing with parental consent

6.74 A court may dispense with the consent of a parent or guardian to adoption or to the making of a placement order on one or both of two possible grounds,[91] namely that:

(1) the parent or guardian cannot be found or is incapable of giving consent;

(2) the welfare of the child requires the consent to be dispensed with.

Cannot be found or is incapable of giving consent

6.75 In order to satisfy this ground, the applicant must show that every reasonable effort has been made to try and contact the parent.

---

88 ACA 2002, s 52(4).
89 Ibid, ss 30–41.
90 Ibid, s 47(5) and (7).
91 Ibid, s 52(1).

Enquiries should be thorough and should include attempts to contact the extended family of the 'missing parent' where the relevant addresses are known.

6.76 The incapacity of a parent 'incapable of giving consent' may relate to the parent's or guardian's mental or physical condition or circumstances at the date of the decision. The court must be satisfied that the parent has not indicated a view on the adoption and is incapable of agreeing to it.

6.77 A parent in the proceedings who is a 'patient' must have a litigation friend to conduct the proceedings on his behalf.[92] A 'patient' is a party to proceedings who, by reason of mental disorder within the meaning of the Mental Health Act 1983, is incapable of managing and administering his property and affairs.[93]

Child's welfare requires consent to be dispensed with

6.78 Consent to the making of a placement order or an adoption order may be dispensed with on the ground that the welfare of the child requires the consent to be dispensed with.[94] The 'welfare' ground is an innovation brought in by ACA 2002 and replaces five alternative grounds for dispensation contained in AA 1976, s 16(2), including that of the parent 'withholding his consent unreasonably'. The manner in which the new ground will be applied will no doubt be the subject of early authority from the higher courts. In particular, it is not clear how much, if at all, the substantial case law established in relation to the 'unreasonableness' ground will be considered relevant to the 'welfare' ground.

6.79 Despite the fact that welfare is brought expressly into the test for dispensing with consent, the consent issue remains separate from the welfare issue; thus the question under s 52(1) is *not* 'does the child's welfare require a placement/adoption order', it is 'does the child's welfare require the parental consent be dispensed with'.

6.80 The child's welfare will be the paramount consideration in determining the issue of dispensing with parental consent. The welfare checklist at ACA 2002, s 1(4) must be applied in determining the consent issue.[95]

6.81 The court must have regard to each element of the welfare checklist. The factors that may indicate that adoption is in the child's

---

92 FP(A)R 2005, r 50.
93 Ibid, r 6(1).
94 ACA 2002, s 52(1)(b).
95 For adoption welfare checklist, see **6.29**.

best interests must be balanced against those that may point away from adoption, for example s 1(4)(c) (likely effect of ceasing to be a member of the original family) or s 1(4)(f) (relationship with relatives and others).

'Requires'

6.82 It is not entirely clear whether the inclusion of the word 'requires' in the welfare test for dispensing with parental consent indicates a simple welfare test (on balance adoption being better for the child) or a whether a higher degree of imperative must be established.

6.83 Previous case law[96] suggests that test may be approached by the judge asking himself whether, having regard to the evidence and applying the current values of our society, the advantages of adoption for the welfare of the child appear sufficiently strong to justify overriding the views and interests of the objecting parent.[97]

6.84 The 'least interventionist' approach in ACA 2002, s 1(6), together with ECHR, Art 8 and the principle of proportionality, are likely to be important factors in considering whether a child's welfare 'requires' the court to dispense with parental consent.

6.85 Commonly encountered factors which may have a bearing on the question of the child's welfare in an appropriate case are: the prospects of rehabilitation to the family, ongoing contact, the child's security, an inherent defect in relation to the parent's ability to care, race, culture and religion, risk of harm to the child, consent given and retracted and, last but not least, the wishes of the child.

Procedure for dispensing with consent

6.86 In a case where the court is asked to dispense with consent, the applicant must give notice of the request in the application form, or at any later stage file a written request setting out the reasons for the request, and must file a statement of facts setting out a summary of the history of the case and any other facts to satisfy the court of the ground(s) for dispensation.[98]

---

96 *Re F (Adoption: Freeing Order); Re C (A Minor) (Adoption: Parental Agreement: Contact)* [1993] 2 FLR 260.

97 Ibid.

98 FP(A)R 2005, r 27(2).

ADOPTION SERVICES

6.87 The range of services that every adoption agency must provide are set out variously in the ACA 2002, the Adoption Agencies Regulations 2005 (AAR 2005)[99] and the Adoption Support Services Regulations 2005.[100] Agencies must also comply with the National Minimum Standards for Voluntary Adoption Agencies and Local Adoption Services (available on the BAAF and DFES websites). Compliance is monitored by the Commission for Social Care Inspection.

6.88 In general the services provided by a local authority, other (ie non-local authority) adoption agency or adoption support agency will fall into one of four categories:

- provision of information, advice and support to prospective adopters and adoptive families;
- assessment of children and prospective adopters;
- provision of advice and support to birth families; and
- maintenance of information relating to adopted children and their birth families.

6.89 Every local authority must set up and maintain an adoption service. Every local authority is therefore also an adoption agency (although not all adoption agencies are local authorities).

Prospective adopters

Advice and information

6.90 Adoption agencies have a duty to provide information to those who are thinking of adopting a child and advice and assistance throughout the adoption process and beyond. They must give prospective adopters clear written information about the assessment and approval process. Agencies must also run a 'preparation programme' that gives prospective adopters the opportunity to meet with others who have adopted children.

6.91 Following a placement the adoption agency must offer the prospective adopters a wide range of support services, including advice on how to help the child come to terms with his history and background, assistance with managing contact with the birth family and support if the placement runs into difficulties or breaks down.

---

99 SI 2005/389.
100 SI 2005/691.

Assessment and the Independent Review Mechanism

6.92 The assessment process is the most tightly regulated of all an adoption agency's functions. The agency must carry out a detailed system of checks and the prospective adopters must undergo a police check and a medical examination and provide references from at least two referees. Most agencies, including local authorities, use BAAF's 'Form F' as a template for their assessment process. The form is available for purchase from the BAAF website.

6.93 Each adoption agency must establish at least one Adoption Panel, which will be made up of a mix of social workers and other professionals, some from within the agency and some who are independent of it. The panel will also include some members who have first hand experience of adoption in their own lives. The panel are required to give recommendations to the agency on three separate topics:

- is a particular child suitable for adoption;
- is a particular adult suitable to be a prospective adopter;
- the plan to match a particular child with a particular prospective adopter(s).

An agency cannot make a decision about any of these three topics until it has considered the recommendation of the panel. Thereafter the agency may or may not decide in accordance with the panel recommendation.

6.94 If an agency informs an applicant that it does not intend to approve him as a prospective adoptive parent, the applicant may in England only ask for a review of the agency's determination via the Independent Review Mechanism, operated by BAAF on behalf of the Secretary of State for Education and Skills. The IRM cannot overturn the agency's decision; it can only make a recommendation that the agency should review its determination.

Matching and placement

6.95 Once the plan for adoption for a child has been confirmed, the agency will begin to look for a match between the child and an adoptive family. Depending on the child's situation and needs, that family may be found within the agency's own pool of prospective adopters or located farther afield.

6.96 The Adoption and Children Act Register is an important tool for agencies seeking to place older children, sibling groups, children with special needs or other children who have traditionally been seen as difficult to place. The Register contains details of children waiting for families, and prospective adopters waiting to adopt children. It has been managed by BAAF since December 2004 and is accessible to adoption agencies who will use it to seek matches either for children they are looking after or for adopters on their books. BAAF also publishes 'Be My Parent', a national newsletter containing details of children seeking adoptive families.

6.97 Once a potential match has been identified the local authority must present it to its Adoption Panel for approval. If the match is approved, the agency will start the process of introducing the child to the family. Depending on the age of the child, this process can take from a few weeks to a couple of months.

The birth family

Counselling and support

6.98 From the time when adoption is identified as the plan for the child, the adoption agency (usually in such cases the local authority) must provide the birth family with a social worker independent of the child's social worker. Via this link the agency must give the birth family support and encourage all members, including siblings, to be involved in the process of providing information to the adoptive family about the child's background and early life. The birth family's views about the adoption must be recorded and parents particularly should have an opportunity to see all information about the birth family that is passed on to the adopters.

6.99 Following the adoption the agency must make available to the parents a post-adoption service, including counselling if appropriate and assistance with any ongoing direct or indirect contact between the birth family and the child.

Life story work

6.100 The term 'life story work' describes the important process of informing an adopted child of details of her life prior to coming to live in the adoptive family. A 'life story book' with words and pictures in age-appropriate terms will be prepared, as will a 'later life letter' which sets out details of the child's natural family in more adult terms. An adoption agency is required to provide the adopters with a copy of the child's permanence report and any other information the agency considers relevant before the proposal to match the child with the prospective adopters is presented to the adoption panel.[101] Before the

---

101 AAR 2005, reg 31(1)(a).

child is placed, the placement plan agreed between the agency and the prospective adopters must indicate the date on which the child's life story book and later life letter are to be passed by the agency to the prospective adopter.[102]

6.101 The birth family should, wherever possible, be given the opportunity to contribute to the life story work done for or with the child, perhaps by providing photographs of the child's early life and important members of the birth family. Involvement of the birth family in this process, where they are able and prepared to participate, is an important part of the post-adoption support services that all adoption agencies must provide.

ACCESS TO CONFIDENTIAL ADOPTION INFORMATION

Confidentiality

6.102 An adoption agency is required to maintain confidentiality with regard to its records.[103] Specified office holders and others have a right of access to the records, and the agency has discretion to provide access for the purpose of carrying out its function as an adoption agency.[104]

Registration and tracing natural family

Adopted Children Register

6.103 Every adoption must be registered in the Adopted Children Register[105] by the Registrar General in the prescribed form.[106] The Register of Births relating to the adopted child will be marked 'adopted'.[107]

6.104 A certified copy of an entry in the Adopted Children Register, if sealed and stamped with the Registrar General's seal, will, without further proof, be received as evidence of the adoption and any other information in the entry as if it were a birth certificate.[108]

---

102 AAR 2005, reg 35 and Sch 5.
103 Ibid, reg 41.
104 Ibid, reg 42.
105 ACA 2002, s 77, Sch 1.
106 The Adopted Children and Adoption Contact Registers Regulations 2005 (ACACRR 2005) (SI 2005/924), reg 2.
107 ACA 2002, s 77, Sch 1.
108 Ibid, s 77(4).

Going behind the adoption curtain: tracing the natural family

Person adopted before 30 December 2005

6.105 An adopted person over the age of 18 years may apply to the Registrar General for such information as is necessary to enable him to obtain a copy of his birth records.[109] For those who were adopted before 30 December 2005, the procedure for tracing birth records is governed by ACA 2002, Sch 2 and regulations.[110] Where a person who was adopted before 12 November 1975 applies for a record of his birth, the Registrar General is not permitted to disclose the information unless the applicant has attended an interview with an adoption counsellor.[111]

6.106 An applicant (who may be the adopted person or a blood relative) may be entitled to receive 'intermediary services' from an adoption agency or an adoption support agency. Intermediary services are defined[112] as a service for the purpose of:

- assisting adopted persons who are over the age of 18 years and who were adopted prior to 30 December 2005 to obtain information in relation to their adoption; and
- facilitating contact between such persons and their relatives.

6.107 The potential emotional and psychological impact of reintroducing an adopted person to their natural family after a long period is such that the intermediary agency is charged with a heavy responsibility in deciding whether it is in fact appropriate to proceed with the process and of managing it if they do proceed.

6.108 Before proceeding with any application an intermediary agency must provide information to the applicant about post-adoption counselling services that are available.[113]

6.109 An intermediary agency may not disclose any information to an applicant about the adopted person ('the subject') without the subject's consent.[114] If the subject has died or is incapable of giving consent, that information may be given to the applicant.[115]

---

109 ACA 2002, s 79(6).

110 (England) the Adoption Information and Intermediary Services (Pre-Commencement Adoptions) Regulations 2005 (AIIS(PC)R 2005) (SI 2005/890).

111 ACA 2002, s 79(6) and Sch 2 para 4.

112 AIIS(PC)R 2005, reg 4.

113 Ibid, reg 10.

114 AIIS(PC)R 2005, reg 7.

115 Ibid.

6.110 An adopted person may put down a written veto (which will be binding on the adoption agencies) to the effect that that he does not wish to be contacted by an intermediary agency in relation to an application under those regulations or that he only wishes to be contacted in specified circumstances.[116]

6.111 Where the subject does not consent to disclosure, or is incapable of consent, or there is a veto, the intermediary agency may nevertheless disclose general non-identifying background information to the applicant, if it considers that it is appropriate to do so.[117]

Person adopted after 30 December 2005

6.112 In relation to a person who has been adopted on or after 30 December 2005, the disclosure of information (known as 'section 56 information') relating to his adoption is governed by ACA 2002, ss 56–65 and regulations.[118] The s 56 information that an adoption agency is required to keep (for 100 years) includes:[119]

(1) the case record set up by the Adoption Agencies Regulations 1983 and/or 2005;
(2) any information that has been supplied by a natural parent or relative or other significant person in the adopted person's life, with the intention that the adopted person may, should he wish, be given that information;
(3) any information supplied by the adoptive parents or other persons which is relevant to matters arising after the making of the adoption order;
(4) any information that the adopted person has requested should be kept;
(5) any information given to the adoption agency in respect of an adopted person by the Registrar General under ACA 2002, s 79(5) (information that would enable an adopted person to obtain a certified copy of the record of his birth);
(6) any information disclosed to the adoption agency about an entry relating to the adopted person on the Adoption Contact Register.

---

116 AIIS(PC)R 2005, reg 8.
117 Ibid, reg 9.
118 (In England) by the Disclosure of Adoption Information (Post-Commencement Adoptions) Regulations 2005 (SI 2005/888); (in Wales) Access to Information (Post-Commencement Adoptions) (Wales) Regulations 2005 (SI 2005/2689).
119 DAI(PCA)R 2005, reg 4.

6.113 An adoption agency is not required to keep information falling within (2)–(4) above if it considers that to do so would be prejudicial to the adopted person's welfare or that it would not be reasonably practicable to keep it.[120]

6.114 Any s 56 information kept by an adoption agency which is about an adopted person or any other person and is, or includes, identifying information about the person in question ('protected information') generally may only be disclosed by the agency to a person (other than that person that the information is about) in pursuance to ACA 2002, ss 56–65.[121]

6.115 An adopted person who has attained the age of 18 years has the right, at his request, to receive from the appropriate adoption agency (in a non-agency case this will mean the local authority to which notice of intention to adopt was given) any information which would enable him to obtain a certified copy of his birth certificate (unless the High Court otherwise orders) or any prescribed information which had been disclosed to his adopters during the adoption process (under ACA 2002, s 54).[122]

6.116 An adoption agency must provide written information about post-adoption counselling in relation to an application for the disclosure of information.[123] If the person requests counselling, the agency has a duty to arrange provision of it.[124]

Adoption Contact Register

6.117 A further register (the Adoption Contact Register) to assist those adoptees and their natural families who wish to express a view about future contact with each other is held by the Registrar General.[125] Part 1 of the ACR contains information provided by the adopted person about his wishes for having contact (or not) with his natural relatives.[126] Part 2 of the ACR contains information about any relative of the adoptee, by blood, half-blood, marriage or civil partnership (but not adoption) who wishes to express a view about contact with the adoptee.[127]

---

120 DAI(PCA)R 2005, reg 4.
121 ACA 2002, s 57(1).
122 Ibid, s 60.
123 DAI(PCA)R 2005, reg 16.
124 Ibid, reg 17.
125 ACA 2002, s 80. Useful guidance is given in BAAF Practice Note 20 'The Adoption Contact Register'.
126 ACA 2002, s 80(2) and (3).
127 Ibid, s 80.

6.118 The system operates by the Registrar General transmitting to the adopted person whose name appears in Part 1, the name and address of any relative entered in Part 2 who has asked for contact.[128] The register is not open to public inspection.[129]

6.119 This facility is intended to ease the practical problems involved in tracing relatives. Natural family members (not only natural parents) who wish to have the possibility of future contact should be advised of the existence of the register. They may have their name and current address entered upon it at any time after the making of the adoption order, and after the entry of the child's name into the Adopted Children Register. An adopted person can only enter his details in Part 1 if he is over 18 years.

PLACING A CHILD FOR ADOPTION

Background

6.120 Prior to ACA 2002, the placing of a child for adoption was largely an administrative process conducted by a local authority or adoption agency either with the agreement of the parent(s) or under the authority provided by a care order (interim or full) or an order freeing a child for adoption. ACA 2002, Chapter 3 establishes a statutory code and legal structure regulating the circumstances in which a child can be placed for adoption and the consequences once such a placement is made. There is provision for substantial court involvement in the process.

6.121 The general effect of the placement provisions in ACA 2002, Ch 3 is two-fold. Firstly, before a placement for adoption can be made a parent must be fully engaged in the decision-making process, either by giving express consent or by having the opportunity to contest the issue in court proceedings. Secondly, if either a parent consents to placement for adoption, or the court makes a 'placement order', and an adoptive placement is then made, the parent's options for later reversing the progress towards adoption or challenging any eventual adoption application are significantly restricted.

6.122 A central aim of the ACA 2002, Ch 3 provisions is to bring the parent's opportunity to challenge the crucial adoption decision forward to a stage before any adoptive placement is made. A feature of the earlier law was that in many cases the first opportunity a parent had to

---

128 ACACRR 2005, reg 8.
129 ACA 2002, s 81(1).

challenge a placement in court might be months or years after the placement had been made, by which time the child would be settled in her new family.

6.123 In contrast to the now repealed provisions 'freeing' a child for adoption, where a child is 'placed for adoption' (by agreement or order) the birth parents remain the child's parents until any final adoption order but they will be required to share parental responsibility with the prospective adopters and the adoption agency.

'Placement for adoption'

6.124 'Placing a child for adoption' by an adoption agency is defined as 'placing a child for adoption with prospective adopters'. The term includes all situations (including pre-ACA placements) where the agency has placed or is placing the child with persons who intend to adopt her. A child who is placed or authorised to be placed for adoption by a local authority is a '*looked after child*' under the provisions of CA 1989, Part III.[130] The local authority will have the continuing responsibility for managing, overseeing and reviewing the child's progress until a future adoption order is made.

6.125 All adoption agencies, whether local authorities or voluntary agencies, must comply with the requirements imposed by AAR 2005, Pt 6 regarding placement for adoption and conducting statutory reviews.

6.126 Local authority foster parents are able to seek formal approval from the local authority as prospective adopters of children being fostered by them. If they are approved, and the agency leaves the child with them as prospective adopters, the placement will become an adoption placement despite the fact that the child will not have actually moved from the foster home.

Two routes to placement for adoption

6.127 ACA 2002 establishes two routes by which an adoption agency may be authorised to place a child for adoption:

- placement with parental consent;
- placement under a placement order.

---

130 ACA 2002, s 18(3).

Placement with parental consent

6.128 ACA 2002, s 19(1) authorises an adoption agency to place a child for adoption where it is satisfied that each parent with parental responsibility or guardian of the child has consented (and has not withdrawn consent) to the child:

- being placed for adoption with prospective adopters identified in the consent; or
- being placed for adoption with any prospective adopters who may be chosen by the agency.

6.129 'Consent' means consent given unconditionally and with full understanding of what is involved.[131]

6.130 Consent to a child being placed for adoption with prospective adopters identified in the consent (under s 19(1)(a)) may be combined with consent to the child subsequently being placed for adoption with any prospective adopters chosen by the agency (under s 19(1)(b)) if the child were to be removed from or returned by the identified adopters.[132]

6.131 Once a child has been placed for adoption pursuant to a consent given under ACA 2002, s 19, he will continue to be regarded as placed there under that provision until he is removed, notwithstanding that a parent may have withdrawn consent at a later stage.[133]

6.132 The consensual route under ACA 2002, s 19(1) cannot be used where an application for a care or supervision order has been made under CA 1989, s 31 and that application has not been disposed of.[134] Where a care order is made after parental consent to placement has been given, the consent no longer gives the agency authority to place the child for adoption.[135] In any circumstances where a care order has been made or an application is pending, and the appropriate local authority is satisfied that the child ought to be placed for adoption, it must apply for a placement order.[136]

6.133 Once a placement order has been made, it is that order, and not any earlier s 19 parental consent, that provides authority for an agency to place the child for adoption.

---

131 ACA 2002, s 52(5) and (6). For parental consent generally, see **6.52**.
132 Ibid, s 19(2).
133 Ibid, s 19(4).
134 Ibid, s 19(3).
135 Ibid.
136 Ibid, s 22(2).

Placing a child under six weeks old

6.134 Any consent 'to the making of an adoption order' given by a mother is ineffective if given less than six weeks after the child's birth.[137] By s 18(1) of the Act, an agency does not need a placement order or formal parental consent before placing a child under six weeks old; and so it seems (although this is not explicit in the Act) that the same approach is taken to placement and applies to both parents. However, according to the regulations an adoption agency may place a child who is less than six weeks old for adoption if each parent or guardian of the child has agreed in writing with the agency that the child may be so placed.[138] Once the child is six weeks old this written agreement must be replaced either by each parent's formal consent, given and witnessed according to the requirements of the Act, or by a placement order.

6.135 In practice an adoption agency is unlikely to place a child under six weeks old for adoption unless it is very confident that the necessary parental consent will be forthcoming in due course and will not be withdrawn. If there is any doubt it will be safer to place the child in a short-term foster placement, and move her to an adoptive placement only when the parents have given consent or a placement order has been obtained.

Form of consent

6.136 Consent to placement for adoption and advance consent to adoption must be given using the relevant statutory form, or a form to like effect.[139]

6.137 In England and Wales any consent form must be witnessed by a CAFCASS officer or, where the child is ordinarily resident in Wales, by a Welsh family proceedings officer.[140] Where a parent is prepared to consent to placement, or give advance consent to adoption, the adoption agency must request CAFCASS, or the Welsh Assembly, to appoint an officer for the consent process and must send the information specified in AAR 2005, Sch 2 together with the request.[141]

Advance consent to adoption

6.138 A parent or guardian of a child who consents to the child being placed for adoption under ACA 2002, s 19 may, at the same time or any

---

137 ACA 2002, s 52(3).
138 AAR 2005, reg 35(4).
139 ACA 2002, s 52(7); FP(A)R 2005, r 28(1)(a). Forms A100–103.
140 See notes on the relevant statutory Form.
141 AAR 2005, reg 20.

subsequent time, consent to the making of a future adoption order.[142] In this context, where the placement consent is for placement with identified prospective adopters the additional consent may be advance consent to adoption by them, or it may be consent to adoption by any prospective adopters who may be chosen by the adoption agency.[143]

6.139 Advance consent to adoption may be withdrawn,[144] but any such withdrawal is ineffective if it takes place after an application for an adoption order has been made.[145]

6.140 A parent who gives advance consent to adoption may, at the same time or any subsequent time, give notice to the adoption agency stating that he does not wish to be informed of any application for an adoption order.[146] Such a notice, once given, may subsequently be withdrawn.[147]

Consequences of parental consent to placement for adoption

6.141 The following important and potentially irrevocable consequences flow from a parent giving consent to the placement of a child for adoption:

- the parent may only oppose any adoption application with the leave of the court;
- the parent's ability to apply for a residence order is restricted;
- the parent's ability to have contact with the child will be determined by the adoption agency or subject to a court order under ACA 2002, s 26;
- parental responsibility is given to the adoption agency (and in due course to prospective adopters with whom the child is placed);
- there are restrictions on a parent's ability to require removal/return of the child.

6.142 Giving consent to placement for adoption has significant consequences for a parent's position in any subsequent adoption application. Where consent to placement has not been withdrawn before an adoption application is made, a parent may only oppose the final

142 ACA 2002, s 20(1).
143 Ibid, s 20(2).
144 Ibid, s 20(3).
145 Ibid, s 52(4).
146 Ibid, s 20(4).
147 Ibid.

adoption order with the leave of the court, and the court may only give leave if there has been a change of circumstances since the s 19 consent was given.[148]

6.143 Where a child is placed for adoption following parental consent under ACA 2002, s 19, or an adoption agency is authorised to place for adoption under that section, a parent or guardian may not apply for a residence order unless an application for adoption has been made and the parent has obtained the court's leave to oppose the adoption order.[149] In the same circumstances, a guardian may not apply for a special guardianship order unless he has obtained the court's leave to oppose the adoption.[150]

Restrictions on changing name or removing from UK a child placed for adoption

6.144 Where a child is placed for adoption pursuant to parental consent under ACA 2002, s 19, or a placement order has been made, no person may:

- cause the child to be known by a new surname; or
- remove the child from the UK,

unless the court gives leave to do so or each parent or guardian of the child gives written consent.[151] A person who provides the child's home may, however, remove the child from the UK for a period of less than one month without the need to obtain parental consent or court leave.[152]

Withdrawal of consent

6.145 Once a parent or guardian has given their consent to the placement of a child for adoption (or advance consent to adoption), the consent may be withdrawn, with the consequence that the agency's authority to place for adoption will cease, at any stage prior to the prospective adopters issuing an adoption application in respect of the child.[153] Consent can only validly be withdrawn by using the statutory form or by notice (which must be in writing) given to the adoption agency.[154] Parental consent cannot be withdrawn if there is a placement

148 ACA 2002, s 47(4), (5), (7).
149 Ibid, s 28(1) and s 47(5); for 'leave to oppose adoption', see **6.54**.
150 Ibid.
151 Ibid, s 28(2), (3).
152 Ibid, s 28(4).
153 Ibid, s 52(4).
154 Ibid, ss 52(8) and 144(1); Form A106.

order in force or an application for a placement order has been made. If a parent withdraws his consent to placement, the local authority has 7 days to make an application for a placement order if the child has not already been placed; 14 days if she has. After that point, if no placement order application has been made, the child must be returned to her parents.[155]

Position of a father without parental responsibility

6.146 In relation to the placement of the child it is only the consent of a parent who has parental responsibility for the child that is relevant.[156] The requirements that must be satisfied in the case of a father without parental responsibility are similar to those that apply when the court considers the application to adopt. Where the identity of the father is known to the adoption agency, and the agency considers that it is appropriate to do so, it is required to contact the father in order to counsel him about adoption and explain the procedure for placement/adoption and the legal implications of adoption.[157] The agency must seek to ascertain his wishes and feelings about the child, the plan for placement/adoption and about contact.[158] They must also ascertain if he wishes to acquire parental responsibility for the child or to apply for a residence or contact order.

6.147 Where an adoption agency is in doubt as to the appropriateness of contacting a father without parental responsibility it may apply to the court for directions on the issue before or after any proceedings have been issued.[159]

6.148 A father who acquires parental responsibility after the agency obtains the mother's consent to placement is deemed to have consented to the child being placed for adoption on the same terms as the mother. This has the advantage of securing the placement for the child; the obvious drawback is that a father who has not managed to acquire parental responsibility before his child reaches the age of six weeks, and whose partner or former partner is determined that the child should be adopted, will have an uphill struggle to contest any subsequent adoption application. It is to be hoped that the local authority's duties to consult unmarried fathers before placing children for adoption will afford some protection.

---

155 ACA 2002, s 31(2) and 32(2).

156 Ibid, s 52(6); for parental consent generally, see **6.52** ff.

157 AAR 2005, reg 14(3) and (4).

158 Ibid.

159 FP(A)R 2005, r 108 (application before proceedings) or Part 9 (application in pending proceedings).

Placement under a placement order

Placement orders

6.149 Given the uncertainty surrounding a consensual placement and the possibility that parental consent may be qualified or withdrawn, it is likely that local authorities will in many cases prefer the security of a placement order. A 'placement order' is 'an order made by the court authorising a local authority to place a child for adoption with any prospective adopters who may be chosen by the authority'.[160]

6.150 While a placement order is in force, parental responsibility for the child is given to the local authority and, while the child is with prospective adopters, also to them.[161] In this respect a placement order is similar to a care order, but with the added feature that the prospective adopters share parental responsibility. The local authority may control the way in which any other person exercises parental responsibility; in reality, it is likely that the prospective adopters will make most of the decisions relating to the child, overseen by the local authority, and that the parents' views will carry relatively little weight.

Conditions for making a placement order

6.151 The court may not make a placement order unless:[162]

- the child is subject to a care order; or
- the court is satisfied that the threshold conditions in CA 1989, s 31(2) (the care or supervision order threshold) are met; or
- the child has no parent or guardian; or
- each parent or guardian has consented to the child being placed for adoption with any prospective adopters who may be chosen by the local authority and has not withdrawn consent, or the court is satisfied that the parent's consent should be dispensed with under ACA 2002, s 52.

Provided that one of these conditions is met, the court will go on to apply the welfare test and checklist in ACA 2002, s 1.

6.152 The statutory definition of the phrase 'care order' includes an interim care order;[163] whether proof of the lower CA 1989, s 38 threshold conditions is sufficient to support the making of a placement order must await judicial clarification. However, it is difficult to see what

---

160 ACA 2002, s 21(1).

161 Ibid, s 25.

162 Ibid, s 21(2), (3).

163 Ibid, Sch 6 and CA 1989, ss 31(11) and 105(1).

circumstances would justify making a placement order while the outcome of care proceedings is still undetermined.

Local authority required to apply for a placement order

6.153 There is a *mandatory* requirement placed upon a local authority to apply for a placement order in the following circumstances:

(1) where a child is placed for adoption, or is being provided with accommodation, by the local authority, and
   - (a) no adoption agency is authorised to place the child for adoption; and
   - (b) it considers that the threshold conditions in CA 1989, s 31(2) are met (or that the child has no parent or guardian); and
   - (c) it is satisfied that the child ought to be placed for adoption.[164]

(2) Where:
   - (a) there is a pending application for a care or supervision order (which has not been disposed of); or
   - (b) the child is the subject of a care order and the appropriate local authority is not authorised to place; and
   - (c) it is satisfied that the child ought to be placed for adoption.[165]

6.154 The purpose of these provisions is to minimise delay for children waiting in care or subject to care proceedings. They do not apply in respect of a child if any person has given notice to a local authority of intention to adopt the child, unless more than four months have gone by since the notice and no adoption application has been made (or it has been withdrawn or dismissed), or if an adoption application has been made and not disposed of.[166]

Status of child pending determination of placement order application

6.155 If a local authority is under a duty to apply for a placement order, or has applied for one and the application has not been disposed of, the subject child is a 'looked after child' under CA 1989, Pt III.[167]

6.156 Where an application for a placement order has been made and has not been disposed of, and no interim care order is in force, the court may give any directions it considers appropriate for the medical or psychiatric examination or other assessment of the child; but a child who is of sufficient understanding to make an informed decision may

---

164 ACA 2002, s 22(1).
165 Ibid.
166 Ibid, s 22(5).
167 Ibid, s 22(4).

refuse to submit to the examination or other assessment.[168] This provision is similar to the court's power to direct assessments under an interim care order.[169]

Consequences of a placement order

6.157 Where a placement order is in force in favour of a local authority the following consequences flow:

(1) The regime for the regulation of contact which applies while an adoption agency is authorised to place a child for adoption applies.
(2) A parent or guardian may not apply for a residence order (and no guardian may apply for a special guardianship order) unless an application for an adoption order has been made and the parent or guardian has obtained the court's leave to oppose the adoption application.[170]
(3) Unless the court gives leave or each parent or guardian gives written consent, no person may:[171]
   (a) cause the child to be known by a new surname;
   (b) remove the child from the UK (save for a period of less than one month by a person who provides the child's home).
(4) Any existing care order on the child does not have effect at any time when the placement order is in force (but will 'revive' if the placement order is revoked).[172]
(5) Any pre-existing CA 1989, s 8 order or supervision order will cease to have effect on the making of a placement order.[173]
(6) No prohibited steps, specific issue or residence order and no supervision or child assessment orders may be made in respect of the child.[174]
(7) No special guardianship order may be made (unless an adoption application has been made and the court has given leave to a person to apply for a special guardianship order or a guardian has been given leave to oppose the adoption).[175]

CARE PROCEEDINGS: HOW DOES A PLAN FOR ADOPTION DEVELOP?

6.158 The ACA 2002 has formalised the process by which a child is placed for adoption. Where a plan for adoption develops within

168 ACA 2002, s 22(6).
169 CA 1989, s 38(6).
170 ACA 2002, s 28(1).
171 Ibid, s 28(2) and (3).
172 Ibid, s 29(1).
173 Ibid, s 29(2).
174 Ibid, s 29(3).
175 Ibid, s 29(5).

ongoing care proceedings, the local authority will not in due course be able to place the child for adoption unless it has been granted a placement order under ACA 2002, s 21. A placement order has a very significant effect upon a parent's ability to challenge any subsequent adoption application. Thus within the compass of care proceedings the plan for the child may develop and, ultimately, the legal rights of the family members may be fundamentally changed by the making of a placement order.

6.159 At the initial stage of a local authority first intervening in a family's care of a child it is unlikely that there will be a ready-made plan for adoption. The process within care proceedings will involve assessment and evaluation of the risks and benefits to the child of remaining with or returning to the natural family. The starting point of any care plan for a child will be a return home to parents, or, if that is not in his best interests, placement within the wider family. Only if the option for family placement is not in accordance with the child's welfare, will an alternative long-term placement be considered appropriate. The priority given to the natural family arises from the duty under domestic law to favour the least interventionist approach[176] and because, under the ECHR Art 8, state intervention in family life must be limited to that for which there is a pressing social need, with any plan being proportionate to that need.

6.160 A local authority is under a duty to apply for a placement order if it is 'satisfied that the child ought to be placed for adoption'.[177] Whilst the legislation is not totally clear, it seems that a local authority cannot come to the conclusion that the child ought to be placed for adoption unless and until it has received a recommendation from its adoption panel on the question of the child's suitability for adoption.[178] In order for the local authority to be in a position to consider applying for a placement order within the timescale of ongoing care proceedings, it is necessary for it to plan its assessment process in time to place the case before the adoption panel at an early stage.

6.161 Where adoption is, or may be, the local authority's care plan for a child, the consideration of adoption may run alongside consideration of other options (for example a return home). Two models have developed for this process. In the first, 'parallel' or 'twin-track' planning, the local authority, while working with the family and continuing to assess a family placement, will nevertheless be preparing the paperwork necessary to proceed with an adoption plan without delay if that becomes the final plan for the child.

---

176 CA 1989, s 1(5) and ACA 2002, s 1(6).

177 ACA 2002, s 22.

178 For adoption panel recommendations, see **6.93**.

6.162 The second model, 'concurrent planning', is a more sophisticated and structured option whereby a young child is placed with specialist foster carers who have been selected and trained to work within a programme of rehabilitation of the child to his family, or, if that is not in his interests, to become his adopters in due course. In this model, the main advantage to the child is not having to move from his foster home to his adoptive home.

CONTACT ON PLACEMENT AND AFTER ADOPTION

Contact arrangements when child is authorised for an adoption placement

6.163 On an agency being authorised to place a child for adoption pursuant to parental consent given under ACA 2002, s 19, or pursuant to a placement order, any existing contact orders under CA 1989 (s 8 or s 34) will cease to have effect[179] and the local authority's obligation to afford reasonable contact to his birth family under CA 1989, s 34 is removed. No further application may be made for a Children Act contact order[180] (save where a s 8 contact application is to be heard together with the application to adopt).[181] However, an application for contact may be made during the currency of an agency's authorisation to place for adoption under ACA 2002, s 26.

6.164 The agency must take into account the wishes and feelings of the parent (and, if appropriate, a father without parental responsibility), the advice of the adoption panel and the adoption welfare checklist in ACA 2002, s 1 before making a decision on contact.[182] The contact arrangements must be kept under review and any proposed changes must be canvassed with parents and others.[183]

6.165 The court must consider on an application for a placement order what arrangements are proposed for allowing contact between the child and members of her birth family or any other relevant person. It must invite the parties to comment on those arrangements and may make a section 26 contact order of its own motion.[184]

6.166 When considering whether to make a section 26 order the court must afford paramount consideration to the child's welfare in

179 ACA 2002, s 26(1), (6).
180 Ibid, s 26(2).
181 Ibid, s 26(5).
182 Ibid, s 27(4); AAR 2005, reg 46.
183 Ibid.
184 ACA 2002, ss 26, 27.

accordance with ACA 2002, s 1. A section 26 contact order has effect while the adoption agency is authorised to place the child for adoption but may be varied or revoked by the court on an application by the child, the agency or the person named in the order.[185]

6.167 The terms of any section 26 order may be departed from by agreement between the agency and any person for whose contact with the child the order provides, provided that the child (if of sufficient age and understanding) agrees, the prospective adopters agree and relevant persons have been informed of the change.[186]

Adoption agency power to refuse to allow contact

6.168 Unlike the position that applies under a care order, there is no requirement upon an adoption agency with authorisation to place the child to allow contact between the child and any person unless such contact is stipulated in an order under ACA 2002, s 26. Consequently, unless to do so would be in conflict with provision in a section 26 order, the agency may refuse contact without having to seek the court's approval.

6.169 In addition, an adoption agency is permitted to refuse to allow contact that would otherwise be required by virtue of a section 26 order, without first obtaining a court order, if it is satisfied that it is necessary to do so in order to safeguard or promote the child's welfare and the refusal is decided upon as a matter of urgency and does not last for more than seven days.[187] The agency is under a duty to inform relevant individuals as soon as any decision to refuse contact is made.[188]

Application for s 26 contact order

6.170 An application for a section 26 contact order may be made by:[189]

- the child;
- the agency;
- any parent or guardian or relative;
- any person in whose favour there was a CA 1989 contact order (which ceased to have effect under s 26(1));
- the person with a residence order in force immediately before the adoption agency was authorised to place;

---

185 ACA 2002, s 27(1).
186 AAR 2005, reg 47(2).
187 ACA 2002, s 27(2).
188 AAR 2005, reg 47.
189 ACA 2002, s 26(3).

- the person who had care of the child by an order under the High Court's inherent jurisdiction before the agency was authorised to place;
- any person with the court's leave.

The procedure is governed by Family Procedure (Adoption) Rules 2005 (FP(A)R 2005),[190] Pt 5; r 23 lists the persons who will be respondents to the application.

6.171 It is worth noting that the pool of applicants and respondents to a section 26 contact application is potentially very wide. Any relative of the child – defined in ACA 2002 s 144 to include grandparents, siblings, uncles and aunts, including those of the half blood and relatives by marriage – is entitled to make a section 26 application and there is no leave requirement. Contrast this with the position under the CA 1989, where even grandparents and siblings need leave to make an application for contact under s 8 or s 34.

6.172 Similarly, the pool of respondents to a section 26 contact application includes those persons 'with whom the child lives or is to live'. It is not entirely clear whether it is envisaged that respondents to such applications will regularly include the child's foster parents and/or the prospective adopters.

6.173 The court may at any time direct that a child, who is not already a respondent to proceedings, be made a respondent where the child wishes to make an application or has evidence to give to the court, or a legal submission to make, which has not been given or made by any other party, or there are other special circumstances.[191] The court may at any time direct that a person or body be made a respondent or be removed as a respondent.[192]

Contact after an adoption order

6.174 The ACA 2002 contains surprisingly little explicit provision for contact after adoption. On making an adoption order the court must consider 'whether there should be arrangements for allowing any person contact with the child; and for that purpose the court must consider any existing or proposed arrangements and obtain any views of the parties to the proceedings'.[193] Otherwise there is no provision in the Act for post-adoption contact and so if the court is persuaded to make an order for ongoing contact it must use s 8 of the CA 1989.

---

190 SI 2005/2795.
191 FP(A)R 2005, r 23(2).
192 Ibid, r 23(3).
193 ACA 2002, s 46(6)

6.175 A parent seeking ongoing contact at a final adoption hearing will want to make use of the 'parent-friendly' ACA 2002 welfare checklist and open up for the court's consideration the child's welfare throughout his life, the impact on him of a loss of the birth family relationships, and the views of his relatives and friends. It would seem likely that this approach will be permitted, given that when deciding on contact as part of the adoption 'package' the court is 'coming to a decision relating to the adoption of a child' (see the definition of this phrase in s 1(7)(a)). However, it may be argued by a local authority opposing contact that as the application is made under s 8 of the CA 1989, only the less comprehensive CA 1989 welfare checklist should apply.

6.176 A parent who wishes to have the benefit of the wider ACA 2002 welfare checklist must make the application for contact in time to be heard together with the adoption application. After the adoption order has been made the courts follow a restrictive approach to contact applications in which priority is given to the need to maintain the stability of the adoptive placement.

ILLEGAL PLACEMENTS AND OTHER PROHIBITED STEPS

6.177 No person other than an adoption agency, or a person acting pursuant to an order of the High Court, may take any of the steps set out in ACA 2002, s 92(2) relating to the adoption of a child (unless, with respect to some of the steps, the proposed adopter is a relative of the child or a partner of a parent). The nine categories of step listed in s 92(2) cover in effect any step in the process of arranging for the adoption of a child and applies to arrangements made anywhere in the world. Anyone who breaches s 92(2) is liable to prosecution. To commit an offence, the step must be taken within the jurisdiction of England and Wales.

6.178 Where steps have been taken in breach of s 92(2), the situation thereby created may only continue if the High Court gives authorisation for it to do so.[194]

6.179 In addition to the steps in ACA 2002, s 92(2) no person other than one prescribed by the Restriction on the Preparation of Adoption Reports Regulations 2005[195] may prepare a report for any person about the suitability of a child for adoption, or of a person to adopt a child or

---

194 ACA 2002, s 92(1).
195 SI 2005/1711.

about the adoption or placement for adoption of a child.[196] The aim of this provision is to outlaw 'home study' reports prepared to support non-agency adoption applications (frequently inter-country adoptions) by any person other than an experienced adoption social worker employed by an adoption agency.

6.180 Finally, it is illegal to make any payment which is made for, or in consideration of, the adoption of a child (or any related activity) unless the payment is expressly permitted by the legislation.[197]

APPLYING FOR AN ADOPTION ORDER

6.181 An application for an adoption order may be made at any of the three levels of family court. The procedure is governed by the Family Procedure (Adoption) Rules 2005 and associated Practice Directions. In particular the main procedure is contained in Part 5 of the Rules.

6.182 The applicant will be the prospective adopter(s) and the respondents will be each parent or guardian with parental responsibility for the child (unless they have given notice stating that they do not wish to be informed of any adoption), any person who has a contact order in their favour, any local authority or adoption agency connected with the child's adoption and, in certain circumstances, the child. In addition the court may direct that any person may be added (or removed) as a respondent. Where the child is a party he will normally be represented by a children's guardian and a solicitor for the child must be appointed.

6.183 The court will hold a 'first directions hearing' at which a number of specific issues listed in r 26 must be considered with a view to ensuring that the case is properly prepared for a timely final hearing.

6.184 Where a request is being made to dispense with a parent's consent to adoption, a written notice to that effect must be filed and a 'statement of facts' reciting the relevant history must be prepared.

6.185 Where a parent has given advance consent to adoption under ACA 2002, s 20 or the child has been placed for adoption pursuant either to parental consent or under a placement order, the parent or guardian may oppose any adoption application only if the court gives him permission to do so. The court may only consider granting permission to such a parent to oppose the adoption if there has been 'a

196 ACA 2002, s 94(1).
197 Ibid, s 95.

change of circumstances' in the intervening period.[198] The result of this provision is that in many cases to which it applies, whilst the parent will be given notice of the adoption application, they will be unable to oppose the application.

6.186 A key statutory requirement is that the court must receive a substantial and comprehensive report upon the child, the natural parents and the adopters before the final hearing can proceed. The report must cover the topics listed in Practice Direction 5C annexed to the rules. As with any other material filed in the proceedings, these reports are confidential within the proceedings.

6.187 Where a parent opposes the making of the adoption order there will be a full final hearing at which the principal issue is likely to be whether or not the parent's consent to adoption should be dispensed with.[199] In other cases, provided that the application is not opposed by the local authority or adoption agency, and provided that the court is satisfied with the written information that has been provided, the adoption hearing is unlikely to be lengthy.

6.188 Where an adoption order is to be made, it is usual for the child and other family members to attend before the judge/magistrates for a formal occasion at which the order is made and, if the court agrees, photographs are taken.

CONSEQUENCES OF AN ADOPTION ORDER

6.189 An adoption order is an order giving parental responsibility for a child to the adopters. The order does not affect parental responsibility so far as it relates to any period prior to the making of the order. Further the making of an adoption order operates to extinguish:

- the parental responsibility which any person (other than the adopters) had prior to the adoption;
- any order under CA 1989 or in wardship proceedings;
- any duty to make payments for the child's maintenance or upbringing relating to the period after the adoption.[200]

6.190 An adopted child is treated in law as if he had been born as a child of the adopters, and he is treated as not being the child of any other person.[201] The only matters that are not affected by adoption are

198 ACA 2002, s 47.

199 See flowchart at **6.53**.

200 ACA 2002, s 46.

201 Ibid, s 67.

the table of kindred and affinity in the Marriage Act 1949 or the Sexual Offences Act 2003 (thus the natural relationships still apply for these purposes), and any provision of the British Nationality Act 1981 and the Immigration Act 1971.

6.191 When an adoption order is made in any court in the UK, the child will automatically become a British citizen if the adopter, or at least one of a couple, is a British citizen on the date of the order.[202] If the applicants wish the child's name to be changed, this can be achieved by stating the child's new name on the adoption application form.

6.192 If provision is to be made for any form of contact between the natural family and the child after an adoption order, this will usually be dealt with without a court order with the plan being spelled out in the local authority report to the court. Alternatively the proposed contact arrangements may be a preliminary recital to any court order. In an exceptional case there may be a need for a court order regulating contact; such an order may be made under CA 1989, s 8 and is a private law contact order. The courts are most unlikely to impose a regime of contact that is not acceptable to the adopters.

Contact after adoption

6.193 In virtually all adoption cases there will be an expectation for some limited indirect contact to continue between the birth family and the adoptive family. This can take the form, for example, of letters or short reports sent once or twice each year (possibly with photographs). Direct face-to-face meetings are not usually contemplated, but where the child is older, and particularly where there is benefit in siblings meeting, such contact may take place. The value of some contact post-adoption is that it permits the child to maintain some concept of the complexity of his identity as he moves through childhood and adolescence. Once a child is an adult, the provisions of the Adoption Contact Register may apply to facilitate reopening contact with the natural family.[203]

---

202 British Nationality Act 1981, s 1(5).

203 For Adoption Contact Register, see **6.117**.

ADOPTIONS WITH AN INTERNATIONAL ELEMENT

6.194 The law relating to international adoptions is complex. What follows is no more than a brief overview of the subject.[204]

6.195 An international element may arise in connection with adoption in the following circumstances:

- a foreign child has been 'adopted' abroad and brought into England and Wales by his adopters;
- a foreign child, who has not been already 'adopted', is brought into England and Wales in order to be adopted here;
- an English/Welsh child is to be sent abroad to be adopted in a foreign country.

Foreign child 'adopted' abroad

6.196 Some foreign adoptions are recognised under English law as being valid adoptions, with the result that the adoption will be seen as valid under English law and the adopters will not need to issue adoption proceedings here. One group of adoptions that are recognised as valid are 'overseas adoptions', being adoptions from one of the 66 states listed in the Adoption (Designation of Overseas Adoptions) Order 1973 (as amended from time to time).[205] Another group of adoptions that are recognised as valid are 'Convention adoptions' made under the 1993 Hague Convention.[206]

6.197 Where a foreign adoption is neither an 'overseas adoption' nor a Convention adoption, it will be necessary for the adopters to make a fresh application for an adoption order in England and Wales in order for their adoptive status to be recognised. The foreign process may be useful evidence in support of their application.

Foreign child brought into England and Wales for adoption

6.198 Stringent procedures and conditions apply to the process of bringing a child into the UK in order to be adopted here. It is a criminal offence, punishable with up to 12 months imprisonment, to bring a child into the UK for adoption unless the regulations have been complied

---

204 For a comprehensive description of Adoptions with an International Element, see Hershman and McFarlane, *Children Law and Practice* (Family Law) Division D, Section 6.

205 ACA 2002, s 66.

206 For 'Convention adoptions' see **6.199**.

with.[207] The key regulations are the Adoptions with a Foreign Element Regulations 2005.[208] In short, they require detailed assessments of the suitability of the adoptive home, and of the child's circumstances, before official approval will be given to any proposed arrangement.[209] Official approval is provided by a certificate issued by the Secretary of State at the Department for Education and Skills. Once the child has arrived in England and Wales, the adopters must notify their local authority of the fact (they will be regarded in the interim period as private foster parents) and must immediately indicate their intention to apply to adopt the child. The local authority is under a duty to monitor the child's welfare. If an adoption order is made, it will be an ordinary domestic adoption order; all of the conditions described earlier in this chapter will apply to the adoption proceedings just as they would if there were no foreign element.

Facilitating the adoption abroad of a child from UK

6.199 A child who is a Commonwealth citizen or who is habitually resident in the UK must not be removed from the UK for the purpose of adoption unless the prospective adopters have obtained an order under ACA 2002, s 84[210] giving them parental responsibility for the child in order to facilitate a foreign adoption. A breach of this restriction, or being involved in making arrangements to breach it, is a criminal offence and may incur up to 12 months imprisonment.[211] In order to obtain a s 84 order the applicant must have complied with the Adoptions with a Foreign Element Regulations 2005 and the child must have had his home with each applicant for the preceding ten weeks.

Convention adoptions

6.200 The 1993 Hague Convention on Protection of Children and Cooperation with respect to International Adoption has full effect in England and Wales. The Convention is essentially a framework setting out minimum standards for the control and regulation of the flow of children between states for adoption. It has been signed or ratified by a total of 62 states. It establishes a detailed system for cooperation between member states and seeks to ensure that adoptions in one member state are recognised as valid in every other Convention state. In the UK the Convention therefore operates to regulate the process in both states and will affect a child coming into the UK from a

207 ACA 2002, s 83.
208 SI 2005/392.
209 Detailed guidance on the process can be found at www.dfes.gov.uk/adoption.
210 Or similar provisions for Scotland or Northern Ireland.
211 ACA 2002, s 85.

Convention country, or vice versa. Depending on the process used, a child may be brought to the UK having already been adopted in another Convention country (in which case the adoption is automatically recognised here) or brought into the UK (without being adopted) for the purpose of achieving a UK adoption (in which case the preliminary vetting process will have been carried out in accordance with the Convention).

7

SECURE ACCOMMODATION

Chapter Summary

- Introduction
- What is secure accommodation?
- Criteria for a secure accommodation order
- Effect of the order
- Children who may (and may not) be kept in secure accommodation
- Procedure
- The local authority's obligations

INTRODUCTION

7.1 The restriction of liberty is a serious matter, whether the subject is an adult or a child. Children are necessarily more likely to have their liberty restricted, by parents, teachers and other adults, to varying degrees depending on their age. Provided that the child is not harmed or put at risk, any restrictions imposed by parents or those acting on their behalf are a matter of parental choice.

7.2 In rare circumstances the state may intervene to restrict a child's liberty by keeping her in 'secure' accommodation. This involves a significant interference with the child's and family's autonomy and engages rights under Articles 5 (liberty) and 8 (respect for one's private and family life) of the European Convention on Human Rights (ECHR). An application to restrict a child's liberty by placing or keeping him in secure accommodation should be made only as a last resort.

7.3 There are a number of contexts in which the state may restrict a child's liberty. Children who are serving prison sentences and children who have been sectioned under the Mental Health Act 1983 are subject to significant restrictions governed by distinct pieces of legislation and generally applicable, with some modifications, to adults as well as children. This chapter is concerned mainly with those children whose accommodation is the direct responsibility of a local authority's social services department, and whose behaviour is so out of control that the local authority seeks to place them in secure accommodation for their own safety or that of others. The statutory provision giving local authorities this power is s 25 of the CA 1989.

WHAT IS SECURE ACCOMMODATION?

Secure accommodation: key features

- Applies only to children already looked after by the local authority
- Criteria:
  - history of absconding *and* likelihood of significant harm if absconds, or
  - likely to injure self or others
- Permissive order: allows the local authority to keep child in secure accommodation; does not require it to do so
- Local authority may keep child in secure accommodation without an order for up to 72 hours in any 28-day period
- Maximum duration of order is 3 months on the first application and 6 months on subsequent applications

7.4 Secure accommodation is defined in CA 1989, s 25 as 'accommodation provided for the purposes of restricting liberty'. Wall J, fleshing out the statutory definition, described it as accommodation 'designed for, or having as its primary purpose', the restriction of a child's liberty.[1] In theory any foster placement involving a young child could be said to be 'secure', in that young children are inevitably subject to a high level of restriction. Foster carers, like parents, will ensure as part of their basic care of the child that his whereabouts are known and he is not permitted to leave the home unsupervised. The difference is that the primary purpose of an ordinary foster placement is not to restrict the child's liberty, even though it may be the carers' responsibility to impose appropriate restrictions as part of their overall care of the child. Accommodation formally designated as 'secure' is

---

1 *Re C (Detention: Medical Treatment)* [1997] 2 FLR 180.

likely only to be appropriate for older children and teenagers whose behaviour is so extreme that the structure and rules of an ordinary foster or children's home are insufficient. In any event a child under the age of 13 may not be placed in secure accommodation in a children's home without the prior approval of the Secretary of State.[2]

7.5 Typically a child subject to a secure accommodation order will be kept in a secure residential unit specifically designed for the purpose and staffed by trained carers. A children's home designated as secure accommodation is subject to regulation and the Secretary of State must approve its use for that purpose.[3]

7.6 However, accommodation not specifically designated as such may also fall within the statutory definition if the effect of keeping a child there is to restrict her liberty. It is a question of fact. The guidance points out that any measure that 'prevents a child from leaving a room or building of his own free will may be deemed by the court to constitute [a] 'restriction of liberty'.[4] A hospital ward secured by a pass key has been held to be secure accommodation,[5] even though it is doubtful whether the restriction of liberty could be said to be such a place's primary purpose.

7.7 It is important to recognise that the phrasing of s 25 *prevents* a local authority from keeping a child in accommodation that restricts her liberty except in the circumstances set out in the statute. It is a prohibitive and not a permissive section and if the criteria cease to apply the local authority must release the child immediately whether or not the order is still in force.

7.8 The section does not entitle the local authority to put a lock on any door and deem it secure accommodation. The types of accommodation that may be used for a planned secure placement are carefully controlled by regulations. Although the definition of secure accommodation is a broad one, the purpose of this is to ensure that every restriction of liberty is subject to the fulfilment of the s 25 criteria.

EXAMPLE

A 16-year-old boy in care is placed in a foster home after his previous placement broke down following a serious assault on his carer. He has a severe alcohol problem and his carers have been warned that when drunk he becomes physically aggressive and violent. Although they take steps

---

2 Children (Secure Accommodation) Regulations 1991 (SI 1991/1505) (C(SA)R 1991), reg 4.

3 C(SA) R 1991, reg 3.

4 Children Act 1989 Guidance and Regulations Volume 4 (HMSO 1991) para 8.10.

5 *A Metropolitan Borough Council v DB* [1997] 1 FLR 767.

to prevent him accessing alcohol, three days into the placement the female carer returns home to find the boy very drunk. His behaviour becomes increasingly erratic and abusive. The carers telephone the police and are told that as no offence has been committed the matter is not a priority and officers will call round in the morning. When the boy goes to his bedroom, muttering threats and swinging his arms around in the air, the male foster carer finds the key and locks his door. The carers then telephone social services.

Provided its criteria are met, section 25 authorises the local authority via its foster carers to restrict the boy's liberty by keeping him in his room. Were it not for this section (subject to any provisions of the criminal law), locking the boy in the room for even a short period would be unlawful. However, the local authority must take immediate steps to find a placement for the boy in approved, secure residential accommodation.

CRITERIA FOR KEEPING A CHILD IN SECURE ACCOMMODATION

7.9 Section 25 applies only to children who are already being looked after by the local authority: that is, children who are in care or being accommodated by the local authority exercising its social services functions.

7.10 There are two alternative grounds for keeping or placing such a child in secure accommodation:

- the child has a history of absconding and is likely to abscond from any other description of accommodation and, if he absconds, is likely to suffer significant harm; or
- if he is kept in any other description of accommodation he is likely to injure himself or other persons.

7.11 'Likely' in this section means the same as it does in section 31 (see Chapter 5). It means that there is a real possibility that cannot sensibly be ignored.

7.12 The welfare of the child is one of the matters the court must take into account. It is not, however, paramount and the welfare checklist does not apply.[6] The effect of this is that the court's role in granting or refusing a secure accommodation order is to exercise a supervisory jurisdiction: that is, to satisfy itself that the local authority is acting appropriately and not to consider every aspect of the child's welfare and

6 *Re M* [1995] 1 FLR 418.

needs afresh. It is worth remembering that s 25 of the CA 1989 falls within Part III of the Act – 'Local Authority Support for Children and Families' – and a decision by a local authority to place a child in secure accommodation can be seen as forming part of its overall duty to promote and safeguard the child's welfare.

7.13 If the statutory criteria are satisfied, the court must make the order: s 25(4). It is not clear how this subsection can be reconciled with the 'no order' principle. Once the order is made the responsibility for ensuring that the power granted by the order is used sparingly, and that the child is only kept in secure accommodation for the minimum period necessary, is that of the local authority.

EFFECT OF A SECURE ACCOMMODATION ORDER

Secure accommodation without an order

7.14 A local authority (or other authority) may keep a child in secure accommodation for a total period of 72 hours, whether or not consecutive, in any 28-day period.

7.15 Special rules apply for calculating and potentially extending the maximum period if it is due to expire between 12 noon the day before a Sunday or bank holiday and 12 noon the day after.[7]

Secure accommodation with an order

7.16 When the child has been remanded to local authority accommodation by a criminal court any secure accommodation order must not extend beyond the period of the remand, and in any event can last for a maximum of 28 days. If the remand period is longer than 28 days a further order of the court must be sought.

7.17 In all other cases the maximum period of a secure accommodation order is 3 months on the first application, and 6 months on any subsequent application. There is no limit to the number of orders that may be made. However in 2003 there were no children in secure units who had been there for longer than 12 months.[8] The court should make the order only for the minimum period necessary.[9] Interim orders may be made, for no longer than the maximum period for a full order.

---

7 See C(SA)R 1991, reg 10(3).

8 www.dfes.gov.uk

9 *Re W* [1993] 1 FLR 692.

CHILDREN WHO MAY (AND MAY NOT) BE KEPT IN SECURE ACCOMMODATION

Age and other restrictions

7.18 The following children may *not* be kept in secure accommodation:

- a child under the age of 13 may not be kept in secure accommodation in a children's home, unless the Secretary of State has given prior approval;[10]
- a child aged 16 and over who is being accommodated by the local authority under s 20;[11]
- a child subject to a child assessment order under s 43 who is being kept away from home pursuant to that order.[12]

The majority of children kept in secure units by a local authority are aged 14 and 15, although the number of 12- and 13-year-olds in secure accommodation is increasing.[13]

Children looked after by the local authority

7.19 Section 25 applies primarily to children who are being looked after by the local authority. This includes children who are subject to care orders, and children who are accommodated by the local authority in its capacity as a provider of social services.[14] Being 'accommodated' means being provided with accommodation for a period in excess of 24 hours. Children who have been remanded by a criminal court to local authority accommodation become 'looked after' children and therefore fall within the scope of s 25, modified as discussed below.

7.20 The fact that a child who is not in care but is being accommodated has been placed in secure accommodation does not affect the right of any person with parental responsibility to remove her from local authority accommodation, secure or otherwise, at any time.[15]

---

10 C(SA)R 1991, reg 4. There appears to be no prohibition on keeping children of this age in secure accommodation elsewhere: for instance in a hospital.

11 Ibid, reg 5(2)(a).

12 Ibid, reg 5(2)(b).

13 www.dfes.gov.uk

14 CA 1989, s 22(1). The latter category includes children who are lost or abandoned or have no person with parental responsibility for them (s 20(1)); who are accommodated with their parents' consent (s 20(7)); and who are subject to emergency protection orders (s 44).

15 Subject to the provisions of s 20(9).

7.21 The local authority has no power to place a child it is *not* looking after in secure accommodation. Faced with a child who meets the criteria for secure accommodation but whose parents do not agree to accommodation under s 20, the local authority's only option is to apply for a care order or an emergency protection order.

EXAMPLE

A local authority has been involved for a number of years with a mother and her daughter, now aged 12. The mother has learning difficulties and the child has previously been on the Child Protection Register under the category of neglect. The local authority has provided a high level of support to the family and until recently took the view that with this help the mother's parenting was 'good enough' and there was no need to issue proceedings for a care or supervision order. In the last month the child's behaviour has escalated and she is not attending school, regularly stays out all night and appears to have become involved with drugs and possibly prostitution. She has told her social worker that if she is put in foster carer she will run away.

Although the child meets at least the second limb of the s 25 criteria (likely to injure herself or others), the child is not being 'looked after' by the local authority. If the mother objects to the child being accommodated, the local authority must apply for a care order. At the same time it may apply for a secure accommodation order. Alternatively, if there is a prospect that a foster placement may succeed, the local authority apply simply for a care order knowing that if it becomes necessary on an emergency basis to place the child in secure accommodation it may do so for a period of up to 72 hours before it becomes necessary for a court to sanction the placement.

Children accommodated by the health or education authorities

7.22 Section 25 also applies, with modifications, to children who are accommodated by health authorities, Primary Care Trusts, NHS trusts or local education authorities; and to children who are being accommodated in care homes or independent hospitals.

7.23 Regulation 7 of the C(SA)R 1991 applies s 25 to these children, modifying the section so that instead of referring to children 'looked after by a local authority' it refers to children accommodated by the relevant health or education authority. The provisions are otherwise the same.

EXAMPLE

A 13-year-old girl is hospitalised suffering from severe anorexia. She has run away from hospital and home on a number of occasions. She agrees to a treatment programme, but on her first night in hospital disappears and is found, disorientated and wearing only pyjamas, at a nearby bus stop the following morning.

The hospital may place the girl on its secure paediatric ward (secured by an electronic pass) for up to 72 hours. If during that time it appears that the criteria for secure accommodation will continue to be met and there is a need to keep the child on the secure ward in the longer-term, the hospital must make an application for a secure accommodation order.

Children who are charged or convicted of a criminal offence

7.24 A distinction must be drawn between children who are defendants in pending proceedings, and children who have been convicted and sentenced. Section 25 applies, with modifications, to the former category as these children remain the responsibility of the local authority. It does not apply to the latter category as responsibility for these children passes to the Youth Justice Board.

Children who have been convicted

7.25 Section 25 does *not* apply to children who have been convicted and given a custodial sentence. These children will fall into one of the following categories:

- children who, following conviction for one of a limited number of very serious offences, are serving long sentences or, following a murder conviction, are detained at Her Majesty's Pleasure;[16]
- children subject to a Detention and Training Order imposed by a criminal court.

The detention of these children is governed by the relevant criminal statute. As some local authorities contract out places in their secure units to the Youth Justice Board, these children may in fact be accommodated together with children who have been accommodated under s 25.

Children who have been charged and/or are on remand

7.26 Section 25 *does* apply, with modifications, to children who are looked after by the local authority following:

- arrest and detention by the police prior to a court appearance; or

16 C(SA)R 1991, reg 5(1).

- remand by a criminal court to local authority accommodation during the course of criminal proceedings.[17]

7.27 The first modification is that in such cases it is not necessary that there should be a history of absconding, or a likelihood of significant harm if the child absconds. It is enough simply to show that the child is 'likely to abscond' or is likely to injure himself or other people if kept in non-secure accommodation.[18]

7.28 The second modification applies only to the second class of children, children who have appeared before a court and are on remand. In these cases secure accommodation is only permissible when:

- the child has been charged with or convicted of a violent or sexual offence, or an offence which in the case of an adult carries a term of 14 years' imprisonment or more; or
- the child has a recent history of absconding while on remand in local authority accommodation, and is charged with or convicted of an imprisonable offence committed on remand.[19]

EXAMPLE

A 14-year-old girl is arrested by the police and charged with a knifepoint robbery. She refuses to give her name or address and the police are of the view that if released she will not answer bail.

The likelihood that the girl will abscond is enough to justify her secure accommodation prior to the court appearance. It is not necessary to show a history of absconding. The girl is placed in a local authority secure unit. Note that s 25 has come into operation and although it is highly unlikely that the period of detention prior to the court appearance would be in excess of 72 hours, if it is, an application to the court will be necessary.

At the first court hearing the youth court remands the girl into local authority accommodation. She is now represented by a solicitor and has given her name and address and the court does not impose a security requirement.[20] *Initially the girl is placed in foster care. She does not settle and after a few days she threatens to leave and stay with friends. She has not previously absconded from any accommodation.*

The local authority may place the girl in secure accommodation. Robbery is both violent and punishable (in the case of an adult) with

---

17 C(SA)R 1991, reg 6(1).

18 Ibid, reg 6(2).

19 Ibid, reg 6(1).

20 Under the CYPA 1969, s 23 the criminal court may itself impose a security requirement. The criteria are different from the s 25 criteria.

a maximum sentence of life imprisonment. The test for secure accommodation in the case of a child on remand is that she is likely to abscond, not that she has a history of doing so. Section 25 is once again in operation and the restrictions on the duration of the placement apply.

The local authority obtains an order enabling it to keep the girl in secure accommodation for 28 days and at the expiry of the 28-day period applies for a further order to cover the further 3 weeks until the trial. At the trial the girl is convicted of the robbery and sentenced to a 12-month Detention and Training order.

Following conviction and sentence s 25 ceases to apply. The girl's continued detention is the responsibility of the Youth Justice Board, albeit that she may well remain in a local authority-run secure unit.

7.29 Of the 420 children in local authority secure units on 31 March 2003, 55 (14%) were remanded to local authority accommodation by a criminal court and 110 (25%) were children in local authority care or accommodated with their parents' consent.[21] The rest were children convicted of offences who were subject to Detention and Training orders or detained for grave crimes, to whom section 25 does not apply.

The appropriate court

7.30 If the child has been remanded to local authority accommodation by a youth court or magistrates' court, the application to place that child in secure accommodation should be made to the youth court that remanded him, or if he was remanded by a magistrates court, to any magistrates court. The rules setting out the procedure in these cases are those that apply to the criminal courts.[22]

7.31 If the Crown Court remanded the child, the application to keep him in secure accommodation should be made not to the Crown Court but to the family proceedings court and the procedure to be followed is the same as that followed in the case of any other looked after child.

Children detained under the Mental Health Act 1983

7.32 A child who has been detained in hospital for assessment or treatment under s 2 or 3 of the Mental Health Act 1983 is not subject to the provisions of s 25. His detention is authorised under the mental health legislation and the provisions of s 25 of the CA 1989 do not apply.

---

21 Dept for Education and Skills, 28 August 2003: www.dfes.gov.uk/rsgateway

22 Magistrates Court (Children and Young Persons) Rules 1992 (SI 1992/2071).

Wards of court

7.33 A child who is a ward of court may not be placed in secure accommodation without the permission of a High Court judge. The criteria for a secure accommodation order and the provisions of s 25 apply to wards in the same way as they do to all other children.

PROCEDURE

7.34 The applicant for a secure accommodation order is the local authority which looks after the child, or the authority or body which is accommodating her. A child accommodated by a health or education authority or in an independent care home may also happen to be looked after by the local authority; if this is the case, only the local authority may apply for a secure accommodation order.[23] The application is made on Form C1 with Supplement C20.

7.35 The application is made in the family proceedings court unless it is made within pending proceedings or as a result of a court-directed investigation, in which case it is made to the court where those proceedings are ongoing.

7.36 The respondents are:

- the child;
- every person believed to have parental responsibility for the child;
- every person believed to have had parental responsibility before the child was placed in care.[24]

Any person may be removed or joined as a respondent.

7.37 Notice of the date, time and place of the hearing must also be given to:

- any local authority providing accommodation for the child;
- any person with whom the child is living; and
- any person providing an authorised refuge where the child is staying.

7.38 The application must be served and the appropriate notice given at least one day before the hearing date. There is no provision for making applications without notice.

---

23 C(SA)(No 2)R 1991 (SI 1991/2034), reg 2.
24 FPR 1991, r 4.7(1).

Representation of the child

7.39 Although applications under s 25 are not 'specified proceedings' for the purposes of s 41 of the CA 1989, there is authority to the effect that in all but the most exceptional cases a children's guardian should be appointed. Where the child is competent to instruct a solicitor and his instructions are at variance with the guardian's views the solicitor must take instructions directly from the child. See Chapter 5 for a full discussion of the roles of the children's guardian and solicitor for the child.

7.40 Because the child's liberty is at stake his rights under Art 5 of the ECHR are engaged (see below) and his right to a fair trial under Art 6 assumes particular significance. He must be informed promptly of the evidence against him and given the opportunity to answer any allegations made.[25] This may mean that the pre-Human Rights Act authorities which discourage the child's attendance at court should be treated with caution.

Challenging the order

7.41 Any party may appeal a secure accommodation order. See Chapter 9 for the appropriate route of appeal.

7.42 Where the criteria for a secure accommodation order cease to apply, but the local authority does not release the child, the appropriate remedy is an action for habeas corpus[26] as the family court has completed its function. If it is alleged that the local authority has failed properly to carry out its duties to review the placement, or has come to an unreasonable decision regarding the continuation of the placement, this action may be coupled with an application for judicial review.

7.43 A challenge to any other aspect of the local authority's exercise of its power under a secure accommodation order should be by judicial review.

THE LOCAL AUTHORITY'S OBLIGATIONS

Educational provision

7.44 The local authority has an obligation to make educational provision for all children it is keeping in secure accommodation. While

---

25 *Re C* [2001] 2 FLR 169.

26 Ie a writ challenging the lawfulness of the continued detention. See Glossary.

this has always been required as a matter of common sense, it now carries additional weight due to the need for secure accommodation orders to be compliant with the Human Rights Act. The interference with the child's right to 'liberty and security of person' under Art 5 of the ECHR can only be justified (other than where the child has been detained by a criminal court) if it is necessary 'for the purpose of educational supervision'.[27] When a court makes a secure accommodation order under s 25 in respect of a child who is not the subject of a criminal charge, it must have the provisions of Art 5 in mind, for it is only the justification of the provision of educational supervision that ensures that s 25 is compatible with the Human Rights Act.

Review

7.45 The local authority must keep the secure placement under review. It must appoint at least three persons, including one who is independent of the local authority, to review the placement within one month of it commencing, and at least every three months thereafter.[28] The local authority must be satisfied throughout the duration of the placement that the criteria for keeping the child in secure accommodation continue to apply and that no other accommodation is appropriate.

Release

7.46 A secure accommodation order permits the local authority to keep the child in secure accommodation; it does not oblige it to do so. If the criteria cease to apply the child must be released, regardless of whether or not the order has expired.

---

27 Article 5(1)(d).
28 C(SA)R 1991 reg 15.

8

WARDSHIP AND THE INHERENT JURISDICTION

Chapter summary

- The High Court's inherent jurisdiction – introduction
- Wardship
  - effects
  - uses of the wardship jurisdiction
- The inherent jurisdiction
  - medical treatment
  - incapacitated adults
  - limitations
- Procedure

THE HIGH COURT'S INHERENT JURISDICTION

8.1 As a superior court of record, the High Court has an inherent jurisdiction to hear all matters of criminal and civil law unless that jurisdiction has been limited by statute or case law. It is a 'catch-all' jurisdiction, used particularly to determine issues that arise in difficult or novel situations where statute and case law do not provide an answer. The High Court's inherent jurisdiction to intervene in questions relating to the welfare and upbringing of children has been said to derive from the Crown's 'right and duty … as parens patriae to take care of those who are not able to take care of themselves'.[1]

8.2 Historically the way in which the High Court exercised its inherent jurisdiction in relation to children was by making the child a ward of court. The primary effect of wardship is that no important decision in the child's life may be taken without reference to the court. Prior to the implementation of the CA 1989 wardship became the standard way of

1 *Re L (an infant)* [1968] 1 All ER 20.

invoking the High Court's inherent jurisdiction in relation to a child, and in children proceedings the two concepts of wardship and inherent jurisdiction became more or less interchangeable.

8.3 As successive governments have legislated and case law has developed, the High Court's inherent jurisdiction has gradually been eroded. In the field of children's law the CA 1989 significantly restricted the court's inherent jurisdiction by codifying the law relating to children and providing a statutory scheme to cover most issues arising in public or private law. Section 100 of the CA 1989 expressly restricts the court's inherent jurisdiction in public law proceedings and prevents local authorities from making any application under the court's inherent jurisdiction unless there is no other way in which the desired result could be achieved.

8.4 The High Court retains a residual jurisdiction, now used most often to resolve such complex and sensitive issues as publicity or medical treatment. This jurisdiction may be exercised within or independently of the wardship jurisdiction.

WARDSHIP

8.5 Since the implementation of the CA 1989, the courts have restricted the use of the wardship jurisdiction to permit it only when no order is available under the Act that will meet the requirements of the case. It has been said that wardship is now an 'exceptional status'[2] requiring exceptional circumstances. Nevertheless, a gap appears to have opened up between public and private law proceedings, where the threshold criteria for local authority intervention has not been met or local authority intervention is otherwise inappropriate, but there is nevertheless a need for judicial supervision in order to protect the child.

Effects of wardship

8.6 A child becomes a ward of court immediately upon issue of an originating summons in wardship. At the first hearing the wardship must be confirmed by court order or it will lapse. The child remains a ward of court until he is 18, unless the wardship is revoked.

8.7 Once a child is a ward, no major step may be taken in her life without the court's consent. 'Major steps' include the following:

- psychiatric or psychological examination or treatment;

---

2 *Re CT* [1993] 2 FLR 278.

- serious medical treatment;
- marriage;
- interview by the police;
- a change of residence;
- a change of school;
- a change of name;
- placement in secure accommodation;
- commencement of adoption proceedings;
- publicity relating to the ward.

8.8 From the moment when the child becomes a ward of court she must not leave or be removed from England and Wales without the court's consent (which may be given generally, on conditions, or for specific purposes). There are some exceptions to this rule. When the ward is habitually resident in another part of the UK, or her parents are involved in matrimonial proceedings in a court in another part of the UK, she may move to that part of the UK without the permission of the court.[3] By s 13 of the CA 1989, where a residence order is in force the holder of the residence order may remove a child from the UK for up to a month, or any person may remove the child for any period with the written consent of all those with parental responsibility. It is not clear in the latter case whether the permission of the court would also be required. Although the wardship court does not have parental responsibility for the child, it is likely that a permanent or long-term removal from the UK would be considered a significant step in the ward's life and, notwithstanding the apparent statutory sanction in s 13, an application to the court would be necessary.

Common uses of the wardship jurisdiction

Medical treatment

8.9 The court's leave is not required for routine medical examinations and treatment; the consent of a person with parental responsibility will be sufficient. However, where 'serious invasive treatment'[4] or other significant intervention is proposed for a ward, an application must be made to the court.

8.10 Where proceedings are underway in respect of the child the court's leave must be obtained before the child is examined by a psychiatrist or psychologist. A ward may not be admitted to hospital

3 Family Law Act 1986, s 38.
4 *Re J* [1990] 3 All ER 930.

under the Mental Health Act 1983 without the authorisation of the court, and the court's leave is required to make the application.[5]

8.11 Where the ward's life or health is seriously at risk the courts have been prepared to override major decisions made even by older, *Gillick*-competent wards. The wardship jurisdiction has been used to sanction in-patient treatment for anorexia nervosa in the case of a 16-year-old girl, and to authorise the use of reasonable force if necessary to detain her for the purposes of such treatment.[6] It has also been used to authorise a heart transplant for a 15-year-old who was refusing to consent to the procedure.[7]

Publicity

8.12 Children who are already involved in proceedings have some statutory protection from publicity. The major statutory restriction is s 97(2) of the CA 1989, which prevents publication of any material that is intended or likely to identify any child involved in CA 1989 proceedings or any address or school of the child. The other sources of statutory protection are set out below.

Protection from publicity: statute

- Children Act 1989, s 97(2): no publication of material intended or likely to identify any child involved in Children Act proceedings
- Family Proceedings Rules, r 4.23: no document in Children Act proceedings may be disclosed to any non-party without leave of the court
- Administration of Justice Act 1960, s 11: general provision permitting the court to direct confidentiality of any name or other matter relating to court proceedings
- Administration of Justice Act 1960, s 12: contempt of court to publish information relating to proceedings before any court sitting in private where the proceedings concern the exercise of the inherent jurisdiction re minors; are brought under the Children Act 1989; or otherwise relate wholly or mainly to the maintenance or upbringing of a minor
- Children and Young Persons Act 1933, s 39: power to direct

5 Mental Health Act 1983, s 33.
6 *Re C (Detention: Medical Treatment)* [1997] 2 FLR 180.
7 *Re M* [1999] 2 FCR 577.

> in any proceedings in any court that no newspaper shall publish the name, address, school or other material calculated to lead to the identification of any child involved in the proceedings; or any picture of the child

8.13 It has been said that wardship can be used in support of the existing statutory protection where 'conferring on the child the status of ward of court will prove a more effective deterrent than the ordinary sanctions of contempt of court which already protect all family proceedings'.[8] Following the implementation of the Human Rights Act 1998, it seems that the court must only exercise its powers under the inherent jurisdiction when the existing safeguards would be inadequate to protect the child from harm.

8.14 The Human Rights Act 1998 requires courts to balance the child's rights under Art 8 of the European Convention on Human Rights (to a private and family life) with the public interest in freedom of speech and specifically rights deriving from Art 10 (freedom of expression). Each right is liable to be qualified and subject to a test of proportionality, and neither has precedence over the other.

8.15 A distinction has been drawn between cases where the anticipated publicity relates directly to the child's upbringing or to issues involving parental responsibility, and where it does not. The court is more likely to exercise its inherent jurisdiction to restrain publicity in the former category of case.[9] Indeed, the Court of Appeal has said that the court 'should not even consider exercising [its inherent] jurisdiction in cases where the publicity is not directed at the child or the child's carers unless it could have an adverse effect on the court's ability to deal properly with the … proceedings in question …'. The exercise of the jurisdiction now requires the court first to decide whether the child's rights under Art 8 are engaged and, if so, then to conduct the necessary balancing exercise between the competing rights under Arts 8 and 10, considering the proportionality of the potential interference with each right considered independently.[10]

Criminal proceedings: Limitation of High Court's jurisdiction

8.16 Where a ward is involved in criminal proceedings, either as a defendant or as a witness, the High Court's power to intervene under the wardship jurisdiction is limited. Unless the ward is 17 or over the court's permission must be obtained to interview or caution him.

---

8 *Re CT* [1993] 2 FLR 278.

9 *Kelly v BBC* [2001] 1 FLR 197.

10 *Re S* [2004] 2 FLR 949.

However, the decision whether or not to charge the ward is a matter for the police alone and decisions relating to bail are a matter for the criminal court. The wardship court cannot intervene in a prosecution decision to call a ward as a witness.[11]

8.17 Publicity issues surrounding a ward who is involved as a victim in criminal proceedings are a matter for the judge in the criminal proceedings to decide, and not the wardship judge.[12]

Child abduction and forced marriage

8.18 Wardship continues to be an effective process for achieving the location and, if necessary, repatriation of children who have been abducted. The use of the inherent jurisdiction opens up the possibility of using the High Court's extensive powers to locate and/or collect a child. In recent times the wardship jurisdiction has been used to protect teenage girls who are at risk of being forced into a marriage by their families.[13]

THE INHERENT JURISDICTION OUTSIDE WARDSHIP

8.19 It is not necessary to make a child a ward of court in order to invoke the High Court's inherent jurisdiction. There may be good reasons not to do so. A child who is in the care of the local authority cannot be made a ward of court,[14] and the court may not use the wardship jurisdiction to place a child in the local authority's care. However, the local authority is permitted to seek the court's guidance regarding a particular issue relating to a child, and the High Court has the power to make injunctions in support of a care order in relation to specific issues, for example concerning any restriction of the parents' ability to exercise parental responsibility.[15] See **8.31** for the High Court's powers with respect to children in care.

8.20 Where the court's guidance or ruling is sought on a discrete issue and there is no likelihood of the court's involvement lasting beyond the resolution of that issue, it may be appropriate to invoke the inherent jurisdiction rather than to make the child a ward of court. Wardship should not be continued beyond the point where it has ceased serving any useful purpose.

---

11 *Re K* [1988] 1 FLR 435.
12 *Re R* [1994] 2 FLR 637.
13 *Re SK* [2005] 2 FLR 230.
14 CA 1989, s 101(2)(c).
15 Supreme Court Act 1981, s 7.

Medical treatment outside wardship

8.21 Other than in an emergency situation, a medical practitioner may not impose treatment on a child without the consent of the parent(s). Without parental consent the medical authorities must apply to the High Court to exercise its inherent jurisdiction to declare the treatment lawful.[16] The position relating to children here differs from that relating to adults, in that while the High Court can in effect 'substitute' its own consent for that of a parent, it cannot do the same in the case of a competent adult.

8.22 In some circumstances it may be necessary to make an application to the court in relation to proposed medical treatment for a child, even though the child is not a ward of court, medical opinion backs the treatment and the parents consent to it. An example is the sterilisation of a child. This may be carried out without court approval if two medical practitioners are satisfied that it is necessary and in the patient's best interests; but if there is any doubt about the lawfulness of the procedure a declaration from the court should be sought.[17] This is the case even if all parties are in agreement. Similarly, it has been held that an application should be made to the court where it was proposed to carry out a termination of pregnancy for a mentally incompetent adult woman, although this was a matter of good practice and not a legal requirement.[18]

Incapacitated adults

8.23 The High Court may exercise its inherent jurisdiction with respect to adults who lack the mental capacity to make certain decisions for themselves. This jurisdiction is equivalent to the jurisdiction with respect to children, in that it also derives from the High Court's power to protect those who cannot protect themselves.

8.24 In the case of an adult it is extremely important to establish whether or not the patient is competent to make decisions for himself. Although the court can override the wishes of even a *Gillick*-competent child, it has no jurisdiction to override a decision taken by a mentally competent adult. Medical practitioners should be careful not to confuse the issue of capacity with the reasonableness or otherwise of the decision taken. In some cases, however, it is not clear where the line should be drawn: the court has been prepared to authorise an adult woman to be anaesthetised for an emergency operation, despite her extreme fear of needles, on the ground that her phobia amounted to a

16 *Glass v UK* [2004] 1 FLR 1019.

17 *Re S* [2000] 2 FLR 389.

18 *D v NHS Trust* [2004] 1 FLR 1110; *R v GMC (ex parte Burke)* EWCA Civ 1003.

psychological condition that affected her capacity to make the decision herself.[19] Similarly, the court has authorised a blood transfusion for a Jehovah's Witness who had signed in advance a directive refusing it.[20]

8.25 The court's inherent jurisdiction with respect to mentally incapacitated adults is limited most significantly by the mental health legislation. The Mental Health Act 1983 provides, for example, for the administration of medical treatment in certain cases without the patient's consent; for the removal of a patient to a place of safety; and for the appointment of a Guardian for the patient.[21] In *Cambridgeshire County Council v R*[22] the High Court refused to exercise its inherent jurisdiction to prevent contact between an adult with learning disabilities with her family, on the grounds that it would be possible to achieve the desired result via a guardianship order under the 1983 Act.

Terminal illness

8.26 The position with respect to a terminally ill child is the same as that in the case of a terminally ill adult, save that an adult who retains full mental capacity may decide for herself whether to accept or refuse treatment, whereas a child is dependent on the consent of his parents or a declaration of the court. The following key principles can be distilled from the authorities:

- The decision of a competent adult to accept or refuse offered treatment is determinative.
- However, medical practitioners are not obliged to administer a specific treatment [other than life-prolonging treatment such as artificial nutrition and hydration] at a patient's (or parent's) request if they feel that such treatment is not in the patient's best interests.[23]
- There is no medical guidance that would require a doctor to withhold life-prolonging treatment from a competent patient who requested it. If there were such guidance it would be unlawful and a doctor who acted in such a way would have no defence to a charge of murder.[24]
- Once an adult is no longer competent to make his own decisions, or in the case of a child, doctors must act in the patient's best

---

19 *Re L* [1997] 2 FLR 837.
20 *HE v A Hospital NHS Trust* [2003] 2 FLR 408.
21 Sections 57–58, 135, and 7 respectively.
22 [1995] 1 FLR 50.
23 *Re J* [1992] 2 FLR 165 (child); *R v GMC (ex parte Burke)* [2005] EWCA Civ 1003 (adult).
24 *R v GMC (ex parte Burke)* [2005] EWCA Civ 1003.

interests. This may include alleviating suffering at expense of prolonging life.[25] Any dispute should be referred to the court.

- The withdrawal of life-prolonging treatment from a patient in a PVS (persistent vegetative state) is lawful where it would be:
  - in accordance with good medical practice;
  - appropriate in the clinical judgment of the treating doctors; and
  - in the patient's best interests.[26]

8.27 In many cases, where there is no disagreement about the appropriate treatment (or withdrawal of treatment), an application to the court for a declaration that the proposed course is lawful is unnecessary. The point was made to the Court of Appeal in *R v GMC (ex parte Burke)*[27] that if such a declaration were necessary in each case where the withdrawal of life-prolonging treatment were proposed, there would be approximately ten applications to the High Court each day. There is still a need to apply to the court in PVS cases for a declaration (a) that the patient is in fact in a persistent vegetative state from which there is no hope of recovery, and (b) that the withdrawal of treatment would be lawful.

8.28 For guidelines and details of the procedure to be followed when seeking a declaration in cases, including PVS and sterilisation cases, where the patient does not have capacity to consent, see Practice Note (Official Solicitor: Declaratory Proceedings: Medical and Welfare Decisions for Adults who Lack Capacity), 1 May 2001.[28]

Limitations on the use of the inherent jurisdiction with respect to children

8.29 The High Court may only exercise its inherent jurisdiction (whether or not in wardship) with respect to a child who is:

- under 18; and
- a British subject; or
- physically present in England and Wales; or
- ordinarily resident in England and Wales.

Even if these conditions are met, where the appropriate forum for decision-making regarding the child is another jurisdiction, the High Court will not be able to exercise jurisdiction over the child.

---

25 For example, *Re C* [1990] 1 FLR 252; *Portsmouth NHS Trust v Wyatt* [2005] 1 FLR 21.

26 *Airedale NHS Trust v Bland* [1993] 1 FLR 1026.

27 [2005] EWCA Civ 1003.

28 Available from the Official Solicitor's website, www.offsol.demon.co.uk

8.30 Examples where the High Court has refused to exercise its inherent jurisdiction, notwithstanding that the jurisdiction exists, include cases where the applicant was attempting to circumvent immigration legislation; where the sole purpose of the proceedings was to generate publicity; and where the proceedings had been issued in an attempt to prevent the arrest of a teenage soldier subject to military law.

Children in care

8.31 The most significant limitation on the High Court's powers under its inherent jurisdiction relates to children who are in the care of a local authority. The courts have always discouraged too much judicial supervision of local authority decision-making with respect to children in their care, although historically it was possible for wardship and a care order to co-exist. A major innovation of the CA 1989 was to transfer responsibility for children in care from the court to the local authority, and to restrict court interference with the local authority's discharge of its duties under a care order.

8.32 Under s 100 of the CA 1989 the court must not exercise its inherent jurisdiction to:

- place a child in the care or under the supervision of a local authority (s 100(2)(a));
- require a child to be accommodated by or on behalf of a local authority (s 100(2)(b));
- make a child who is the subject of a care order a ward of court (s 100(2)(c));
- confer on any local authority power to determine any question in connection with any aspect of parental responsibility for a child (s 100(2)(d)).

8.33 A local authority may only apply for any exercise of the High Court's inherent jurisdiction with the leave of the court, and the court may only grant leave if it is satisfied that:

- the result which the authority wishes to achieve cannot be achieved through the making of any order which the local authority is entitled to apply for (s 100(4)(a)); and
- there is reasonable cause to believe that if the court's inherent jurisdiction is not exercised with respect to the child he is likely to suffer significant harm (s 100(4)(b)).

EXAMPLE

At the conclusion of care proceedings the High Court is proposing to make a final care order in respect of a 9-year-old boy who is living in foster care. The local authority is very concerned that the boy's father, who has been consistently violent towards him, should not have contact and should not be aware of where the boy is living. The local authority is worried that the mother, who is having limited contact with the boy, may pass on information to the father. It seeks leave to invoke the High Court's inherent jurisdiction.

The High Court cannot use its inherent jurisdiction to make an order about contact: the local authority has available to it s 34 of the CA 1989 and must apply under this section for an order giving it leave to refuse contact to the father. However, there is no order available to the local authority that would achieve the desired result of preventing the mother from telling the father where the child is. Its only route is to ask the High Court to grant an injunction forbidding the mother to pass on information that might lead to the father discovering the child's whereabouts.

8.34 The restriction on local authority applications applies whether or not the child is in care. There may be cases where the local authority seeks a declaration from the court on whether a proposed course of action, for example a medical procedure, would be lawful. In such a case the local authority must still overcome the leave restriction in s 100(4) and in particular must satisfy the court that, for example, a child assessment order or specific issue order would not achieve the desired result. It may be that where the child is not in care, and a specific issue order is therefore available,[29] this will be the more appropriate route. Both routes have been used to permit blood transfusions where the child's parents refused to consent to the procedure.[30]

8.35 The courts have consistently (pre- and post-CA 1989) discouraged attempts to review, by way of the inherent jurisdiction, a local authority's decision-making under a care order. The appropriate route of challenge to a decision of the local authority is via an application for judicial review, provided that it can be shown that the local authority has acted illegally, improperly or irrationally.

PROCEDURE

8.36 An originating summons in wardship, and an application under the court's inherent jurisdiction, must each be issued in the High Court. Any person with an interest in the child may issue an originating summons. Once a summons in wardship is issued the child immediately

29 CA 1989, s 9(1).

30 *Re S* [1993] 1 FLR 376 (inherent jurisdiction); *Re R* [1993] 2 FLR 757 (specific issue order).

becomes a ward of court;[31] an application for a hearing must be made within 21 days, and at that hearing the court must confirm the wardship or it will lapse.

8.37 The court may exercise its inherent jurisdiction, including by making a child a ward of court, of its own motion without an application.

8.38 The originating summons must be accompanied by an affidavit sworn by the plaintiff setting out the grounds for the application. The defendants are those with a genuine interest in the child, including, where the application is made to resolve a specific dispute, the parties to the dispute. The child himself will not be made a party unless there are specific reasons for doing so.

8.39 Applications in wardship or under the inherent jurisdiction may be made without notice. This may be appropriate in cases where there is an emergency and it is not possible or appropriate to give notice. Out of hours the application should be made by telephone to the urgent applications judge, who may be contacted on 020 7947 6000.

31 Supreme Court Act 1981, s 41(2).

9

CHALLENGING THE LOCAL AUTHORITY

Chapter summary

- Parental veto
- Independent Reviewing Officer
- Making a complaint
- Powers of the Secretary of State
- Children's Commissioner
- Local Government Ombudsman
- Judicial Review
- Appeals
- Human Rights Act 1998

9.1 The content of the preceding chapters will have demonstrated the extent of the far-reaching powers conferred by Parliament upon local authorities to order the lives of children for whom they are given statutory responsibilities. These powers in some cases, although reviewable by judicial review, are otherwise largely unsupervised by the courts. The potential impact of these powers upon individual families may be devastating. It is thus important for all involved to be aware of the various avenues available for a local authority's actions, or proposed actions, to be questioned or challenged.

9.2 Rather than being embodied in a unified code, the options for challenging a local authority are made up of a cocktail of provisions from various sources. In summary they are:

- exercise any power of **parental veto** that may be available;
- raise the issue at the next Looked After Children **Review meeting** (if the child is accommodated by the local authority or in care);[1]
- ask for the decision to be reviewed by **a more senior officer** in the local authority hierarchy;

1 For LAC Reviews, see **3.24**.

- seeking the intervention of the local authority's **Independent Reviewing Officer**;
- follow any **general complaints procedure** established by the local authority;
- follow the **complaints procedure** established by the local authority under **CA 1989, s 26**;
- contact a local **councillor**, the chair or vice-chair of the social services committee, or any other councillor;
- seek the intervention of the local **Member of Parliament**;
- write to the appropriate central **government department** (normally the Department for Education and Skills) or the **Minister for Children**;
- refer the matter to the **Children's Commissioner**;
- refer the matter to the **Local Government Ombudsman**;
- seek **judicial review** of the particular action, or failure to take action, of the local authority;
- **apply to the court** (if the case falls into the limit range where a CA 1989 application is available);
- **appeal** against the original court order;
- make a claim under the **Human Rights Act 1998**;
- refer the matter to the **European Court of Human Rights**.

We will now look at some of these options in more detail.

PARENTAL VETO

9.3 Whether a child is being looked after by a local authority pursuant to a care order or simply being accommodated, his parents will still have parental responsibility with respect to him. If there is a care order the local authority will also share parental responsibility for the child and has the power to determine the extent to which any other holder of parental responsibility may exercise his parental responsibility for the child.[2]

9.4 The prime example of parental veto is the right of any person with parental responsibility to choose to remove a child (who is not under a care order) from accommodation being provided by the local authority under CA 1989, s 19.

9.5 Where a child is in care, notwithstanding the local authority's general powers under a care order, a person with parental responsibility

2 CA 1989, s 33(3). Those who may have parental responsibility for a child include a parent, guardian, special guardian or step-parent.

may refuse to give consent to medical treatment, religious instruction, marriage, travel out of the jurisdiction, a name change, adoption (or placement for adoption).

9.6 A child may also exercise a right of veto, to refuse to be involved in a certain course of action proposed by a local authority in accordance with the *Gillick* principle.[3]

INDEPENDENT REVIEWING OFFICER

9.7 Once a full care order has been made, the responsibility for developing and implementing the care plan for the child is that of the local authority and not the court. As a result of difficulties that have arisen in past cases where the local authority has either failed to implement an agreed plan, or markedly deviated from the plan, the role of 'independent reviewing officer' ('IRO') has now been introduced with the principal aim of monitoring the performance of the authority's functions in respect of the care plan.[4] The IRO must (so far as is reasonably practicable) attend and chair any meetings held in connection with the review of the child's case and has a responsibility for ensuring that the process is conducted in accordance with the regulations and that, in particular, the child's views are understood and taken into account.[5]

9.8 If the child whose case is being reviewed wishes to take proceedings under CA 1989 on his own account, the IRO's role is to assist the child to obtain legal advice; or to establish whether an appropriate adult is willing to provide such assistance or bring the proceedings on the child's behalf.[6]

9.9 In addition, if the IRO considers that it is appropriate to do so he/she must refer the case to CAFCASS with a view to that agency taking proceedings under the Human Rights Act 1998, s 7, or for judicial review or any other proceedings in order to bring issues relating to the care plan before a court.[7]

---

3 For the *Gillick* principle, see **5.35**.

4 For earlier case law see *Re S (Care Order: Implementation of Care Plan); Re W (Care Order: Adequacy of Care Plan)* [2001] UKHL 10; [2002] 1 FLR 815.

5 Review of Children's Cases Regulations 1991 (SI 1991/895), reg 2A.

6 Ibid.

7 CA 1989, s 26(2A); CAFCASS (Reviewed Case Referral) Regulations 2004 (SI 2004/2187); *CAFCASS Practice Note: Cases Referred by Independent Reviewing Officers* [2005] Fam Law 60.

9.10 The potential for the IRO to influence the successful implementation of the child's care plan is not to be underestimated. Early experience of the IRO system has failed to see cases being referred back to the courts as contemplated by the legislation. One difficulty may be that IR Officers are appointed by (and have to work with) the local authority whose work is being reviewed.

MAKING A COMPLAINT

9.11 There are three different complaints procedures relating to local authority decisions:

- complaint to the local authority under CA 1989, s 26(3) (support for families and children);
- complaint to the local authority under Local Authority Social Services Complaints (England) Regulations (LASSC(E)R) 2006[8] (or in Wales, the Social Services Complaints Procedure (Wales) Regulations (SSCP(W)R) 2005[9]) in relation to all matters not within the scope of CA 1989, s 26(3); or
- complaint in relation to children's homes and voluntary organisations within their procedure.

It is important to note that the procedure established by s 26(3) does not include CA 1989, Parts IV and V (child protection provisions).

9.12 CA 1989, s 26(3) requires local authorities to establish a procedure for considering representations and complaints about the discharge of their functions from the following persons:

- the child;
- a parent;
- any person with parental responsibility;
- a local authority foster-carer;
- any other such person who the local authority considers has sufficient interest in the child's welfare to warrant his representation being considered;

in relation to any child being looked after or in need.

---

8 SI 2006/1681.
9 SI 2005/3366.

9.13 The s 26(3) duty therefore covers not only the accommodation of a child, and the decision whether or not to commence care proceedings, but also day care and services for family support and aftercare provisions. The s 26(3) duty extends to those for whom provision is made by the Adoption Service under ACA 2002.

9.14 Voluntary organisations and registered children's homes are also required to have a procedure for considering representations (including complaints) about children's services.

9.15 The s 26(3) procedure involves an independent person in the process with the aim of ensuring that the child, parents and others are sufficiently involved in the process (which is also an important requirement of ECHR law). The procedure does not affect any other rights and is not to be regarded as a formal appeals process. Detailed provision is made by the Representations Procedure (Children) Regulations 1991. Each local authority should have accessible information available about its complaints procedures.

9.16 In essence, where a qualifying representation or complaint is made the local authority, having appointed an independent person to investigate the matter, will issue a response within 28 days. If the complainant is dissatisfied with the response, he may have the matter reconsidered by a panel appointed by the local authority (which must include at least one independent person). The panel must make its recommendations within a further 28 days. The local authority, on receipt of the recommendations, must, together with the independent person, consider what action should be taken in relation to the child in the light of the representation/complaint. The procedure is summarised on the following charts:

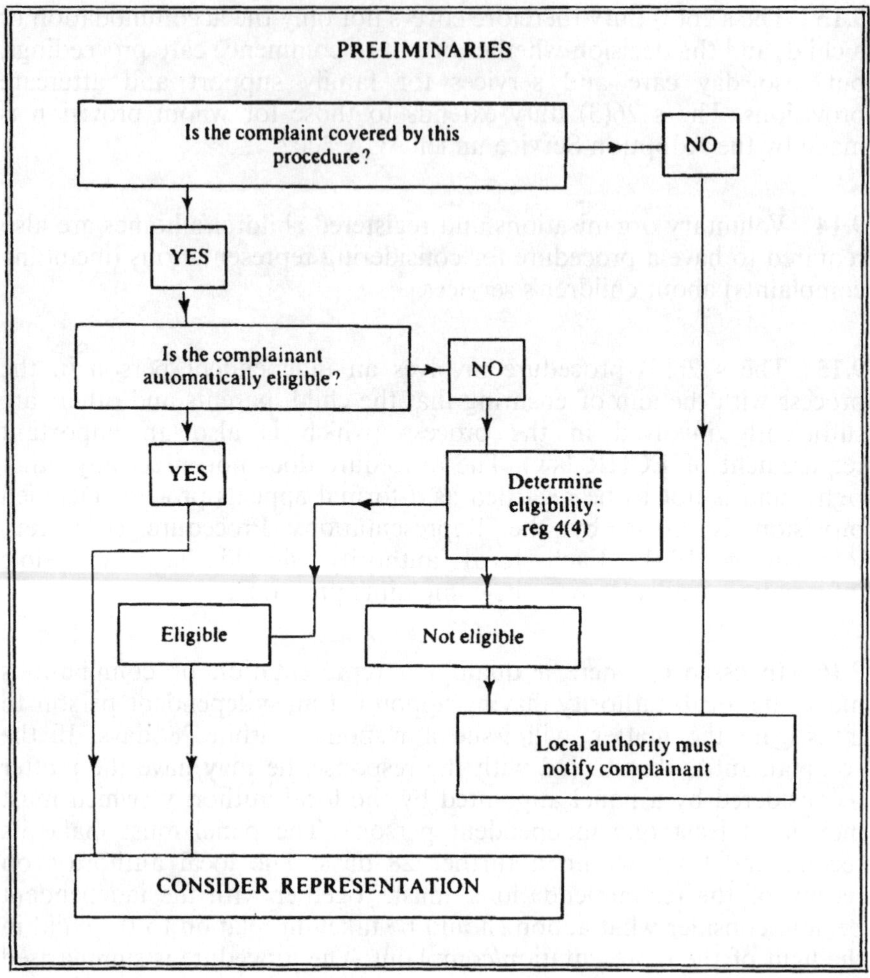
PRELIMINARIES
Is the complaint covered by this procedure?
NO
YES
Is the complainant automatically eligible?
NO
YES
Determine eligibility: reg 4(4)
Eligible
Not eligible
Local authority must notify complainant
CONSIDER REPRESENTATION

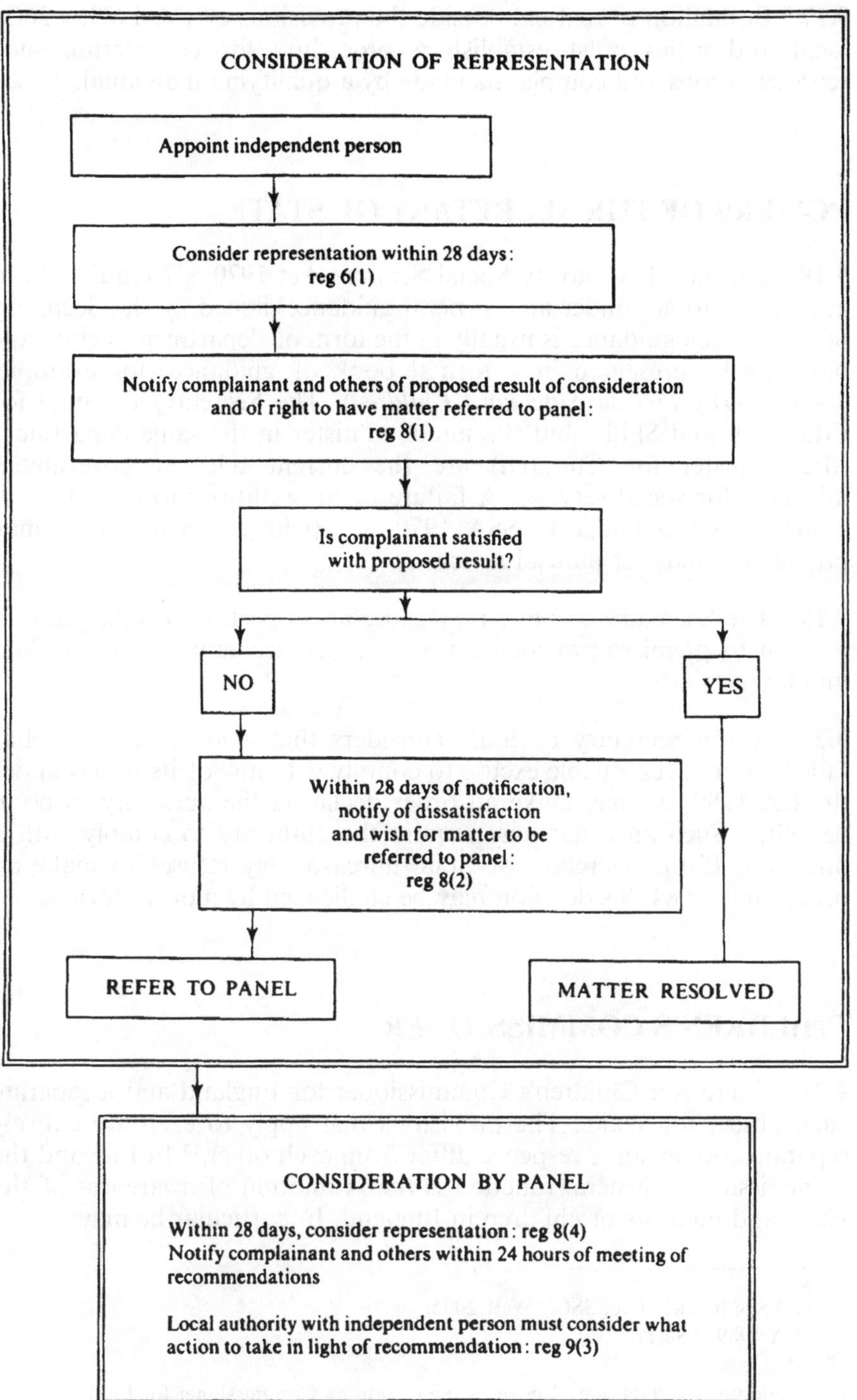
CONSIDERATION OF REPRESENTATION
Appoint independent person
Consider representation within 28 days: reg 6(1)
Notify complainant and others of proposed result of consideration and of right to have matter referred to panel: reg 8(1)
Is complainant satisfied with proposed result?
NO
YES
Within 28 days of notification, notify of dissatisfaction and wish for matter to be referred to panel: reg 8(2)
REFER TO PANEL
MATTER RESOLVED
CONSIDERATION BY PANEL
Within 28 days, consider representation: reg 8(4)
Notify complainant and others within 24 hours of meeting of recommendations
Local authority with independent person must consider what action to take in light of recommendation: reg 9(3)

9.17 In relation to matters outside the provisions of CA 1989, s 26(3) local authorities must establish a procedure for considering such representations and complaints made by a qualifying individual.[10]

POWERS OF THE SECRETARY OF STATE

9.18 The Local Authority Social Services Act 1970, s 7 requires local authorities to act under any 'general guidance' issued by the Secretary of State. Such guidance is usually in the form of departmental circulars, but may be presented in a formal book of guidance (for example, *Working Together to Safeguard Children*). The Secretary of State for Education and Skills, and the junior minister in the same department (the Minister for Children) are the current relevant government ministers for social services. A failure of an authority to comply with guidance issued under LASSA 1970, s 7 (which is mandatory) may provide grounds for judicial review.

9.19 The Secretary of State may cause an inspection to take place in relation to premises provided for a child (eg accommodation or child minding).[11]

9.20 If the Secretary of State considers that a local authority has failed without reasonable excuse to comply with any of its duties under the CA 1989, he may make an order declaring the authority to be in default.[12] Such an order may require the authority to comply with a direction. If the Secretary of State unreasonably refuses to make an order under s 84, his decision may be challenged by judicial review.

CHILDREN'S COMMISSIONER

9.21 There is a Children's Commissioner for England and a separate such officer for Wales. The provisions that apply to each are entirely separate and, in some respects, differ from each other.[13] In England the Commissioner's general function is the promotion of awareness of the views and interests of children in England. In particular he may:

---

10 LASSCR(E)R 2006; SSCP(W)R 2005.

11 CA 1989, s 80(1).

12 Ibid, s 84.

13 Children Act 2004, Part 1 governs the Children's Commissioner for England; Care Standards Act 2000, Part V and Children's Commissioner for Wales Act 2001 (and the Children's Commissioner for Wales Regulations 2001 (SI 2001/2787)) make provision for Wales.

(a) encourage persons exercising functions or engaged in activities affecting children to take account of their views and interests;
(b) advise the Secretary of State on the views and interests of children;
(c) consider or research the operation of complaints procedures so far as they relate to children;
(d) consider or research any other matter relating to the interests of children;
(e) publish a report on any matter considered or researched by him.

9.22 Where the English Children's Commissioner considers that the case of an individual child raises issues of public policy of relevance to other children, he may hold an inquiry into that case for the purpose of investigating and making recommendations about those issues. He may, however, only hold such an inquiry if to do so would not duplicate the work of another person.

9.23 The Children's Commissioner for Wales has wider powers than his English counterpart and may offer advice and support to specific children, where those children are provided with relevant services in Wales or in respect of whom regulated children's services are provided in Wales.

LOCAL GOVERNMENT OMBUDSMAN

9.24 The Ombudsman appointed by Parliament under the Local Government Act 1974, s 23 is an independent and impartial person whose role is to investigate complaints of injustice through maladministration by a local authority. 'Maladministration' means failure to follow agreed policies or procedures, failure to provide information or advice, providing inaccurate information or advice, or causing unjustified delays.[14] The focus of the Ombudsman's investigation will normally be the process of any decision making, rather than the merits of the decision itself.

9.25 A complaint may only be made to the Ombudsman after the matter has been raised with the local authority and, thereafter, a local councillor. If that has not provided a satisfactory outcome, then a referral may be made to the Ombudsman either directly or via a councillor.[15] He does not normally deal with issues relating to court proceedings or where there is a statutory right of appeal. Any conclusion made by the Ombudsman takes the form of a recommendation to the local authority.

---

14 Local Government Act 1974, s 26.
15 www.lgo.org.uk. Advice line: 0845 602 1983.

JUDICIAL REVIEW

9.26 Judicial review is the process whereby the High Court exercises its supervisory jurisdiction to review the legality and validity of the actions and decisions of persons or bodies exercising administrative powers whether of a legislative, executive or judicial/adjudicatory character. Thus the jurisdiction is over the proceedings and decisions of inferior courts, tribunals and other bodies performing public acts and duties.

9.27 Judicial review is not a system of appeal. A claim for judicial review is a claim for the High Court to review the lawfulness of an enactment, or a decision, action or failure to act in relation to a public function. Judicial review is about the legality and fairness of the process that has been adopted and not about the merits of the decision itself. In general the High Court may quash (that is extinguish) the decision of an inferior body where that body has acted:

- illegally (an error of law, or an abuse of power or jurisdiction);
- irrationally (acting on irrelevant matters or unreasonably); or
- improperly (acting in breach of rules of natural justice and fairness).

9.28 Judicial review proceedings take place within the context of the HRA 1998 and may be consolidated with a claim under that Act.

9.29 An application for judicial review is a two-stage process, in which the claimant must first obtain permission to make the application. Permission will only be granted if the claimant has:

- 'sufficient interest' in the matter to which the application relates;
- a prima facie case;
- made the application promptly (and in any event within three months from the day when grounds to apply arose);
- (usually) exhausted alternative remedies of redress; and
- shown that the decision is one that is capable of challenge by judicial review.

9.30 A favourable result for a judicial review claimant may be a mandatory order, a prohibiting order, a quashing order, a declaration and/or an injunction or damages.[16]

9.31 Judicial review is a highly developed area of public law, detailed consideration of which is well beyond the scope of this work.[17]

---

16 Supreme Court Act 1981, s 31.

17 For further description of judicial review, see Hershman and McFarlane, *Children: Law and Practice* (Family Law) Division K.

APPEALS

9.32 An appeal to the High Court lies from a decision under CA 1989 made by a family proceedings court. There is no requirement that permission to appeal is obtained, therefore the appeal is as of right and will be a rehearing.

9.33 In the county court an appeal from a decision of a district judge may be made to a circuit judge. In the High Court an appeal from a district judge may be made to a High Court judge. In both cases the appellant does not need permission to appeal. The appeal must be brought within 21 days of the order complained of being made. An appeal from a circuit judge or from a High Court judge in a CA 1989 case goes to the Court of Appeal Civil Division. Permission to appeal must either be given by the judge of the lower court or by the Court of Appeal. Any appeal process must be started within 21 days of the order complained of being made. A further appeal from the Court of Appeal lies to the House of Lords on a point of law and only with the leave of the Court of Appeal or of the House of Lords.

9.34 As a general rule, appeals against court decisions about a child's welfare are difficult to sustain if they are not founded upon a point of law, or show that the lower court went outside the band of reasonable conclusions that were open to it. Where a court is exercising its discretion as between two or more equally balanced options for a child, it will be very difficult to show the appeal court that the lower court was 'plainly wrong' for preferring option A over option B. The more finely balanced the case, the less likely there can be an arguable appeal.

HUMAN RIGHTS ACT 1998

9.35 The events in Europe in the 1930s and 1940s provided the impetus for the establishment of an international structure to protect the human rights of individual citizens against the actions of a Member State. The Convention for the Protection of Human Rights and Fundamental Freedoms (the 'ECHR') was signed in November 1950 and ratified by the UK in March 1951. The ECHR structure and law is distinct and separate from European Community Law and the European Court of Justice.

9.36 From October 2000 the Human Rights Act 1998 (HRA 1998) has been fully in force in the UK. The broad effect of the HRA 1998 is to require that UK domestic law is interpreted, and that public authorities act, in a manner that is compatible with the ECHR, with the result that a citizen may rely directly upon the ECHR in proceedings before UK domestic courts. The HRA 1998 does not strictly 'incorporate' the

ECHR into UK domestic law. So far as it is possible to do so, primary legislation and subordinate legislation *must* be read and given effect to in a way that is *compatible* with the Convention rights.[18]

9.37 Whilst it has impact upon many areas of domestic life, the ECHR is a comparatively short document containing brief statements of basic human rights, each set out in a numbered 'article'. Over the past 50 years, the European Court of Human Rights (ECtHR) in Strasbourg has interpreted and applied the Convention to a myriad of different factual circumstances, with the result that the ECHR is now applied widely and with detailed consequences in a way that, to English eyes, would not necessarily be suggested from the brief wording of the ECHR itself.

9.38 In relation to the intervention of public authorities in the lives of children and their families the two key articles of the ECHR are Art 6 (fair trial) and Art 8 (family life). These two articles are considered in summary terms below. Other ECHR articles that may be engaged in a child care case are:

- Art 2: Right to life
- Art 3: Prohibition of torture, inhuman or degrading treatment or punishment
- Art 5: Right to liberty and security of person
- Art 12: Right to marry and found a family
- Art 14: Prohibition of discrimination.

Article 6: Right to a fair trial

9.39 ECHR Art 6 states:

> '1. In the determination of his civil rights and obligations or of any criminal charge against him, everyone is entitled to a fair and public hearing within a reasonable time by an independent and impartial tribunal established by law. Judgment shall be pronounced publicly but the press and public may be excluded from all or part of the trial in the interest of morals, public order or national security in a democratic society, where the interests of juveniles or the protection of the private life of the parties so require, or to the extent strictly necessary in the opinion of the court in special circumstances where publicity would prejudice the interests of justice.'

The principal features of Art 6 are:

- the right to effective access to a court or tribunal;
- the tribunal must be independent and impartial;
- the hearing must be within a reasonable time;

---

18 HRA 1998, s 3(1).

- there must be 'equality of arms' as between the litigants;
- the parties must be present and able to participate at the hearing;
- a party must know the case against him;
- in general the hearing should be in public with a public judgment; and
- the judgment should include a reasoned decision.

9.40 Article 6 applies where there is a 'determination' affecting a person's civil rights, thus there must be a right, recognised by domestic law, involved and there must have been some determination relating to that right.

Article 8: Right to respect for private and family life

9.41 ECHR Art 8 states:

> '1. Everyone has the right to respect for his private and family life, his home and his correspondence.
> 2. There shall be no interference by a public authority with the exercise of this right except such as is in accordance with the law and is necessary in a democratic society in the interests of national security, public safety or the economic well-being of the country, for the prevention of disorder or crime, for the protection of health or morals, or for the protection of the rights and freedoms of others.'

The preliminary question of whether rights to 'family life' are engaged with respect to a local authority's intervention in relation to children is likely to be answered in the affirmative. Thus, where, for example, a child is removed into care, there will clearly be an interference with rights to family life sufficient to trigger consideration under Art 8. The focus of such consideration will therefore be conducted under Art 8.2 where, in order for the state's interference to be 'justified' (and therefore not in breach of Art 8), the following four conditions must be fulfilled:

(a) the interference must be in accordance with the domestic law (for example under CA 1989);
(b) the interference must serve a legitimate purpose (for example the protection of children from harm);
(c) the interference must be '*necessary in a democratic society*'; and
(d) the interference must not be discriminatory.

9.42 Of those four conditions (a) and (b) are likely to be met where a local authority is seeking to take a child into care and the key to determining whether or not Art 8 is breached is likely to be (c), namely whether or not the interference is necessary in a democratic society. This latter consideration imports the need to identify some 'pressing social need' and requires a state of affairs which is more than simply that a certain action is 'useful' or 'desirable'; it must be 'necessary'. Further, in determining whether any intervention is 'necessary' not only the need to intervene but also the degree and type of intervention must be considered. The intervention must be 'proportionate' to the need: a sledgehammer is not required to crack a nut.

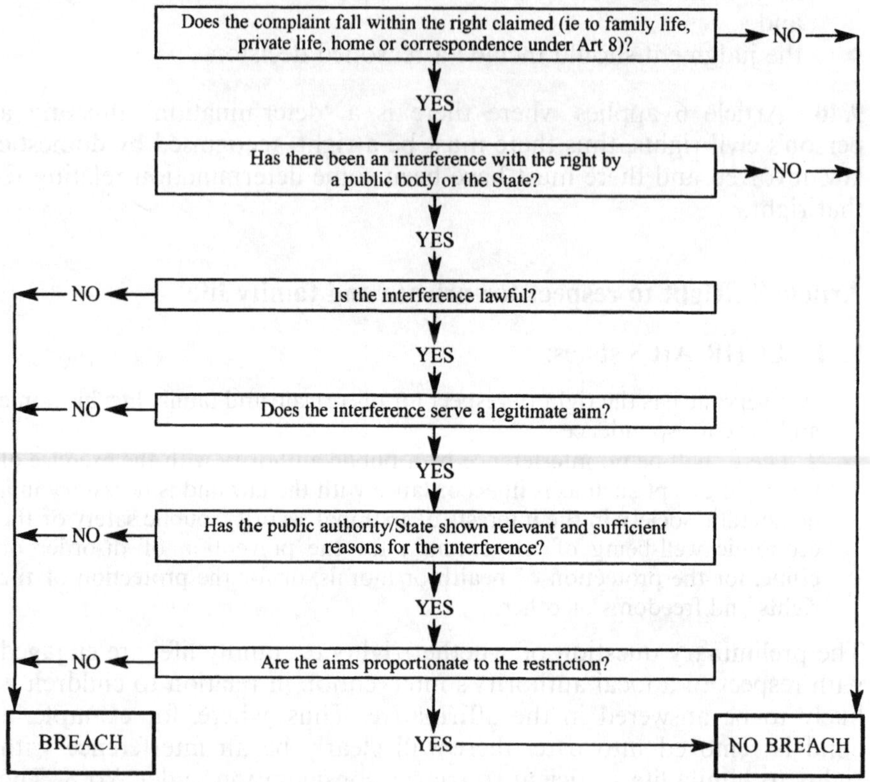

Checkchart

	Question	Answer	Breach?
1	Does the complaint fall within the right claimed? (eg to family life or private life under Art 8)	Yes No	Go to 2 Breach ✗
2	Has there been an interference with the right by a public body or the State? (eg removal of child from care of parents)	Yes No	Go to 3 Breach ✗
3	Is the interference lawful?	Yes No	Go to 4 Breach ✓
4	Does the interference serve a legitimate aim? (eg the protection of the child from harm)	Yes No	Go to 5 Breach ✓
5	Has the public authority/State shown relevant and sufficient reasons for the interference? (eg is there a pressing social need to remove a child from the parents?)	Yes No	Go to 6 Breach ✓
6	Are those reasons proportionate to the restriction? (eg is the plan of adoption with no contact appropriate in the circumstances of the case?)	Yes No	Breach ✗ Breach ✓

Applying the ECHR in domestic courts under the HRA 1998

9.43 The principal effect of the HRA 1998 is that every action of a local authority (as a public authority) and every decision of a court in family proceedings (and indeed the proceedings themselves) must be compatible with the ECHR. Only where it is impossible to act in a compatible manner, or achieve an interpretation of the law that is compatible, can another course be taken. Where a number of options are all compatible, then a court or an authority will have, so far as the HRA 1998 is concerned, discretion to choose between them.

9.44 Consideration of the ECHR will thus arise during the ordinary process of every care case and every set of family proceedings before a court in England and Wales, without any of the parties having to bring a separate action under the HRA 1998. Where ECHR issues arise in pending proceedings, they should be dealt with within those proceedings. The HRA 1998 does, however, provide the option for separate, freestanding, proceedings to be brought in reliance upon ECHR claims (for example where there are no relevant current proceedings pending before a court). HRA 1998, s 6 renders it 'unlawful' for a public body (which would include a local authority) to act, or intend to act, in a manner that is incompatible with the ECHR. Where a person claims that a public body (other than a judicial authority) has acted or proposes to act 'unlawfully' in this context, he may bring proceedings under HRA 1998, s 7 in the High Court or a county court.

9.45 Where a local authority under a full care order has operated the care plan in a manner that may be incompatible with the ECHR rights of the child and family members, it is appropriate for freestanding HRA 1998 proceedings to be brought in order to allow the court to review the matter.[19]

9.46 If the proceedings result in a finding of 'unlawful' activity by the defendant public body, the court has the power to grant such relief or remedy, or make such order, within its powers, as it considers just and appropriate.[20]

Reference to the European Court of Human Rights

9.47 As an option of last resort, a claim that the state (in the guise, for example, of the local authority or the court) has acted in breach of the

---

19 *Re M (Care: Challenging Decisions by Local Authority)* [2001] 2 FLR 1300 (approved by the House of Lords in *Re S (Care Order: Implementation of Care Plan); Re W (Care Order: Adequacy of Care Plan)* [2001] UKHL 10; [2002] 1 FLR 815).

20 HRA 1998, s 8.

ECHR may be the subject of an application directly to the ECtHR in Strasbourg. Such an application will normally only be admitted for consideration by the ECtHR if all the legal remedies available within England and Wales have been exhausted. The claim, if it is accepted by the ECtHR as 'admissible', will take a number of years to proceed to final determination. The effect of a final determination in favour of the claimant will be a finding that the state has been in breach of one or more Articles of the ECHR and, in an appropriate case, modest damages may be awarded. It is not within the ECtHR's power to quash the original decision and the result back in England and Wales may be an amendment to the law in due course: an outcome which will not of itself achieve the return of a child 'unlawfully' removed by a local authority some years earlier.

APPENDICES

Appendix 1

CHILDREN ACT 1989

(1989 c 41)

Part I
Introductory

1 Welfare of the child

(1) When a court determines any question with respect to –

(a) the upbringing of a child; or
(b) the administration of a child's property or the application of any income arising from it,

the child's welfare shall be the court's paramount consideration.

(2) In any proceedings in which any question with respect to the upbringing of a child arises, the court shall have regard to the general principle that any delay in determining the question is likely to prejudice the welfare of the child.

(3) In the circumstances mentioned in subsection (4), a court shall have regard in particular to –

(a) the ascertainable wishes and feelings of the child concerned (considered in the light of his age and understanding);
(b) his physical, emotional and educational needs;
(c) the likely effect on him of any change in his circumstances;
(d) his age, sex, background and any characteristics of his which the court considers relevant;
(e) any harm which he has suffered or is at risk of suffering;
(f) how capable each of his parents, and any other person in relation to whom the court considers the question to be relevant, is of meeting his needs;
(g) the range of powers available to the court under this Act in the proceedings in question.

(4) The circumstances are that –

(a) the court is considering whether to make, vary or discharge a section 8 order, and the making, variation or discharge of the order is opposed by any party to the proceedings; or
(b) the court is considering whether to make, vary or discharge a special guardianship order or an order under Part IV.

(5) Where a court is considering whether or not to make one or more orders under this Act with respect to a child, it shall not make the order or any of the orders unless it considers that doing so would be better for the child than making no order at all.

2 Parental responsibility for children

(1) Where a child's father and mother were married to each other at the time of his birth, they shall each have parental responsibility for the child.

(2) Where a child's father and mother were not married to each other at the time of his birth –

(a) the mother shall have parental responsibility for the child;
(b) the father shall have parental responsibility for the child if he has acquired it (and has not ceased to have it) in accordance with the provisions of this Act.

(3) References in this Act to a child whose father and mother were, or (as the case may be) were not, married to each other at the time of his birth must be read with section 1 of the Family Law Reform Act 1987 (which extends their meaning).

(4) The rule of law that a father is the natural guardian of his legitimate child is abolished.

(5) More than one person may have parental responsibility for the same child at the same time.

(6) A person who has parental responsibility for a child at any time shall not cease to have that responsibility solely because some other person subsequently acquires parental responsibility for the child.

(7) Where more than one person has parental responsibility for a child, each of them may act alone and without the other (or others) in meeting that responsibility; but nothing in this Part shall be taken to affect the operation of any enactment which requires the consent of more than one person in a matter affecting the child.

(8) The fact that a person has parental responsibility for a child shall not entitle him to act in any way which would be incompatible with any order made with respect to the child under this Act.

(9) A person who has parental responsibility for a child may not surrender or transfer any part of that responsibility to another but may arrange for some or all of it to be met by one or more persons acting on his behalf.

(10) The person with whom any such arrangement is made may himself be a person who already has parental responsibility for the child concerned.

(11) The making of any such arrangement shall not affect any liability of the person making it which may arise from any failure to meet any part of his parental responsibility for the child concerned.

3 Meaning of "parental responsibility"

(1) In this Act "parental responsibility" means all the rights, duties, powers, responsibilities and authority which by law a parent of a child has in relation to the child and his property.

(2) It also includes the rights, powers and duties which a guardian of the child's estate (appointed, before the commencement of section 5, to act generally) would have had in relation to the child and his property.

(3) The rights referred to in subsection (2) include, in particular, the right of the guardian to receive or recover in his own name, for the benefit of the child, property of whatever description and wherever situated which the child is entitled to receive or recover.

(4) The fact that a person has, or does not have, parental responsibility for a child shall not affect –

(a) any obligation which he may have in relation to the child (such as a statutory duty to maintain the child); or
(b) any rights which, in the event of the child's death, he (or any other person) may have in relation to the child's property.

(5) A person who –

(a) does not have parental responsibility for a particular child; but
(b) has care of the child,

may (subject to the provisions of this Act) do what is reasonable in all the circumstances of the case for the purpose of safeguarding or promoting the child's welfare.

4 Acquisition of parental responsibility by father

(1) Where a child's father and mother were not married to each other at the time of his birth, the father shall acquire parental responsibility for the child if –

(a) he becomes registered as the child's father under any of the enactments specified in subsection (1A);
(b) he and the child's mother make an agreement (a "parental responsibility agreement") providing for him to have parental responsibility for the child; or
(c) the court, on his application, orders that he shall have parental responsibility for the child.

(1A) The enactments referred to in subsection (1)(a) are –

(a) paragraphs (a), (b) and (c) of section 10(1) and of section 10A(1) of the Births and Deaths Registration Act 1953;
(b) paragraphs (a), (b)(i) and (c) of section 18(1), and sections 18(2)(b) and 20(1)(a) of the Registration of Births, Deaths and Marriages (Scotland) Act 1965; and
(c) sub-paragraphs (a), (b) and (c) of Article 14(3) of the Births and Deaths Registration (Northern Ireland) Order 1976.

(1B) The Secretary of State may by order amend subsection (1A) so as to add further enactments to the list in that subsection.

(2) No parental responsibility agreement shall have effect for the purposes of this Act unless –

(a) it is made in the form prescribed by regulations made by the Lord Chancellor; and
(b) where regulations are made by the Lord Chancellor prescribing the manner in which such agreements must be recorded, it is recorded in the prescribed manner.

(2A) A person who has acquired parental responsibility under subsection (1) shall cease to have that responsibility only if the court so orders.

(3) The court may make an order under subsection (2A) on the application –

(a) of any person who has parental responsibility for the child; or
(b) with leave of the court, of the child himself,

subject, in the case of parental responsibility acquired under subsection (1)(c), to section 12(4).

(4) The court may only grant leave under subsection (3)(b) if it is satisfied that the child has sufficient understanding to make the proposed application.

4A Acquisition of parental responsibility by step-parent

(1) Where a child's parent ("parent A") who has parental responsibility for the child is married to, or a civil partner of, a person who is not the child's parent ("the step-parent") –

(a) parent A or, if the other parent of the child also has parental responsibility for the child, both parents may by agreement with the step-parent provide for the step-parent to have parental responsibility for the child; or
(b) the court may, on the application of the step-parent, order that the step-parent shall have parental responsibility for the child.

(2) An agreement under subsection (1)(a) is also a "parental responsibility agreement", and section 4(2) applies in relation to such agreements as it applies in relation to parental responsibility agreements under section 4.

(3) A parental responsibility agreement under subsection (1)(a), or an order under subsection (1)(b), may only be brought to an end by an order of the court made on the application –

(a) of any person who has parental responsibility for the child; or
(b) with the leave of the court, of the child himself.

(4) The court may only grant leave under subsection (3)(b) if it is satisfied that the child has sufficient understanding to make the proposed application.

5 Appointment of guardians

(1) Where an application with respect to a child is made to the court by any individual, the court may by order appoint that individual to be the child's guardian or special guardian if –

(a) the child has no parent with parental responsibility for him; or
(b) a residence order has been made with respect to the child in favour of a parent or guardian of his who has died while the order was in force; or
(c) paragraph (*b*) does not apply, and the child's only or last surviving special guardian dies.

(2) The power conferred by subsection (1) may also be exercised in any family proceedings if the court considers that the order should be made even though no application has been made for it.

(3) A parent who has parental responsibility for his child may appoint another individual to be the child's guardian in the event of his death.

(4) A guardian of a child may appoint another individual to take his place as the child's guardian in the event of his death; and a special guardian of a child may appoint another individual to be the child's guardian in the event of his death.

(5) An appointment under subsection (3) or (4) shall not have effect unless it is made in writing, is dated and is signed by the person making the appointment or –

- (a) in the case of an appointment made by a will which is not signed by the testator, is signed at the direction of the testator in accordance with the requirements of section 9 of the Wills Act 1837; or
- (b) in any other case, is signed at the direction of the person making the appointment, in his presence and in the presence of two witnesses who each attest the signature.

(6) A person appointed as a child's guardian under this section shall have parental responsibility for the child concerned.

(7) Where –

- (a) on the death of any person making an appointment under subsection (3) or (4), the child concerned has no parent with parental responsibility for him; or
- (b) immediately before the death of any person making such an appointment, a residence order in his favour was in force with respect to the child or he was the child's only (or last surviving) special guardian,

the appointment shall take effect on the death of that person.

(8) Where, on the death of any person making an appointment under subsection (3) or (4) –

- (a) the child concerned has a parent with parental responsibility for him; and
- (b) subsection (7)(b) does not apply,

the appointment shall take effect when the child no longer has a parent who has parental responsibility for him.

(9) Subsections (1) and (7) do not apply if the residence order referred to in paragraph (b) of those subsections was also made in favour of a surviving parent of the child.

(10) Nothing in this section shall be taken to prevent an appointment under subsection (3) or (4) being made by two or more persons acting jointly.

(11) Subject to any provision made by rules of court, no court shall exercise the High Court's inherent jurisdiction to appoint a guardian of the estate of any child.

(12) Where the rules of court are made under subsection (11) they may prescribe the circumstances in which, and conditions subject to which, an appointment of such a guardian may be made.

(13) A guardian of a child may only be appointed in accordance with the provisions of this section.

6 Guardians: revocation and disclaimer

(1) An appointment under section 5(3) or (4) revokes an earlier such appointment (including one made in an unrevoked will or codicil) made by the same person in respect of the same child, unless it is clear (whether as the result of an express provision in the later appointment or by any necessary implication) that the purpose of the later appointment is to appoint an additional guardian.

(2) An appointment under section 5(3) or (4) (including one made in an unrevoked will or codicil) is revoked if the person who made the appointment revokes it by a written and dated instrument which is signed –

(a) by him; or
(b) at his direction, in his presence and in the presence of two witnesses who each attest the signature.

(3) An appointment under section 5(3) or (4) (other than one made in a will or codicil) is revoked if, with the intention of revoking the appointment, the person who made it –

(a) destroys the instrument by which it was made; or
(b) has some other person destroy that instrument in his presence.

(3A) An appointment under section 5(3) or (4) (including one made in an unrevoked will or codicil) is revoked if the person appointed is the spouse of the person who made the appointment and either –

(a) a decree of a court of civil jurisdiction in England and Wales dissolves or annuls the marriage, or
(b) the marriage is dissolved or annulled and the divorce or annulment is entitled to recognition in England and Wales by virtue of Part II of the Family Law Act 1986,

unless a contrary intention appears by the appointment.

(3B) An appointment under section 5(3) or (4) (including one made in an unrevoked will or codicil) is revoked if the person appointed is the civil partner of the person who made the appointment and either –

(a) an order of a court of civil jurisdiction in England and Wales dissolves or annuls the civil partnership, or
(b) the civil partnership is dissolved or annulled and the dissolution or annulment is entitled to recognition in England and Wales by virtue of Chapter 3 of Part 5 of the Civil Partnership Act 2004,

unless a contrary intention appears by the appointment.

(4) For the avoidance of doubt, an appointment under section 5(3) or (4) made in a will or codicil is revoked if the will or codicil is revoked.

(5) A person who is appointed as a guardian under section 5(3) or (4) may disclaim his appointment by an instrument in writing signed by him and made within a reasonable time of his first knowing that the appointment has taken effect.

(6) Where regulations are made by the Lord Chancellor prescribing the manner in which such disclaimers must be recorded, no such disclaimer shall have effect unless it is recorded in the prescribed manner.

(7) Any appointment of a guardian under section 5 may be brought to an end at any time by order of the court –

(a) on the application of any person who has parental responsibility for the child;
(b) on the application of the child concerned, with leave of the court; or
(c) in any family proceedings, if the court considers that it should be brought to an end even though no application has been made.

7 Welfare reports

(1) A court considering any question with respect to a child under this Act may –

(a) ask an officer of the Service or a Welsh family proceedings officer; or
(b) ask a local authority to arrange for –
   (i) an officer of the authority; or
   (ii) such other person (other than an officer of the Service or a Welsh family proceedings officer) as the authority considers appropriate,

to report to the court on such matters relating to the welfare of that child as are required to be dealt with in the report.

(2) The Lord Chancellor may make regulations specifying matters which, unless the court orders otherwise, must be dealt with in any report under this section.

(3) The report may be made in writing, or orally, as the court requires.

(4) Regardless of any enactment or rule of law which would otherwise prevent it from doing so, the court may take account of –

(*a*) any statement contained in the report; and
(*b*) any evidence given in respect of the matters referred to in the report,

in so far as the statement or evidence is, in the opinion of the court, relevant to the question which it is considering.

(5) It shall be the duty of the authority or officer of the Service or a Welsh family proceedings officer to comply with any request for a report under this section.

Part III
Local Authority Support For Children And Families

Provision of services for children and their families

17 Provision of services for children in need, their families and others

(1) It shall be the general duty of every local authority (in addition to the other duties imposed on them by this Part) –

(a) to safeguard and promote the welfare of children within their area who are in need; and

(b) so far as is consistent with that duty, to promote the upbringing of such children by their families,

by providing a range and level of services appropriate to those children's needs.

(2) For the purpose principally of facilitating the discharge of their general duty under this section, every local authority shall have the specific duties and powers set out in Part I of Schedule 2.

(3) Any service provided by an authority in the exercise of functions conferred on them by this section may be provided for the family of a particular child in need or for any member of his family, if it is provided with a view to safeguarding or promoting the child's welfare.

(4) The Secretary of State may by order amend any provision of Part I of Schedule 2 or add any further duty or power to those for the time being mentioned there.

(4A) Before determining what (if any) services to provide for a particular child in need in the exercise of functions conferred on them by this section, a local authority shall, so far as is reasonably practicable and consistent with the child's welfare –

(a) ascertain the child's wishes and feelings regarding the provision of those services; and

(b) give due consideration (having regard to his age and understanding) to such wishes and feelings of the child as they have been able to ascertain.

(5) Every local authority –

(a) shall facilitate the provision by others (including in particular voluntary organisations) of services which the authority have power to provide by virtue of this section, or section 18, 20, 23, 23B to 23D, 24A or 24B; and

(b) may make such arrangements as they see fit for any person to act on their behalf in the provision of any such service.

(6) The services provided by a local authority in the exercise of functions conferred on them by this section may include providing accommodation and giving assistance in kind or, in exceptional circumstances, in cash.

(7) Assistance may be unconditional or subject to conditions as to the repayment of the assistance or of its value (in whole or in part).

(8) Before giving any assistance or imposing any conditions, a local authority shall have regard to the means of the child concerned and of each of his parents.

(9) No person shall be liable to make any repayment of assistance or of its value at any time when he is in receipt of income support under Part VII of the Social Security Contributions and Benefits Act 1992, of any element of child tax credit other than the family element, of working tax credit or of an income-based jobseeker's allowance.

(10) For the purposes of this Part a child shall be taken to be in need if –

- (a) he is unlikely to achieve or maintain, or to have the opportunity of achieving or maintaining, a reasonable standard of health or development without the provision for him of services by a local authority under this Part;
- (b) his health or development is likely to be significantly impaired, or further impaired, without the provision for him of such services; or
- (c) he is disabled,

and "family," in relation to such a child, includes any person who has parental responsibility for the child and any other person with whom he has been living.

(11) For the purposes of this Part, a child is disabled if he is blind, deaf or dumb or suffers from mental disorder of any kind or is substantially and permanently handicapped by illness, injury or congenital deformity or such other disability as may be prescribed; and in this Part –

"development" means physical, intellectual, emotional, social or behavioural development; and
"health" means physical or mental health.

(12) The Treasury may by regulations prescribe circumstances in which a person is to be treated for the purposes of this Part (or for such of those purposes as are prescribed) as in receipt of any element of child tax credit other than the family element or of working tax credit.

17A Direct payments

(1) The Secretary of State may by regulations make provision for and in connection with requiring or authorising the responsible authority in the case of a person of a prescribed description who falls within subsection (2) to make, with that person's consent, such payments to him as they may determine in accordance with the regulations in respect of his securing the provision of the service mentioned in that subsection.

(2) A person falls within this subsection if he is –

- (a) a person with parental responsibility for a disabled child,
- (b) a disabled person with parental responsibility for a child, or
- (c) a disabled child aged 16 or 17,

and a local authority ('the responsible authority') have decided for the purposes of section 17 that the child's needs (or, if he is such a disabled child, his needs) call for the provision by them of a service in exercise of functions conferred on them under that section.

(3) Subsections (3) to (5) and (7) of section 57 of the 2001 Act shall apply, with any necessary modifications, in relation to regulations under this section as they apply in relation to regulations under that section.

(4) Regulations under this section shall provide that, where payments are made under the regulations to a person falling within subsection (5) –

(a) the payments shall be made at the rate mentioned in subsection (4)(a) of section 57 of the 2001 Act (as applied by subsection (3)); and
(b) subsection (4)(b) of that section shall not apply.

(5) A person falls within this subsection if he is –

(a) a person falling within subsection (2)(a) or (b) and the child in question is aged 16 or 17, or
(b) a person who is in receipt of income support, under Part 7 of the Social Security Contributions and Benefits Act 1992, of any element of child tax credit other than the family element, of working tax credit or of an income-based jobseeker's allowance.

(6) In this section –

'the 2001 Act' means the Health and Social Care Act 2001;
'disabled' in relation to an adult has the same meaning as that given by section 17(11) in relation to a child;
'prescribed' means specified in or determined in accordance with regulations under this section (and has the same meaning in the provisions of the 2001 Act mentioned in subsection (3) as they apply by virtue of that subsection).

18 Day care for pre-school and other children

(1) Every local authority shall provide such day care for children in need within their area who are –

(a) aged five or under; and
(b) not yet attending schools,

as is appropriate.

(2) A local authority may provide day care for children within their area who satisfy the conditions mentioned in subsection (1)(a) and (b) even though they are not in need.

(3) A local authority may provide facilities (including training, advice, guidance and counselling) for those –

(a) caring for children in day care; or
(b) who at any time accompany such children while they are in day care.

(4) In this section 'day care' means any form of care or supervised activity provided for children during the day (whether or not it is provided on a regular basis).

(5) Every local authority shall provide for children in need within their area who are attending any school such care or supervised activities as is appropriate –

(a) outside school hours; or
(b) during school holidays.

(6) A local authority may provide such care or supervised activities for children within their area who are attending any school even though those children are not in need.

(7) In this section 'supervised activity' means an activity supervised by a responsible person.

Provision of accommodation for children

20 Provision of accommodation for children: general

(1) Every local authority shall provide accommodation for any child in need within their area who appears to them to require accommodation as a result of –

(a) there being no person who has parental responsibility for him;
(aa) who is a special guardian of the child; or
(b) his being lost or having been abandoned; or
(c) the person who has been caring for him being prevented (whether or not permanently, and for whatever reason) from providing him with suitable accommodation or care.

(2) Where a local authority provide accommodation under subsection (1) for a child who is ordinarily resident in the area of another local authority, that other local authority may take over the provision of accommodation for the child within –

(a) three months of being notified in writing that the child is being provided with accommodation; or
(b) such other longer period as may be prescribed.

(3) Every local authority shall provide accommodation for any child in need within their area who has reached the age of sixteen and whose welfare the authority consider is likely to be seriously prejudiced if they do not provide him with accommodation.

(4) A local authority may provide accommodation for any child within their area (even though a person who has parental responsibility for him is able to provide him with accommodation) if they consider that to do so would safeguard or promote the child's welfare.

(5) A local authority may provide accommodation for any person who has reached the age of sixteen but is under twenty-one in any community home which takes children who have reached the age of sixteen if they consider that to do so would safeguard or promote his welfare.

(6) Before providing accommodation under this section, a local authority shall, so far as is reasonably practicable and consistent with the child's welfare –

(a) ascertain the child's wishes and feelings regarding the provision of accommodation; and

(b) give due consideration (having regard to his age and understanding) to such wishes and feelings of the child as they have been able to ascertain.

(7) A local authority may not provide accommodation under this section for any child if any person who –

(a) has parental responsibility for him; and
(b) is willing and able to –
  (i) provide accommodation for him; or
  (ii) arrange for accommodation to be provided for him,

objects.

(8) Any person who has parental responsibility for a child may at any time remove the child from accommodation provided by or on behalf of the local authority under this section.

(9) Subsections (7) and (8) do not apply while any person –

(*a*) in whose favour a residence order is in force with respect to the child; or
(b) who has care of the child by virtue of an order made in the exercise of the High Court's inherent jurisdiction with respect to children,

agrees to the child being looked after in accommodation provided by or on behalf of the local authority.

(10) Where there is more than one such person as is mentioned in subsection (9), all of them must agree.

(11) Subsections (7) and (8) do not apply where a child who has reached the age of sixteen agrees to being provided with accommodation under this section.

21 Provision of accommodation for children in police protection or detention or on remand etc

(1) Every local authority shall make provision for the reception and accommodation of children who are removed or kept away from home under Part V.

(2) Every local authority shall receive, and provide accommodation for, children –

(a) in police protection whom they are requested to receive under section 46(3)(f);
(b) whom they are requested to receive under section 38(6) of the Police and Criminal Evidence Act 1984;
(c) who are –
  (i) on remand under paragraph 7(5) of Schedule 7 to the Powers of Criminal Courts (Sentencing) Act 2000 or section 23(1) of the Children and Young Persons Act 1969; or
  (ii) the subject of a supervision order imposing a local authority residence requirement under paragraph 5 of Schedule 6 to that Act,

and with respect to whom they are the designated authority.

(3) Where a child has been –

- (a) removed under Part V; or
- (b) detained under section 38 of the Police and Criminal Evidence Act 1984,

and he is not being provided with accommodation by a local authority or in a hospital vested in the Secretary of State or a Primary Care Trust or otherwise made available pursuant to arrangements made by a Health Authority or a Primary Care Trust, any reasonable expenses of accommodating him shall be recoverable from the local authority in whose area he is ordinarily resident.

Duties of local authorities in relation to children looked after by them

22 General duty of local authority in relation to children looked after by them

(1) In this Act, any reference to a child who is looked after by a local authority is a reference to a child who is –

- (a) in their care; or
- (b) provided with accommodation by the authority in the exercise of any functions (in particular those under this Act) which are social services functions within the meaning of the Local Authority Social Services Act 1970, apart from functions under sections 17, 23B and 24B.

(2) In subsection (1) "accommodation" means accommodation which is provided for a continuous period of more than 24 hours.

(3) It shall be the duty of a local authority looking after any child –

- (a) to safeguard and promote his welfare; and
- (b) to make such use of services available for children cared for by their own parents as appears to the authority reasonable in his case.

(3A) The duty of a local authority under subsection (3)(a) to safeguard and promote the welfare of a child looked after by them includes in particular a duty to promote the child's educational achievement.

(4) Before making any decision with respect to a child whom they are looking after, or proposing to look after, a local authority shall, so far as is reasonably practicable, ascertain the wishes and feelings of –

- (a) the child;
- (b) his parents;
- (c) any person who is not a parent of his but who has parental responsibility for him; and
- (d) any other person whose wishes and feelings the authority consider to be relevant,

regarding the matter to be decided.

(5) In making any such decision a local authority shall give due consideration –

(a) having regard to his age and understanding, to such wishes and feelings of the child as they have been able to ascertain;
(b) to such wishes and feelings of any person mentioned in subsection (4)(b) to (d) as they have been able to ascertain; and
(c) to the child's religious persuasion, racial origin and cultural and linguistic background.

(6) If it appears to a local authority that it is necessary, for the purposes of protecting members of the public from serious injury, to exercise their powers with respect to a child whom they are looking after in a manner which may not be consistent with their duties under this section, they may do so.

(7) If the Secretary of State considers it necessary, for the purpose of protecting members of the public from serious injury, to give directions to a local authority with respect to the exercise of their powers with respect to a child whom they are looking after, he may give such directions to the authority.

(8) Where any such directions are given to an authority they shall comply with them even though doing so is inconsistent with their duties under this section.

23 Provision of accommodation and maintenance by local authority for children whom they are looking after

(1) It shall be the duty of any local authority looking after a child –

(a) when he is in their care, to provide accommodation for him; and
(b) to maintain him in other respects apart from providing accommodation for him.

(2) A local authority shall provide accommodation and maintenance for any child whom they are looking after by –

(a) placing him (subject to subsection (5) and any regulations made by the Secretary of State) with –
  (i) a family;
  (ii) a relative of his; or
  (iii) any other suitable person,

on such terms as to payment by the authority and otherwise as the authority may determine (subject to section 49 of the Children Act 2004);

(*aa*) maintaining him in an appropriate children's home;
(*f*) making such other arrangements as –
  (i) seem appropriate to them; and
  (ii) comply with any regulations made by the Secretary of State.

(2A) Where under subsection (2)(aa) a local authority maintains a child in a home provided, equipped and maintained by the Secretary of State under section 82(5), it shall do so on such terms as the Secretary of State may from time to time determine.

(3) Any person with whom a child has been placed under subsection (2)(*a*) is referred to in this Act as a local authority foster parent unless he falls within subsection (4).

(4) A person falls within this subsection if he is –

(a) a parent of the child;
(b) a person who is not a parent of the child but who has parental responsibility for him; or
(c) where the child is in care and there was a residence order in force with respect to him immediately before the care order was made, a person in whose favour the residence order was made.

(5) Where a child is in the care of a local authority, the authority may only allow him to live with a person who falls within subsection (4) in accordance with regulations made by the Secretary of State.

(5A) For the purposes of subsection (5) a child shall be regarded as living with a person if he stays with that person for a continuous period of more than 24 hours.

(6) Subject to any regulations made by the Secretary of State for the purposes of this subsection, any local authority looking after a child shall make arrangements to enable him to live with –

(a) a person falling within subsection (4); or
(b) a relative, friend or other person connected with him,

unless that would not be reasonably practicable or consistent with his welfare.

(7) Where a local authority provide accommodation for a child whom they are looking after, they shall, subject to the provisions of this Part and so far as is reasonably practicable and consistent with his welfare, secure that –

(a) the accommodation is near his home; and
(b) where the authority are also providing accommodation for a sibling of his, they are accommodated together.

(8) Where a local authority provide accommodation for a child whom they are looking after and who is disabled, they shall, so far as is reasonably practicable, secure that the accommodation is not unsuitable to his particular needs.

(9) Part II of Schedule 2 shall have effect for the purposes of making further provision as to children looked after by local authorities and in particular as to the regulations that may be made under subsections (2)(*a*) and (*f*) and (5).

(10) In this Act –

"appropriate children's home" means a children's home in respect of which a person is registered under Part II of the Care Standards Act 2000; and
"children's home" has the same meaning as in that Act.

Advice and assistance for certain children and young persons

23A The responsible authority and relevant children

(1) The responsible local authority shall have the functions set out in section 23B in respect of a relevant child.

(2) In subsection (1) "relevant child" means (subject to subsection (3)) a child who –

(a) is not being looked after by any local authority;

(b) was, before last ceasing to be looked after, an eligible child for the purposes of paragraph 19B of Schedule 2; and
(c) is aged sixteen or seventeen.

(3) The Secretary of State may prescribe –

(a) additional categories of relevant children; and
(b) categories of children who are not to be relevant children despite falling within subsection (2).

(4) In subsection (1) the "responsible local authority" is the one which last looked after the child.

(5) If under subsection (3)(*a*) the Secretary of State prescribes a category of relevant children which includes children who do not fall within subsection (2)(*b*) (for example, because they were being looked after by a local authority in Scotland), he may in the regulations also provide for which local authority is to be the responsible local authority for those children.

23B Additional functions of the responsible authority in respect of relevant children

(1) It is the duty of each local authority to take reasonable steps to keep in touch with a relevant child for whom they are the responsible authority, whether he is within their area or not.

(2) It is the duty of each local authority to appoint a personal adviser for each relevant child (if they have not already done so under paragraph 19C of Schedule 2).

(3) It is the duty of each local authority, in relation to any relevant child who does not already have a pathway plan prepared for the purposes of paragraph 19B of Schedule 2 –

(a) to carry out an assessment of his needs with a view to determining what advice, assistance and support it would be appropriate for them to provide him under this Part; and
(b) to prepare a pathway plan for him.

(4) The local authority may carry out such an assessment at the same time as any assessment of his needs is made under any enactment referred to in sub-paragraphs (a) to (c) of paragraph 3 of Schedule 2, or under any other enactment.

(5) The Secretary of State may by regulations make provision as to assessments for the purposes of subsection (3).

(6) The regulations may in particular make provision about –

(*a*) who is to be consulted in relation to an assessment;
(*b*) the way in which an assessment is to be carried out, by whom and when;
(*c*) the recording of the results of an assessment;
(*d*) the considerations to which the local authority are to have regard in carrying out an assessment.

(7) The authority shall keep the pathway plan under regular review.

(8) The responsible local authority shall safeguard and promote the child's welfare and, unless they are satisfied that his welfare does not require it, support him by –

(a) maintaining him;
(b) providing him with or maintaining him in suitable accommodation; and
(c) providing support of such other descriptions as may be prescribed.

(9) Support under subsection (8) may be in cash.

(10) The Secretary of State may by regulations make provision about the meaning of "suitable accommodation" and in particular about the suitability of landlords or other providers of accommodation.

(11) If the local authority have lost touch with a relevant child, despite taking reasonable steps to keep in touch, they must without delay –

(a) consider how to re-establish contact; and
(b) take reasonable steps to do so,

and while the child is still a relevant child must continue to take such steps until they succeed.

(12) Subsections (7) to (9) of section 17 apply in relation to support given under this section as they apply in relation to assistance given under that section.

(13) Subsections (4) and (5) of section 22 apply in relation to any decision by a local authority for the purposes of this section as they apply in relation to the decisions referred to in that section.

23C Continuing functions in respect of former relevant children

(1) Each local authority shall have the duties provided for in this section towards –

(a) a person who has been a relevant child for the purposes of section 23A (and would be one if he were under eighteen), and in relation to whom they were the last responsible authority; and
(b) a person who was being looked after by them when he attained the age of eighteen, and immediately before ceasing to be looked after was an eligible child,

and in this section such a person is referred to as a "former relevant child".

(2) It is the duty of the local authority to take reasonable steps –

(a) to keep in touch with a former relevant child whether he is within their area or not; and
(b) if they lose touch with him, to re-establish contact.

(3) It is the duty of the local authority –

(a) to continue the appointment of a personal adviser for a former relevant child; and
(b) to continue to keep his pathway plan under regular review.

(4) It is the duty of the local authority to give a former relevant child –

(a) assistance of the kind referred to in section 24B(1), to the extent that his welfare requires it;
(b) assistance of the kind referred to in section 24B(2), to the extent that his welfare and his educational or training needs require it;
(c) other assistance, to the extent that his welfare requires it.

(5) The assistance given under subsection (4)(c) may be in kind or, in exceptional circumstances, in cash.

(6) Subject to subsection (7), the duties set out in subsections (2), (3) and (4) subsist until the former relevant child reaches the age of twenty-one.

(7) If the former relevant child's pathway plan sets out a programme of education or training which extends beyond his twenty-first birthday –

(a) the duty set out in subsection (4)(b) continues to subsist for so long as the former relevant child continues to pursue that programme; and
(b) the duties set out in subsections (2) and (3) continue to subsist concurrently with that duty.

(8) For the purposes of subsection (7)(*a*) there shall be disregarded any interruption in a former relevant child's pursuance of a programme of education or training if the local authority are satisfied that he will resume it as soon as is reasonably practicable.

(9) Section 24B(5) applies in relation to a person being given assistance under subsection (4)(b) as it applies in relation to a person to whom section 24B(3) applies.

(10) Subsections (7) to (9) of section 17 apply in relation to assistance given under this section as they apply in relation to assistance given under that section.

Personal advisers and pathway plans

23D Personal advisers

(1) The Secretary of State may by regulations require local authorities to appoint a personal adviser for children or young persons of a prescribed description who have reached the age of sixteen but not the age of twenty-one who are not –

(a) children who are relevant children for the purposes of section 23A;
(b) the young persons referred to in section 23C; or
(c) the children referred to in paragraph 19C of Schedule 2.

(2) Personal advisers appointed under or by virtue of this Part shall (in addition to any other functions) have such functions as the Secretary of State prescribes.

23E Pathway plans

(1) In this Part, a reference to a "pathway plan" is to a plan setting out –

(a) in the case of a plan prepared under paragraph 19B of Schedule 2 –
   (i) the advice, assistance and support which the local authority intend to provide a child under this Part, both while they are looking after him and later; and
   (ii) when they might cease to look after him; and
(b) in the case of a plan prepared under section 23B, the advice, assistance and support which the local authority intend to provide under this Part,

and dealing with such other matters (if any) as may be prescribed.

(2) The Secretary of State may by regulations make provision about pathway plans and their review.

Advice and assistance for certain children and young persons

24 Persons qualifying for advice and assistance

(1) In this Part "a person qualifying for advice and assistance" means a person to whom subsection (1A) or (1B) applies.

(1A) This subsection applies to a person –

(a) who has reached the age of sixteen but not the age of twenty-one;
(b) with respect to whom a special guardianship order is in force (or, if he has reached the age of eighteen, was in force when he reached that age); and
(c) who was, immediately before the making of that order, looked after by a local authority.

(1B) This subsection applies to a person to whom subsection (1A) does not apply, and who –

(a) is under twenty-one; and
(b) at any time after reaching the age of sixteen but while still a child was, but is no longer, looked after, accommodated or fostered.

(2) In subsection (1B)(b), "looked after, accommodated or fostered" means –

(a) looked after by a local authority;
(b) accommodated by or on behalf of a voluntary organisation;
(c) accommodated in a registered children's home;
(d) accommodated for a consecutive period of at least three months –
   (i) by any Health Authority, Special Health Authority, Primary Care Trust or local education authority, or
   (ii) in any residential care home, nursing home or mental nursing home or in any accommodation provided by a National Health Service trust or an NHS foundation trust; or
(e) privately fostered.

(3) Subsection (2)(*d*) applies even if the period of three months mentioned there began before the child reached the age of sixteen.

(4) In the case of a person qualifying for advice and assistance by virtue of subsection (2)(*a*), it is the duty of the local authority which last looked after

him to take such steps as they think appropriate to contact him at such times as they think appropriate with a view to discharging their functions under sections 24A and 24B.

(5) In each of sections 24A and 24B, the local authority under the duty or having the power mentioned there ("the relevant authority") is –

(za) in the case of a person to whom subsection (1A) applies, a local authority determined in accordance with regulations made by the Secretary of State;

(a) in the case of a person qualifying for advice and assistance by virtue of subsection (2)(a), the local authority which last looked after him; or

(b) in the case of any other person qualifying for advice and assistance, the local authority within whose area the person is (if he has asked for help of a kind which can be given under section 24A or 24B).

24A Advice and assistance

(1) The relevant authority shall consider whether the conditions in subsection (2) are satisfied in relation to a person qualifying for advice and assistance.

(2) The conditions are that –

(a) he needs help of a kind which they can give under this section or section 24B; and

(b) in the case of a person to whom section 24(1A) applies, or to whom section 24(1B) applies and who was not being looked after by any local authority, they are satisfied that the person by whom he was being looked after does not have the necessary facilities for advising or befriending him.

(3) If the conditions are satisfied –

(a) they shall advise and befriend him if he is a person to whom section 24(1A) applies, or he is a person to whom section 24(1B) applies and he was being looked after by a local authority or was accommodated by or on behalf of a voluntary organisation; and

(b) in any other case they may do so.

(4) Where as a result of this section a local authority are under a duty, or are empowered, to advise and befriend a person, they may also give him assistance.

(5) The assistance may be in kind and, in exceptional circumstances, assistance may be given –

(a) by providing accommodation, if in the circumstances assistance may not be given in respect of the accommodation under section 24B, or

(b) in cash.

(6) Subsections (7) to (9) of section 17 apply in relation to assistance given under this section or section 24B as they apply in relation to assistance given under that section.

24B Employment, education and training

(1) The relevant local authority may give assistance to any person who qualifies for advice and assistance by virtue of section 24(1A) or section 24(2)(*a*) by contributing to expenses incurred by him in living near the place where he is, or will be, employed or seeking employment.

(2) The relevant local authority may give assistance to a person to whom subsection (3) applies by –

(a) contributing to expenses incurred by the person in question in living near the place where he is, or will be, receiving education or training; or

(b) making a grant to enable him to meet expenses connected with his education or training.

(3) This subsection applies to any person who –

(a) is under twenty-four; and

(b) qualifies for advice and assistance by virtue of section 24(1A) or section 24(2)(a), or would have done so if he were under twenty-one.

(4) Where a local authority are assisting a person under subsection (2) they may disregard any interruption in his attendance on the course if he resumes it as soon as is reasonably practicable.

(5) Where the local authority are satisfied that a person to whom subsection (3) applies who is in full-time further or higher education needs accommodation during a vacation because his term-time accommodation is not available to him then, they shall give him assistance by –

(a) providing him with suitable accommodation during the vacation; or

(b) paying him enough to enable him to secure such accommodation himself.

(6) The Secretary of State may prescribe the meaning of "full-time", "further education", "higher education" and "vacation" for the purposes of subsection (5).

24C Information

(1) Where it appears to a local authority that a person –

(a) with whom they are under a duty to keep in touch under section 23B, 23C or 24; or

(b) whom they have been advising and befriending under section 24A; or

(c) to whom they have been giving assistance under section 24B,

proposes to live, or is living, in the area of another local authority, they must inform that other authority.

(2) Where a child who is accommodated –

(a) by a voluntary organisation or in a registered children's home;

(b) by any Health Authority, Special Health Authority, Primary Care Trust or local education authority; or

(c) in any residential care home, nursing home or mental nursing home or any accommodation provided by a National Health Service trust or an NHS foundation trust,

ceases to be so accommodated, after reaching the age of sixteen, the organisation, authority or (as the case may be) person carrying on the home shall inform the local authority within whose area the child proposes to live.

(3) Subsection (2) only applies, by virtue of paragraph (b) or (c), if the accommodation has been provided for a consecutive period of at least three months.

24D Representations: sections 23A to 24B

(1) Every local authority shall establish a procedure for considering representations (including complaints) made to them by –

(a) a relevant child for the purposes of section 23A or a young person falling within section 23C;
(b) a person qualifying for advice and assistance; or
(c) a person falling within section 24B(2),

about the discharge of their functions under this Part in relation to him.

(1A) Regulations may be made by the Secretary of State imposing time limits on the making of representations under subsection (1).

(2) In considering representations under subsection (1), a local authority shall comply with regulations (if any) made by the Secretary of State for the purposes of this subsection.

Secure accommodation

25 Use of accommodation for restricting liberty

(1) Subject to the following provisions of this section, a child who is being looked after by a local authority may not be placed, and, if placed, may not be kept, in accommodation provided for the purpose of restricting liberty ("secure accommodation") unless it appears –

(a) that –
    (i) he has a history of absconding and is likely to abscond from any other description of accommodation; and
    (ii) if he absconds, he is likely to suffer significant harm, or
(b) that if he is kept in any other description of accommodation he is likely to injure himself or other persons.

(2) The Secretary of State may by regulations –

(a) specify a maximum period –
    (i) beyond which a child may not be kept in secure accommodation without the authority of the court; and
    (ii) for which the court may authorise a child to be kept in secure accommodation;

(b) empower the court from time to time to authorise a child to be kept in secure accommodation for such further period as the regulations may specify; and
(c) provide that applications to the court under this section shall be made only by local authorities.

(3) It shall be the duty of a court hearing an application under this section to determine whether any relevant criteria for keeping a child in secure accommodation are satisfied in his case.

(4) If a court determines that any such criteria are satisfied, it shall make an order authorising the child to be kept in secure accommodation and specifying the maximum period for which he may be so kept.

(5) On any adjournment of the hearing of an application under this section, a court may make an interim order permitting the child to be kept during the period of the adjournment in secure accommodation.

(6) No court shall exercise the powers conferred by this section in respect of a child who is not legally represented in that court unless, having been informed of his right to apply for representation funded by the Legal Services Commission as part of the Community Legal Service or Criminal Defence Service and having had the opportunity to do so, he refused or failed to apply.

(7) The Secretary of State may by regulations provide that –

(a) this section shall or shall not apply to any description of children specified in the regulations;
(b) this section shall have effect in relation to children of a description specified in the regulations subject to such modifications as may be so specified;
(c) such other provisions as may be so specified shall have effect for the purpose of determining whether a child of a description specified in the regulations may be placed or kept in secure accommodation.

(8) The giving of an authorisation under this section shall not prejudice any power of any court in England and Wales or Scotland to give directions relating to the child to whom the authorisation relates.

(9) This section is subject to section 20(8).

Supplemental

26 Review of cases and inquiries into representations

(1) The Secretary of State may make regulations requiring the case of each child who is being looked after by a local authority to be reviewed in accordance with the provisions of the regulations.

(2) The regulations may, in particular, make provision –

(a) as to the manner in which each case is to be reviewed;
(b) as to the considerations to which the local authority are to have regard in reviewing each case;

(c) as to the time when each case is first to be reviewed and the frequency of subsequent reviews;
(d) requiring the authority, before conducting any review, to seek the views of –
  (i) the child;
  (ii) his parents;
  (iii) any person who is not a parent of his but who has parental responsibility for him; and
  (iv) any other person whose views the authority consider to be relevant, including, in particular, the views of those persons in relation to any particular matter which is to be considered in the course of the review;
(e) requiring the authority, in the case of a child who is in their care –
  (i) to keep the section 31A plan for the child under review and, if they are of the opinion that some change is required, to revise the plan, or make a new plan, accordingly,
  (ii) to consider whether an application should be made to discharge the care order;
(f) requiring the authority, in the case of a child in accommodation provided by the authority –
  (i) if there is no plan for the future care of the child, to prepare one,
  (ii) if there is such a plan for the child, to keep it under review and, if they are of the opinion that some change is required, to revise the plan or make a new plan, accordingly,
  (iii) to consider whether the accommodation accords with the requirements of this Part;
(g) requiring the authority to inform the child, so far as is reasonably practicable, of any steps he may take under this Act;
(h) requiring the authority to make arrangements, including arrangements with such other bodies providing services as it considers appropriate, to implement any decision which they propose to make in the course, or as a result, of the review;
(i) requiring the authority to notify details of the result of the review and of any decision taken by them in consequence of the review to –
  (i) the child;
  (ii) his parents;
  (iii) any person who is not a parent of his but who has had parental responsibility for him; and
  (iv) any other person whom they consider ought to be notified;
(j) requiring the authority to monitor the arrangements which they have made with a view to ensuring that they comply with the regulations;
(k) for the authority to appoint a person in respect of each case to carry out in the prescribed manner the functions mentioned in subsection (2A) and any prescribed function.

(2A) The functions referred to in subsection (2)(k) are –

(a) participating in the review of the case in question,
(b) monitoring the performance of the authority's functions in respect of the review,
(c) referring the case to an officer of the Children and Family Court

Advisory and Support Service, if the person appointed under subsection (2)(k) considers it appropriate to do so.

(2B) A person appointed under subsection (2)(k) must be a person of a prescribed description.

(2C) In relation to children whose cases are referred to officers under subsection (2A)(c), the Lord Chancellor may by regulations –

- (a) extend any functions of the officers in respect of family proceedings (within the meaning of section 12 of the Criminal Justice and Court Services Act 2000) to other proceedings,
- (b) require any functions of the officers to be performed in the manner prescribed by the regulations.

(3) Every local authority shall establish a procedure for considering any representations (including any complaint) made to them by –

- (a) any child who is being looked after by them or who is not being looked after by them but is in need;
- (b) a parent of his;
- (c) any person who is not a parent of his but who has parental responsibility for him;
- (d) any local authority foster parent;
- (e) such other person as the authority consider has a sufficient interest in the child's welfare to warrant his representations being considered by them,

about the discharge of the authority of any of their qualifying functions in relation to the child.

(3A) The following are qualifying functions for the purposes of subsection (3) –

- (a) functions under this Part,
- (b) such functions under Part 4 or 5 as are specified by the Secretary of State in regulations.

(3B) The duty under subsection (3) extends to representations (including complaints) made to the authority by –

- (a) any person mentioned in section 3(1) of the Adoption and Children Act 2002 (persons for whose needs provision is made by the Adoption Service) and any other person to whom arrangements for the provision of adoption support services (within the meaning of that Act) extend,
- (b) such other person as the authority consider has sufficient interest in a child who is or may be adopted to warrant his representations being considered by them,

about the discharge by the authority of such functions under the Adoption and Children Act 2002 as are specified by the Secretary of State in regulations.

(3C) The duty under subsection (3) extends to any representations (including complaints) which are made to the authority by –

- (a) a child with respect to whom a special guardianship order is in force,
- (b) a special guardian or a parent of such a child,

(c) any other person the authority consider has a sufficient interest in the welfare of such a child to warrant his representations being considered by them, or
(d) any person who has applied for an assessment under section 14F(3) or (4), about the discharge by the authority of such functions under section 14F as may be specified by the Secretary of State in regulations.

(4) The procedure shall ensure that at least one person who is not a member or officer of the authority takes part in –

(a) the consideration; and
(b) any discussions which are held by the authority about the action (if any) to be taken in relation to the child in the light of the consideration

but this subsection is subject to subsection (5A).

(4A) Regulations may be made by the Secretary of State imposing time limits on the making of representations under this section.

(5) In carrying out any consideration of representations under this section a local authority shall comply with any regulations made by the Secretary of State for the purpose of regulating the procedure to be followed.

(5A) Regulations under subsection (5) may provide that subsection (4) does not apply in relation to any consideration or discussion which takes place as part of a procedure for which provision is made by the regulations for the purpose of resolving informally the matters raised in the representations.

(6) The Secretary of State may make regulations requiring local authorities to monitor the arrangements that they have made with a view to ensuring that they comply with any regulations made for the purposes of subsection (5).

(7) Where any representation has been considered under the procedure established by a local authority under this section, the authority shall –

(a) have due regard to the findings of those considering the representation; and
(b) take such steps as are reasonably practicable to notify (in writing) –
   (i) the person making the representation;
   (ii) the child (if the authority consider that he has sufficient understanding); and
   (iii) such other persons (if any) as appear to the authority to be likely to be affected,

of the authority's decision in the matter and their reasons for taking that decision and of any action which they have taken, or propose to take.

(8) Every local authority shall give such publicity to their procedure for considering representations under this section as they consider appropriate.

26A Advocacy services

(1) Every local authority shall make arrangements for the provision of assistance to –

(a) persons who make or intend to make representations under section 24D; and
(b) children who make or intend to make representations under section 26.

(2) The assistance provided under the arrangements shall include assistance by way of representation.

(3) The arrangements –

(a) shall secure that a person may not provide assistance if he is a person who is prevented from doing so by regulations made by the Secretary of State; and
(b) shall comply with any other provision made by the regulations in relation to the arrangements.

(4) The Secretary of State may make regulations requiring local authorities to monitor the steps that they have taken with a view to ensuring that they comply with regulations made for the purposes of subsection (3).

(5) Every local authority shall give such publicity to their arrangements for the provision of assistance under this section as they consider appropriate.

27 Co-operation between authorities

(1) Where it appears to a local authority that any authority mentioned in subsection (3) could, by taking any specified action, help in the exercise of any of their functions under this Part, they may request the help of that other authority, specifying the action in question.

(2) An authority whose help is so requested shall comply with the request if it is compatible with their own statutory or other duties and obligations and does not unduly prejudice the discharge of any of their functions.

(3) The authorities are –

(a) any local authority;
(b) any local education authority;
(c) any local housing authority;
(d) any Health Authority, Special Health Authority, Primary Care Trust, National Health Service trust or NHS foundation trust; and
(e) any person authorised by the Secretary of State for the purposes of this section.

28 Consultation with local education authorities

(1) Where –

(a) a child is being looked after by a local authority; and
(b) the authority propose to provide accommodation for him in an establishment at which education is provided for children who are accommodated there,

they shall, so far as is reasonably practicable, consult the appropriate local education authority before doing so.

(2) Where any such proposal is carried out, the local authority shall, as soon as is reasonably practicable, inform the appropriate local education authority of the arrangements that have been made for the child's accommodation.

(3) Where the child ceases to be accommodated as mentioned in subsection (1)(b), the local authority shall inform the appropriate local education authority.

(4) In this section "the appropriate local education authority" means –

- (a) the local education authority within whose area the local authority's area falls; or
- (b) where the child has special educational needs and a statement of his needs is maintained under Part IV of the Education Act 1996, the local education authority who maintain the statement.

29 Recoupment of cost of providing services etc

(1) Where a local authority provide any service under section 17 or 18, other than advice, guidance or counselling, they may recover from a person specified in subsection (4) such charge for the service as they consider reasonable.

(2) Where the authority are satisfied that that person's means are insufficient for it to be reasonably practicable for him to pay the charge, they shall not require him to pay more than he can reasonably be expected to pay.

(3) No person shall be liable to pay any charge under subsection (1) for a service provided under section 17 or section 18(1) or (5) at any time when he is in receipt of income support under Part VII of the Social Security Contributions and Benefits Act 1992, of any element of child tax credit other than the family element, of working tax credit or of an income-based jobseeker's allowance.

(3A) No person shall be liable to pay any charge under subsection (1) for a service provided under section 18(2) or (6) at any time when he is in receipt of income support under Part VII of the Social Security and Benefits Act 1992 or of an income-based jobseeker's allowance.

(4) The persons are –

- (a) where the service is provided for a child under sixteen, each of his parents;
- (b) where it is provided for a child who has reached the age of sixteen, the child himself; and
- (c) where it is provided for a member of the child's family, that member.

(5) Any charge under subsection (1) may, without prejudice to any other method of recovery, be recovered summarily as a civil debt.

(6) Part III of Schedule 2 makes provision in connection with contributions towards the maintenance of children who are being looked after by local authorities and consists of the re-enactment with modifications of provisions in Part V of the Child Care Act 1980.

(7) Where a local authority provide any accommodation under section 20(1) for a child who was (immediately before they began to look after him)

ordinarily resident within the area of another local authority, they may recover from that other authority any reasonable expenses incurred by them in providing the accommodation and maintaining him.

(8) Where a local authority provide accommodation under section 21(1) or (2)(a) or (b) for a child who is ordinarily resident within the area of another local authority and they are not maintaining him in –

(a) a community home provided by them;
(b) a controlled community home; or
(c) a hospital vested in the Secretary of State or a Primary Care Trust, or any other hospital made available pursuant to arrangements made by a Strategic Health Authority, Health Authority or a Primary Care Trust,

they may recover from that other authority any reasonable expenses incurred by them in providing the accommodation and maintaining him.

(9) Except where subsection (10) applies, where a local authority comply with any request under section 27(2) in relation to a child or other person who is not ordinarily resident within their area, they may recover from the local authority in whose area the child or person is ordinarily resident any reasonable expenses incurred by them in respect of that person.

(10) Where a local authority ("authority A") comply with any request under section 27(2) from another local authority ("authority B") in relation to a child or other person –

(a) whose responsible authority is authority B for the purposes of section 23B or 23C; or
(b) whom authority B are advising or befriending or to whom they are giving assistance by virtue of section 24(5)(a),

authority A may recover from authority B any reasonable expenses incurred by them in respect of that person.

30 Miscellaneous

(1) Nothing in this Part shall affect any duty imposed on a local authority by or under any other enactment.

(2) Any question arising under section 20(2), 21(3) or 29(7) to (9) as to the ordinary residence of a child shall be determined by agreement between the local authorities concerned or, in default of agreement, by the Secretary of State.

(3) Where the functions conferred on a local authority by this Part and the functions of a local education authority are concurrent, the Secretary of State may by regulations provide by which authority the functions are to be exercised.

(4) The Secretary of State may make regulations for determining, as respects any local education authority functions specified in the regulations, whether a child who is being looked after by a local authority is to be treated, for purposes so specified, as a child of parents of sufficient resources or as a child of parents without resources.

Part IV
Care and Supervision

General

31 Care and supervision orders

(1) On the application of any local authority or authorised person, the court may make an order –

(a) placing the child with respect to whom the application is made in the care of a designated local authority; or
(b) putting him under the supervision of a designated local authority.

(2) A court may only make a care order or supervision order if it is satisfied –

(a) that the child concerned is suffering, or is likely to suffer, significant harm; and
(b) that the harm, or likelihood of harm, is attributable to –
 (i) the care given to the child, or likely to be given to him if the order were not made, not being what it would be reasonable to expect a parent to give to him; or
 (ii) the child's being beyond parental control.

(3) No care order or supervision order may be made with respect to a child who has reached the age of seventeen (or sixteen, in the case of a child who is married).

(3A) No care order may be made with respect to a child until the court has considered a section 31A plan.

(4) An application under this section may be made on its own or in any other family proceedings.

(5) The court may –

(a) on an application for a care order, make a supervision order;
(b) on an application for a supervision order, make a care order.

(6) Where an authorised person proposes to make an application under this section he shall –

(a) if it is reasonably practicable to do so; and
(b) before making the application,

consult the local authority appearing to him to be the authority in whose area the child concerned is ordinarily resident.

(7) An application made by an authorised person shall not be entertained by the court if, at the time when it is made, the child concerned is –

(a) the subject of an earlier application for a care order, or supervision order, which has not been disposed of; or
(b) subject to –
 (i) a care order or supervision order;
 (ii) an order under section 63(1) of the Powers of Criminal Courts (Sentencing) Act 2000; or

(iii) a supervision requirement within the meaning of Part II of the Children (Scotland) Act 1995.

(8) The local authority designated in a care order must be –

(a) the authority within whose area the child is ordinarily resident; or
(b) where the child does not reside in the area of a local authority, the authority within whose area any circumstances arose in consequence of which the order is being made.

(9) In this section –

"authorised person" means –
(a) the National Society for the Prevention of Cruelty to Children and any of its officers; and
(b) any person authorised by order of the Secretary of State to bring proceedings under this section and any officer of a body which is so authorised;

"harm" means ill-treatment or the impairment of health or development including, for example, impairment suffered from seeing or hearing the ill-treatment of another;
"development" means physical, intellectual, emotional, social or behavioural development;
"health" means physical or mental health; and
"ill-treatment" includes sexual abuse and forms of ill-treatment which are not physical.

(10) Where the question of whether harm suffered by a child is significant turns on the child's health or development, his health or development shall be compared with that which could reasonably be expected of a similar child.

(11) In this Act –

"a care order" means (subject to section 105(1)) an order under subsection (1)(*a*) and (except where express provision to the contrary is made) includes an interim care order made under section 38; and
"a supervision order" means an order under subsection (1)(b) and (except where express provision to the contrary is made) includes an interim supervision order made under section 38.

31A Care orders: care plans

(1) Where an application is made on which a care order might be made with respect to a child, the appropriate local authority must, within such time as the court may direct, prepare a plan ("a care plan") for the future care of the child.

(2) While the application is pending, the authority must keep any care plan prepared by them under review and, if they are of the opinion some change is required, revise the plan, or make a new plan, accordingly.

(3) A care plan must give any prescribed information and do so in the prescribed manner.

(4) For the purposes of this section, the appropriate local authority, in relation to a child in respect of whom a care order might be made, is the local authority proposed to be designated in the order.

(5) In section 31(3A) and this section, references to a care order do not include an interim care order.

(6) A plan prepared, or treated as prepared, under this section is referred to in this Act as a "section 31A plan".

32 Period within which application for order under this Part must be disposed of

(1) A court hearing an application for an order under this Part shall (in the light of any rules made by virtue of subsection (2)) –

(a) draw up a timetable with a view to disposing of the application without delay; and
(b) give such directions as it considers appropriate for the purpose of ensuring, so far as is reasonably practicable, that that timetable is adhered to.

(2) Rules of court may –

(a) specify periods within which specified steps must be taken in relation to such proceedings; and
(b) make other provision with respect to such proceedings for the purpose of ensuring, so far as is reasonably practicable, that they are disposed of without delay.

Care orders

33 Effect of care order

(1) Where a care order is made with respect to a child it shall be the duty of the local authority designated by the order to receive the child into their care and to keep him in their care while the order remains in force.

(2) Where –

(a) a care order has been made with respect to a child on the application of an authorised person; but
(b) the local authority designated by the order was not informed that that person proposed to make the application,

the child may be kept in the care of that person until received into the care of the authority.

(3) While a care order is in force with respect to a child, the local authority designated by the order shall –

(a) have parental responsibility for the child; and
(b) have the power (subject to the following provisions of this section) to determine the extent to which
  (i) a parent, guardian or special guardian of the child; or
  (ii) a person who by virtue of section 4A has parental responsibility for the child

may meet his parental responsibility for him.

(4) The authority may not exercise the power in subsection (3)(b) unless they are satisfied that it is necessary to do so in order to safeguard or promote the child's welfare.

(5) Nothing in subsection (3)(b) shall prevent a person mentioned in that provision who has care of the child from doing what is reasonable in all the circumstances of the case for the purpose of safeguarding or promoting his welfare.

(6) While a care order is in force with respect to a child, the local authority designated by the order shall not –

(a) cause the child to be brought up in any religious persuasion other than that in which he would have been brought up if the order had not been made; or
(b) have the right –
  (i) (*repealed*)
  (ii) to agree or refuse to agree to the making of an adoption order, or an order under section 84 of the Adoption and Children Act 2002, with respect to the child; or
  (iii) to appoint a guardian for the child.

(7) While a care order is in force with respect to a child, no person may –

(a) cause the child to be known by a new surname; or
(b) remove him from the United Kingdom,

without either the written consent of every person who has parental responsibility for the child or the leave of the court.

(8) Subsection (7)(b) does not –

(a) prevent the removal of such a child, for a period of less than one month, by the authority in whose care he is; or
(b) apply to arrangements for such a child to live outside England and Wales (which are governed by paragraph 19 of Schedule 2).

(9) The power in subsection (3)(b) is subject (in addition to being subject to the provisions of this section) to any right, duty, power, responsibility or authority which a person mentioned in that provision has in relation to the child and his property by virtue of any other enactment.

34 Parental contact etc with children in care

(1) Where a child is in the care of a local authority, the authority shall (subject to the provisions of this section) allow the child reasonable contact with –

(a) his parents;
(b) any guardian or special guardian of his;
(ba) any person who by virtue of section 4A has parental responsibility for him;
(c) where there was a residence order in force with respect to the child immediately before the care order was made, the person in whose favour the order was made; and
(d) where, immediately before the care order was made, a person had

care of the child by virtue of an order made in the exercise of the High Court's inherent jurisdiction with respect to children, that person.

(2) On an application made by the authority or the child, the court may make such order as it considers appropriate with respect to the contact which is to be allowed between the child and any named person.

(3) On an application made by –

(a) any person mentioned in paragraph (a) to (d) of subsection (1); or
(b) any person who has obtained the leave of the court to make the application,

the court may make such order as it considers appropriate with respect to the contact which is to be allowed between the child and that person.

(4) On an application made by the authority or the child, the court may make an order authorising the authority to refuse to allow contact between the child and any person who is mentioned in paragraphs (a) to (d) of subsection (1) and named in the order.

(5) When making a care order with respect to a child, or in any family proceedings in connection with a child who is in the care of a local authority, the court may make an order under this section, even though no application for such an order has been made with respect to the child, if it considers that the order should be made.

(6) An authority may refuse to allow the contact that would otherwise be required by virtue of subsection (1) or an order under this section if –

(a) they are satisfied that it is necessary to do so in order to safeguard or promote the child's welfare; and
(b) the refusal –
  (i) is decided upon as a matter of urgency; and
  (ii) does not last for more than seven days.

(7) An order under this section may impose such conditions as the court considers appropriate.

(8) The Secretary of State may by regulations make provision as to –

(a) the steps to be taken by a local authority who have exercised their power under subsection (6);
(b) the circumstances in which, and conditions subject to which, the terms of any order under this section may be departed from by agreement between the local authority and the person in relation to whom the order is made;
(c) notification by a local authority of any variation or suspension of arrangements made (otherwise than under an order under this section) with a view to affording any person contact with a child to whom this section applies.

(9) The court may vary or discharge any order made under this section on the application of the authority, the child concerned or the person named in the order.

(10) An order under this section may be made either at the same time as the care order itself or later.

(11) Before making a care order with respect to any child the court shall –

(a) consider the arrangements which the authority have made, or propose to make, for affording any person contact with a child to whom this section applies; and

(b) invite the parties to the proceedings to comment on those arrangements.

Supervision orders

35 Supervision orders

(1) While a supervision order is in force it shall be the duty of the supervisor –

(a) to advise, assist and befriend the supervised child;

(b) to take such steps as are reasonably necessary to give effect to the order; and

(c) where –

(i) the order is not wholly complied with; or

(ii) the supervisor considers that the order may no longer be necessary,

to consider whether or not to apply to the court for its variation or discharge.

(2) Parts I and II of Schedule 3 make further provision with respect to supervision orders.

36 Education supervision orders

(1) On the application of any local education authority, the court may make an order putting the child with respect to whom the application is made under the supervision of a designated local education authority.

(2) In this Act "an education supervision order" means an order under subsection (1).

(3) A court may only make an education supervision order if it is satisfied that the child concerned is of compulsory school age and is not being properly educated.

(4) For the purposes of this section, a child is being properly educated only if he is receiving efficient full-time education suitable to his age, ability and aptitude and any special educational needs he may have.

(5) Where a child is –

(a) the subject of a school attendance order which is in force under section 437 of the Education Act 1996 and which has not been complied with; or

(b) is not attending regularly within the meaning of section 444 of that Act –

(i) a school at which he is a registered pupil,

(ii) any place at which education is provided for him in the circumstances mentioned in subsection (1) of section 444ZA of that Act, or
(iii) any place which he is required to attend in the circumstances mentioned in subsection (2) of that section,

then, unless it is proved that he is being properly educated, it shall be assumed that he is not.

(6) An education supervision order may not be made with respect to a child who is in the care of a local authority.

(7) The local education authority designated in an education supervision order must be –

(a) the authority within whose area the child concerned is living or will live; or
(b) where –
   (i) the child is a registered pupil at a school; and
   (ii) the authority mentioned in paragraph (a) and the authority within whose area the school is situated agree,

the latter authority.

(8) Where a local education authority propose to make an application for an education supervision order they shall, before making the application, consult the appropriate local authority.

(9) The appropriate local authority is –

(a) in the case of a child who is being provided with accommodation by, or on behalf of, a local authority, that authority; and
(b) in any other case, the local authority within whose area the child concerned lives, or will live.

(10) Part III of Schedule 3 makes further provision with respect to education supervision orders.

Powers of court

37 Powers of court in certain family proceedings

(1) Where, in any family proceedings in which a question arises with respect to the welfare of any child, it appears to the court that it may be appropriate for a care or supervision order to be made with respect to him, the court may direct the appropriate authority to undertake an investigation of the child's circumstances.

(2) Where the court gives a direction under this section the local authority concerned shall, when undertaking the investigation, consider whether they should –

(a) apply for a care order or for a supervision order with respect to the child;
(b) provide services or assistance for the child or his family; or
(c) take any other action with respect to the child.

(3) Where a local authority undertake an investigation under this section, and decide not to apply for a care order or supervision order with respect to the child concerned, they shall inform the court of –

(a) their reasons for so deciding;
(b) any service or assistance which they have provided, or to intend to provide, for the child and his family; and
(c) any other action which they have taken, or propose to take, with respect to the child.

(4) The information shall be given to the court before the end of the period of eight weeks beginning with the date of the direction, unless the court otherwise directs.

(5) The local authority named in a direction under subsection (1) must be –

(a) the authority in whose area the child is ordinarily resident; or
(b) where the child is not ordinarily resident in the area of a local authority, the authority within whose area any circumstances arose in consequence of which the direction is being given.

(6) If, on the conclusion of any investigation or review under this section, the authority decide not to apply for a care order or supervision order with respect to the child –

(a) they shall consider whether it would be appropriate to review the case at a later date; and
(b) if they decide that it would be, they shall determine the date on which that review is to begin.

38 Interim orders

(1) Where –

(a) in any proceedings on an application for a care order or supervision order, the proceedings are adjourned; or
(b) the court gives a direction under section 37(1).

the court may make an interim care order or an interim supervision order with respect to the child concerned.

(2) A court shall not make an interim care order or interim supervision order under this section unless it is satisfied that there are reasonable grounds for believing that circumstances with respect to the child are as mentioned in section 31(2).

(3) Where, in any proceedings on an application for a care order or supervision order, a court makes a residence order with respect to the child concerned, it shall also make an interim supervision order with respect to him unless satisfied that his welfare will be satisfactorily safeguarded without an interim order being made.

(4) An interim order made under or by virtue of this section shall have effect for such period as may be specified in the order, but shall in any event cease to have effect on whichever of the following events first occurs –

(a) the expiry of the period of eight weeks beginning with the date on which the order is made;
(b) if the order is the second or subsequent such order made with respect to the same child in the same proceedings, the expiry of the relevant period;
(c) in a case which falls within subsection (1)(a), the disposal of the application;
(d) in a case which falls within subsection (1)(b), the disposal of an application for a care order or a supervision order made by the authority with respect to the child;
(e) in a case which falls within subsection (1)(b) and in which –
    (i) the court has given a direction under section 37(4), but
    (ii) no application for a care order or supervision order has been made with respect to the child,

the expiry of the period fixed by that direction.

(5) In subsection (4)(b) "the relevant period" means –

(a) the period of four weeks beginning with the date on which the order in question is made; or
(b) the period of eight weeks beginning with the date on which the first order was made if that period ends later than the period mentioned in paragraph (a).

(6) Where the court makes an interim care order, or interim supervision order, it may give such directions (if any) as it considers appropriate with regard to the medical or psychiatric examination or other assessment of the child; but if the child is of sufficient understanding to make an informed decision he may refuse to submit to the examination or other assessment.

(7) A direction under subsection (6) may be to the effect that there is to be –

(a) no such examination or assessment; or
(*b*) no such examination or assessment unless the court directs otherwise.

(8) A direction under subsection (6) may be –

(a) given when the interim order is made or at any time while it is in force; and
(b) varied at any time on the application of any person falling within any class of person prescribed by rules of court for the purposes of this subsection.

(9) Paragraphs 4 and 5 of Schedule 3 shall not apply in relation to an interim supervision order.

(10) Where a court makes an order under or by virtue of this section it shall, in determining the period for which the order is to be in force, consider whether any party who was, or might have been, opposed to the making of the order was in a position to argue his case against the order in full.

38A Power to include exclusion requirement in interim care order

(1) Where –

(a) on being satisfied that there are reasonable grounds for believing that the circumstances with respect to a child are as mentioned in section 31(2)(a) and (b)(i), the court makes an interim care order with respect to a child, and
(b) the conditions mentioned in subsection (2) are satisfied,

the court may include an exclusion requirement in the interim care order.

(2) The conditions are –
(a) that there is reasonable cause to believe that, if a person ("the relevant person") is excluded from a dwelling-house in which the child lives, the child will cease to suffer, or cease to be likely to suffer, significant harm, and
(b) that another person living in the dwelling-house (whether a parent of the child or some other person) –
(i) is able and willing to give to the child the care which it would be reasonable to expect a parent to give him, and
(ii) consents to the inclusion of the exclusion requirement.

(3) For the purposes of this section an exclusion requirement is any one or more of the following –
(a) a provision requiring the relevant person to leave a dwelling-house in which he is living with the child,
(b) a provision prohibiting the relevant person from entering a dwelling-house in which the child lives, and
(c) a provision excluding the relevant person from a defined area in which a dwelling-house in which the child lives is situated.

(4) The court may provide that the exclusion requirement is to have effect for a shorter period than the other provisions of the interim care order.

(5) Where the court makes an interim care order containing an exclusion requirement, the court may attach a power of arrest to the exclusion requirement.

(6) Where the court attaches a power of arrest to an exclusion requirement of an interim care order, it may provide that the power of arrest is to have effect for a shorter period than the exclusion requirement.

(7) Any period specified for the purposes of subsection (4) or (6) may be extended by the court (on one or more occasions) on an application to vary or discharge the interim care order.

(8) Where a power of arrest is attached to an exclusion requirement of an interim care order by virtue of subsection (5), a constable may arrest without warrant any person whom he has reasonable cause to believe to be in breach of the requirement.

(9) Sections 47(7), (11) and (12) and 48 of, and Schedule 5 to, the Family Law Act 1996 shall have effect in relation to a person arrested under subsection (8) of this section as they have effect in relation to a person arrested under section 47(6) of that Act.

(10) If, while an interim care order containing an exclusion requirement is in force, the local authority have removed the child from the dwelling-house from

which the relevant person is excluded to other accommodation for a continuous period of more than 24 hours, the interim care order shall cease to have effect in so far as it imposes the exclusion requirement.

38B Undertakings relating to interim care orders

(1) In any case where the court has power to include an exclusion requirement in an interim care order, the court may accept an undertaking from the relevant person.

(2) No power of arrest may be attached to any undertaking given under subsection (1).

(3) An undertaking given to a court under subsection (1) –

- (a) shall be enforceable as if it were an order of the court, and
- (b) shall cease to have effect if, while it is in force, the local authority have removed the child from the dwelling-house from which the relevant person is excluded to other accommodation for a continuous period of more than 24 hours.

(4) This section has effect without prejudice to the powers of the High Court and county court apart from this section.

(5) In this section "exclusion requirement" and "relevant person" have the same meaning as in section 38A.

39 Discharge and variation etc of care orders and supervision orders

(1) A care order may be discharged by the court on the application of –

- (a) any person who has parental responsibility for the child;
- (b) the child himself; or
- (c) the local authority designated by the order.

(2) A supervision order may be varied or discharged by the court on the application of –

- (a) any person who has parental responsibility for the child;
- (b) the child himself; or
- (c) the supervisor.

(3) On the application of a person who is not entitled to apply for the order to be discharged, but who is a person with whom the child is living, a supervision order may be varied by the court in so far as it imposes a requirement which affects that person.

(3A) On the application of a person who is not entitled to apply for the order to be discharged, but who is a person to whom an exclusion requirement contained in the order applies, an interim care order may be varied or discharged by the court in so far as it imposes the exclusion requirement.

(3B) Where a power of arrest has been attached to an exclusion requirement of an interim care order, the court may, on the application of any person entitled to apply for the discharge of the order so far as it imposes the exclusion requirement, vary or discharge the order in so far as it confers a power of arrest (whether or not any application has been made to vary or discharge any other provision of the order).

(4) Where a care order is in force with respect to a child the court may, on the application of any person entitled to apply for the order to be discharged, substitute a supervision order for the care order.

(5) When a court is considering whether to substitute one order for another under subsection (4) any provision of this Act which would otherwise require section 31(2) to be satisfied at the time when the proposed order is substituted or made shall be disregarded.

40 Orders pending appeals in cases about care or supervision orders

(1) Where –

(a) a court dismisses an application for a care order; and
(b) at the time when the court dismisses the application, the child concerned is the subject of an interim care order,

the court may make a care order with respect to the child to have effect subject to such directions (if any) as the court may see fit to include in the order.

(2) Where –

(a) a court dismisses an application for a care order, or an application for a supervision order; and
(b) at the time when the court dismisses the application, the child concerned is the subject of an interim supervision order,

the court may make a supervision order with respect to the child to have effect subject to such directions (if any) as the court sees fit to include in the order.

(3) Where a court grants an application to discharge a care order or supervision order, it may order that –

(a) its decision is not to have effect; or
(b) the care order, or supervision order, is to continue to have effect but subject to such directions as the court sees fit to include in the order.

(4) An order made under this section shall only have effect for such a period, not exceeding the appeal period, as may be specified in the order.

(5) Where –

(a) an appeal is made against any decision of a court under this section; or
(b) any application is made to the appellate court in connection with a proposed appeal against that decision,

the appellate court may extend the period for which the order in question is to have effect, but not so as to extend it beyond the end of the appeal period.

(6) In this section "the appeal period" means –

(a) where an appeal is made against the decision in question, the period between the making of that decision and the determination of the appeal; and

(b) otherwise, the period during which an appeal may be made against the decision.

Representation of child

41 Representation of child and of his interests in certain proceedings

(1) For the purpose of any specified proceedings, the court shall appoint an officer of the Service or a Welsh family proceedings officer for the child concerned unless satisfied that it is not necessary to do so in order to safeguard his interests.

(2) The officer of the Service or a Welsh family proceedings officer shall –

(a) be appointed in accordance with rules of court; and
(b) be under a duty to safeguard the interests of the child in the manner prescribed by such rules.

(3) Where –

(*a*) the child concerned is not represented by a solicitor; and
(*b*) any of the conditions mentioned in subsection (4) is satisfied,

the court may appoint a solicitor to represent him.

(4) The conditions are that –

(a) no officer of the Service or Welsh family proceedings officer has been appointed for the child;
(b) the child has sufficient understanding to instruct a solicitor and wishes to do so;
(c) it appears to the court that it would be in the child's best interests for him to be represented by a solicitor.

(5) Any solicitor appointed under or by virtue of this section shall be appointed, and shall represent the child, in accordance with rules of court.

(6) In this section "specified proceedings" means any proceedings –

(a) on an application for a care order or supervision order;
(b) in which the court has given a direction under section 37(1) and has made, or is considering whether to make, an interim care order;
(c) on an application for the discharge of a care order or the variation or discharge of a supervision order;
(d) on an application under section 39(4);
(e) in which the court is considering whether to make a residence order with respect to a child who is the subject of a care order;
(f) with respect to contact between a child who is the subject of a care order and any other person;
(g) under Part V;
(h) on an appeal against –
  (i) the making of, or refusal to make, a care order, supervision order or any order under section 34;
  (ii) the making of, or refusal to make, a residence order with respect to a child who is the subject of a care order; or

(iii) the variation or discharge of, or refusal of an application to vary or discharge, an order of a kind mentioned in sub-paragraph (i) or (ii);
(iv) the refusal of an application under section 39(4);
(v) the making of, or refusal to make, an order under Part V;

(hh) on an application for the making or revocation of a placement order (within the meaning of section 21 of the Adoption and Children Act 2002); or

(i) which are specified for the time being, for the purposes of this section, by rules of court.

(6A) The proceedings which may be specified under subsection (6)(i) include (for example) proceedings for the making, varying or discharging of a section 8 order.

(10) Rules of court may make this provision as to –

(a) the assistance which any officer of the Service or Welsh family proceedings officer may be required by the court to give to it;
(b) the consideration to be given by any officer of the Service or Welsh family proceedings officer, where an order of a specified kind has been made in the proceedings in question, as to whether to apply for the variation or discharge of the order;
(c) the participation of officers of the Service or Welsh family proceedings officers in reviews, of a kind specified in the rules, which are conducted by the court.

(11) Regardless of any enactment or rule of law which would otherwise prevent it from doing so, the court may take account of –

(a) any statement contained in a report made by an officer of the Service or a Welsh family proceedings officer who is appointed under this section for the purpose of the proceedings in question; and
(b) any evidence given in respect of the matters referred to in the report,

in so far as the statement or evidence is, in the opinion of the court, relevant to the question which the court is considering.

42 Right of officer of the Service to have access to local authority records

(1) Where an officer of the Service or Welsh family proceedings officer has been appointed under section 41 he shall have the right at all reasonable times to examine and take copies of –

(a) any records of, or held by, a local authority or an authorised person which were compiled in connection with the making, or proposed making, by any person of any application under this Act with respect to the child concerned;
(b) any records of, or held by, a local authority which were compiled in connection with any functions which are social services functions within the meaning of the Local Authority Social Services Act 1970, so far as those records relate to that child; or

(c) any records of, or held by, an authorised person which were compiled in connection with the activities of that person, so far as those records relate to that child.

(2) Where an officer of the Service or Welsh family proceedings officer takes a copy of any record which he is entitled to examine under this section, that copy or any part of it shall be admissible as evidence of any matter referred to in any –

(a) report which he makes to the court in the proceedings in question; or
(b) evidence which he gives in those proceedings.

(3) Subsection (2) has effect regardless of any enactment or rule of law which would otherwise prevent the record in question being admissible in evidence.

(4) In this section "authorised person" has the same meaning as in section 31.

Part V
Protection of Children

43 Child assessment orders

(1) On the application of a local authority or authorised person for an order to be made under this section with respect to a child, the court may make the order if, but only if, it is satisfied that –

(a) the applicant has reasonable cause to suspect that the child is suffering, or is likely to suffer, significant harm;
(b) an assessment of the state of the child's health or development, or of the way in which he has been treated, is required to enable the applicant to determine whether or not the child is suffering, or is likely to suffer, significant harm; and
(c) it is unlikely that such an assessment will be made, or be satisfactory, in the absence of an order under this section.

(2) In this Act "a child assessment order" means an order under this section.

(3) A court may treat an application under this section as an application for an emergency protection order.

(4) No court shall make a child assessment order if it is satisfied –

(a) that there are grounds for making an emergency protection order with respect to the child; and
(b) that it ought to make such an order rather than a child assessment order.

(5) A child assessment order shall –

(a) specify a date by which the assessment is to begin; and
(b) have effect for such period, not exceeding 7 days beginning with that date, as may be specified in the order.

(6) Where a child assessment order is in force with respect to a child it shall be the duty of any person who is in a position to produce the child –

(a) to produce him to such person as may be named in the order; and

(b) to comply with such directions relating to the assessment of the child as the court thinks fit to specify in the order.

(7) A child assessment order authorises any person carrying out the assessment, or any part of the assessment, to do so in accordance with the terms of the order.

(8) Regardless of subsection (7), if the child is of sufficient understanding to make an informed decision he may refuse to submit to a medical or psychiatric examination or other assessment.

(9) The child may only be kept away from home –

(a) in accordance with directions specified in the order;
(b) if it is necessary for the purposes of the assessment; and
(c) for such period or periods as may be specified in the order.

(10) Where the child is to be kept away from home, the order shall contain such directions as the court thinks fit with regard to the contact that he must be allowed to have with other persons while away from home.

(11) Any person making an application for a child assessment order shall take such steps as are reasonably practicable to ensure that notice of the application is given to –

(a) the child's parents;
(b) any person who is not a parent of his but who has parental responsibility for him;
(c) any other person caring for the child;
(d) any person in whose favour a contact order is in force with respect to the child;
(e) any person who is allowed to have contact with the child by virtue of an order under section 34; and
(f) the child,

before the hearing of the application.

(12) Rules of court may make provision as to the circumstances in which –

(a) any of the persons mentioned in subsection (11); or
(b) such other person as may be specified in the rules,

may apply to the court for a child assessment order to be varied or discharged.

(13) In this section "authorised person" means a person who is an authorised person for the purposes of section 31.

44 Orders for emergency protection of children

(1) Where any person ("the applicant") applies to the court for an order to be made under this section with respect to a child, the court may make the order if, but only if, it is satisfied that –

(a) there is reasonable cause to believe that the child is likely to suffer significant harm if –
  (i) he is not removed to accommodation provided by or on behalf of the applicant; or

(ii) he does not remain in the place in which he is then being accommodated;

(b) in the case of an application made by the local authority –

(i) enquiries are being made with respect to the child under section 47(1)(b); and

(ii) those enquiries are being frustrated by access to the child being unreasonably refused to a person authorised to seek access and that the applicant has reasonable cause to believe that access to the child is required as a matter of urgency; or

(c) in the case of an application made by an authorised person –

(i) the applicant has reasonable cause to suspect that a child is suffering, or is likely to suffer, significant harm;

(ii) the applicant is making enquiries with respect to the child's welfare; and

(iii) those enquiries are being frustrated by access to the child being unreasonably refused to a person authorised to seek access and the applicant has reasonable cause to believe that access to the child is required as a matter of urgency.

(2) In this section –

(a) "authorised person" means a person who is an authorised person for the purposes of section 31; and

(b) "a person authorised to seek access" means –

(i) in the case of an application by a local authority, an officer of the local authority or a person authorised by the local authority to act on their behalf in connection with the enquiries; or

(ii) in the case of an application by an authorised person, that person.

(3) Any person –

(*a*) seeking access to a child in connection with enquiries of a kind mentioned in subsection (1); and

(*b*) purporting to be a person authorised to do so,

shall, on being asked to do so, produce some duly authenticated document as evidence that he is such a person.

(4) While an order under this section ("an emergency protection order") is in force it –

(a) operates as a direction to any person who is in a position to do so to comply with any request to produce the child to the applicant;

(b) authorises –

(i) the removal of the child at any time to accommodation provided by or on behalf of the applicant and his being kept there; or

(ii) the prevention of the child's removal from any hospital, or other place, in which he was being accommodated immediately before the making of the order; and

(c) gives the applicant parental responsibility for the child.

(5) Where an emergency protection order is in force with respect to a child, the applicant –

- (a) shall only exercise the power given by virtue of subsection (4)(b) in order to safeguard the welfare of the child;
- (b) shall take, and shall only take, such action in meeting his parental responsibility for the child as is reasonably required to safeguard or promote the welfare of the child (having regard in particular to the duration of the order); and
- (c) shall comply with the requirements of any regulations made by the Secretary of State for the purposes of this subsection.

(6) Where the court makes an emergency protection order, it may give such directions (if any) as it considers appropriate with respect to –

- (a) the contact which is, or is not, to be allowed between the child and any named person;
- (b) the medical or psychiatric examination or other assessment of the child.

(7) Where any direction is given under subsection (6)(b), the child may, if he is of sufficient understanding to make an informed decision, refuse to submit to the examination or other assessment.

(8) A direction under subsection (6)(a) may impose conditions and one under subsection (6)(b) may be to the effect that there is to be –

- (a) no such examination or assessment; or
- (b) no such examination or assessment unless the court directs otherwise.

(9) A direction under subsection (6) may be –

- (a) given when the emergency protection order is made or at any time while it is in force; and
- (b) varied at any time on the application of any person falling within any class of person prescribed by rules of court for the purposes of this subsection.

(10) Where an emergency protection order is in force with respect to a child and –

- (a) the applicant has exercised the power given by subsection (4)(b)(i) but it appears to him that it is safe for the child to be returned; or
- (b) the applicant has exercised the power given by subsection (4)(b)(ii) but it appears to him that it is safe for the child to be allowed to be removed from the place in question,

he shall return the child or (as the case may be) allow him to be removed.

(11) Where he is required by subsection (10) to return the child the applicant shall –

- (a) return him to the care of the person from whose care he was removed; or
- (b) if that is not reasonably practicable, return him to the care of –
  - (i) a parent of his;

(ii) any person who is not a parent of his but who has parental responsibility for him; or

(iii) such other person as the applicant (with the agreement of the court) considers appropriate.

(12) Where the applicant has been required by subsection (10) to return the child, or to allow him to be removed, he may again exercise his powers with respect to the child (at any time while the emergency protection order remains in force) if it appears to him that a change in the circumstances of the case makes it necessary for him to do so.

(13) Where an emergency protection order has been made with respect to a child, the applicant shall, subject to any direction given under subsection (6), allow the child reasonable contact with –

(a) his parents;

(b) any person who is not a parent of his but who has parental responsibility for him;

(c) any person with whom he was living immediately before the making of the order;

(d) any person in whose favour a contact order is in force with respect to him;

(e) any person who is allowed to have contact with the child by virtue of an order under section 34; and

(f) any person acting on behalf of any of those persons.

(14) Wherever it is reasonably practicable to do so, an emergency protection order shall name the child; and where it does not name him it shall describe him as clearly as possible.

(15) A person shall be guilty of an offence if he intentionally obstructs any person exercising the power under subsection (4)(b) to remove, or prevent the removal of, a child.

(16) A person guilty of an offence under subsection (15) shall be liable on summary conviction to a fine not exceeding level 3 on the standard scale.

44A Power to include exclusion requirement in emergency protection order

(1) Where –

(a) on being satisfied as mentioned in section 44(1)(a), (b) or (*c*), the court makes an emergency protection order with respect to a child, and

(b) the conditions mentioned in subsection (2) are satisfied,

the court may include an exclusion requirement in the emergency protection order.

(2) The conditions are –

(a) that there is reasonable cause to believe that, if a person ("the relevant person") is excluded from a dwelling-house in which the child lives, then –

(i) in the case of an order made on the ground mentioned in

section 44(1)(a), the child will not be likely to suffer significant harm, even though the child is not removed as mentioned in section 44(1)(a)(i) or does not remain as mentioned in section 44(1)(a)(ii), or

(ii) in the case of an order made on the ground mentioned in paragraph (b) or (c) of section 44(1), the enquiries referred to in that paragraph will cease to be frustrated, and

(b) that another person living in the dwelling-house (whether a parent of the child or some other person) –

(i) is able and willing to give to the child the care which it would be reasonable to expect a parent to give him, and

(ii) consents to the inclusion of the exclusion requirement.

(3) For the purposes of this section an exclusion requirement is any one or more of the following –

(a) a provision requiring the relevant person to leave a dwelling-house in which he is living with the child,

(b) a provision prohibiting the relevant person from entering a dwelling-house in which the child lives, and

(*c*) a provision excluding the relevant person from a defined area in which a dwelling-house in which the child lives is situated.

(4) The court may provide that the exclusion requirement is to have effect for a shorter period than the other provisions of the order.

(5) Where the court makes an emergency protection order containing an exclusion requirement, the court may attach a power of arrest to the exclusion requirement.

(6) Where the court attaches a power of arrest to an exclusion requirement of an emergency protection order, it may provide that the power of arrest is to have effect for a shorter period than the exclusion requirement.

(7) Any period specified for the purposes of subsection (4) or (6) may be extended by the court (on one or more occasions) on an application to vary or discharge the emergency protection order.

(8) Where a power of arrest is attached to an exclusion requirement of an emergency protection order by virtue of subsection (5), a constable may arrest without warrant any person whom he has reasonable cause to believe to be in breach of the requirement.

(9) Sections 47(7), (11) and (12) and 48 of, and Schedule 5 to, the Family Law Act 1996 shall have effect in relation to a person arrested under subsection (8) of this section as they have effect in relation to a person arrested under section 47(6) of that Act.

(10) If, while an emergency protection order containing an exclusion requirement is in force, the applicant has removed the child from the dwelling-house from which the relevant person is excluded to other accommodation for a continuous period of more than 24 hours, the order shall cease to have effect in so far as it imposes the exclusion requirement.

44B Undertakings relating to emergency protection orders

(1) In any case where the court has power to include an exclusion requirement in an emergency protection order, the court may accept an undertaking from the relevant person.

(2) No power of arrest may be attached to any undertaking given under subsection (1).

(3) An undertaking given to a court under subsection (1) –

(a) shall be enforceable as if it were an order of the court, and
(b) shall cease to have effect if, while it is in force, the applicant has removed the child from the dwelling-house from which the relevant person is excluded to other accommodation for a continuous period of more than 24 hours.

(4) This section has effect without prejudice to the powers of the High Court and county court apart from this section.

(5) In this section "exclusion requirement" and "relevant person" have the same meaning as in section 44A.

45 Duration of emergency protection orders and other supplemental provisions

(1) An emergency protection order shall have effect for such period, not exceeding eight days, as may be specified in the order.

(2) Where –

(a) the court making an emergency protection order would, but for this subsection, specify a period of eight days as the period for which the order is to have effect; but
(b) the last of those eight days is a public holiday (that is to say, Christmas Day, Good Friday, a bank holiday or a Sunday),

the court may specify a period which ends at noon on the first later day which is not such a holiday.

(3) Where an emergency protection order is made on an application under section 46(7), the period of eight days mentioned in subsection (1) shall begin with the first day on which the child was taken into police protection under section 46.

(4) Any person who –

(a) has parental responsibility for a child as the result of an emergency protection order; and
(b) is entitled to apply for a care order with respect to the child,

may apply to the court for the period during which the emergency protection order is to have effect to be extended.

(5) On an application under subsection (4) the court may extend the period during which the order is to have effect by such period, not exceeding seven

days, as it thinks fit, but may do so only if it has reasonable cause to believe that the child concerned is likely to suffer significant harm if the order is not extended.

(6) An emergency protection order may only be extended once.

(7) Regardless of any enactment or rule of law which would otherwise prevent it from doing so, a court hearing an application for, or with respect to, an emergency protection order may take account of –

(a) any statement contained in any report made to the court in the course of, or in connection with, the hearing; or
(b) any evidence given during the hearing,

which is, in the opinion of the court, relevant to the application.

(8) Any of the following may apply to the court for an emergency protection order to be discharged –

(a) the child;
(b) a parent of his;
(c) any person who is not a parent of his but who has parental responsibility for him; or
(d) any person with whom he was living immediately before the making of the order.

(8A) On the application of a person who is not entitled to apply for the order to be discharged, but who is a person to whom an exclusion requirement contained in the order applies, an emergency protection order may be varied or discharged by the court in so far as it imposes the exclusion requirement.

(8B) Where a power of arrest has been attached to an exclusion requirement of an emergency protection order, the court may, on the application of any person entitled to apply for the discharge of the order so far as it imposes the exclusion requirement, vary or discharge the order in so far as it confers a power of arrest (whether or not any application has been made to vary or discharge any other provision of the order).

(9) No application for the discharge of an emergency protection order shall be heard by the court before the expiry of the period of 72 hours beginning with the making of the order.

(10) No appeal may be made against –

(a) the making of, or refusal to make, an emergency protection order;
(b) the extension of, or refusal to extend, the period during which such an order is to have effect;
(c) the discharge of, or refusal to discharge, such an order; or
(d) the giving of, or refusal to give, any direction in connection with such an order.

(11) Subsection (8) does not apply –

(a) where the person who would otherwise be entitled to apply for the emergency protection order to be discharged –
   (i) was given notice (in accordance with rules of court) of the hearing at which the order was made; and
   (ii) was present at that hearing; or

(b) to any emergency protection order the effective period of which has been extended under subsection (5).

(12) A court making an emergency protection order may direct that the applicant may, in exercising any powers which he has by virtue of the order, be accompanied by a registered medical practitioner, registered nurse or registered health visitor, if he so chooses.

46 Removal and accommodation of children by police in cases of emergency

(1) Where a constable has reasonable cause to believe that a child would otherwise be likely to suffer significant harm, he may –

(a) remove the child to suitable accommodation and keep him there; or

(b) take such steps as are reasonable to ensure that the child's removal from any hospital, or other place, in which he is then being accommodated is prevented.

(2) For the purposes of this Act, a child with respect to whom a constable has exercised his powers under this section is referred to as having been taken into police protection.

(3) As soon as is reasonably practicable after taking a child into police protection, the constable concerned shall –

(a) inform the local authority within whose area the child was found of the steps that have been, and are proposed to be, taken with respect to the child under this section and the reasons for taking them;

(b) give details to the authority within whose area the child is ordinarily resident ("the appropriate authority") of the place at which the child is being accommodated;

(c) inform the child (if he appears capable of understanding) –

(i) of the steps that have been taken with respect to him under this section and of the reasons for taking them; and;

(ii) of the further steps that may be taken with respect to him under this section;

(d) take such steps as are reasonably practicable to discover the wishes and feelings of the child;

(e) secure that the case is inquired into by an officer designated for the purposes of this section by the chief officer of the police area concerned; and

(f) where the child was taken into police protection by being removed to accommodation which is not provided –

(i) by or on behalf of a local authority; or

(ii) as a refuge, in compliance with the requirements of section 51,

secure that he is moved to accommodation which is so provided.

(4) As soon as is reasonably practicable after taking a child into police protection, the constable concerned shall take such steps as are reasonably practicable to inform –

(a) the child's parents;

(b) every person who is not a parent of his but who has parental responsibility for him; and

(c) any other person with whom the child was living immediately before being taken into police protection,

of the steps that he has taken under this section with respect to the child, the reasons for taking them and the further steps that may be taken with respect to him under this section.

(5) On completing any inquiry under subsection (3)(e), the officer conducting it shall release the child from police protection unless he considers that there is still reasonable cause for believing that the child would be likely to suffer significant harm if released.

(6) No child may be kept in police protection for more than 72 hours.

(7) While a child is being kept in police protection, the designated officer may apply on behalf of the appropriate authority for an emergency protection order to be made under section 44 with respect to the child.

(8) An application may be made under subsection (7) whether or not the authority know of it or agree to its being made.

(9) While a child is being kept in police protection –

(a) neither the constable concerned nor the designated officer shall have parental responsibility for him; but

(b) the designated officer shall do what is reasonable in all the circumstances of the case for the purpose of safeguarding or promoting the child's welfare (having regard in particular to the length of the period during which the child will be so protected).

(10) Where a child has been taken into police protection, the designated officer shall allow –

(a) the child's parents;

(b) any person who is not a parent of the child but who has parental responsibility for him;

(c) any person with whom the child was living immediately before he was taken into police protection;

(d) any person in whose favour a contact order is in force with respect to the child;

(e) any person who is allowed to have contact with the child by virtue of an order under section 34; and

(f) any person acting on behalf of any of those persons,

to have such contact (if any) with the child as, in the opinion of the designated officer, is both reasonable and in the child's best interests.

(11) Where a child who has been taken into police protection is in accommodation provided by, or on behalf of, the appropriate authority, subsection (10) shall have effect as if it referred to the authority rather than to the designated officer.

47 Local authority's duty to investigate

(1) Where a local authority –

(a) are informed that a child who lives, or is found, in their area –
   (i) is the subject of an emergency protection order; or
   (ii) is in police protection; or
   (iii) has contravened a ban imposed by a curfew notice within the meaning of Chapter I of Part I of the Crime And Disorder Act 1998; or
(b) have reasonable cause to suspect that a child who lives, or is found, in their area is suffering, or is likely to suffer, significant harm,

the authority shall make, or cause to be made, such enquiries as they consider necessary to enable them to decide whether they should take any action to safeguard or promote the child's welfare.

In the case of a child falling within paragraph (a)(iii) above, the enquiries shall be commenced as soon as practicable and, in any event, within 48 hours of the authority receiving the information.

(2) Where a local authority have obtained an emergency protection order with respect to a child, they shall make, or cause to be made, such enquiries as they consider necessary to enable them to decide what action they should take to safeguard or promote the child's welfare.

(3) The enquiries shall, in particular, be directed towards establishing –

(a) whether the authority should make any application to the court, or exercise any of their other powers under this Act or section 11 of the Crime and Disorder Act 1998 (child safety orders), with respect to the child;
(b) whether, in the case of a child –
   (i) with respect to whom an emergency protection order has been made; and
   (ii) who is not in accommodation provided by or on behalf of the authority,

it would be in the child's best interests (while an emergency protection order remains in force) for him to be in such accommodation; and
(c) whether, in the case of a child who has been taken into police protection, it would be in the child's best interests for the authority to ask for an application to be made under section 46(7).

(4) Where enquiries are being made under subsection (1) with respect to a child, the local authority concerned shall (with a view to enabling them to determine what action, if any, to take with respect to him) take such steps as are reasonably practicable –

(*a*) to obtain access to him; or
(*b*) to ensure that access to him is obtained, on their behalf, by a person authorised by them for the purpose,

unless they are satisfied that they already have sufficient information with respect to him.

(5) Where, as a result of any such enquiries, it appears to the authority that there are matters connected with the child's education which should be investigated, they shall consult the relevant local education authority.

(5A) For the purposes of making a determination under this section as to the action to be taken with respect to a child, a local authority shall, so far as is reasonably practicable and consistent with the child's welfare –

(a) ascertain the child's wishes and feelings regarding the action to be taken with respect to him; and
(b) give due consideration (having regard to his age and understanding) to such wishes and feelings of the child as they have been able to ascertain.

(6) Where, in the course of enquiries made under this section –

(a) any officer of the local authority concerned; or
(b) any person authorised by the authority to act on their behalf in connection with those enquiries –
    (i) is refused access to the child concerned; or
    (ii) is denied information as to his whereabouts,

the authority shall apply for an emergency protection order, a child assessment order, a care order or a supervision order with respect to the child unless they are satisfied that his welfare can be satisfactorily safeguarded without their doing so.

(7) If, on the conclusion of any enquiries or review made under this section, the authority decide not to apply for an emergency protection order, a care order, a child assessment order or a supervision order they shall –

(a) consider whether it would be appropriate to review the case at a later date; and
(b) if they decide that it would be, determine the date on which that review is to begin.

(8) Where, as a result of complying with this section, a local authority conclude that they should take action to safeguard or promote the child's welfare they shall take that action (so far as it is both within their power and reasonably practicable for them to do so).

(9) Where a local authority are conducting enquiries under this section, it shall be the duty of any person mentioned in subsection (11) to assist them with those enquiries (in particular by providing relevant information and advice) if called upon by the authority to do so.

(10) Subsection (9) does not oblige any person to assist a local authority where doing so would be unreasonable in all the circumstances of the case.

(11) The persons are –

(a) any local authority;
(b) any local education authority;
(c) any local housing authority;
(d) any Health Authority, Special Health Authority, Primary Care Trust, National Health Service trust or NHS foundation trust; and
(e) any person authorised by the Secretary of State for the purposes of this section.

(12) Where a local authority are making enquiries under this section with respect to a child who appears to them to be ordinarily resident within the area of another authority, they shall consult that other authority, who may undertake the necessary enquiries in their place.

48 Powers to assist in discovery of children who may be in need of emergency protection

(1) Where it appears to a court making an emergency protection order that adequate information as to the child's whereabouts –

(a) is not available to the applicant for the order; but
(b) is available to another person,

it may include in the order a provision requiring that other person to disclose, if asked to do so by the applicant, any information that he may have as to the child's whereabouts.

(2) No person shall be excused from complying with such a requirement on the ground that complying might incriminate him or his spouse or civil partner of an offence; but a statement of admission made in complying shall not be admissible in evidence against either of them in proceedings for any offence other than perjury.

(3) An emergency protection order may authorise the applicant to enter premises specified by the order and search for the child with respect to whom the order is made.

(4) Where the court is satisfied that there is reasonable cause to believe that there may be another child on those premises with respect to whom an emergency protection order ought to be made, it may make an order authorising the applicant to search for that other child on those premises.

(5) Where –

(a) an order has been made under subsection (4);
(b) the child concerned has been found on the premises; and
(c) the applicant is satisfied that the grounds for making an emergency protection order exist with respect to him,

the order shall have effect as if it were an emergency protection order.

(6) Where an order has been made under subsection (4), the applicant shall notify the court of its effect.

(7) A person shall be guilty of an offence if he intentionally obstructs any person exercising the power of entry and search under subsection (3) or (4).

(8) A person guilty of an offence under subsection (7) shall be liable on summary conviction to a fine not exceeding level 3 on the standard scale.

(9) Where, on an application made by any person for a warrant under this section, it appears to the court –

(a) that a person attempting to exercise powers under an emergency protection order has been prevented from doing so by being refused entry to the premises concerned or access to the child concerned; or
(b) that any such person is likely to be so prevented from exercising any such powers,

it may issue a warrant authorising any constable to assist the person mentioned in paragraph (a) or (b) in the exercise of those powers, using reasonable force if necessary.

(10) Every warrant issued under this section shall be addressed to, and executed by, a constable who shall be accompanied by the person applying for the warrant if –

(a) that person so desires; and
(b) the court by whom the warrant is issued does not direct otherwise.

(11) A court granting an application for a warrant under this section may direct that the constable concerned may, in executing the warrant, be accompanied by a registered medical practitioner, registered nurse or registered health visitor if he so chooses.

(12) An application for a warrant under this section shall be made in the manner and form prescribed by rules of court.

(13) Wherever it is reasonably practicable to do so, an order under subsection (4), an application for a warrant under this section and any such warrant shall name the child; and where it does not name him it shall describe him as clearly as possible.

49 Abduction of children in care etc

(1) A person shall be guilty of an offence if, knowingly and without lawful authority or reasonable excuse, he –

(a) takes a child to whom this section applies away from the responsible person;
(b) keeps such a child away from the responsible person; or
(c) induces, assists or incites such a child to run away or stay away from the responsible person.

(2) This section applies in relation to a child who is –

(a) in care;
(b) the subject of an emergency protection order; or
(c) in police protection,

and in this section "the responsible person" means any person who for the time being has care of him by virtue of the care order, the emergency protection order, or section 46, as the case may be.

(3) A person guilty of an offence under this section shall be liable on summary conviction to imprisonment for a term not exceeding six months, or to a fine not exceeding level 5 on the standard scale, or to both.

50 Recovery of abducted children etc

(1) Where it appears to the court that there is reason to believe that a child to whom this section applies –

(a) has been unlawfully taken away or is being unlawfully kept away from the responsible person;
(b) has run away or is staying away from the responsible person; or
(c) is missing,

the court may make an order under this section ("a recovery order").

(2) This section applies to the same children to whom section 49 applies and in this section "the responsible person" has the same meaning as in section 49.

(3) A recovery order –

- (a) operates as a direction to any person who is in a position to do so to produce the child on request to any authorised person;
- (b) authorises the removal of the child by any authorised person;
- (c) requires any person who has information as to the child's whereabouts to disclose that information, if asked to do so, to a constable or an officer of the court;
- (d) authorises a constable to enter any premises specified in the order and search for the child, using reasonable force if necessary.

(4) The court may make a recovery order on the application of –

- (a) any person who has parental responsibility for the child by virtue of a care order or emergency protection order; or
- (b) where the child is in police protection, the designated officer.

(5) A recovery order shall name the child and –

- (a) any person who has parental responsibility for the child by virtue of a care order or emergency protection order; or
- (b) where the child is in police protection, the designated officer.

(6) Premises may only be specified under subsection (3)(*d*) if it appears to the court that there are reasonable grounds for believing the child to be on them.

(7) In this section –

"an authorised person" means –
- (a) any person specified by the court;
- (b) any constable;
- (c) any person who is authorised –
  - (i) after the recovery order is made; and
  - (ii) by a person who has parental responsibility for the child by virtue of a care order or an emergency protection order,

to exercise any power under a recovery order; and

"the designated officer" means the officer designated for the purposes of section 46.

(8) Where a person is authorised as mentioned in subsection (7)(c) –

- (a) the authorisation shall identify the recovery order; and
- (b) any person claiming to be so authorised shall, if asked to do so, produce some duly authenticated document showing that he is so authorised.

(9) A person shall be guilty of an offence if he intentionally obstructs an authorised person exercising the power under subsection (3)(b) to remove a child.

(10) A person guilty of an offence under this section shall be liable on summary conviction to a fine not exceeding level 3 on the standard scale.

(11) No person shall be excused from complying with any request made under subsection (3)(*c*) on the ground that complying with it might incriminate him

or his spouse or civil partner of an offence; but a statement or admission made in complying shall not be admissible in evidence against either of them in proceedings for an offence other than perjury.

51 Refuges for children at risk

(1) Where it is proposed to use a voluntary home or private children's home to provide a refuge for children who appear to be at risk of harm, the Secretary of State may issue a certificate under this section with respect to that home.

(2) Where a local authority or voluntary organisation arrange for a foster parent to provide such a refuge, the Secretary of State may issue a certificate under this section with respect to that foster parent.

(3) In subsection (2) "foster parent" means a person who is, or who from time to time is, a local authority foster parent or a foster parent with whom children are placed by a voluntary organisation.

(4) The Secretary of State may by regulations –

(a) make provision as to the manner in which certificates may be issued;
(b) impose requirements which must be complied with while any certificate is in force; and
(c) provide for the withdrawal of certificates in prescribed circumstances.

(5) Where a certificate is in force with respect to a home, none of the provisions mentioned in subsection (7) shall apply in relation to any person providing a refuge for any child in that home.

(6) Where a certificate is in force with respect to a foster parent, none of those provisions shall apply in relation to the provision by him of a refuge for any child in accordance with arrangements made by the local authority or voluntary organisation.

(7) The provisions are –

(a) section 49;
(b) sections 82 (recovery of certain fugitive children) and 83 (harbouring) of the Children (Scotland) Act 1995, so far as they apply in relation to anything done in England and Wales;
(c) section 32(3) of the Children and Young Persons Act 1969 (compelling, persuading, inciting or assisting any person to be absent from detention etc), so far as it applies in relation to anything done in England and Wales;
(d) section 2 of the Child Abduction Act 1984.

52 Rules and regulations

(1) Without prejudice to section 93 or any other power to make such rules, rules of court may be made with respect to the procedure to be followed in connection with proceedings under this Part.

(2) The rules may in particular make provision –

(a) as to the form in which any application is to be made or direction is to be given;

(b) prescribing the persons who are to be notified of –

(i) the making, or extension, of an emergency protection order; or

(ii) the making of an application under section 45(4) or (8) or 46(7); and

(c) as to the content of any such notification and the manner in which, and person by whom, it is to be given.

(3) The Secretary of State may by regulations provide that, where –

(a) an emergency protection order has been made with respect to a child;

(b) the applicant for the order was not the local authority within whose area the child is ordinarily resident; and

(c) that local authority are of the opinion that it would be in the child's best interests for the applicant's responsibilities under the order to be transferred to them,

that authority shall (subject to their having complied with any requirements imposed by the regulations) be treated, for the purposes of this Act, as though they and not the original applicant had applied for, and been granted, the order.

(4) Regulations made under subsection (3) may, in particular, make provision as to –

(*a*) the considerations to which the local authority shall have regard in forming an opinion as mentioned in subsection (3)(*c*); and

(*b*) the time at which responsibility under any emergency protection order is to be treated as having been transferred to a local authority.

Appendix 2

ADOPTION AND CHILDREN ACT 2002

Part 1
Adoption

Chapter 1 Introductory

1 Considerations applying to the exercise of powers

(1) This section applies whenever a court or adoption agency is coming to a decision relating to the adoption of a child.

(2) The paramount consideration of the court or adoption agency must be the child's welfare, throughout his life.

(3) The court or adoption agency must at all times bear in mind that, in general, any delay in coming to the decision is likely to prejudice the child's welfare.

(4) The court or adoption agency must have regard to the following matters (among others) –

(a) the child's ascertainable wishes and feelings regarding the decision (considered in the light of the child's age and understanding),
(b) the child's particular needs,
(c) the likely effect on the child (throughout his life) of having ceased to be a member of the original family and become an adopted person,
(d) the child's age, sex, background and any of the child's characteristics which the court or agency considers relevant,
(e) any harm (within the meaning of the Children Act 1989) which the child has suffered or is at risk of suffering,
(f) the relationship which the child has with relatives, and with any other person in relation to whom the court or agency considers the relationship to be relevant, including –
  (i) the likelihood of any such relationship continuing and the value to the child of its doing so,
  (ii) the ability and willingness of any of the child's relatives, or of any such person, to provide the child with a secure environment in which the child can develop, and otherwise to meet the child's needs,
  (iii) the wishes and feelings of any of the child's relatives, or of any such person, regarding the child.

(5) In placing the child for adoption, the adoption agency must give due consideration to the child's religious persuasion, racial origin and cultural and linguistic background.

(6) The court or adoption agency must always consider the whole range of powers available to it in the child's case (whether under this Act or the Children Act 1989); and the court must not make any order under this Act unless it considers that making the order would be better for the child than not doing so.

(7) In this section, "coming to a decision relating to the adoption of a child", in relation to a court, includes –

(a) coming to a decision in any proceedings where the orders that might be made by the court include an adoption order (or the revocation of such an order), a placement order (or the revocation of such an order) or an order under section 26 (or the revocation or variation of such an order),

(b) coming to a decision about granting leave in respect of any action (other than the initiation of proceedings in any court) which may be taken by an adoption agency or individual under this Act,

but does not include coming to a decision about granting leave in any other circumstances.

(8) For the purposes of this section –

(a) references to relationships are not confined to legal relationships,

(b) references to a relative, in relation to a child, include the child's mother and father.

Chapter 3
Placement for Adoption and Adoption Orders

Placement of children by adoption agency for adoption

18 Placement for adoption by agencies

(1) An adoption agency may –

(a) place a child for adoption with prospective adopters, or

(b) where it has placed a child with any persons (whether under this Part or not), leave the child with them as prospective adopters,

but, except in the case of a child who is less than six weeks old, may only do so under section 19 or a placement order.

(2) An adoption agency may only place a child for adoption with prospective adopters if the agency is satisfied that the child ought to be placed for adoption.

(3) A child who is placed or authorised to be placed for adoption with prospective adopters by a local authority is looked after by the authority.

(4) If an application for an adoption order has been made by any persons in respect of a child and has not been disposed of –

(a) an adoption agency which placed the child with those persons may leave the child with them until the application is disposed of, but

(b) apart from that, the child may not be placed for adoption with any prospective adopters.

"Adoption order" includes a Scottish or Northern Irish adoption order.

(5) References in this Act (apart from this section) to an adoption agency placing a child for adoption –

(a) are to its placing a child for adoption with prospective adopters, and
(b) include, where it has placed a child with any persons (whether under this Act or not), leaving the child with them as prospective adopters;

and references in this Act (apart from this section) to a child who is placed for adoption by an adoption agency are to be interpreted accordingly.

(6) References in this Chapter to an adoption agency being, or not being, authorised to place a child for adoption are to the agency being or (as the case may be) not being authorised to do so under section 19 or a placement order.

(7) This section is subject to sections 30 to 35 (removal of children placed by adoption agencies).

19 Placing children with parental consent

(1) Where an adoption agency is satisfied that each parent or guardian of a child has consented to the child –

(a) being placed for adoption with prospective adopters identified in the consent, or
(b) being placed for adoption with any prospective adopters who may be chosen by the agency,

and has not withdrawn the consent, the agency is authorised to place the child for adoption accordingly.

(2) Consent to a child being placed for adoption with prospective adopters identified in the consent may be combined with consent to the child subsequently being placed for adoption with any prospective adopters who may be chosen by the agency in circumstances where the child is removed from or returned by the identified prospective adopters.

(3) Subsection (1) does not apply where –

(a) an application has been made on which a care order might be made and the application has not been disposed of, or
(b) a care order or placement order has been made after the consent was given.

(4) References in this Act to a child placed for adoption under this section include a child who was placed under this section with prospective adopters and continues to be placed with them, whether or not consent to the placement has been withdrawn.

(5) This section is subject to section 52 (parental etc consent).

20 Advance consent to adoption

(1) A parent or guardian of a child who consents to the child being placed for adoption by an adoption agency under section 19 may, at the same or any subsequent time, consent to the making of a future adoption order.

(2) Consent under this section –

(a) where the parent or guardian has consented to the child being placed for adoption with prospective adopters identified in the consent, may be consent to adoption by them, or
(b) may be consent to adoption by any prospective adopters who may be chosen by the agency.

(3) A person may withdraw any consent given under this section.

(4) A person who gives consent under this section may, at the same or any subsequent time, by notice given to the adoption agency –

(a) state that he does not wish to be informed of any application for an adoption order, or
(b) withdraw such a statement.

(5) A notice under subsection (4) has effect from the time when it is received by the adoption agency but has no effect if the person concerned has withdrawn his consent.

(6) This section is subject to section 52 (parental etc consent).

21 Placement orders

(1) A placement order is an order made by the court authorising a local authority to place a child for adoption with any prospective adopters who may be chosen by the authority.

(2) The court may not make a placement order in respect of a child unless –

(a) the child is subject to a care order,
(b) the court is satisfied that the conditions in section 31(2) of the 1989 Act (conditions for making a care order) are met, or
(c) the child has no parent or guardian.

(3) The court may only make a placement order if, in the case of each parent or guardian of the child, the court is satisfied –

(a) that the parent or guardian has consented to the child being placed for adoption with any prospective adopters who may be chosen by the local authority and has not withdrawn the consent, or
(b) that the parent's or guardian's consent should be dispensed with.

This subsection is subject to section 52 (parental etc consent).

(4) A placement order continues in force until –

(a) it is revoked under section 24,
(b) an adoption order is made in respect of the child, or
(c) the child marries, forms a civil partnership or attains the age of 18 years.

"Adoption order" includes a Scottish or Northern Irish adoption order.

22 Applications for placement orders

(1) A local authority must apply to the court for a placement order in respect of a child if –

(a) the child is placed for adoption by them or is being provided with accommodation by them,
(b) no adoption agency is authorised to place the child for adoption,
(c) the child has no parent or guardian or the authority consider that the conditions in section 31(2) of the 1989 Act are met, and
(d) the authority are satisfied that the child ought to be placed for adoption.

(2) If –

(a) an application has been made (and has not been disposed of) on which a care order might be made in respect of a child, or
(b) a child is subject to a care order and the appropriate local authority are not authorised to place the child for adoption,

the appropriate local authority must apply to the court for a placement order if they are satisfied that the child ought to be placed for adoption.

(3) If –

(*a*) a child is subject to a care order, and
(*b*) the appropriate local authority are authorised to place the child for adoption under section 19,

the authority may apply to the court for a placement order.

(4) If a local authority –

(a) are under a duty to apply to the court for a placement order in respect of a child, or
(b) have applied for a placement order in respect of a child and the application has not been disposed of,

the child is looked after by the authority.

(5) Subsections (1) to (3) do not apply in respect of a child –

(a) if any persons have given notice of intention to adopt, unless the period of four months beginning with the giving of the notice has expired without them applying for an adoption order or their application for such an order has been withdrawn or refused, or
(b) if an application for an adoption order has been made and has not been disposed of.

"Adoption order" includes a Scottish or Northern Irish adoption order.

(6) Where –

(a) an application for a placement order in respect of a child has been made and has not been disposed of, and
(b) no interim care order is in force,

the court may give any directions it considers appropriate for the medical or psychiatric examination or other assessment of the child; but a child who is of sufficient understanding to make an informed decision may refuse to submit to the examination or other assessment.

(7) The appropriate local authority –

(a) in relation to a care order, is the local authority in whose care the child is placed by the order, and
(b) in relation to an application on which a care order might be made, is the local authority which makes the application.

23 Varying placement orders

(1) The court may vary a placement order so as to substitute another local authority for the local authority authorised by the order to place the child for adoption.

(2) The variation may only be made on the joint application of both authorities.

24 Revoking placement orders

(1) The court may revoke a placement order on the application of any person.

(2) But an application may not be made by a person other than the child or the local authority authorised by the order to place the child for adoption unless –

(a) the court has given leave to apply, and
(b) the child is not placed for adoption by the authority.

(3) The court cannot give leave under subsection (2)(a) unless satisfied that there has been a change in circumstances since the order was made.

(4) If the court determines, on an application for an adoption order, not to make the order, it may revoke any placement order in respect of the child.

(5) Where –

(a) an application for the revocation of a placement order has been made and has not been disposed of, and
(b) the child is not placed for adoption by the authority,

the child may not without the court's leave be placed for adoption under the order.

25 Parental responsibility

(1) This section applies while –

(a) a child is placed for adoption under section 19 or an adoption agency is authorised to place a child for adoption under that section, or
(b) a placement order is in force in respect of a child.

(2) Parental responsibility for the child is given to the agency concerned.

(3) While the child is placed with prospective adopters, parental responsibility is given to them.

(4) The agency may determine that the parental responsibility of any parent or guardian, or of prospective adopters, is to be restricted to the extent specified in the determination.

26 Contact

(1) On an adoption agency being authorised to place a child for adoption, or placing a child for adoption who is less than six weeks old, any provision for contact under the 1989 Act ceases to have effect.

(2) While an adoption agency is so authorised or a child is placed for adoption –

(a) no application may be made for any provision for contact under that Act, but
(b) the court may make an order under this section requiring the person with whom the child lives, or is to live, to allow the child to visit or stay with the person named in the order, or for the person named in the order and the child otherwise to have contact with each other.

(3) An application for an order under this section may be made by –

(a) the child or the agency,
(b) any parent, guardian or relative,
(c) any person in whose favour there was provision for contact under the 1989 Act which ceased to have effect by virtue of subsection (1),
(d) if a residence order was in force immediately before the adoption agency was authorised to place the child for adoption or (as the case may be) placed the child for adoption at a time when he was less than six weeks old, the person in whose favour the order was made,
(e) if a person had care of the child immediately before that time by virtue of an order made in the exercise of the High Court's inherent jurisdiction with respect to children, that person,
(f) any person who has obtained the court's leave to make the application.

(4) When making a placement order, the court may on its own initiative make an order under this section.

(5) This section does not prevent an application for a contact order under section 8 of the 1989 Act being made where the application is to be heard together with an application for an adoption order in respect of the child.

(6) In this section, "provision for contact under the 1989 Act" means a contact order under section 8 of that Act or an order under section 34 of that Act (parental contact with children in care).

27 Contact: supplementary

(1) An order under section 26 –

(a) has effect while the adoption agency is authorised to place the child for adoption or the child is placed for adoption, but
(b) may be varied or revoked by the court on an application by the child, the agency or a person named in the order.

(2) The agency may refuse to allow the contact that would otherwise be required by virtue of an order under that section if –

(a) it is satisfied that it is necessary to do so in order to safeguard or promote the child's welfare, and
(b) the refusal is decided upon as a matter of urgency and does not last for more than seven days.

(3) Regulations may make provision as to –

(a) the steps to be taken by an agency which has exercised its power under subsection (2),
(b) the circumstances in which, and conditions subject to which, the terms of any order under section 26 may be departed from by agreement between the agency and any person for whose contact with the child the order provides,
(c) notification by an agency of any variation or suspension of arrangements made (otherwise than under an order under that section) with a view to allowing any person contact with the child.

(4) Before making a placement order the court must –

(a) consider the arrangements which the adoption agency has made, or proposes to make, for allowing any person contact with the child, and
(b) invite the parties to the proceedings to comment on those arrangements.

(5) An order under section 26 may provide for contact on any conditions the court considers appropriate.

28 Further consequences of placement

(1) Where a child is placed for adoption under section 19 or an adoption agency is authorised to place a child for adoption under that section –

(a) a parent or guardian of the child may not apply for a residence order unless an application for an adoption order has been made and the parent or guardian has obtained the court's leave under subsection (3) or (5) of section 47,
(b) if an application has been made for an adoption order, a guardian of the child may not apply for a special guardianship order unless he has obtained the court's leave under subsection (3) or (5) of that section.

(2) Where –

(a) a child is placed for adoption under section 19 or an adoption agency is authorised to place a child for adoption under that section, or
(b) a placement order is in force in respect of a child,

then (whether or not the child is in England and Wales) a person may not do either of the following things, unless the court gives leave or each parent or guardian of the child gives written consent.

(3) Those things are –

(a) causing the child to be known by a new surname, or

(b) removing the child from the United Kingdom.

(4) Subsection (3) does not prevent the removal of a child from the United Kingdom for a period of less than one month by a person who provides the child's home.

29 Further consequences of placement orders

(1) Where a placement order is made in respect of a child and either –

(a) the child is subject to a care order, or
(b) the court at the same time makes a care order in respect of the child,

the care order does not have effect at any time when the placement order is in force.

(2) On the making of a placement order in respect of a child, any order mentioned in section 8(1) of the 1989 Act, and any supervision order in respect of the child, ceases to have effect.

(3) Where a placement order is in force –

(a) no prohibited steps order, residence order or specific issue order, and
(b) no supervision order or child assessment order,

may be made in respect of the child.

(4) Subsection (3)(a) does not apply in respect of a residence order if –

(a) an application for an adoption order has been made in respect of the child, and
(b) the residence order is applied for by a parent or guardian who has obtained the court's leave under subsection (3) or (5) of section 47 or by any other person who has obtained the court's leave under this subsection.

(5) Where a placement order is in force, no special guardianship order may be made in respect of the child unless –

(a) an application has been made for an adoption order, and
(b) the person applying for the special guardianship order has obtained the court's leave under this subsection or, if he is a guardian of the child, has obtained the court's leave under section 47(5).

(6) Section 14A(7) of the 1989 Act applies in respect of an application for a special guardianship order for which leave has been given as mentioned in subsection (5)(b) with the omission of the words "the beginning of the period of three months ending with".

(7) Where a placement order is in force –

(a) section 14C(1)(b) of the 1989 Act (special guardianship: parental responsibility) has effect subject to any determination under section 25(4) of this Act,
(b) section 14C(3) and (4) of the 1989 Act (special guardianship: removal of child from UK etc) does not apply.

Preliminaries to adoption

42 Child to live with adopters before application

(1) An application for an adoption order may not be made unless –

- (a) if subsection (2) applies, the condition in that subsection is met,
- (b) if that subsection does not apply, the condition in whichever is applicable of subsections (3) to (5) applies.

(2) If –

- (a) the child was placed for adoption with the applicant or applicants by an adoption agency or in pursuance of an order of the High Court, or
- (b) the applicant is a parent of the child,

the condition is that the child must have had his home with the applicant or, in the case of an application by a couple, with one or both of them at all times during the period of ten weeks preceding the application.

(3) If the applicant or one of the applicants is the partner of a parent of the child, the condition is that the child must have had his home with the applicant or, as the case may be, applicants at all times during the period of six months preceding the application.

(4) If the applicants are local authority foster parents, the condition is that the child must have had his home with the applicants at all times during the period of one year preceding the application.

(5) In any other case, the condition is that the child must have had his home with the applicant or, in the case of an application by a couple, with one or both of them for not less than three years (whether continuous or not) during the period of five years preceding the application.

(6) But subsections (4) and (5) do not prevent an application being made if the court gives leave to make it.

(7) An adoption order may not be made unless the court is satisfied that sufficient opportunities to see the child with the applicant or, in the case of an application by a couple, both of them together in the home environment have been given –

- (a) where the child was placed for adoption with the applicant or applicants by an adoption agency, to that agency,
- (b) in any other case, to the local authority within whose area the home is.

(8) In this section and sections 43 and 44(1) –

- (a) references to an adoption agency include a Scottish or Northern Irish adoption agency,
- (b) references to a child placed for adoption by an adoption agency are to be read accordingly.

43 Reports where child placed by agency

Where an application for an adoption order relates to a child placed for adoption by an adoption agency, the agency must –

(a) submit to the court a report on the suitability of the applicants and on any other matters relevant to the operation of section 1, and
(b) assist the court in any manner the court directs.

44 Notice of intention to adopt

(1) This section applies where persons (referred to in this section as "proposed adopters") wish to adopt a child who is not placed for adoption with them by an adoption agency.

(2) An adoption order may not be made in respect of the child unless the proposed adopters have given notice to the appropriate local authority of their intention to apply for the adoption order (referred to in this Act as a "notice of intention to adopt").

(3) The notice must be given not more than two years, or less than three months, before the date on which the application for the adoption order is made.

(4) Where –

(a) if a person were seeking to apply for an adoption order, subsection (4) or (5) of section 42 would apply, but
(b) the condition in the subsection in question is not met,

the person may not give notice of intention to adopt unless he has the court's leave to apply for an adoption order.

(5) On receipt of a notice of intention to adopt, the local authority must arrange for the investigation of the matter and submit to the court a report of the investigation.

(6) In particular, the investigation must, so far as practicable, include the suitability of the proposed adopters and any other matters relevant to the operation of section 1 in relation to the application.

(7) If a local authority receive a notice of intention to adopt in respect of a child whom they know was (immediately before the notice was given) looked after by another local authority, they must, not more than seven days after the receipt of the notice, inform the other local authority in writing that they have received the notice.

(8) Where –

(a) a local authority have placed a child with any persons otherwise than as prospective adopters, and
(b) the persons give notice of intention to adopt,

the authority are not to be treated as leaving the child with them as prospective adopters for the purposes of section 18(1)(b).

(9) In this section, references to the appropriate local authority, in relation to any proposed adopters, are –

(a) in prescribed cases, references to the prescribed local authority,
(b) in any other case, references to the local authority for the area in which, at the time of giving the notice of intention to adopt, they have their home,

and "prescribed" means prescribed by regulations.

45 Suitability of adopters

(1) Regulations under section 9 may make provision as to the matters to be taken into account by an adoption agency in determining, or making any report in respect of, the suitability of any persons to adopt a child.

(2) In particular, the regulations may make provision for the purpose of securing that, in determining the suitability of a couple to adopt a child, proper regard is had to the need for stability and permanence in their relationship.

The making of adoption orders

46 Adoption orders

(1) An adoption order is an order made by the court on an application under section 50 or 51 giving parental responsibility for a child to the adopters or adopter.

(2) The making of an adoption order operates to extinguish –

(a) the parental responsibility which any person other than the adopters or adopter has for the adopted child immediately before the making of the order,
(b) any order under the 1989 Act or the Children (Northern Ireland) Order 1995 (SI 1995/755 (NI 2)),
(c) any order under the Children (Scotland) Act 1995 other than an excepted order, and
(d) any duty arising by virtue of an agreement or an order of a court to make payments, so far as the payments are in respect of the adopted child's maintenance or upbringing for any period after the making of the adoption order.

"Excepted order" means an order under section 9, 11(1)(d) or 13 of the Children (Scotland) Act 1995 or an exclusion order within the meaning of section 76(1) of that Act.

(3) An adoption order –

(a) does not affect parental responsibility so far as it relates to any period before the making of the order, and
(b) in the case of an order made on an application under section 51(2) by the partner of a parent of the adopted child, does not affect the parental responsibility of that parent or any duties of that parent within subsection (2)(d).

(4) Subsection (2)(d) does not apply to a duty arising by virtue of an agreement –

(a) which constitutes a trust, or
(b) which expressly provides that the duty is not to be extinguished by the making of an adoption order.

(5) An adoption order may be made even if the child to be adopted is already an adopted child.

(6) Before making an adoption order, the court must consider whether there should be arrangements for allowing any person contact with the child; and for that purpose the court must consider any existing or proposed arrangements and obtain any views of the parties to the proceedings.

47 Conditions for making adoption orders

(1) An adoption order may not be made if the child has a parent or guardian unless one of the following three conditions is met; but this section is subject to section 52 (parental etc consent).

(2) The first condition is that, in the case of each parent or guardian of the child, the court is satisfied –

(a) that the parent or guardian consents to the making of the adoption order,
(b) that the parent or guardian has consented under section 20 (and has not withdrawn the consent) and does not oppose the making of the adoption order, or
(c) that the parent's or guardian's consent should be dispensed with.

(3) A parent or guardian may not oppose the making of an adoption order under subsection (2)(b) without the court's leave.

(4) The second condition is that –

(a) the child has been placed for adoption by an adoption agency with the prospective adopters in whose favour the order is proposed to be made,
(b) either –
   (i) the child was placed for adoption with the consent of each parent or guardian and the consent of the mother was given when the child was at least six weeks old, or
   (ii) the child was placed for adoption under a placement order, and
(c) no parent or guardian opposes the making of the adoption order.

(5) A parent or guardian may not oppose the making of an adoption order under the second condition without the court's leave.

(6) The third condition is that the child is free for adoption by virtue of an order made –

(a) in Scotland, under section 18 of the Adoption (Scotland) Act 1978, or
(b) in Northern Ireland, under Article 17(1) or 18(1) of the Adoption (Northern Ireland) Order 1987 (SI 1987/2203 (NI 22)).

(7) The court cannot give leave under subsection (3) or (5) unless satisfied that there has been a change in circumstances since the consent of the parent or guardian was given or, as the case may be, the placement order was made.

(8) An adoption order may not be made in relation to a person who is or has been married.

(8A) An adoption order may not be made in relation to a person who is or has been a civil partner.

(9) An adoption order may not be made in relation to a person who has attained the age of 19 years.

48 Restrictions on making adoption orders

(1) The court may not hear an application for an adoption order in relation to a child, where a previous application to which subsection (2) applies made in relation to the child by the same persons was refused by any court, unless it appears to the court that, because of a change in circumstances or for any other reason, it is proper to hear the application.

(2) This subsection applies to any application –

(a) for an adoption order or a Scottish or Northern Irish adoption order, or

(b) for an order for adoption made in the Isle of Man or any of the Channel Islands.

49 Applications for adoption

(1) An application for an adoption order may be made by –

(a) a couple, or

(b) one person,

but only if it is made under section 50 or 51 and one of the following conditions is met.

(2) The first condition is that at least one of the couple (in the case of an application under section 50) or the applicant (in the case of an application under section 51) is domiciled in a part of the British Islands.

(3) The second condition is that both of the couple (in the case of an application under section 50) or the applicant (in the case of an application under section 51) have been habitually resident in a part of the British Islands for a period of not less than one year ending with the date of the application.

(4) An application for an adoption order may only be made if the person to be adopted has not attained the age of 18 years on the date of the application.

(5) References in this Act to a child, in connection with any proceedings (whether or not concluded) for adoption, (such as "child to be adopted" or "adopted child") include a person who has attained the age of 18 years before the proceedings are concluded.

50 Adoption by couple

(1) An adoption order may be made on the application of a couple where both of them have attained the age of 21 years.

(2) An adoption order may be made on the application of a couple where –

(a) one of the couple is the mother or the father of the person to be adopted and has attained the age of 18 years, and
(b) the other has attained the age of 21 years.

51 Adoption by one person

(1) An adoption order may be made on the application of one person who has attained the age of 21 years and is not married or a civil partner.

(2) An adoption order may be made on the application of one person who has attained the age of 21 years if the court is satisfied that the person is the partner of a parent of the person to be adopted.

(3) An adoption order may be made on the application of one person who has attained the age of 21 years and is married if the court is satisfied that –

(a) the person's spouse cannot be found,
(b) the spouses have separated and are living apart, and the separation is likely to be permanent, or
(c) the person's spouse is by reason of ill-health, whether physical or mental, incapable of making an application for an adoption order.

(3A) An adoption order may be made on the application of one person who has attained the age of 21 years and is a civil partner if the court is satisfied that—

(a) the person's civil partner cannot be found,
(b) the civil partners have separated and are living apart, and the separation is likely to be permanent, or
(c) the person's civil partner is by reason of ill-health, whether physical or mental, incapable of making an application for an adoption order.

(4) An adoption order may not be made on an application under this section by the mother or the father of the person to be adopted unless the court is satisfied that –

(a) the other natural parent is dead or cannot be found,
(b) by virtue of section 28 of the Human Fertilisation and Embryology Act 1990 (disregarding subsections (5A) to (5I) of that section), there is no other parent, or
(c) there is some other reason justifying the child's being adopted by the applicant alone,

and, where the court makes an adoption order on such an application, the court must record that it is satisfied as to the fact mentioned in paragraph (*a*) or (*b*) or, in the case of paragraph (*c*), record the reason.

Placement and adoption: general

52 Parental etc consent

(1) The court cannot dispense with the consent of any parent or guardian of a child to the child being placed for adoption or to the making of an adoption order in respect of the child unless the court is satisfied that –

(a) the parent or guardian cannot be found or is incapable of giving consent, or
(b) the welfare of the child requires the consent to be dispensed with.

(2) The following provisions apply to references in this Chapter to any parent or guardian of a child giving or withdrawing –

(a) consent to the placement of a child for adoption, or
(b) consent to the making of an adoption order (including a future adoption order).

(3) Any consent given by the mother to the making of an adoption order is ineffective if it is given less than six weeks after the child's birth.

(4) The withdrawal of any consent to the placement of a child for adoption, or of any consent given under section 20, is ineffective if it is given after an application for an adoption order is made.

(5) "Consent" means consent given unconditionally and with full understanding of what is involved; but a person may consent to adoption without knowing the identity of the persons in whose favour the order will be made.

(6) "Parent" (except in subsections (9) and (10) below) means a parent having parental responsibility.

(7) Consent under section 19 or 20 must be given in the form prescribed by rules, and the rules may prescribe forms in which a person giving consent under any other provision of this Part may do so (if he wishes).

(8) Consent given under section 19 or 20 must be withdrawn –

(a) in the form prescribed by rules, or
(b) by notice given to the agency.

(9) Subsection (10) applies if –

(a) an agency has placed a child for adoption under section 19 in pursuance of consent given by a parent of the child, and
(b) at a later time, the other parent of the child acquires parental responsibility for the child.

(10) The other parent is to be treated as having at that time given consent in accordance with this section in the same terms as those in which the first parent gave consent.

Chapter 4
Status of Adopted Children

66 Meaning of adoption in Chapter 4

(1) In this Chapter "adoption" means –

(a) adoption by an adoption order or a Scottish or Northern Irish adoption order,
(b) adoption by an order made in the Isle of Man or any of the Channel Islands,
(c) an adoption effected under the law of a Convention country outside the British Islands, and certified in pursuance of Article 23(1) of the Convention (referred to in this Act as a "Convention adoption"),
(d) an overseas adoption, or
(e) an adoption recognised by the law of England and Wales and effected under the law of any other country;

and related expressions are to be interpreted accordingly.

(2) But references in this Chapter to adoption do not include an adoption effected before the day on which this Chapter comes into force (referred to in this Chapter as "the appointed day").

(3) Any reference in an enactment to an adopted person within the meaning of this Chapter includes a reference to an adopted child within the meaning of Part 4 of the Adoption Act 1976.

67 Status conferred by adoption

(1) An adopted person is to be treated in law as if born as the child of the adopters or adopter.

(2) An adopted person is the legitimate child of the adopters or adopter and, if adopted by –

(a) a couple, or
(b) one of a couple under section 51(2),

is to be treated as the child of the relationship of the couple in question.

(3) An adopted person –

(a) if adopted by one of a couple under section 51(2), is to be treated in law as not being the child of any person other than the adopter and the other one of the couple, and
(b) in any other case, is to be treated in law, subject to subsection (4), as not being the child of any person other than the adopters or adopter;

but this subsection does not affect any reference in this Act to a person's natural parent or to any other natural relationship.

(4) In the case of a person adopted by one of the person's natural parents as sole adoptive parent, subsection (3)(b) has no effect as respects entitlement to property depending on relationship to that parent, or as respects anything else depending on that relationship.

(5) This section has effect from the date of the adoption.

(6) Subject to the provisions of this Chapter and Schedule 4, this section –

(a) applies for the interpretation of enactments or instruments passed or made before as well as after the adoption, and so applies subject to any contrary indication, and

(*b*) has effect as respects things done, or events occurring, on or after the adoption.

68 Adoptive relatives

(1) A relationship existing by virtue of section 67 may be referred to as an adoptive relationship, and –

(a) an adopter may be referred to as an adoptive parent or (as the case may be) as an adoptive father or adoptive mother,

(b) any other relative of any degree under an adoptive relationship may be referred to as an adoptive relative of that degree.

(2) Subsection (1) does not affect the interpretation of any reference, not qualified by the word "adoptive", to a relationship.

(3) A reference (however expressed) to the adoptive mother and father of a child adopted by –

(a) a couple of the same sex, or

(b) a partner of the child's parent, where the couple are of the same sex,

is to be read as a reference to the child's adoptive parents.

Chapter 6
Adoptions with a Foreign Element

Bringing children into and out of the United Kingdom

83 Restriction on bringing children in

(1) This section applies where a person who is habitually resident in the British Islands (the "British resident") –

(a) brings, or causes another to bring, a child who is habitually resident outside the British Islands into the United Kingdom for the purpose of adoption by the British resident, or

(b) at any time brings, or causes another to bring, into the United Kingdom a child adopted by the British resident under an external adoption effected within the period of six months ending with that time.

The references to adoption, or to a child adopted, by the British resident include a reference to adoption, or to a child adopted, by the British resident and another person.

(2) But this section does not apply if the child is intended to be adopted under a Convention adoption order.

(3) An external adoption means an adoption, other than a Convention adoption, of a child effected under the law of any country or territory outside the British Islands, whether or not the adoption is –

(a) an adoption within the meaning of Chapter 4, or
(b) a full adoption (within the meaning of section 88(3)).

(4) Regulations may require a person intending to bring, or to cause another to bring, a child into the United Kingdom in circumstances where this section applies –

(a) to apply to an adoption agency (including a Scottish or Northern Irish adoption agency) in the prescribed manner for an assessment of his suitability to adopt the child, and
(b) to give the agency any information it may require for the purpose of the assessment.

(5) Regulations may require prescribed conditions to be met in respect of a child brought into the United Kingdom in circumstances where this section applies.

(6) In relation to a child brought into the United Kingdom for adoption in circumstances where this section applies, regulations may –

(a) provide for any provision of Chapter 3 to apply with modifications or not to apply,
(b) if notice of intention to adopt has been given, impose functions in respect of the child on the local authority to which the notice was given.

(7) If a person brings, or causes another to bring, a child into the United Kingdom at any time in circumstances where this section applies, he is guilty of an offence if –

(a) he has not complied with any requirement imposed by virtue of subsection (4), or
(b) any condition required to be met by virtue of subsection (5) is not met,

before that time, or before any later time which may be prescribed.

(8) A person guilty of an offence under this section is liable –

(a) on summary conviction to imprisonment for a term not exceeding six months, or a fine not exceeding the statutory maximum, or both,
(b) on conviction on indictment, to imprisonment for a term not exceeding twelve months, or a fine, or both.

(9) In this section, "prescribed" means prescribed by regulations and "regulations" means regulations made by the Secretary of State, after consultation with the Assembly.

84 Giving parental responsibility prior to adoption abroad

(1) The High Court may, on an application by persons who the court is satisfied intend to adopt a child under the law of a country or territory outside the British Islands, make an order giving parental responsibility for the child to them.

(2) An order under this section may not give parental responsibility to persons who the court is satisfied meet those requirements as to domicile, or habitual residence, in England and Wales which have to be met if an adoption order is to be made in favour of those persons.

(3) An order under this section may not be made unless any requirements prescribed by regulations are satisfied.

(4) An application for an order under this section may not be made unless at all times during the preceding ten weeks the child's home was with the applicant or, in the case of an application by two people, both of them.

(5) Section 46(2) to (4) has effect in relation to an order under this section as it has effect in relation to adoption orders.

(6) Regulations may provide for any provision of this Act which refers to adoption orders to apply, with or without modifications, to orders under this section.

(7) In this section, "regulations" means regulations made by the Secretary of State, after consultation with the Assembly.

85 Restriction on taking children out

(1) A child who –

(a) is a Commonwealth citizen, or
(b) is habitually resident in the United Kingdom,

must not be removed from the United Kingdom to a place outside the British Islands for the purpose of adoption unless the condition in subsection (2) is met.

(2) The condition is that –

(a) the prospective adopters have parental responsibility for the child by virtue of an order under section 84, or
(b) the child is removed under the authority of an order under section 49 of the Adoption (Scotland) Act 1978 or Article 57 of the Adoption (Northern Ireland) Order 1987 (SI 1987/2203 (NI 22)).

(3) Removing a child from the United Kingdom includes arranging to do so; and the circumstances in which a person arranges to remove a child from the United Kingdom include those where he –

(a) enters into an arrangement for the purpose of facilitating such a removal of the child,
(b) initiates or takes part in any negotiations of which the purpose is the conclusion of an arrangement within paragraph (a), or

(c) causes another person to take any step mentioned in paragraph (a) or (b).

An arrangement includes an agreement (whether or not enforceable).

(4) A person who removes a child from the United Kingdom in contravention of subsection (1) is guilty of an offence.

(5) A person is not guilty of an offence under subsection (4) of causing a person to take any step mentioned in paragraph (a) or (b) of subsection (3) unless it is proved that he knew or had reason to suspect that the step taken would contravene subsection (1).

But this subsection only applies if sufficient evidence is adduced to raise an issue as to whether the person had the knowledge or reason mentioned.

(6) A person guilty of an offence under this section is liable –

(a) on summary conviction to imprisonment for a term not exceeding six months, or a fine not exceeding the statutory maximum, or both,
(b) on conviction on indictment, to imprisonment for a term not exceeding twelve months, or a fine, or both.

(7) In any proceedings under this section –

(a) a report by a British consular officer or a deposition made before a British consular officer and authenticated under the signature of that officer is admissible, upon proof that the officer or the deponent cannot be found in the United Kingdom, as evidence of the matters stated in it, and
(b) it is not necessary to prove the signature or official character of the person who appears to have signed any such report or deposition.

86 Power to modify sections 83 and 85

(1) Regulations may provide for section 83 not to apply if –

(a) the adopters or (as the case may be) prospective adopters are natural parents, natural relatives or guardians of the child in question (or one of them is), or
(b) the British resident in question is a partner of a parent of the child,

and any prescribed conditions are met.

(2) Regulations may provide for section 85(1) to apply with modifications, or not to apply, if –

(a) the prospective adopters are parents, relatives or guardians of the child in question (or one of them is), or
(b) the prospective adopter is a partner of a parent of the child,

and any prescribed conditions are met.

(3) On the occasion of the first exercise of the power to make regulations under this section –

(a) the statutory instrument containing the regulations is not to be made unless a draft of the instrument has been laid before, and approved by a resolution of, each House of Parliament, and

(b) accordingly section 140(2) does not apply to the instrument.

(4) In this section, "prescribed" means prescribed by regulations and "regulations" means regulations made by the Secretary of State after consultation with the Assembly.

Overseas adoptions

87 Overseas adoptions

(1) In this Act, "overseas adoption" –

(a) means an adoption of a description specified in an order made by the Secretary of State, being a description of adoptions effected under the law of any country or territory outside the British Islands, but

(b) does not include a Convention adoption.

(2) Regulations may prescribe the requirements that ought to be met by an adoption of any description effected after the commencement of the regulations for it to be an overseas adoption for the purposes of this Act.

(3) At any time when such regulations have effect, the Secretary of State must exercise his powers under this section so as to secure that subsequently effected adoptions of any description are not overseas adoptions for the purposes of this Act if he considers that they are not likely within a reasonable time to meet the prescribed requirements.

(4) In this section references to this Act include the Adoption Act 1976.

(5) An order under this section may contain provision as to the manner in which evidence of any overseas adoption may be given.

(6) In this section –

"adoption" means an adoption of a child or of a person who was a child at the time the adoption was applied for,

"regulations" means regulations made by the Secretary of State after consultation with the Assembly.

Miscellaneous

88 Modification of section 67 for Hague Convention adoptions

(1) If the High Court is satisfied, on an application under this section, that each of the following conditions is met in the case of a Convention adoption, it may direct that section 67(3) does not apply, or does not apply to any extent specified in the direction.

(2) The conditions are –

(a) that under the law of the country in which the adoption was effected, the adoption is not a full adoption,

(b) that the consents referred to in Article 4(c) and (d) of the Convention have not been given for a full adoption or that the United Kingdom is not the receiving State (within the meaning of Article 2 of the Convention),

(c) that it would be more favourable to the adopted child for a direction to be given under subsection (1).

(3) A full adoption is an adoption by virtue of which the child is to be treated in law as not being the child of any person other than the adopters or adopter.

(4) In relation to a direction under this section and an application for it, sections 59 and 60 of the Family Law Act 1986 (declarations under Part 3 of that Act as to marital status) apply as they apply in relation to a direction under that Part and an application for such a direction.

89 Annulment etc of overseas or Hague Convention adoptions

(1) The High Court may, on an application under this subsection, by order annul a Convention adoption or Convention adoption order on the ground that the adoption is contrary to public policy.

(2) The High Court may, on an application under this subsection –

(a) by order provide for an overseas adoption or a determination under section 91 to cease to be valid on the ground that the adoption or determination is contrary to public policy or that the authority which purported to authorise the adoption or make the determination was not competent to entertain the case, or

(b) decide the extent, if any, to which a determination under section 91 has been affected by a subsequent determination under that section.

(3) The High Court may, in any proceedings in that court, decide that an overseas adoption or a determination under section 91 is to be treated, for the purposes of those proceedings, as invalid on either of the grounds mentioned in subsection (2)(a).

(4) Subject to the preceding provisions, the validity of a Convention adoption, Convention adoption order or overseas adoption or a determination under section 91 cannot be called in question in proceedings in any court in England and Wales.

90 Section 89: supplementary

(1) Any application for an order under section 89 or a decision under subsection (2)(b) or (3) of that section must be made in the prescribed manner and within any prescribed period.

"Prescribed" means prescribed by rules.

(2) No application may be made under section 89(1) in respect of an adoption unless immediately before the application is made –

(a) the person adopted, or

(b) the adopters or adopter,

habitually reside in England and Wales.

(3) In deciding in pursuance of section 89 whether such an authority as is mentioned in section 91 was competent to entertain a particular case, a court is bound by any finding of fact made by the authority and stated by the authority to be so made for the purpose of determining whether the authority was competent to entertain the case.

91 Overseas determinations and orders

(1) Subsection (2) applies where any authority of a Convention country (other than the United Kingdom) or of the Channel Islands, the Isle of Man or any British overseas territory has power under the law of that country or territory –

(a) to authorise, or review the authorisation of, an adoption order made in that country or territory, or

(b) to give or review a decision revoking or annulling such an order or a Convention adoption.

(2) If the authority makes a determination in the exercise of that power, the determination is to have effect for the purpose of effecting, confirming or terminating the adoption in question or, as the case may be, confirming its termination.

(3) Subsection (2) is subject to section 89 and to any subsequent determination having effect under that subsection.

Chapter 7
Miscellaneous

Restrictions

92 Restriction on arranging adoptions etc

(1) A person who is neither an adoption agency nor acting in pursuance of an order of the High Court must not take any of the steps mentioned in subsection (2).

(2) The steps are –

(a) asking a person other than an adoption agency to provide a child for adoption,

(b) asking a person other than an adoption agency to provide prospective adopters for a child,

(c) offering to find a child for adoption,

(d) offering a child for adoption to a person other than an adoption agency,

(e) handing over a child to any person other than an adoption agency with a view to the child's adoption by that or another person,

(f) receiving a child handed over to him in contravention of paragraph (e),

(g) entering into an agreement with any person for the adoption of a child, or for the purpose of facilitating the adoption of a child, where no adoption agency is acting on behalf of the child in the adoption,

(h) initiating or taking part in negotiations of which the purpose is the conclusion of an agreement within paragraph (g),

(i) causing another person to take any of the steps mentioned in paragraphs (a) to (h).

(3) Subsection (1) does not apply to a person taking any of the steps mentioned in paragraphs (d), (e), (g), (h) and (i) of subsection (2) if the following condition is met.

(4) The condition is that –

(a) the prospective adopters are parents, relatives or guardians of the child (or one of them is), or

(b) the prospective adopter is the partner of a parent of the child.

(5) References to an adoption agency in subsection (2) include a prescribed person outside the United Kingdom exercising functions corresponding to those of an adoption agency, if the functions are being exercised in prescribed circumstances in respect of the child in question.

(6) The Secretary of State may, after consultation with the Assembly, by order make any amendments of subsections (1) to (4), and any consequential amendments of this Act, which he considers necessary or expedient.

(7) In this section –

(a) "agreement" includes an arrangement (whether or not enforceable),

(b) "prescribed" means prescribed by regulations made by the Secretary of State after consultation with the Assembly.

93 Offence of breaching restrictions under section 92

(1) If a person contravenes section 92(1), he is guilty of an offence; and, if that person is an adoption society, the person who manages the society is also guilty of the offence.

(2) A person is not guilty of an offence under subsection (1) of taking the step mentioned in paragraph (f) of section 92(2) unless it is proved that he knew or had reason to suspect that the child was handed over to him in contravention of paragraph (e) of that subsection.

(3) A person is not guilty of an offence under subsection (1) of causing a person to take any of the steps mentioned in paragraphs (a) to (h) of section 92(2) unless it is proved that he knew or had reason to suspect that the step taken would contravene the paragraph in question.

(4) But subsections (2) and (3) only apply if sufficient evidence is adduced to raise an issue as to whether the person had the knowledge or reason mentioned.

(5) A person guilty of an offence under this section is liable on summary conviction to imprisonment for a term not exceeding six months, or a fine not exceeding £10,000, or both.

94 Restriction on reports

(1) A person who is not within a prescribed description may not, in any prescribed circumstances, prepare a report for any person about the suitability of a child for adoption or of a person to adopt a child or about the adoption, or placement for adoption, of a child.

"Prescribed" means prescribed by regulations made by the Secretary of State after consultation with the Assembly.

(2) If a person –

(a) contravenes subsection (1), or
(b) causes a person to prepare a report, or submits to any person a report which has been prepared, in contravention of that subsection,

he is guilty of an offence.

(3) If a person who works for an adoption society –

(a) contravenes subsection (1), or
(b) causes a person to prepare a report, or submits to any person a report which has been prepared, in contravention of that subsection,

the person who manages the society is also guilty of the offence.

(4) A person is not guilty of an offence under subsection (2)(b) unless it is proved that he knew or had reason to suspect that the report would be, or had been, prepared in contravention of subsection (1).

But this subsection only applies if sufficient evidence is adduced to raise an issue as to whether the person had the knowledge or reason mentioned.

(5) A person guilty of an offence under this section is liable on summary conviction to imprisonment for a term not exceeding six months, or a fine not exceeding level 5 on the standard scale, or both.

95 Prohibition of certain payments

(1) This section applies to any payment (other than an excepted payment) which is made for or in consideration of –

(a) the adoption of a child,
(b) giving any consent required in connection with the adoption of a child,
(c) removing from the United Kingdom a child who is a Commonwealth citizen, or is habitually resident in the United Kingdom, to a place outside the British Islands for the purpose of adoption,
(d) a person (who is neither an adoption agency nor acting in pursuance of an order of the High Court) taking any step mentioned in section 92(2),
(e) preparing, causing to be prepared or submitting a report the preparation of which contravenes section 94(1).

(2) In this section and section 96, removing a child from the United Kingdom has the same meaning as in section 85.

(3) Any person who –

(a) makes any payment to which this section applies,
(b) agrees or offers to make any such payment, or
(c) receives or agrees to receive or attempts to obtain any such payment,

is guilty of an offence.

(4) A person guilty of an offence under this section is liable on summary conviction to imprisonment for a term not exceeding six months, or a fine not exceeding £10,000, or both.

96 Excepted payments

(1) A payment is an excepted payment if it is made by virtue of, or in accordance with provision made by or under, this Act, the Adoption (Scotland) Act 1978 or the Adoption (Northern Ireland) Order 1987 (SI 1987/2203 (NI 22)).

(2) A payment is an excepted payment if it is made to a registered adoption society by –

(a) a parent or guardian of a child, or
(b) a person who adopts or proposes to adopt a child,

in respect of expenses reasonably incurred by the society in connection with the adoption or proposed adoption of the child.

(3) A payment is an excepted payment if it is made in respect of any legal or medical expenses incurred or to be incurred by any person in connection with an application to a court which he has made or proposes to make for an adoption order, a placement order, or an order under section 26 or 84.

(4) A payment made as mentioned in section 95(1)(c) is an excepted payment if –

(a) the condition in section 85(2) is met, and
(b) the payment is made in respect of the travel and accommodation expenses reasonably incurred in removing the child from the United Kingdom for the purpose of adoption.

Appendix 3

FAMILY PROCEEDINGS RULES 1991

SI 1991/1247

PART IV
Proceedings Under the Children Act 1989

4.1 Interpretation and application

(1) In this Part of these rules, unless a contrary intention appears –

a section or schedule referred to means the section or schedule so numbered in the Act of 1989;

"a section 8 order" has the meaning assigned to it by section 8(2);

"application" means an application made under or by virtue of the Act of 1989 or under these rules, and "applicant" shall be construed accordingly;

"child", in relation to proceedings to which this Part applies –

(a) means, subject to sub-paragraph (b), a person under the age of 18 with respect to whom the proceedings are brought, and

(b) where the proceedings are under Schedule 1, also includes a person who has reached the age of 18;

"children and family reporter" means an officer of the service or a Welsh family proceedings officer who has been asked to prepare a welfare report under section 7(1)(a);

"children's guardian" –

(a) means an officer of the service or a Welsh family proceedings officer appointed under section 41 for the child with respect to whom the proceedings are brought; but

(b) does not include such an officer appointed in relation to proceedings specified by Part IVA;

"directions appointment" means a hearing for directions under rule 4.14(2);

"emergency protection order" means an order under section 44;

"leave" includes permission and approval;

"note" includes a record made by mechanical means;

"parental responsibility" has the meaning assigned to it by section 3;

"recovery order" means an order under section 50;

"special guardianship order" has the meaning assigned to it by section 14A;

"specified proceedings" has the meaning assigned to it by section 41(6) and rule 4.2(2); and

"welfare officer" means a person who has been asked to prepare a welfare report under section 7(1)(b).

(2) Except where the contrary intention appears, the provisions of this Part apply to proceedings in the High Court and the county courts –

(a) on an application for a section 8 order;
(b) on an application for a care order or a supervision order;
(c) on an application under section 4(1)(c), 4(3), 4A(1)(*b*), 4A(3), 5(1), 6(7), 13(1), 14A, 14C(3), 14D, 16(6), 33(7), 34(2), 34(3), 34(4), 34(9), 36(1), 38(8)(b), 39(1), 39(2), 39(3), 39(4), 43(1), 43(12), 44, 45, 46(7), 48(9), 50(1) or 102(1);
(d) under Schedule 1, except where financial relief is also sought by or on behalf of an adult;
(e) on an application under paragraph 19(1) of Schedule 2;
(f) on an application under paragraph 6(3), 15(2) or 17(1) of Schedule 3;
(g) on an application under paragraph 11(3) or 16(5) of Schedule 14; or
(h) under section 25.

4.2 Matters prescribed for the purposes of the Act of 1989

(1) The parties to proceedings in which directions are given under section 38(6), and any person named in such a direction, form the prescribed class for the purposes of section 38(8) (application to vary directions made with interim care or interim supervision order).

(2) The following proceedings are specified for the purposes of section 41 in accordance with subsection (6)(i) thereof –

(a) proceedings under section 25;
(b) applications under section 33(7);
(c) proceedings under paragraph 19(1) of Schedule 2;
(d) applications under paragraph 6(3) of Schedule 3;
(e) appeals against the determination of proceedings of a kind set out in sub-paragraphs (a) to (d).

(3) The applicant for an order that has been made under section 43(1) and the persons referred to in section 43(11) may, in any circumstances, apply under section 43(12) for a child assessment order to be varied or discharged.

(4) The following persons form the prescribed class for the purposes of section 44(9) (application to vary directions) –

(a) the parties to the application for the order in respect of which it is sought to vary the directions;
(b) the children's guardian;
(c) the local authority in whose area the child concerned is ordinarily resident;
(d) any person who is named in the directions.

4.3 Application for leave to commence proceedings

(1) Where the leave of the court is required to bring any proceedings to which this Part applies, the person seeking leave shall file –

(a) a written request for leave in Form C2 setting out the reasons for the application; and

(b) a draft of the application (being the documents referred to in rule 4.4(1A)) for the making of which leave is sought together with sufficient copies for one to be served on each respondent.

(2) On considering a request for leave filed under paragraph (1), the court shall –

(a) grant the request, whereupon the proper officer shall inform the person making the request of the decision, or
(b) direct that a date be fixed for the hearing of the request, whereupon the proper officer shall fix such a date and give such notice as the court directs to the person making the request and any local authority that is preparing, or has prepared, a report under section 14A(8) or (9) and such other persons as the court requires to be notified, of the date so fixed.

(3) Where leave is granted to bring proceedings to which this Part applies the application shall proceed in accordance with rule 4.4; but paragraph (1)(a) of that rule shall not apply.

(4) In the case of a request for leave to bring proceedings under Schedule 1, the draft application under paragraph (1) shall be accompanied by a statement setting out the financial details which the person seeking leave believes to be relevant to the request and containing a declaration that it is true to the maker's best knowledge and belief, together with sufficient copies for one to be served on each respondent.

4.4 Application

(1) Subject to paragraph (4), an applicant shall –

(a) file the documents referred to in paragraph (1A) below (which documents shall together be called the "application") together with sufficient copies for one to be served on each respondent, and
(b) serve a copy of the application together with Form C6 and such (if any) of Forms C7 and C10A as are given to him by the proper officer under paragraph (2)(b) on each respondent such number of days prior to the date fixed under paragraph (2)(a) as is specified for that application in column (ii) of Appendix 3 to these rules.

(1A) The documents to be filed under paragraph (1)(a) above are –

(*a*) (i) whichever is appropriate of Forms C1, C2, C3, C4 or C51, and
(ii) such of the supplemental Forms C10 or C11 to C20 as may be appropriate, and
(iii) in the case of an application for a section 8 order or an order under section 4(1)(c) where question 7 on Form C1, or question 4 on Form C2, is answered in the affirmative, supplemental Form C1A, or
(b) where there is no appropriate form a statement in writing of the order sought,

and where the application is made in respect of more than one child, all the children shall be included in one application.

(2) On receipt of the documents filed under paragraph (1)(a) the proper officer shall –

(a) fix the date for a hearing or a directions appointment, allowing sufficient time for the applicant to comply with paragraph (1)(b),
(b) endorse the date so fixed upon Form C6 and, where appropriate, Form C6A, and
(c) return forthwith to the applicant the copies of the application and Form C10A if filed with it, together with Form C6 and such of Forms C6A and C7 as are appropriate, and, in the case of an application for a section 8 order or an order under section 4(1)(c), Form C1A.

(3) The applicant shall, at the same time as complying with paragraph (1)(*b*), serve Form C6A on the persons set out for the relevant class of proceedings in column (iv) of Appendix 3 to these rules.

(4) An application for –

(a) a section 8 order,
(b) an emergency protection order,
(c) a warrant under section 48(9),
(d) a recovery order, or
(e) a warrant under section 102(1)

may be made ex parte in which case the applicant shall –

(i) file the application in the appropriate form in Appendix 1 to these rules –
  (a) where the application is made by telephone, within 24 hours after the making of the application, or
  (b) in any other case, at the time when the application is made, and
(ii) in the case of an application for a section 8 order or an emergency protection order, serve a copy of the application on each respondent within 48 hours after the making of the order.

(5) Where the court refuses to make an order on an ex parte application it may direct that the application be made inter partes.

(6) In the case of proceedings under Schedule 1, the application under paragraph (1) shall be accompanied by a statement in Form C10A setting out the financial details which the applicant believes to be relevant to the application, together with sufficient copies for one to be served on each respondent.

4.5 Withdrawal of application

(1) An application may be withdrawn only with leave of the court.

(2) Subject to paragraph (3), a person seeking leave to withdraw an application shall file and serve on the parties a written request for leave setting out the reasons for the request.

(3) The request under paragraph (2) may be made orally to the court if the parties and either the children's guardian or the welfare officer or children and family reporter are present.

(4) Upon receipt of a written request under paragraph (2) the court shall –

(a) if –
(i) the parties consent in writing,
(ii) the children's guardian has had an opportunity to make representations,
and
(iii) the court thinks fit,
grant the request, in which case the proper officer shall notify the parties, any local authority that is preparing, or has prepared, a report under section 14A(8) or (9), the children's guardian and the welfare officer or children and family reporter of the granting of the request, or
(b) direct that a date be fixed for the hearing of the request in which case the proper officer shall give at least 7 days' notice to the parties, any local authority that is preparing, or has prepared, a report under section 14A(8) or (9), the children's guardian and the welfare officer or children and family reporter, of the date fixed.

4.6 Transfer

(1) Where an application is made, in accordance with the provisions of the Allocation Order, to a county court for an order transferring proceedings from a magistrates' court following the refusal of the magistrates' court to order such a transfer, the applicant shall –

(a) file the application in Form C2, together with a copy of the certificate issued by the magistrates' court, and
(b) serve a copy of the documents mentioned in sub-paragraph (*a*) personally on all parties to the proceedings which it is sought to have transferred,

within 2 days after receipt by the applicant of the certificate.

(2) Within 2 days after receipt of the documents served under paragraph (1)(b), any party other than the applicant may file written representations.

(3) The court shall, not before the fourth day after the filing of the application under paragraph (1), unless the parties consent to earlier consideration, consider the application and either –

(a) grant the application, whereupon the proper officer shall inform the parties and any local authority that is preparing, or has prepared, a report under section 14A(8) or (9) of that decision, or
(b) direct that a date be fixed for the hearing of the application, whereupon the proper officer shall fix such a date and give not less than 1 day's notice to the parties and any local authority that is preparing, or has prepared, a report under section 14A(8) or (9) of the date so fixed.

(4) Where proceedings are transferred from a magistrates' court to a county court in accordance with the provisions of the Allocation Order, the county court shall consider whether to transfer those proceedings to the High Court in accordance with that Order and either –

(a) determine that such an order need not be made,
(b) make such an order,
(c) order that a date be fixed for the hearing of the question whether such an order should be made, whereupon the proper officer shall give such notice to the parties and any local authority that is preparing, or has prepared, a report under section 14A(8) or (9) as the court directs of the date so fixed, or
(d) invite the parties to make written representations, within a specified period, as to whether such an order should be made; and upon receipt of the representations the court shall act in accordance with sub-paragraph (a), (b) or (c).

(5) The proper officer shall notify the parties and any local authority that is preparing, or has prepared, a report under section 14A(8) or (9) of an order transferring the proceedings from a county court or from the High Court made in accordance with the provisions of the Allocation Order.

(6) Before ordering the transfer of proceedings from a county court to a magistrates' court in accordance with the Allocation Order, the county court shall notify the magistrates' court of its intention to make such an order and invite the views of the clerk to the justices on whether such an order should be made.

(7) An order transferring proceedings from a county court to a magistrates' court in accordance with the Allocation Order shall –

(a) be in Form C49, and
(b) be served by the court on the parties.

(8) In this rule "the Allocation Order" means the Children (Allocation of Proceedings) Order 1991 or any Order replacing that Order.

4.7 Parties

(1) The respondents to proceedings to which this Part applies shall be those persons set out in the relevant entry in column (iii) of Appendix 3 to these rules.

(2) In proceedings to which this Part applies, a person may file a request in Form C2 that he or another person –

(a) be joined as a party, or
(b) cease to be a party.

(3) On considering a request under paragraph (2) the court shall, subject to paragraph (4) –

(a) grant it without a hearing or representations, save that this shall be done only in the case of a request under paragraph (2)(*a*), whereupon the proper officer shall inform the parties and any local authority that is preparing, or has prepared, a report under section 14A(8) or (9) and the person making the request of that decision, or
(b) order that a date be fixed for the consideration of the request,

whereupon the proper officer shall give notice of the date so fixed, together with a copy of the request –

(i) in the case of a request under paragraph (2)(*a*), to the applicant and any local authority that is preparing, or has prepared, a report under section 14A(8) or (9), and

(ii) in the case of a request under paragraph (2)(*b*), to the parties and any local authority that is preparing, or has prepared, a report under section 14A(8) or (9), or

(c) invite the parties or any of them to make written representations, within a specified period, as to whether the request should be granted; and upon the expiry of the period the court shall act in accordance with sub-paragraph (a) or (b).

(4) Where a person with parental responsibility requests that he be joined under paragraph (2)(a), the court shall grant his request.

(5) In proceedings to which this Part applies the court may direct –

(a) that a person who would not otherwise be a respondent under these rules be joined as a party to the proceedings, or

(b) that a party to the proceedings cease to be a party.

4.8 Service

(1) Subject to the requirement in rule 4.6(1)(b) of personal service, where service of a document is required under this Part (and not by a provision to which section 105(8) (Service of notice or other document under the Act) applies) it may be effected –

(a) if the person to be served is not known by the person serving to be acting by solicitor –

(i) by delivering it to him personally, or

(ii) by delivering it at, or by sending it by first-class post to, his residence or his last known residence, or

(b) if the person to be served is known by the person serving to be acting by solicitor –

(i) by delivering the document at, or sending it by first-class post to, the solicitor's address for service,

(ii) where the solicitor's address for service includes a numbered box at a document exchange, by leaving the document at that document exchange or at a document exchange which transmits documents on every business day to that document exchange, or

(iii) by sending a legible copy of the document by facsimile transmission to the solicitor's office.

(2) In this rule "first-class post" means first-class post which has been pre-paid or in respect of which pre-payment is not required.

(3) Where a child who is a party to proceedings to which this Part applies is not prosecuting or defending them without a next friend or guardian ad litem under rule 9.2A and is required by these rules or other rules of court to serve a document, service shall be effected by –

(a) the solicitor acting for the child, or
(b) where there is no such solicitor, the children's guardian or the guardian ad litem, or
(c) where there is neither such a solicitor nor a children's guardian nor a guardian ad litem, the court.

(4) Service of any document on a child who is not prosecuting or defending the proceedings concerned without a next friend or guardian ad litem under rule 9.2A shall, subject to any direction of the court, be effected by service on –

(a) the solicitor acting for the child, or
(b) where there is no such solicitor, the children's guardian or the guardian ad litem, or
(c) where there is neither such a solicitor nor a children's guardian nor a guardian ad litem, with leave of the court, the child.

(5) Where the court refuses leave under paragraph (4)(c) it shall give a direction under paragraph (8).

(6) A document shall, unless the contrary is proved, be deemed to have been served –

(a) in the case of service by first-class post, on the second business day after posting, and
(b) in the case of service in accordance with paragraph (1)(b)(ii), on the second business day after the day on which it is left at the document exchange.

(7) At or before the first directions appointment in, or hearing of, proceedings to which this Part applies the applicant shall file a statement in Form C9 that service of –

(a) a copy of the application and other documents referred to in rule 4.4(1)(b) has been effected on each respondent, and
(b) notice of the proceedings has been effected under rule 4.4(3);

and the statement shall indicate –

(i) the manner, date, time and place of service, or
(ii) where service was effected by post, the date, time and place of posting.

(8) In proceedings to which this Part applies, where these rules or other rules of court require a document to be served, the court may, without prejudice to any power under rule 4.14, direct that –

(a) the requirement shall not apply;
(b) the time specified by the rules for complying with the requirement shall be abridged to such extent as may be specified in the direction;
(c) service shall be effected in such manner as may be specified in the direction.

4.9 Answer to application

(1) Within 14 days of service of an application for an order under section 4(1)(c), an application for a section 8 order, a special guardianship order or an application under Schedule 1, each respondent shall file, and serve

on the parties, an acknowledgement of the application in Form C7 and, if both parts of question 6 or question 7 (or both) on Form C7 are answered in the affirmative, Form C1A.

(2) (*revoked*)

(3) Following service of an application to which this Part applies, other than an application under rule 4.3, for an order under section 4(1)(c) or for a section 8 order or special guardianship order, a respondent may, subject to paragraph (4), file a written answer, which shall be served on the other parties.

(4) An answer under paragraph (3) shall, except in the case of an application under section 25, 31, 34, 38, 43, 44, 45, 46, 48 or 50, be filed, and served, not less than 2 days before the date fixed for the hearing of the application.

4.10 Appointment of children's guardian

(1) As soon as practicable after the commencement of specified proceedings, or the transfer of such proceedings to the court, the court shall appoint a children's guardian, unless –

(a) such an appointment has already been made by the court which made the transfer and is subsisting, or
(b) the court considers that such an appointment is not necessary to safeguard the interests of the child.

(2) At any stage in specified proceedings a party may apply, without notice to the other parties unless the court directs otherwise, for the appointment of a children's guardian.

(3) The court shall grant an application under paragraph (2) unless it considers such an appointment not to be necessary to safeguard the interests of the child, in which case it shall give its reasons; and a note of such reasons shall be taken by the proper officer.

(4) At any stage in specified proceedings the court may, of its own motion, appoint a children's guardian.

(4A) The court may, in specified proceedings, appoint more than one children's guardian in respect of the same child.

(5) The proper officer shall, as soon as practicable, notify the parties and any welfare officer or children and family reporter of an appointment under this rule or, as the case may be, of a decision not to make such an appointment.

(6) Upon the appointment of a children's guardian the proper officer shall, as soon as practicable, notify him of the appointment and serve on him copies of the application and of documents filed under rule 4.17(1).

(7) A children's guardian appointed by the court under this rule shall not –

(a) be a member, officer or servant of a local authority which, or an authorised person (within the meaning of section 31(9)) who, is a party to the proceedings;
(b) be, or have been, a member, officer or servant of a local authority or voluntary organisation (within the meaning of section 105(1)) who has been directly concerned in that capacity in arrangements relating

to the care, accommodation or welfare of the child during the five years prior to the commencement of the proceedings; or

(c) be a serving probation officer who has, in that capacity, been previously concerned with the child or his family.

(8) When appointing a children's guardian the court shall consider the appointment of anyone who has previously acted as children's guardian of the same child.

(9) The appointment of a children's guardian under this rule shall continue for such time as is specified in the appointment or until terminated by the court.

(10) When terminating an appointment in accordance with paragraph (9), the court shall give its reasons in writing for so doing.

(11) Where the court appoints a children's guardian in accordance with this rule or refuses to make such an appointment, the court or the proper officer shall record the appointment or refusal in Form C47.

4.11 Powers and duties of officers of the service and Welsh family proceedings officers

(1) In carrying out his duty under section 7(1)(*a*) or section 41(2), the officer of the service or the Welsh family proceedings officer shall have regard to the principle set out in section 1(2) and the matters set out in section 1(3)(a) to (f) as if for the word "court" in that section there were substituted the words "officer of the service or the Welsh family proceedings officer".

(2) The officer of the service or the Welsh family proceedings officer shall make such investigations as may be necessary for him to carry out his duties and shall, in particular –

(a) contact or seek to interview such persons as he thinks appropriate or as the court directs;

(b) obtain such professional assistance as is available to him which he thinks appropriate or which the court directs him to obtain.

(3) In addition to his duties, under other paragraphs of this rule, or rules 4.11A and 4.11B, the officer of the service or the Welsh family proceedings officer shall provide to the court such other assistance as it may require.

(4) A party may question the officer of the service or the Welsh family proceedings officer about oral or written advice tendered by him to the court.

4.11A Additional powers and duties of children's guardian

(1) The children's guardian shall –

(a) appoint a solicitor to represent the child unless such a solicitor has already been appointed; and

(b) give such advice to the child as is appropriate having regard to his understanding and, subject to rule 4.12(1)(a), instruct the solicitor representing the child on all matters relevant to the interests of the child including possibilities for appeal, arising in the course of the proceedings.

(2) Where the children's guardian is an officer of the service authorised by the Service in the terms mentioned by and in accordance with section 15(1) of the Criminal Justice and Court Services Act 2000, paragraph 1(a) shall not require him to appoint a solicitor for the child if he intends to have conduct of the proceedings on behalf of the child unless –

(a) the child wishes to instruct a solicitor direct; and
(b) the children's guardian or the court considers that he is of sufficient understanding to do so.

(2A) Where the children's guardian is a Welsh family proceedings officer authorised by the National Assembly for Wales in the terms mentioned by and in accordance with section 37(1) of the Children Act 2004, paragraph (1)(a) shall not require him to appoint a solicitor for the child if he intends to have conduct of the proceedings on behalf of the child unless –

(a) the child wishes to instruct a solicitor direct; and
(b) the children's guardian or the court considers that he is of sufficient understanding to do so.

(3) Where it appears to the children's guardian that the child –

(a) is instructing his solicitor direct, or
(b) intends to conduct and is capable of conducting the proceedings on his own behalf,

he shall inform the court and from then he –

(i) shall perform all of his duties set out in rule 4.11 and this rule, other than duties under paragraph (1)(a) of this rule, and such other duties as the court may direct;
(ii) shall take such part in the proceedings as the court may direct; and
(iii) may, with leave of the court, have legal representation in the conduct of those duties.

(4) Unless excused by the court, the children's guardian shall attend all directions appointments in and hearings of the proceedings and shall advise the court on the following matters –

(a) whether the child is of sufficient understanding for any purpose including the child's refusal to submit to a medical or psychiatric examination or other assessment that the court has power to require, direct or order;
(b) the wishes of the child in respect of any matter relevant to the proceedings, including his attendance at court;
(c) the appropriate forum for the proceedings;
(d) the appropriate timing of the proceedings or any part of them;
(e) the options available to it in respect of the child and the suitability of each such option including what order should be made in determining the application; and
(f) any other matter concerning which the court seeks his advice or concerning which he considers that the court should be informed.

(5) The advice given under paragraph (4) may, subject to any order of the court, be given orally or in writing; and if the advice be given orally, a note of it shall be taken by the court or the proper officer.

(6) The children's guardian shall, where practicable, notify any person whose joinder as a party to those proceedings would be likely, in the opinion of the children's guardian, to safeguard the interests of the child of that person's right to apply to be joined under rule 4.7(2) and shall inform the court –

(a) of any such notification given;
(b) of anyone whom he attempted to notify under this paragraph but was unable to contact; and
(c) of anyone whom he believes may wish to be joined to the proceedings.

(7) The children's guardian shall, unless the court otherwise directs, not less than 14 days before the date fixed for the final hearing of the proceedings –

(a) file a written report advising on the interests of the child; and
(b) serve a copy of the filed report on the other parties and any local authority that is preparing, or has prepared, a report under section 14A(8) or (9).

(8) The children's guardian shall serve and accept service of documents on behalf of the child in accordance with rule 4.8(3)(b) and (4)(b) and, where the child has not himself been served, and has sufficient understanding, advise the child of the contents of any document so served.

(9) If the children's guardian inspects records of the kinds referred to in section 42, he shall bring to the attention of –

(a) the court; and
(b) unless the court otherwise directs, the other parties to the proceedings,

all records and documents which may, in his opinion, assist in the proper determination of the proceedings.

(10) The children's guardian shall ensure that, in relation to a decision made by the court in the proceedings –

(a) if he considers it appropriate to the age and understanding of the child, the child is notified of that decision; and
(b) if the child is notified of the decision, it is explained to the child in a manner appropriate to his age and understanding.

4.11B Additional powers and duties of a children and family reporter

(1) The children and family reporter shall –

(a) notify the child of such contents of his report (if any) as he considers appropriate to the age and understanding of the child, including any reference to the child's own views on the application and the recommendation of the children and family reporter; and
(b) if he does notify the child of any contents of his report, explain them to the child in a manner appropriate to his age and understanding.

(2) Where the court has –

(a) directed that a written report be made by a children and family reporter; and

(b) notified the children and family reporter that his report is to be considered at a hearing,

the children and family reporter shall –

(i) file the report; and

(ii) serve a copy on the other parties, any local authority that is preparing, or has prepared, a report under section 14A(8) or (9) and on the children's guardian (if any),

by such time as the court may direct and if no direction is given, not less than 14 days before that hearing.

(3) The court may direct that the children and family reporter attend any hearing at which his report is to be considered.

(4) The children and family reporter shall advise the court if he considers that the joinder of a person as a party to the proceedings would be likely to safeguard the interests of the child.

(5) The children and family reporter shall consider whether it is in the best interests of the child for the child to be made a party to the proceedings.

(6) If the children and family reporter considers the child should be made a party to the proceedings he shall notify the court of his opinion together with the reasons for that opinion.

4.12 Solicitor for child

(1) A solicitor appointed under section 41(3) or in accordance with rule 4.11A(1)(a) shall represent the child –

(a) in accordance with instructions received from the children's guardian (unless the solicitor considers, having taken into account the views of the children's guardian and any direction of the court under rule 4.11A(3), that the child wishes to give instructions which conflict with those of the children's guardian and that he is able, having regard to his understanding, to give such instructions on his own behalf in which case he shall conduct the proceedings in accordance with instructions received from the child), or

(b) where no children's guardian has been appointed for the child and the condition in section 41(4)(*b*) is satisfied, in accordance with instructions received from the child, or

(c) in default of instructions under (*a*) or (*b*), in furtherance of the best interests of the child.

(2) A solicitor appointed under section 41(3) or in accordance with rule 4.11A(1)(a) shall serve and accept service of documents on behalf of the child in accordance with rule 4.8(3)(*a*) and (4)(a) and, where the child has not himself been served and has sufficient understanding, advise the child of the contents of any document so served.

(3) Where the child wishes an appointment of a solicitor under section 41(3) or in accordance with rule 4.11A(1)(a) to be terminated, he may apply to the court for an order terminating the appointment; and the solicitor and the children's guardian shall be given an opportunity to make representations.

(4) Where the children's guardian wishes an appointment of a solicitor under section 41(3) to be terminated, he may apply to the court for an order terminating the appointment; and the solicitor and, if he is of sufficient understanding, the child, shall be given an opportunity to make representations.

(5) When terminating an appointment in accordance with paragraph (3) or (4), the court shall give its reasons for so doing, a note of which shall be taken by the court or the proper officer.

(6) Where the court appoints a solicitor under section 41(3) or refuses to make such an appointment, the court or the proper officer shall record the appointment or refusal in Form C48.

4.13 Welfare officer

(1) Where the court has directed that a written report be made by a welfare officer in accordance with section 7(1)(b), the report shall be filed at or by such time as the court directs or, in the absence of such a direction, at least 14 days before a relevant hearing; and the proper officer shall, as soon as practicable, serve a copy of the report on the parties, any local authority that is preparing, or has prepared, a report under section 14A(8) or (9) and any children's guardian.

(2) In paragraph (1), a hearing is relevant if the proper officer has given the welfare officer notice that his report is to be considered at it.

(3) After the filing of a report by a welfare officer, the court may direct that the welfare officer attend any hearing at which the report is to be considered; and

(a) except where such a direction is given at a hearing attended by the welfare officer the proper officer shall inform the welfare officer of the direction; and
(b) at the hearing at which the report is considered any party may question the welfare officer about his report.

(3A) The welfare officer shall consider whether it is in the best interests of the child for the child to be made a party to the proceedings.

(3B) If the welfare officer considers the child should be made a party to the proceedings he shall notify the court of his opinion together with the reasons for that opinion.

(4) This rule is without prejudice to any power to give directions under rule 4.14.

4.14 Directions

(1) In this rule, "party" includes the children's guardian and, where a request or direction concerns a report under —

(a) section 7, the welfare officer or children and family reporter; or
(b) section 14A(8) or (9), the local authority preparing that report.

(2) In proceedings to which this Part applies the court may, subject to paragraph (3), give, vary or revoke directions for the conduct of the proceedings, including –

(a) the timetable for the proceedings;
(b) varying the time within which or by which an act is required, by these rules or by other rules of court, to be done;
(c) the attendance of the child;
(d) the appointment of a children's guardian, a guardian ad litem, or of a solicitor under section 41(3);
(e) the service of documents;
(f) the submission of evidence including experts' reports;
(g) the preparation of welfare reports under section 7;
(h) the transfer of the proceedings to another court;
(i) consolidation with other proceedings;
(j) the preparation of reports under section 14A(8) or (9);
(k) the attendance of the person who prepared the report under section 14A(8) or (9) at any hearing at which the report is to be considered.

(3) Directions under paragraph (2) may be given, varied or revoked either –

(a) of the court's own motion having given the parties notice of its intention to do so, and an opportunity to attend and be heard or to make written representations,
(b) on the written request in Form C2 of a party specifying the direction which is sought, filed and served on the other parties, or
(c) on the written request in Form C2 of a party specifying the direction which is sought, to which the other parties consent and which they or their representatives have signed.

(4) In an urgent case the request under paragraph (3)(b) may, with the leave of the court, be made –

(a) orally, or
(b) without notice to the parties, or
(c) both as in sub-paragraph (a) and as in sub-paragraph (b).

(5) On receipt of a written request under paragraph (3)(b) the proper officer shall fix a date for the hearing of the request and give not less than 2 days' notice in Form C6 to the parties of the date so fixed.

(6) On considering a request under paragraph (3)(c) the court shall either –

(a) grant the request, whereupon the proper officer shall inform the parties of the decision, or
(b) direct that a date be fixed for the hearing of the request, whereupon the proper officer shall fix such a date and give not less than 2 days' notice to the parties of the date so fixed.

(7) A party may apply for an order to be made under section 11(3) or, if he is entitled to apply for such an order, under section 38(1) in accordance with paragraph (3)(b) or (c).

(8) Where a court is considering making, of its own motion, a section 8 order, or an order under section 14A, 14D, 31, 34 or 38, the power to give directions under paragraph (2) shall apply.

(9) Directions of a court which are still in force immediately prior to the transfer of proceedings to which this Part applies to another court shall

continue to apply following the transfer, subject to any changes of terminology which are required to apply those directions to the court to which the proceedings are transferred, unless varied or discharged by directions under paragraph (2).

(10) The court or the proper officer shall take a note of the giving, variation or revocation of a direction under this rule and serve, as soon as practicable, a copy of the note on any party who was not present at the giving, variation or revocation.

4.15 Timing of proceedings

(1) Where these rules or other rules of court provide a period of time within which or by which a certain act is to be performed in the course of proceedings to which this Part applies, that period may not be extended otherwise than by direction of the court under rule 4.14.

(2) At the –

(a) transfer to a court of proceedings to which this Part applies,
(b) postponement or adjournment of any hearing or directions appointment in the course of proceedings to which this Part applies, or
(c) conclusion of any such hearing or directions appointment other than one at which the proceedings are determined, or so soon thereafter as is practicable,

the court or the proper officer shall –

(i) fix a date upon which the proceedings shall come before the court again for such purposes as the court directs, which date shall, where paragraph (*a*) applies, be as soon as possible after the transfer, and
(ii) give notice to the parties, any local authority that is preparing, or has prepared, a report under section 14A(8) or (9), the children's guardian or the welfare officer or children and family reporter of the date so fixed.

4.16 Attendance at directions appointment and hearing

(1) Subject to paragraph (2), a party shall attend a directions appointment of which he has been given notice in accordance with rule 4.14(5) unless the court otherwise directs.

(2) Proceedings or any part of them shall take place in the absence of any party, including the child, if –

(a) the court considers it in the interests of the child, having regard to the matters to be discussed or the evidence likely to be given, and
(b) the party is represented by a children's guardian or solicitor;

and when considering the interests of the child under sub-paragraph (*a*) the court shall give the children's guardian, the solicitor for the child and, if he is of sufficient understanding, the child an opportunity to make representations.

(3) Subject to paragraph (4), where at the time and place appointed for a hearing or directions appointment the applicant appears but one or more of the respondents do not, the court may proceed with the hearing or appointment.

(4) The court shall not begin to hear an application in the absence of a respondent unless –

(a) it is proved to the satisfaction of the court that he received reasonable notice of the date of the hearing; or

(b) the court is satisfied that the circumstances of the case justify proceeding with the hearing.

(5) Where, at the time and place appointed for a hearing or directions appointment one or more of the respondents appear but the applicant does not, the court may refuse the application or, if sufficient evidence has previously been received, proceed in the absence of the applicant.

(6) Where at the time and place appointed for a hearing or directions appointment neither the applicant nor any respondent appears, the court may refuse the application.

(7) Unless the court otherwise directs, a hearing of, or directions appointment in, proceedings to which this Part applies shall be in chambers.

4.17 Documentary evidence

(1) Subject to paragraphs (4) and (5), in proceedings to which this Part applies a party shall file and serve on the parties, any local authority that is preparing, or has prepared, a report under section 14A(8) or (9), any welfare officer or children and family reporter and any children's guardian of whose appointment he has been given notice under rule 4.10(5) –

(*a*) written statements of the substance of the oral evidence which the party intends to adduce at a hearing of, or a directions appointment in, those proceedings, which shall –

- (i) be dated,
- (ii) be signed by the person making the statement,
- (iii) contain a declaration that the maker of the statement believes it to be true and understands that it may be placed before the court; and
- (iv) show in the top right hand corner of the first page –
  - (a) the initials and surname of the person making the statement,
  - (*b*) the number of the statement in relation to the maker,
  - (c) the date on which the statement was made, and
  - (d) the party on whose behalf it is filed; and

(b) copies of any documents, including experts' reports, upon which the party intends to rely at a hearing of, or a directions appointment in, those proceedings,

at or by such time as the court directs or, in the absence of a direction, before the hearing or appointment.

(2) A party may, subject to any direction of the court about the timing of statements under this rule, file and serve on the parties a statement which is supplementary to a statement served under paragraph (1).

(3) At a hearing or a directions appointment a party may not, without the leave of the court –

(a) adduce evidence, or
(b) seek to rely on a document,

in respect of which he has failed to comply with the requirements of paragraph (1).

(4) In proceedings for a section 8 order or a special guardianship order a party shall –

(a) neither file nor serve any document other than as required or authorised by these rules, and
(b) in completing a form prescribed by these rules, neither give information, nor make a statement, which is not required or authorised by that form,

without the leave of the court.

(5) In proceedings for a section 8 order or a special guardianship order no statement or copy may be filed under paragraph (1) until such time as the court directs.

4.17A Disclosure of report under section 14A(8) or (9)

(1) In proceedings for a special guardianship order, the local authority shall file the report under section 14A(8) or (9) within the timetable fixed by the court.

(2) The court shall consider whether to give a direction that the report under section 14A(8) or (9) be disclosed to each party to the proceedings.

(3) Before giving such a direction the court shall consider whether any information should be deleted including information which reveals the party's address in a case where he has declined to reveal it in accordance with rule 10.21 (disclosure of addresses).

(4) The court may direct that the report will not be disclosed to a party.

(5) The proper officer shall serve a copy of the report filed under paragraph (1) –

(i) in accordance with any direction given under paragraph (2); and
(ii) on any children's guardian, welfare officer or children and family reporter.

4.18 Expert evidence – examination of child

(1) No person may, without the leave of the court, cause the child to be medically or psychiatrically examined, or otherwise assessed, for the purpose of the preparation of expert evidence for use in the proceedings.

(2) An application for leave under paragraph (1) shall, unless the court otherwise directs, be served on all parties to the proceedings and on the children's guardian.

(3) Where the leave of the court has not been given under paragraph (1), no evidence arising out of an examination or assessment to which that paragraph applies may be adduced without the leave of the court.

4.19 Amendment

(1) Subject to rule 4.17(2), a document which has been filed or served in proceedings to which this Part applies, may not be amended without the leave of the court which shall, unless the court otherwise directs, be requested in writing.

(2) On considering a request for leave to amend a document the court shall either –

(a) grant the request, whereupon the proper officer shall inform the person making the request of that decision, or

(b) invite the parties or any of them to make representations, within a specified period, as to whether such an order should be made.

(3) A person amending a document shall file it and serve it on those persons on whom it was served prior to amendment; and the amendments shall be identified.

4.20 Oral evidence

The court or the proper officer shall keep a note of the substance of the oral evidence given at a hearing of, or directions appointment in, proceedings to which this Part applies.

4.21 Hearing

(1) The court may give directions as to the order of speeches and evidence at a hearing or directions appointment, in the course of proceedings to which this Part applies.

(2) Subject to directions under paragraph (1), at a hearing of, or directions appointment in, proceedings to which this Part applies, the parties and the children's guardian shall adduce their evidence in the following order –

(a) the applicant,
(b) any party with parental responsibility for the child,
(c) other respondents,
(d) the children's guardian,
(e) the child, if he is a party to the proceedings and there is no children's guardian.

(2A) At the hearing at which the report under section 14A(8) or (9) is considered a party to whom the report, or part of it, has been disclosed may question the person who prepared the report about it.

(3) After the final hearing of proceedings to which this Part applies, the court shall deliver its judgment as soon as is practicable.

(4) When making an order or when refusing an application, the court shall –

(a) where it makes a finding of fact state such finding and complete Form C22; and
(b) state the reasons for the court's decision.

(5) An order made in proceedings to which this Part applies shall be recorded, by the court or the proper officer, either in the appropriate form in Appendix 1 to these rules or, where there is no such form, in writing.

(6) Subject to paragraph (7), a copy of an order made in accordance with paragraph (5) shall, as soon as practicable after it has been made, be served by the proper officer on the parties to the proceedings in which it was made and on any person with whom the child is living, and where applicable, on the local authority that prepared the report under section 14A(8) or (9).

(7) Within 48 hours after the making ex parte of –

(a) a section 8 order, or
(b) an order under section 44, 48(4), 48(9) or 50,

the applicant shall serve a copy of the order in the appropriate form in Appendix 1 to these Rules on –

(i) each party,
(ii) any person who has actual care of the child or who had such care immediately prior to the making of the order, and
(iii) in the case of an order referred to in sub-paragraph (*b*), the local authority in whose area the child lives or is found.

(8) At a hearing of, or directions appointment in, an application which takes place outside the hours during which the court office is normally open, the court or the proper officer shall take a note of the substance of the proceedings.

4.21A Attachment of penal notice

CCR Order 29, rule 1 (committal for breach of order or undertaking) shall apply to section 8 orders and orders under section 14A, 14B(2)(b), 14C(3)(b), or 14D as if for paragraph (3) of that rule there were substituted the following –

> "(3) In the case of a section 8 order (within the meaning of section 8(2) of the Children Act 1989) or an order under section 14A, 14B(2)(b), 14C(3)(b), or 14D of the Children Act 1989 enforceable by committal order under paragraph (1), the judge or the district judge may, on the application of the person entitled to enforce the order, direct that the proper officer issue a copy of the order, endorsed with or incorporating a notice as to the consequences of disobedience, for service in accordance with paragraph (2); and no copy of the order shall be issued with any such notice endorsed or incorporated save in accordance with such a direction.".

4.22 Appeals

(1) Where an appeal lies –

(a) to the High Court under section 94, or

(b) from any decision of a district judge to the judge of the court in which the decision was made,

it shall be made in accordance with the following provisions; and references to "the court below" are references to the court from which, or person from whom, the appeal lies.

(2) The appellant shall file and serve on the parties to the proceedings in the court below, and on any children's guardian and where applicable, on the local authority that prepared a report under section 14A(8) or (9) –

(a) notice of the appeal in writing, setting out the grounds upon which he relies;
(b) a certified copy of the summons or application and of the order appealed against, and of any order staying its execution;
(c) a copy of any notes of the evidence;
(d) a copy of any reasons given for the decision.

(2A) In relation to an appeal to the High Court under section 94, the documents required to be filed by paragraph (2) shall, –

(a) where the care centre listed in column (ii) of Schedule 2 to the Children (Allocation of Proceedings) Order 1991 against the entry in column (i) relating to the petty sessions area or London commission area in which the court below is situated –
   (i) is the principal registry, or
   (ii) has a district registry in the same place,

be filed in that registry, and

(b) in any other case, be filed in the district registry, being in the same place as a care centre within the meaning of article 2(c) of the said Order, which is nearest to the court below.

(3) The notice of appeal shall be filed and served in accordance with paragraph (2)(*a*) –

(a) within 14 days after the determination against which the appeal is brought, or
(b) in the case of an appeal against an order under section 38(1), within 7 days after the making of the order, or
(c) with the leave of the court to which, or judge to whom, the appeal is to be brought, within such other time as that court or judge may direct.

(4) The documents mentioned in paragraph (2)(b) to (d) shall, subject to any direction of the court to which, or judge to whom, the appeal is to be brought, be filed and served as soon as practicable after the filing and service of the notice of appeal under paragraph (2)(a).

(5) Subject to paragraph (6), a respondent who wishes –

(a) to contend on the appeal that the decision of the court below should be varied, either in any event or in the event of the appeal being allowed in whole or in part, or
(b) to contend that the decision of the court below should be affirmed on grounds other than those relied upon by that court, or

(c) to contend by way of cross-appeal that the decision of the court below was wrong in whole or in part,

shall, within 14 days of receipt of notice of the appeal, file and serve on all other parties to the appeal a notice in writing, setting out the grounds upon which he relies.

(6) No notice under paragraph (5) may be filed or served in an appeal against an order under section 38.

(7) In the case of an appeal mentioned in paragraph (1)(*a*) an application to –

(a) withdraw the appeal,
(b) have the appeal dismissed with the consent of all the parties, or
(c) amend the grounds of appeal,

may be heard by a district judge.

(8) An appeal of the kind mentioned in paragraph (1)(a) shall, unless the President otherwise directs, be heard and determined by a single judge.

4.23

(*revoked*)

4.24 Notification of consent

(1) Consent for the purposes of –

(a) section 16(3), or
(b) section 38A(2)(b)(ii) or 44A(2)(b)(ii), or
(c) paragraph 19(3)(c) or (d) of Schedule 2,

shall be given either –

(i) orally in court, or
(ii) in writing to the court signed by the person giving his consent.

(2) Any written consent given for the purposes of subsection (2) of section 38A or section 44A, shall include a statement that the person giving consent –

(a) is able and willing to give to the child the care which it would be reasonable to expect a parent to give him; and
(b) understands that the giving of consent could lead to the exclusion of the relevant person from the dwelling-house in which the child lives.

4.24A Exclusion requirements: interim care orders and emergency protection orders

(1) This rule applies where the court includes an exclusion requirement in an interim care order or an emergency protection order.

(2) The applicant for an interim care order or emergency protection order shall –

(a) prepare a separate statement of the evidence in support of the application for an exclusion requirement;

(b) serve the statement personally on the relevant person with a copy of the order containing the exclusion requirement (and of any power of arrest which is attached to it);
(c) inform the relevant person of his right to apply to vary or discharge the exclusion requirement.

(3) Where a power of arrest is attached to an exclusion requirement in an interim care order or an emergency protection order, a copy of the order shall be delivered to the officer for the time being in charge of the police station for the area in which the dwelling-house in which the child lives is situated (or of such other station as the court may specify) together with a statement showing that the relevant person has been served with the order or informed of its terms (whether by being present when the order was made or by telephone or otherwise).

(4) Rules 3.9(5), 3.9A (except paragraphs (1) and (3)) and 3.10 shall apply, with the necessary modifications, for the service, variation, discharge and enforcement of any exclusion requirement to which a power of arrest is attached as they apply to an order made on an application under Part IV of the Family Law Act 1996.

(5) The relevant person shall serve the parties to the proceedings with any application which he makes for the variation or discharge of the exclusion requirement.

(6) Where an exclusion requirement ceases to have effect whether –

(a) as a result of the removal of a child under section 38A(10) or 44A(10),
(b) because of the discharge of the interim care order or emergency protection order, or
(c) otherwise,

the applicant shall inform –

(i) the relevant person,
(ii) the parties to the proceedings
(iii) any officer to whom a copy of the order was delivered under paragraph (3), and
(iv) (where necessary) the court.

(7) Where the court includes an exclusion requirement in an interim care order or an emergency protection order of its own motion, paragraph (2) shall apply with the omission of any reference to the statement of the evidence.

4.25 Secure accommodation – evidence

In proceedings under section 25, the court shall, if practicable, arrange for copies of all written reports before it to be made available before the hearing to –

(a) the applicant;
(b) the parent or guardian of the child;
(c) any legal representative of the child;
(d) the children's guardian; and
(e) the child, unless the court otherwise directs;

and copies of such reports may, if the court considers it desirable, be shown to any person who is entitled to notice of the proceedings in accordance with these rules.

4.26 Investigation under section 37

(1) This rule applies where a direction is given to an appropriate authority by the High Court or a county court under section 37(1).

(2) On giving a direction the court shall adjourn the proceedings and the court or the proper officer shall record the direction in Form C40.

(3) A copy of the direction recorded under paragraph (2) shall, as soon as practicable after the direction is given, be served by the proper officer on the parties to the proceedings in which the direction is given and, where the appropriate authority is not a party, on that authority.

(4) When serving the copy of the direction on the appropriate authority the proper officer shall also serve copies of such of the documentary evidence which has been, or is to be, adduced in the proceedings as the court may direct.

(5) Where a local authority informs the court of any of the matters set out in section 37(3)(*a*) to (*c*) it shall do so in writing.

4.27 Direction to local education authority to apply for education supervision order

(1) For the purposes of section 40(3) and (4) of the Education Act 1944 a direction by the High Court or a county court to a local education authority to apply for an education supervision order shall be given in writing.

(2) Where, following such a direction, a local education authority informs the court that they have decided not to apply for an education supervision order, they shall do so in writing.

4.27A Stay under the Council Regulation

(1) An application for an order under Article 19 of the Council Regulation shall be made to a district judge, who may determine the application or refer the application, or any question arising thereon, to a judge for his decision.

(2) Where at any time after an application under rule 4.4 is made, it appears to the court that, under Articles 16 to 19 of the Council Regulation, the court does not have jurisdiction to hear the application and is required or may be required to stay the proceedings, the court will stay the proceedings and fix a date for a hearing to determine the questions of jurisdiction and whether there should be a stay or other order and shall serve notice of the hearing on the parties to the proceedings.

(3) The court must give reasons for its decision under Articles 16 to 19 of the Council Regulation and, where it makes a finding of fact state such a finding of fact.

(4) A declaration under Article 17 of the Council Regulation that the court has no jurisdiction over the proceedings shall be recorded by the court or proper officer in writing.

(5) The court may, if all parties agree, deal with any question about the jurisdiction of the court without a hearing.

4.28 Transitional provision

Nothing in any provision of this Part of these rules shall affect any proceedings which are pending (within the meaning of paragraph 1 of Schedule 14 to the Act of 1989) immediately before these rules come into force.

Appendix 4

FAMILY PROCEDURE (ADOPTION) RULES 2005

SI 2005/2795

Part 1
Overriding Objective

1 The overriding objective

(1) These Rules are a new procedural code with the overriding objective of enabling the court to deal with cases justly, having regard to the welfare issues involved.

(2) Dealing with a case justly includes, so far as is practicable –

(a) ensuring that it is dealt with expeditiously and fairly;
(b) dealing with the case in ways which are proportionate to the nature, importance and complexity of the issues;
(c) ensuring that the parties are on an equal footing;
(d) saving expense; and
(e) allotting to it an appropriate share of the court's resources, while taking into account the need to allot resources to other cases.

2 Application by the court of the overriding objective

The court must seek to give effect to the overriding objective when it –

(a) exercises any power given to it by these Rules; or
(b) interprets any rule.

3 Duty of the parties

The parties are required to help the court to further the overriding objective.

4 Court's duty to manage cases

(1) The court must further the overriding objective by actively managing cases.

(2) Active case management includes –

(a) encouraging the parties to co-operate with each other in the conduct of the proceedings;
(b) identifying at an early stage –
  (i) the issues; and

(ii) who should be a party to the proceedings;

(c) deciding promptly –

(i) which issues need full investigation and hearing and which do not; and

(ii) the procedure to be followed in the case;

(d) deciding the order in which issues are to be resolved;

(e) encouraging the parties to use an alternative dispute resolution procedure if the court considers that appropriate and facilitating the use of such procedure;

(f) helping the parties to settle the whole or part of the case;

(g) fixing timetables or otherwise controlling the progress of the case;

(h) considering whether the likely benefits of taking a particular step justify the cost of taking it;

(i) dealing with as many aspects of the case as it can on the same occasion;

(j) dealing with the case without the parties needing to attend at court;

(k) making use of technology; and

(l) giving directions to ensure that the case proceeds quickly and efficiently.

Part 3
General Case Management Powers

12 The court's general powers of management

(1) The list of powers in this rule is in addition to any powers given to the court by any other rule or practice direction or by any other enactment or any powers it may otherwise have.

(2) Except where these Rules provide otherwise, the court may –

(a) extend or shorten the time for compliance with any rule, practice direction or court direction (even if an application for extension is made after the time for compliance has expired);

(b) adjourn or bring forward a hearing;

(c) require a party or a party's legal representative to attend the court;

(d) hold a hearing and receive evidence by telephone or by using any other method of direct oral communication;

(e) direct that part of any proceedings be dealt with as separate proceedings;

(f) stay the whole or part of any proceedings or judgment either generally or until a specified date or event;

(g) consolidate proceedings;

(h) hear two or more applications on the same occasion;

(i) direct a separate hearing of any issue;

(j) decide the order in which issues are to be heard;

(k) exclude an issue from consideration;

(l) dismiss or give judgment on an application after a decision on a preliminary issue;

(m) direct any party to file and serve an estimate of costs; and

(n) take any other step or give any other direction for the purpose of managing the case and furthering the overriding objective.

(3) The court may not extend the period within which a section 89 order must be made.

(4) Paragraph (2)(f) does not apply to proceedings in a magistrates' court.

13 Exercise of powers of court's own initiative

(1) Except where an enactment provides otherwise, the court may exercise the powers in rule 12 on an application or of its own initiative.

(Part 9 sets out the procedure for making an application.)

(2) Where the court proposes to exercise its powers of its own initiative –

(a) it may give any person likely to be affected an opportunity to make representations; and
(b) where it does so it must specify the time by and the manner in which the representations must be made.

(3) Where the court proposes to hold a hearing to decide whether to exercise its powers of its own initiative it must give each party likely to be affected at least 3 days' notice of the hearing.

(4) The court may exercise its powers of its own initiative, without hearing the parties or giving them an opportunity to make representations.

(5) Where the court has exercised its powers under paragraph (4) –

(a) a party affected by the direction may apply to have it set aside or varied; and
(b) the direction must contain a statement of the right to make such an application.

(6) An application under paragraph (5)(a) must be made –

(a) within such period as may be specified by the court; or
(b) if the court does not specify a period, within 7 days beginning with the date on which the order was served on the party making the application.

(7) If the High Court or a county court of its own initiative dismisses an application (including an application for permission to appeal) and it considers that the application is totally without merit –

(a) the court's order must record that fact; and
(b) the court must at the same time consider whether it is appropriate to make a civil restraint order.

14 Court officer's power to refer to the court

Where these Rules require a step to be taken by a court officer –

(a) the court officer may consult the court before taking that step;
(b) the step may be taken by the court instead of the court officer.

15 General power of the court to rectify matters where there has been an error of procedure

Where there has been an error of procedure such as a failure to comply with a rule or practice direction –

(a) the error does not invalidate any step taken in the proceedings unless the court so orders; and
(b) the court may make an order to remedy the error.

16 Power of the court to make civil restraint orders

The relevant practice direction sets out –

(a) the circumstances in which the High Court or a county court has the power to make a civil restraint order against a party to proceedings;
(b) the procedure where a party applies for a civil restraint order against another party; and
(c) the consequences of the court making a civil restraint order.

Part 5
Procedure For Applications In Adoption, Placement And Related Proceedings

22 Application of this Part

The rules in this Part apply to the following proceedings –

(a) adoption proceedings;
(b) placement proceedings; or
(c) proceedings for –
   (i) the making of a contact order under section 26;
   (ii) the variation or revocation of a contact order under section 27;
   (iii) an order giving permission to change a child's surname or remove a child from the United Kingdom under section 28(2) and (3);
   (iv) a section 84 order;
   (v) a section 88 direction;
   (vi) a section 89 order; or
   (vii) any other order that may be referred to in a practice direction.

(Parts 9 and 10 set out the procedure for making an application in proceedings not dealt with in this Part.)

23 Who the parties are

(1) In relation to the proceedings set out in column 1 of each of the following tables, column 2 of Table 1 sets out who the application may be made by and column 2 of Table 2 sets out who the respondents to those proceedings will be.

TABLE 1

Proceedings for	Applicants
An adoption order (section 46)	The prospective adopters (section 50 and 51).
A section 84 order	The prospective adopters asking for parental responsibility prior to adoption abroad.
A placement order (section 21)	A local authority (section 22).
An order varying a placement order (section 23)	The joint application of the local authority authorised by the placement order to place the child for adoption and the local authority which is to be substituted for that authority (section 23).
An order revoking a placement order (section 24)	The child;
	the local authority authorised to place the child for adoption; or
	where the child is not placed for adoption by the authority, any other person who has the permission of the court to apply (section 24).
A contact order (section 26)	The child;
	the adoption agency;
	any parent, guardian or relative;
	any person in whose favour there was provision for contact under the 1989 Act which ceased to have effect on an adoption agency being authorised to place a child for adoption, or placing a child for adoption who is less than six weeks old (section 26(1));
	a person in whose favour there was a residence order in force immediately before the adoption agency was authorised to place the child for adoption or placed the child for adoption at a time when he was less than six weeks old;
	a person who by virtue of an order made in the exercise of the High Court's inherent jurisdiction with respect to children had care of the child immediately before that time; or
	any person who has the permission of the court to make the application (section 26).
An order varying or revoking a contact order (section 27)	The child;
	the adoption agency; or
	any person named in the contact order (section 27(1)).

Proceedings for	Applicants
An order permitting the child's name to be changed or the removal of the child from the United Kingdom (section 28(2) and (3))	Any person including the adoption agency or the local authority authorised to place, or which has placed, the child for adoption (section 28(2)).
A section 88 direction	The adopted child; the adopters; any parent; or any other person.
A section 89 order	The adopters; the adopted person; any parent; the relevant Central Authority; the adoption agency; the local authority to whom notice under section 44 (notice of intention to adopt or apply for a section 84 order) has been given; the Secretary of State for the Home Department; or any other person.

TABLE 2

Proceedings for	Respondents
An adoption order (section 46) or a section 84 order	Each parent who has parental responsibility for the child or guardian of the child unless he has given notice under section 20(4)(*a*) (statement of wish not to be informed of any application for an adoption order) which has effect; any person in whose favour there is provision for contact; any adoption agency having parental responsibility for the child under section 25; any adoption agency which has taken part at any stage in the arrangements for adoption of the child; any local authority to whom notice under section 44 (notice of intention to adopt or apply for a section 84 order) has been given; any local authority or voluntary organisation which has parental responsibility for, is looking after, or is caring for, the child; and the child where – permission has been granted to a parent or guardian to oppose the making of the adoption order (section 47(3) or 47(5)); he opposes the making of an adoption order;

Proceedings for	Respondents
	a children and family reporter recommends that it is in the best interests of the child to be a party to the proceedings and that recommendation is accepted by the court; he is already an adopted child; any party to the proceedings or the child is opposed to the arrangements for allowing any person contact with the child, or a person not being allowed contact with the child after the making of the adoption order; the application is for a Convention adoption order or a section 84 order; he has been brought into the United Kingdom in the circumstances where section 83(1) applies (restriction on bringing children in); the application is for an adoption order other than a Convention adoption order and the prospective adopters intend the child to live in a country or territory outside the British Islands after the making of the adoption order; or the prospective adopters are relatives of the child.
A placement order (section 21)	Each parent who has parental responsibility for the child or guardian of the child; any person in whose favour an order under the 1989 Act is in force in relation to the child; any adoption agency or voluntary organisation which has parental responsibility for, is looking after, or is caring for, the child; the child; and the parties or any persons who are or have been parties to proceedings for a care order in respect of the child where those proceedings have led to the application for the placement order.
An order varying a placement order (section 23)	The parties to the proceedings leading to the placement order which it is sought to have varied except the child who was the subject of those proceedings; and any person in whose favour there is provision for contact.
An order revoking a placement order (section 24)	The parties to the proceedings leading to the placement order which it is sought to have revoked; and any person in whose favour there is provision for contact.
A contact order (section 26)	The adoption agency authorised to place the child for adoption or which has placed the child for adoption; the person with whom the child lives or is to live; each parent with parental responsibility for the child or guardian of the child; and the child where –

Proceedings for	Respondents
	the adoption agency authorised to place the child for adoption or which has placed the child for adoption or a parent with parental responsibility for the child opposes the making of the contact order under section 26; he opposes the making of the contact order under section 26; existing provision for contact is to be revoked; relatives of the child do not agree to the arrangements for allowing any person contact with the child, or a person not being allowed contact with the child; or he is suffering or is at risk of suffering harm within the meaning of the 1989 Act.
An order varying or revoking a contact order (section 27)	The parties to the proceedings leading to the contact order which it is sought to have varied or revoked; and any person named in the contact order.
An order permitting the child's name to be changed or the removal of the child from the United Kingdom (section 28(2) and (3))	The parties to proceedings leading to any placement order; the adoption agency authorised to place the child for adoption or which has placed the child for adoption; any prospective adopters with whom the child is living; and each parent with parental responsibility for the child or guardian of the child.
A section 88 direction	The adopters; the parents; the adoption agency; the local authority to whom notice under section 44 (notice of intention to apply for a section 84 order) has been given; and the Attorney-General.
A section 89 order	The adopters; the parents; the adoption agency; and the local authority to whom notice under section 44 (notice of intention to adopt or apply for a section 84 order) has been given.

(2) The court may at any time direct that a child, who is not already a respondent to proceedings, be made a respondent to proceedings where –

(a) the child –

(i) wishes to make an application; or

(ii) has evidence to give to the court or a legal submission to make which has not been given or made by any other party; or
(b) there are other special circumstances.

(3) The court may at any time direct that –

(a) any other person or body be made a respondent to proceedings; or
(b) a respondent be removed.

(4) If the court makes a direction for the addition or removal of a party, it may give consequential directions about –

(a) serving a copy of the application form on any new respondent;
(b) serving relevant documents on the new party; and
(c) the management of the proceedings.

24 What the court or a court officer will do when the application has been issued

(1) As soon as practicable after the application has been issued in proceedings –

(a) the court will –
  (i) if section 48(1) (restrictions on making adoption orders) applies, consider whether it is proper to hear the application;
  (ii) subject to paragraph (4), set a date for the first directions hearing;
  (iii) appoint a children's guardian in accordance with rule 59;
  (iv) appoint a reporting officer in accordance with rule 69;
  (v) consider whether a report relating to the welfare of the child is required, and if so, request such a report in accordance with rule 73;
  (vi) set a date for the hearing of the application; and
  (vii) do anything else that may be set out in a practice direction; and
(b) a court officer will –
  (i) subject to receiving confirmation in accordance with paragraph (2)(b)(ii), give notice of any directions hearing set by the court to the parties and to any children's guardian, reporting officer or children and family reporter;
  (ii) serve a copy of the application form (but, subject to sub-paragraphs (iii) and (iv), not the documents attached to it) on the persons referred to in the relevant practice direction;
  (iii) send a copy of the certified copy of the entry in the register of live-births or Adopted Children Register and any health report attached to an application for an adoption order to –
    (aa) any children's guardian, reporting officer or children and family reporter; and
    (bb) the local authority to whom notice under section 44 (notice of intention to adopt or apply for a section 84 order) has been given;
  (iv) if notice under rule 27 has been given (request to dispense with consent of parent or guardian), in accordance with that rule inform the parent or guardian of the request and send a copy of the statement of facts to –

(aa) the parent or guardian;
(bb) any children's guardian, reporting officer or children and family reporter;
(cc) any local authority to whom notice under section 44 (notice of intention to adopt or apply for a section 84 order) has been given; and
(dd) any adoption agency which has placed the child for adoption; and

(v) do anything else that may be set out in a practice direction.

(2) In addition to the matters referred to in paragraph (1), as soon as practicable after an application for an adoption order or a section 84 order has been issued the court or the court officer will –

(a) where the child is not placed for adoption by an adoption agency –
(i) ask either the Service or the Assembly to file any relevant form of consent to an adoption order or a section 84 order; and
(ii) ask the local authority to prepare a report on the suitability of the prospective adopters if one has not already been prepared; and

(b) where the child is placed for adoption by an adoption agency, ask the adoption agency to –
(i) file any relevant form of consent to –
(aa) the child being placed for adoption;
(bb) an adoption order;
(cc) a future adoption order under section 20; or
(dd) a section 84 order;
(ii) confirm whether a statement has been made under section 20(4)(a) (statement of wish not to be informed of any application for an adoption order) and if so, to file that statement;
(iii) file any statement made under section 20(4)(b) (withdrawal of wish not to be informed of any application for an adoption order) as soon as it is received by the adoption agency; and
(iv) prepare a report on the suitability of the prospective adopters if one has not already been prepared.

(3) In addition to the matters referred to in paragraph (1), as soon as practicable after an application for a placement order has been issued –

(a) the court will consider whether a report giving the local authority's reasons for placing the child for adoption is required, and if so, will direct the local authority to prepare such a report; and
(b) the court or the court officer will ask either the Service or the Assembly to file any form of consent to the child being placed for adoption.

(4) Where it considers it appropriate the court may, instead of setting a date for a first directions hearing, give the directions provided for by rule 26.

25 Date for first directions hearing

Unless the court directs otherwise, the first directions hearing must be within 4 weeks beginning with the date on which the application is issued.

26 The first directions hearing

(1) At the first directions hearing in the proceedings the court will –

(a) fix a timetable for the filing of –
  (i) any report relating to the suitability of the applicants to adopt a child;
  (ii) any report from the local authority;
  (iii) any report from a children's guardian, reporting officer or children and family reporter;
  (iv) if a statement of facts has been filed, any amended statement of facts;
  (v) any other evidence, and

give directions relating to the reports and other evidence;

(b) consider whether an alternative dispute resolution procedure is appropriate and, if so, give directions relating to the use of such procedure;

(c) consider whether the child or any other person should be a party to the proceedings and, if so, give directions in accordance with rule 23(2) or (3) joining that child or person as a party;

(d) give directions relating to the appointment of a litigation friend for any patient or non-subject child unless a litigation friend has already been appointed;

(e) consider whether the case needs to be transferred to another court and, if so, give directions to transfer the proceedings to another court in accordance with any order made by the Lord Chancellor under Part I of Schedule 11 to the 1989 Act;

(f) give directions about –
  (i) tracing parents or any other person the court considers to be relevant to the proceedings;
  (ii) service of documents;
  (iii) subject to paragraph (2), disclosure as soon as possible of information and evidence to the parties; and
  (iv) the final hearing; and

(2) Rule 77(2) applies to any direction given under paragraph (1)(f)(iii) as it applies to a direction given under rule 77(1).

(3) In addition to the matters referred to in paragraph (1), the court will give any of the directions listed in the relevant practice direction in proceedings for –

(a) a Convention adoption order;
(b) a section 84 order;
(c) a section 88 direction;
(d) a section 89 order; or
(e) an adoption order where section 83(1) applies (restriction on bringing children in).

(4) The parties or their legal representatives must attend the first directions hearing unless the court directs otherwise.

(5) Directions may also be given at any stage in the proceedings –

(a) of the court's own initiative; or

(b) on the application of a party or any children's guardian or, where the direction concerns a report by a reporting officer or children and family reporter, the reporting officer or children and family reporter.

(6) For the purposes of giving directions or for such purposes as the court directs –

(a) the court may set a date for a further directions hearing or other hearing; and
(b) the court officer will give notice of any date so fixed to the parties and to any children's guardian, reporting officer or children and family reporter.

(7) After the first directions hearing the court will monitor compliance with the court's timetable and directions by the parties.

27 Requesting the court to dispense with the consent of any parent or guardian

(1) The following paragraphs apply where the applicant wants to ask the court to dispense with the consent of any parent or guardian of a child to –

(a) the child being placed for adoption;
(b) the making of an adoption order except a Convention adoption order; or
(c) the making of a section 84 order.

(2) The applicant requesting the court to dispense with the consent must –

(a) give notice of the request in the application form or at any later stage by filing a written request setting out the reasons for the request; and
(b) file a statement of facts setting out a summary of the history of the case and any other facts to satisfy the court that –
  (i) the parent or guardian cannot be found or is incapable of giving consent; or
  (ii) the welfare of the child requires the consent to be dispensed with.

(3) If a serial number has been assigned to the applicant under rule 20, the statement of facts supplied under paragraph (2)(b) must be framed so that it does not disclose the identity of the applicant.

(4) On receipt of the notice of the request –

(a) a court officer will –
  (i) inform the parent or guardian of the request; and
  (ii) send a copy of the statement of facts filed in accordance with paragraph (2)(b) to –
    (aa) the parent or guardian;
    (bb) any children's guardian, reporting officer or children and family reporter;
    (cc) any local authority to whom notice under section 44 (notice of intention to adopt or apply for a section 84 order) has been given; and

(dd) any adoption agency which has placed the child for adoption; and

(b) if the applicant considers that the parent or guardian is incapable of giving consent, the court will consider whether to –

(i) appoint a litigation friend for the parent or guardian under rule 55(1); or

(ii) give directions for an application to be made under rule 55(3),

unless a litigation friend is already appointed for that parent or guardian.

28 Consent

(1) Consent of any parent or guardian of a child –

(a) under section 19, to the child being placed for adoption; and
(b) under section 20, to the making of a future adoption order

must be given in the form required by the relevant practice direction or a form to the like effect.

(2) Subject to paragraph (3), consent –

(a) to the making of an adoption order; or
(b) to the making of a section 84 order,

may be given in the form required by the relevant practice direction or a form to the like effect.

(3) Any consent to a Convention adoption order must be in a form which complies with the internal law relating to adoption of the Convention country of which the child is habitually resident.

(4) Any form of consent executed in Scotland must be witnessed by a Justice of the Peace or a Sheriff.

(5) Any form of consent executed in Northern Ireland must be witnessed by a Justice of the Peace.

(6) Any form of consent executed outside the United Kingdom must be witnessed by –

(a) any person for the time being authorised by law in the place where the document is executed to administer an oath for any judicial or other legal purpose;
(b) a British Consular officer;
(c) a notary public; or
(d) if the person executing the document is serving in any of the regular armed forces of the Crown, an officer holding a commission in any of those forces.

29 Reports by the adoption agency or local authority

(1) The adoption agency or local authority must file the report on the suitability of the applicant to adopt a child within the timetable fixed by the court.

(2) A local authority that is directed to prepare a report on the placement of the child for adoption must file that report within the timetable fixed by the court.

(3) The reports must cover the matters specified in the relevant practice direction.

(4) The court may at any stage request a further report or ask the adoption agency or local authority to assist the court in any other manner.

(5) A court officer will send a copy of any report referred to in this rule to any children's guardian, reporting officer or children and family reporter.

(6) Any report to the court under this rule will be confidential.

30 Health reports

(1) Reports by a registered medical practitioner ("health reports") made not more than three months earlier on the health of the child and of each applicant must be attached to an application for an adoption order or a section 84 order except where –

- (a) the child was placed for adoption with the applicant by an adoption agency;
- (b) the applicant or one of the applicants is a parent of the child; or
- (c) the applicant is the partner of a parent of the child.

(2) Health reports must contain the matters set out in the relevant practice direction.

(3) Any health report will be confidential.

31 Notice of final hearing

A court officer will give notice to the parties, any children's guardian, reporting officer or children and family reporter and to any other person that may be referred to in a practice direction –

- (a) of the date and place where the application will be heard; and
- (b) of the fact that, unless the person wishes or the court requires, the person need not attend.

32 The final hearing

(1) Any person who has been given notice in accordance with rule 31 may attend the final hearing and, subject to paragraph (2), be heard on the question of whether an order should be made.

(2) A person whose application for the permission of the court to oppose the making of an adoption order under section 47(3) or (5) has been refused is not entitled to be heard on the question of whether an order should be made.

(3) Any member or employee of a party which is a local authority, adoption agency or other body may address the court at the final hearing if he is authorised to do so.

(4) The court may direct that any person must attend a final hearing.

(5) Paragraphs (6) and (7) apply to –

(a) an adoption order;
(b) a section 84 order; or
(c) a section 89 order.

(6) Subject to paragraphs (7) and (8), the court cannot make an order unless the applicant and the child personally attend the final hearing.

(7) The court may direct that the applicant or the child need not attend the final hearing.

(8) In a case of adoption by a couple under section 50 the court may make an adoption order after personal attendance of one only of the applicants if there are special circumstances.

(9) The court cannot make a placement order unless a legal representative of the applicant attends the final hearing.

33 Proof of identity of the child

(1) Unless the contrary is shown, the child referred to in the application will be deemed to be the child referred to in the form of consent –

(a) to the child being placed for adoption;
(b) to the making of an adoption order; or
(c) to the making of a section 84 order

where the conditions in paragraph (2) apply.

(2) The conditions are –

(a) the application identifies the child by reference to a full certified copy of an entry in the registers of live-births;
(b) the form of consent identifies the child by reference to a full certified copy of an entry in the registers of live-births attached to the form; and
(c) the copy of the entry in the registers of live-births referred to in sub-paragraph (a) is the same or relates to the same entry in the registers of live-births as the copy of the entry in the registers of live-births attached to the form of consent.

(3) Where the child is already an adopted child paragraph (2) will have effect as if for the references to the registers of live-births there were substituted references to the Adopted Children Register.

(4) Subject to paragraph (7), where the precise date of the child's birth is not proved to the satisfaction of the court, the court will determine the probable date of birth.

(5) The probable date of the child's birth may be specified in the placement order, adoption order or section 84 order as the date of his birth.

(6) Subject to paragraph (7), where the child's place of birth cannot be proved to the satisfaction of the court –

(a) he may be treated as having been born in the registration district of the court where it is probable that the child may have been born in –
   (i) the United Kingdom;
   (ii) the Channel Islands; or
   (iii) the Isle of Man; or

(b) in any other case, the particulars of the country of birth may be omitted from the placement order, adoption order or section 84 order.

(7) A placement order identifying the probable date and place of birth of the child will be sufficient proof of the date and place of birth of the child in adoption proceedings and proceedings for a section 84 order.

Part 7
Litigation Friend, Children's Guardian, Reporting Officer and Children and Family Reporter

Section 1 – Litigation Friend

49 Application of this Section

(1) This Section –

(a) contains special provisions which apply in proceedings involving non-subject children and patients; and
(b) sets out how a person becomes a litigation friend.

(2) The provisions of this Section also apply to a child who does not have a children's guardian, in which case, any reference to a "non-subject child" in these Rules is to be taken as including a child.

50 Requirement for litigation friend in proceedings

(1) Subject to rule 51, a non-subject child must have a litigation friend to conduct proceedings on his behalf.

(2) A patient must have a litigation friend to conduct proceedings on his behalf.

51 Circumstances in which the non-subject child does not need a litigation friend

(1) A non-subject child may conduct proceedings without a litigation friend –

(a) where he has obtained the court's permission to do so; or
(b) where a solicitor –
   (i) considers that the non-subject child is able, having regard to his understanding, to give instructions in relation to the proceedings; and
   (ii) has accepted instructions from that child to act for him in the proceedings and, if the proceedings have begun, he is already acting.

(2) An application for permission under paragraph (1)(a) may be made by the non-subject child without notice.

(3) Where a non-subject child has a litigation friend in proceedings and he wishes to conduct the remaining stages of the proceedings without a litigation friend, the non-subject child may apply to the court, on notice to the litigation friend, for permission for that purpose and for the removal of the litigation friend.

(4) Where the court is considering whether to –

(a) grant permission under paragraph (1)(a); or
(b) grant permission under paragraph (3) and remove a litigation friend

it will grant the permission sought and, as the case may be, remove the litigation friend if it considers that the non-subject child concerned has sufficient understanding to conduct the proceedings concerned or proposed without a litigation friend.

(5) In exercising its powers under paragraph (4) the court may require the litigation friend to take such part in the proceedings as the court directs.

(6) The court may revoke any permission granted under paragraph (1)(a) where it considers that the non-subject child does not have sufficient understanding to participate as a party in the proceedings concerned without a litigation friend.

(7) Where a solicitor is acting for a non-subject child in proceedings without a litigation friend by virtue of paragraph (1)(b) and either of the conditions specified in paragraph (1)(b)(i) or (ii) cease to be fulfilled, he must inform the court immediately.

(8) Where –

(a) the court revokes any permission under paragraph (6); or
(b) either of the conditions specified in paragraph (1)(b)(i) or (ii) is no longer fulfilled

the court may, if it considers it necessary in order to protect the interests of the non-subject child concerned, appoint a person to be that child's litigation friend.

52 Stage of proceedings at which a litigation friend becomes necessary

(1) This rule does not apply where a non-subject child is conducting proceedings without a litigation friend in accordance with rule 51.

(2) A person may not without the permission of the court take any step in proceedings except –

(a) filing an application form; or
(b) applying for the appointment of a litigation friend under rule 55

until the non-subject child or patient has a litigation friend.

(3) If a party becomes a patient during proceedings, no party may take any step in proceedings without the permission of the court until the patient has a litigation friend.

53 Who may be a litigation friend for a patient without a court order

(1) This rule does not apply if the court has appointed a person to be a litigation friend.

(2) A person authorised under Part VII of the Mental Health Act 1983 to conduct legal proceedings in the name of a patient or on his behalf is entitled to be the litigation friend of the patient in any proceedings to which his authority extends.

(3) If nobody has been appointed by the court or, in the case of a patient, authorised under Part VII of the Mental Health Act 1983, a person may act as a litigation friend if he –

(a) can fairly and competently conduct proceedings on behalf of the non-subject child or patient;
(b) has no interest adverse to that of the non-subject child or patient; and
(c) subject to paragraph (4), undertakes to pay any costs which the non-subject child or patient may be ordered to pay in relation to the proceedings, subject to any right he may have to be repaid from the assets of the non-subject child or patient.

(4) Paragraph (3)(c) does not apply to the Official Solicitor, an officer of the Service or a Welsh family proceedings officer.

54 How a person becomes a litigation friend without a court order

(1) If the court has not appointed a litigation friend, a person who wishes to act as a litigation friend must follow the procedure set out in this rule.

(2) A person authorised under Part VII of the Mental Health Act 1983 must file an official copy of the order or other document which constitutes his authorisation to act.

(3) Any other person must file a certificate of suitability stating that he satisfies the conditions specified in rule 53(3).

(4) A person who is to act as a litigation friend must file –

(a) the authorisation; or
(b) the certificate of suitability

at the time when he first takes a step in the proceedings on behalf of the non-subject child or patient.

(5) A court officer will send the certificate of suitability to every person on whom, in accordance with rule 37(1) (service on parent, guardian etc), the application form should be served.

(6) This rule does not apply to the Official Solicitor, an officer of the Service or a Welsh family proceedings officer.

55 How a person becomes a litigation friend by court order

(1) The court may make an order appointing –

(a) the Official Solicitor;
(b) in the case of a non-subject child, an officer of the Service or a Welsh family proceedings officer (if he consents); or
(c) some other person (if he consents)

as a litigation friend.

(2) An order appointing a litigation friend may be made by the court of its own initiative or on the application of –

(a) a person who wishes to be a litigation friend; or
(b) a party to the proceedings.

(3) The court may at any time direct that a party make an application for an order under paragraph (2).

(4) An application for an order appointing a litigation friend must be supported by evidence.

(5) Unless the court directs otherwise, a person appointed under this rule to be a litigation friend for a non-subject child or patient will be treated as a party for the purpose of any provision in these Rules requiring a document to be served on, or sent to, or notice to be given to, a party to the proceedings.

(6) Subject to rule 53(4), the court may not appoint a litigation friend under this rule unless it is satisfied that the person to be appointed complies with the conditions specified in rule 53(3).

56 Court's power to change litigation friend and to prevent person acting as litigation friend

(1) The court may –

(a) direct that a person may not act as a litigation friend;
(b) terminate a litigation friend's appointment; or
(c) appoint a new litigation friend in substitution for an existing one.

(2) An application for an order under paragraph (1) must be supported by evidence.

(3) Subject to rule 53(4), the court may not appoint a litigation friend under this rule unless it is satisfied that the person to be appointed complies with the conditions specified in rule 53(3).

57 Appointment of litigation friend by court order – supplementary

(1) A copy of the application for an order under rule 55 or 56 must be sent by a court officer to every person on whom, in accordance with rule 37(1) (service on parent, guardian etc), the application form should be served.

(2) Where an application for an order under rule 55 is in respect of a patient, the court officer must also send a copy of the application to the patient unless the court directs otherwise.

(3) A copy of an application for an order under rule 56 must also be sent to –

(a) the person who is the litigation friend, or who is purporting to act as the litigation friend, when the application is made; and
(b) the person who it is proposed should be the litigation friend, if he is not the applicant.

58 Procedure where appointment of litigation friend comes to an end

(1) When a non-subject child who is not a patient reaches the age of 18, a litigation friend's appointment comes to an end.

(2) When a party ceases to be a patient, the litigation friend's appointment continues until it is brought to an end by a court order.

(3) An application for an order under paragraph (2) may be made by –

(a) the former patient;
(b) the litigation friend; or
(c) a party.

(4) A court officer will send a notice to the other parties stating that the appointment of the non-subject child or patient's litigation friend to act has ended.

Section 2 – Children's Guardian

59 Appointment of children's guardian

(1) In proceedings to which Part 5 applies, the court will appoint a children's guardian where the child is a party to the proceedings unless it is satisfied that it is not necessary to do so to safeguard the interests of the child.

(2) At any stage in proceedings where the child is a party to the proceedings –

(a) a party may apply, without notice to the other parties unless the court directs otherwise, for the appointment of a children's guardian; or
(b) the court may of its own initiative appoint a children's guardian.

(3) The court will grant an application under paragraph (2)(a) unless it considers that such an appointment is not necessary to safeguard the interests of the child.

(4) When appointing a children's guardian the court will consider the appointment of anyone who has previously acted as a children's guardian of the same child.

60 What the court or a court officer will do once the court has made a decision about appointing a children's guardian

(1) Where the court refuses an application under rule 59(2)(a) it will give reasons for the refusal and the court or a court officer will –

(a) record the refusal and the reasons for it; and
(b) as soon as practicable, notify the parties and either the Service or the Assembly of a decision not to appoint a children's guardian.

(2) Where the court appoints a children's guardian under rule 59 a court officer will record the appointment and, as soon as practicable, will –

(a) inform the parties and either the Service or the Assembly; and
(b) unless it has already been sent, send the children's guardian a copy of the application and copies of any document filed with the court in the proceedings.

(3) A court officer also has a continuing duty to send the children's guardian a copy of any other document filed with the court during the course of the proceedings.

61 Termination of the appointment of the children's guardian

(1) The appointment of a children's guardian under rule 59 continues for such time as is specified in the appointment or until terminated by the court.

(2) When terminating an appointment in accordance with paragraph (1), the court will give reasons for doing so, a note of which will be taken by the court or a court officer.

62 Powers and duties of the children's guardian

(1) The children's guardian is to act on behalf of the child upon the hearing of any application in proceedings to which Part 5 applies with the duty of safeguarding the interests of the child.

(2) The children's guardian must also provide the court with such other assistance as it may require.

63 How the children's guardian exercises his duties – investigations and appointment of solicitor

(1) The children's guardian must make such investigations as are necessary for him to carry out his duties and must, in particular –

(a) contact or seek to interview such persons as he thinks appropriate or as the court directs; and
(b) obtain such professional assistance as is available to him which he thinks appropriate or which the court directs him to obtain.

(2) The children's guardian must –

(a) appoint a solicitor for the child unless a solicitor has already been appointed;
(b) give such advice to the child as is appropriate having regard to his understanding; and
(c) where appropriate instruct the solicitor representing the child on all matters relevant to the interests of the child, including possibilities for appeal, arising in the course of proceedings.

(3) Where the children's guardian is authorised in the terms mentioned by and in accordance with section 15(1) of the Criminal Justice and Court Services Act 2000 or section 37(1) of the Children Act 2004 (right of officer of the

Service or Welsh family proceedings officer to conduct litigation or exercise a right of audience), paragraph (2)(a) will not apply if he intends to have conduct of the proceedings on behalf of the child unless –

(a) the child wishes to instruct a solicitor direct; and
(b) the children's guardian or the court considers that he is of sufficient understanding to do so.

64 Where the child instructs a solicitor or conducts proceedings on his own behalf

(1) Where it appears to the children's guardian that the child –

(a) is instructing his solicitor direct; or
(b) intends to conduct and is capable of conducting the proceedings on his own behalf

he must inform the court of that fact.

(2) Where paragraph (1) applies, the children's guardian –

(a) must perform the duties set out in rules 62, 63, 65 to 67 and this rule, other than those duties in rule 63(2)(a) and (c), and such other duties as the court may direct;
(b) must take such part in the proceedings as the court may direct; and
(c) may, with the permission of the court, have legal representation in the conduct of those duties.

65 How the children's guardian exercises his duties – attendance at court, advice to the court and reports

(1) The children's guardian or the solicitor appointed under section 41(3) of the 1989 Act or in accordance with rule 63(2)(a) must attend all directions hearings unless the court directs otherwise.

(2) The children's guardian must advise the court on the following matters –

(a) whether the child is of sufficient understanding for any purpose including the child's refusal to submit to a medical or psychiatric examination or other assessment that the court has the power to require, direct or order;
(b) the wishes of the child in respect of any matter relevant to the proceedings including his attendance at court;
(c) the appropriate forum for the proceedings;
(d) the appropriate timing of the proceedings or any part of them;
(e) the options available to it in respect of the child and the suitability of each such option including what order should be made in determining the application; and
(f) any other matter on which the court seeks his advice or on which he considers that the court should be informed.

(3) The advice given under paragraph (2) may, subject to any direction of the court, be given orally or in writing.

(4) The children's guardian must –

(a) unless the court directs otherwise, file a written report advising on the interests of the child in accordance with the timetable set by the court; and

(b) where practicable, notify any person the joining of whom as a party to those proceedings would be likely, in his opinion, to safeguard the interests of the child, of the court's power to join that person as a party under rule 23 and must inform the court –

  (i) of any notification;

  (ii) of anyone whom he attempted to notify under this paragraph but was unable to contact; and

  (iii) of anyone whom he believes may wish to be joined to the proceedings.

(5) Any report to the court under this rule will be confidential.

(Part 9 sets out the procedure for making an application to be joined as a party in proceedings.)

66 How the children's guardian exercises his duties –service of documents and inspection of records

(1) The children's guardian must –

(a) serve documents on behalf of the child in accordance with rule 37(2)(b); and

(b) accept service of documents on behalf of the child in accordance with the table in rule 37(1),

and, where the child has not himself been served and has sufficient understanding, advise the child of the contents of any document so served.

(2) Where the children's guardian inspects records of the kinds referred to in –

(a) section 42 of the 1989 Act (right to have access to local authority records); or

(b) section 103 (right to have access to adoption agency records)

he must bring all records and documents which may, in his opinion, assist in the proper determination of the proceedings to the attention of –

  (i) the court; and

  (ii) unless the court directs otherwise, the other parties to the proceedings.

67 How the children's guardian exercises his duties –communication of a court's decision to the child

The children's guardian must ensure that, in relation to a decision made by the court in the proceedings –

(a) if he considers it appropriate to the age and understanding of the child, the child is notified of that decision; and

(b) if the child is notified of the decision, it is explained to the child in a manner appropriate to his age and understanding.

68 Solicitor for child

(1) A solicitor appointed under section 41(3) of the 1989 Act or in accordance with rule 63(2)(a) must represent the child –

(a) in accordance with instructions received from the children's guardian unless the solicitor considers, having taken into account the views of the children's guardian and any direction of the court under rule 64(2) –

(i) that the child wishes to give instructions which conflict with those of the children's guardian; and

(ii) that he is able, having regard to his understanding, to give such instructions on his own behalf,

in which case the solicitor must conduct the proceedings in accordance with instructions received from the child;

(b) where no children's guardian has been appointed and the condition in section 41(4)(b) of the 1989 Act is satisfied, in accordance with instructions received from the child; or

(c) in default of instructions under sub-paragraph (a) or (b), in furtherance of the best interests of the child.

(2) A solicitor appointed under section 41(3) of the 1989 Act or in accordance with rule 63(2)(a) must –

(a) serve documents on behalf of the child in accordance with rule 37(2)(a); and

(b) accept service of documents on behalf of the child in accordance with the table in rule 37(1),

and, where the child has not himself been served and has sufficient understanding, advise the child of the contents of any document so served.

(3) Where the child wishes an appointment of a solicitor under section 41(3) of the 1989 Act or in accordance with rule 63(2)(a) to be terminated –

(a) he may apply to the court for an order terminating the appointment; and

(b) the solicitor and the children's guardian will be given an opportunity to make representations.

(4) Where the children's guardian wishes an appointment of a solicitor under section 41(3) of the 1989 Act or in accordance with rule 63(2)(a) to be terminated –

(a) he may apply to the court for an order terminating the appointment; and

(b) the solicitor and, if he is of sufficient understanding, the child, will be given an opportunity to make representations.

(5) When terminating an appointment in accordance with paragraph (3) or (4), the court will give its reasons for so doing, a note of which will be taken by the court or a court officer.

(6) The court or a court officer will record the appointment under section 41(3) of the 1989 Act or in accordance with rule 63(2)(a) or the refusal to make the appointment.

Section 3 – Reporting Officer

69 When the court appoints a reporting officer

In proceedings to which Part 5 applies, the court will appoint a reporting officer where –

(a) it appears that a parent or guardian of the child is willing to consent to the placing of the child for adoption, to the making of an adoption order or to a section 84 order; and
(b) that parent or guardian is in England or Wales.

70 Appointment of the same reporting officer in respect of two or more parents or guardians

The same person may be appointed as the reporting officer for two or more parents or guardians of the child.

71 The duties of the reporting officer

The reporting officer must witness the signature by a parent or guardian on the document in which consent is given to –

(a) the placing of the child for adoption;
(b) the making of an adoption order; or
(c) the making of a section 84 order.

72 How the reporting officer exercises his duties

(1) The reporting officer must –

(a) ensure so far as reasonably practicable that the parent or guardian is –
  (i) giving consent unconditionally; and
  (ii) with full understanding of what is involved;
(b) investigate all the circumstances relevant to a parent's or guardian's consent to the placing of the child for adoption or to the making of an adoption order or a section 84 order; and
(c) on completing his investigations the reporting officer must –
  (i) make a report in writing to the court in accordance with the timetable set by the court, drawing attention to any matters which, in his opinion, may be of assistance to the court in considering the application; or
  (ii) make an interim report to the court if a parent or guardian of the child is unwilling to consent to the placing of the child for adoption or to the making of an adoption order or section 84 order.

(2) On receipt of an interim report under paragraph (1)(c)(ii) a court officer must inform the applicant that a parent or guardian of the child is unwilling to consent to the placing of the child for adoption or to the making of an adoption order or section 84 order.

(3) The reporting officer may at any time before the final hearing make an interim report to the court if he considers necessary and ask the court for directions.

(4) The reporting officer must attend all directions hearings unless the court directs otherwise.

(5) Any report to the court under this rule will be confidential.

Section 4 – Children and Family Reporter

73 Request by court for a welfare report in respect of the child

(1) In proceedings to which Part 5 applies, where the court is considering an application for an order in proceedings the court may ask a children and family reporter to prepare a report on matters relating to the welfare of the child.

(2) It is the duty of a children and family reporter to –

(a) comply with any request for a report under this rule; and
(b) provide the court with such other assistance as it may require.

(3) Any report to the court under this rule will be confidential.

74 How the children and family reporter exercises his powers and duties

(1) The children and family reporter must make such investigations as may be necessary for him to perform his powers and duties and must, in particular –

(a) contact or seek to interview such persons as he thinks appropriate or as the court directs; and
(b) obtain such professional assistance as is available to him which he thinks appropriate or which the court directs him to obtain.

(2) The children and family reporter must –

(a) notify the child of such contents of his report (if any) as he considers appropriate to the age and understanding of the child, including any reference to the child's own views on the application and his recommendation; and
(b) if he does notify the child of any contents of his report, explain them to the child in a manner appropriate to his age and understanding.

(3) The children and family reporter must –

(a) attend all directions hearings unless the court directs otherwise;
(b) advise the court of the child's wishes and feelings;
(c) advise the court if he considers that the joining of a person as a party to the proceedings would be likely to safeguard the interests of the child;
(d) consider whether it is in the best interests of the child for the child to be made a party to the proceedings, and if so, notify the court of his opinion together with the reasons for that opinion; and
(e) where the court has directed that a written report be made, file the report in accordance with the timetable set by the court.

Section 5 – Who can Act as Children's Guardian, Reporting Officer and Children and Family Reporter

75 Persons who may not be appointed as children's guardian, reporting officer or children and family reporter

(1) In adoption proceedings or proceedings for a section 84 order or a section 89 order, a person may not be appointed as a children's guardian, reporting officer or children and family reporter if he –

(a) is a member, officer or servant of a local authority which is a party to the proceedings;
(b) is, or has been, a member, officer or servant of a local authority or voluntary organisation who has been directly concerned in that capacity in arrangements relating to the care, accommodation or welfare of the child during the five years prior to the commencement of the proceedings; or
(c) is a serving probation officer who has, in that capacity, been previously concerned with the child or his family.

(2) In placement proceedings, a person described in paragraph (1)(b) or (c) may not be appointed as a children's guardian, reporting officer or children and family reporter.

76 Appointment of the same person as children's guardian, reporting officer and children and family reporter

The same person may be appointed to act as one or more of the following –

(a) the children's guardian;
(b) the reporting officer; and
(c) the children and family reporter.

Part 17
Experts

154 Duty to restrict expert evidence

Expert evidence shall be restricted to that which is reasonably required to resolve the proceedings.

155 Interpretation

A reference to an "expert" in this Part –

(a) is a reference to an expert who has been instructed to give or prepare evidence for the purpose of court proceedings; and
(b) does not include –
  (i) a person who is within a prescribed description for the purposes of section 94(1) of the Act (persons who may prepare a report for any person about the suitability of a child for

adoption or of a person to adopt a child or about the adoption, or placement for adoption, of a child); or

(ii) an officer of the Service or a Welsh family proceedings officer when acting in that capacity.

(Regulation 3 of the Restriction on the Preparation of Adoption Reports Regulations 2005 (SI 2005/1711) sets out which persons are within a prescribed description for the purposes of section 94(1) of the Act.)

156 Experts – overriding duty to the court

(1) It is the duty of an expert to help the court on the matters within his expertise.

(2) This duty overrides any obligation to the person from whom he has received instructions or by whom he is paid.

157 Court's power to restrict expert evidence

(1) No party may call an expert or put in evidence an expert's report without the court's permission.

(2) When a party applies for permission under this rule he must identify –

(a) the field in which he wishes to rely on expert evidence; and
(b) where practicable the expert in that field on whose evidence he wishes to rely.

(3) If permission is granted under this rule it shall be in relation only to the expert named or the field identified under paragraph (2).

(4) The court may limit the amount of the expert's fees and expenses that the party who wishes to rely on the expert may recover from any other party.

158 General requirement for expert evidence to be given in a written report

Expert evidence is to be given in a written report unless the court directs otherwise.

159 Written questions to experts

(1) A party may put to –

(a) an expert instructed by another party; or
(b) a single joint expert appointed under rule 160,

written questions about his report.

(2) Written questions under paragraph (1) –

(a) may be put once only;
(b) must be put within 5 days beginning with the date on which the expert's report was served; and
(c) must be for the purpose only of clarification of the report,

unless in any case –
(i) the court gives permission;
(ii) the other party agrees; or
(iii) any practice direction provides otherwise.

(3) An expert's answers to questions put in accordance with paragraph (1) shall be treated as part of the expert's report.

(4) Where –

(a) a party has put a written question to an expert instructed by another party in accordance with this rule; and
(b) the expert does not answer that question,

the court may make one or both of the following orders in relation to the party who instructed the expert –
(i) that the party may not rely on the evidence of that expert; or
(ii) that the party may not recover the fees and expenses of that expert from any other party.

160 Court's power to direct that evidence is to be given by a single joint expert

(1) Where two or more parties wish to submit expert evidence on a particular issue, the court may direct that the evidence on that issue is to given by one expert only.

(2) The parties wishing to submit the expert evidence are called "the instructing parties".

(3) Where the instructing parties cannot agree who should be the expert, the court may –

(a) select the expert from a list prepared or identified by the instructing parties; or
(b) direct that the expert be selected in such other manner as the court may direct.

161 Instructions to a single joint expert

(1) Where the court gives a direction under rule 160 for a single joint expert to be used, each instructing party may give instructions to the expert.

(2) When an instructing party gives instructions to the expert he must, at the same time, send a copy of the instructions to the other instructing parties.

(3) The court may give directions about –

(a) the payment of the expert's fees and expenses; and
(b) any inspection, examination or experiments which the expert wishes to carry out.

(4) The court may, before an expert is instructed, limit the amount that can be paid by way of fees and expenses to the expert.

(5) Unless the court otherwise directs, the instructing parties are jointly and severally liable for the payment of the expert's fees and expenses.

162 Power of court to direct a party to provide information

(1) Where a party has access to information which is not reasonably available to the other party, the court may direct the party who has access to the information to prepare and file a document recording the information.

(2) A court officer will send a copy of that document to the other party.

163 Contents of report

(1) An expert's report must comply with the requirements set out in the relevant practice direction.

(2) At the end of an expert's report there must be a statement that –

(a) the expert understands his duty to the court; and
(b) he has complied with that duty.

(3) The expert's report must state the substance of all material instructions, whether written or oral, on the basis of which the report was written.

(4) The instructions referred to in paragraph (3) shall not be privileged against disclosure.

164 Use by one party of expert's report disclosed by another

Where a party has disclosed an expert's report, any party may use that expert's report as evidence at the final hearing.

165 Discussions between experts

(1) The court may, at any stage, direct a discussion between experts for the purpose of requiring the experts to –

(a) identify and discuss the expert issues in the proceedings; and
(b) where possible, reach an agreed opinion on those issues.

(2) The court may specify the issues which the experts must discuss.

(3) The court may direct that following a discussion between the experts they must prepare a statement for the court showing –

(a) those issues on which they agree; and
(b) those issues on which they disagree and a summary of their reasons for disagreeing.

166 Consequence of failure to disclose expert's report

A party who fails to disclose an expert's report may not use the report at the final hearing or call the expert to give evidence orally unless the court gives permission.

167 Expert's right to ask court for directions

(1) An expert may file a written request for directions to assist him in carrying out his function as an expert.

(2) An expert must, unless the court directs otherwise, provide a copy of any proposed request for directions under paragraph (1) –

- (a) to the party instructing him, at least 7 days before he files the request; and
- (b) to all other parties, at least 4 days before he files it.

(3) The court, when it gives directions, may also direct that a party be served with a copy of the directions.

Appendix 5

PROTOCOL FOR JUDICIAL CASE MANAGEMENT IN PUBLIC LAW CHILDREN ACT CASES

1	2	3
The Application	**The First Hearing in the FPC**	**Allocation Hearing & Directions**
Day 1 to Day 3	**On (or before) Day 6**	**By Day 11 (CC) 15(HC)**
Objective: LA to provide sufficient information to identify issues/make early welfare and case management decisions	**Objective:** To decide what immediate steps are necessary/contested ICO/preventing delay/appropriate court	**Objective:** To make provision for continuous/consistent judicial case management
Action: • LA file Application in Form C1/C3 ***on Day 1*** [1.1] • Directions on Issue by Court - fixing the hearing - Appointment of Guardian ***on Day 1*** [1.2] • Allocation of Guardian by Cafcass ***by Day 3*** [1.2-3] • Appointment of Solicitor for the child - no appointment of Guardian - Notification to parties of name of Guardian/solicitor ***on Day 3*** [1.4] • LA File and serve Documents ***by Day 3*** [1.5]	**Action:** • Parties [2.2] • Contested Interim Care Orders [2.3] • Transfer [2.4] and transfer arrangements [2.5] Initial Case Management and Checklist [2.6] including: - Case Management Conference - Final Hearing - Pre-Hearing Review - Evidence - Disclosure - Core Assessment - Standard Directions Form ***by Day 6***	**Action:** **Care Centre court officer shall:** • Allocate 1-2 Judges (including final hearing judge) [3.2] • Attach SDF with proposed date for CMC, Final Hearing and PHR ***by Day 8*** [3.2]: **Judge (at Allocation Hearing) considers:** • Transfer, ICO, CM Checklist, dates for CMC, Final Hearing, PHR, Disclosure, Core Assessment, SDF ***by Day 11*** [3.4] • Case Management Documents [3.4]

5 days

▼ 1 Day ▼

In High Court:

- Court Officer ***by Day 12*** [3.6]
- Case Management Judge ***by Day 15*** [3.7]

Within 54 days

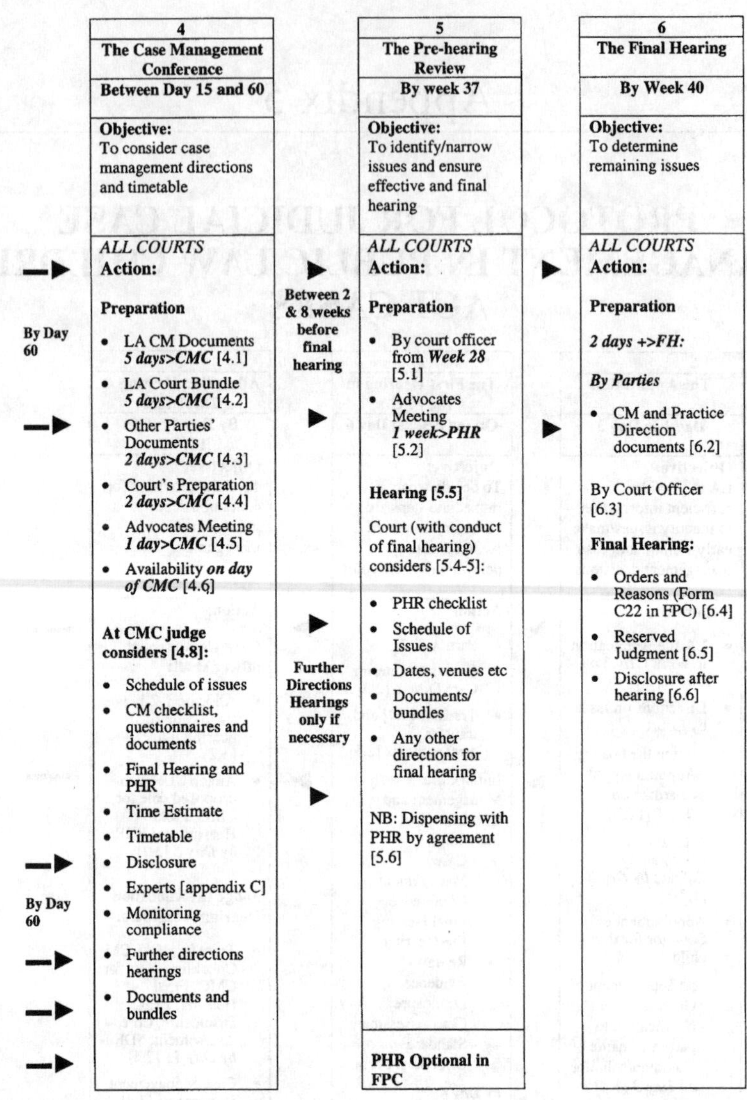
4
The Case Management Conference
Between Day 15 and 60
Objective:
To consider case management directions and timetable
ALL COURTS
Action:
Preparation
By Day 60
• LA CM Documents 5 days>CMC [4.1]
• LA Court Bundle 5 days>CMC [4.2]
• Other Parties' Documents 2 days>CMC [4.3]
• Court's Preparation 2 days>CMC [4.4]
• Advocates Meeting 1 day>CMC [4.5]
• Availability on day of CMC [4.6]
At CMC judge considers [4.8]:
• Schedule of issues
• CM checklist, questionnaires and documents
• Final Hearing and PHR
• Time Estimate
• Timetable
• Disclosure
• Experts [appendix C]
By Day 60
• Monitoring compliance
• Further directions hearings
• Documents and bundles
Between 2 & 8 weeks before final hearing
Further Directions Hearings only if necessary
5
The Pre-hearing Review
By week 37
Objective:
To identify/narrow issues and ensure effective and final hearing
ALL COURTS
Action:
Preparation
• By court officer from Week 28 [5.1]
• Advocates Meeting 1 week>PHR [5.2]
Hearing [5.5]
Court (with conduct of final hearing) considers [5.4-5]:
• PHR checklist
• Schedule of Issues
• Dates, venues etc
• Documents/ bundles
• Any other directions for final hearing
NB: Dispensing with PHR by agreement [5.6]
PHR Optional in FPC
6
The Final Hearing
By Week 40
Objective:
To determine remaining issues
ALL COURTS
Action:
Preparation
2 days +>FH:
By Parties
• CM and Practice Direction documents [6.2]
By Court Officer [6.3]
Final Hearing:
• Orders and Reasons (Form C22 in FPC) [6.4]
• Reserved Judgment [6.5]
• Disclosure after hearing [6.6]

DAYS

Where target times are expressed in days, the days are "court business days" in accordance with the Rules (principles of application para 10)

STEP 1: The Application

Objective — Target time: by DAY 3

To provide sufficient information about the Local Authority's (LA) case to enable:

- The parties and the Court to identify the issues
- The Court to make early welfare and case management decisions about the child

	Action	Party and Timing	
1.1	LA Application When a decision is made to apply for a care or supervision order the LA shall: • File with the Court an application in form C1 • Set out in form C13 under 'Reasons' a summary of all facts and matters relied upon, in particular, those necessary to satisfy the threshold criteria and/or • Refer in the Reasons to any annexed schedules setting out the facts and matters relied upon • Not state that the Reasons are those contained in the evidence filed or to be filed.	LA	on DAY 1
1.2	Directions on Issue On the day the application is filed (DAY 1) the Court shall: • Issue the application • Issue a notice in form C6 to the LA fixing a time and a date for the First Hearing which shall be not later than on DAY 6 • Appoint a Guardian (unless satisfied that it is not necessary to do so to safeguard the child's interests) • Inform CAFCASS of the decision to appoint and the request to allocate a Guardian	Court	on DAY 1

	Action	Party and Timing	
1.3	Allocation of the Guardian by CAFCASS Within 2 days of issue (by DAY 3) CAFCASS shall inform the Court of: • The name of the allocated Guardian or • The likely date upon which an application will be made.	CAFCASS	by DAY 3
1.4	Appointment of the Solicitor for the Child When a Guardian is allocated the Guardian shall on that day: • Appoint a solicitor for the child • Inform the Court of the name of the solicitor appointed • In the event that the Guardian's allocation is delayed and the Court has already appointed a solicitor, ensure that effective legal representation is maintained	Guardian	on DAY 3
	Where a Guardian is not allocated within 2 days of issue, the Court shall on DAY 3: • Consider when a Guardian will be allocated • Decide whether to appoint a solicitor for the child	FPC	on DAY 3
	In any event on the day the appointment is made the Court shall: • Notify all parties on form C47 of the names of the Guardian and/or the solicitor for the child who have been appointed.	FPC	on DAY 3
1.5	LA Documents Within 2 days of issue (by DAY 3) the LA shall file and serve on all parties, the solicitor for the child and CAFCASS the following documents: • The forms Cl and C13 and any supplementary forms and notices issued by the Court • Any relevant court orders relating to the child (together with the relevant Justices Facts and Reasons in form C22 and any relevant judgments that exist)	LA	by DAY 3

Action	Party and Timing
• The initial social work statement (appendix B/3) • The social work chronology (appendix B/2) • The core or initial assessment reports (appendix F) • Any other additional evidence including specialist assessments or reports which then exist and which are relied upon by the LA.	

STEP 2: The First Hearing in the FPC

Objective — Target time: by DAY 6

To decide what immediate steps are necessary to safeguard the welfare of the child by:

- Determining contested interim care order applications/with whom the child will live
- Identifying how to prevent delay
- Identifying the appropriate Court
- Transferring to the appropriate Court

	Action	Party and Timing	
2.1	**The First Hearing**	FPC	on DAY 6
	The First Hearing shall take place in the Family Proceedings Court (FPC) on or before **DAY 6**. At every First Hearing the **FPC** shall: • Consider who should be a **party** to the proceedings (step 2.2) • Make arrangements for contested **interim care applications** to be determined (step 2.3) • Consider whether the proceedings should be **transferred** to the Care Centre or another FPC (step 2.4) • Where the proceedings are not transferred, make **initial case management** decisions (step 2.6).		

	Action	Party and Timing	
2.2	**Parties and Service** At the First Hearing the **FPC** shall: • Obtain confirmation that all those who are entitled to be parties have been served • Consider whether any other person should be joined as a party • Give directions relating to party status and the service of documents upon parties.	FPC	on DAY 6
2.3	**Contested Interim Care Orders** In any proceedings where the application for an interim care order (ICO) is not agreed at the First Hearing, the **FPC** shall: • Decide whether to grant an order and if so what order; or • List the application for an urgent contested interim hearing in an FPC prior to the Case Management Conference (CMC); and • Give such case management directions as are necessary to ensure that the interim hearing will be effective; or • Transfer the proceedings to be heard at the Care Centre.	FPC	on DAY 6
2.4	**Urgency and Transfer** At the First Hearing the **FPC** shall: • Hear submissions as to complexity, gravity and urgency • Consider whether transfer to another Court is appropriate and in any event determine any application made by a party for transfer • Give reasons for any transfer decision made and record the information provided by the parties relating to transfer on **form C22** (including any intention to apply for transfer to the High Court) • Send the court file and the Order of transfer in **form C49** to the receiving court within **1 day** of the First Hearing (by **DAY 7**)	FPC	on DAY 6

	Action	Party and Timing
2.5	**Proceedings Transferred to the Care Centre** Where a decision is made to transfer to the Care Centre, the **FPC** shall: • In accordance with the arrangements set out in the **Care Centre Plan** (CCP) and the **FPC Plan** (FPCP) (**appendix E**), immediately inform the court officer at the Care Centre of the transfer and of the reasons set out on **form C22** • Obtain a date and time from the court officer for an **Allocation Hearing**/contested interim hearing in the Care Centre which shall be between **3** and **5** days of the decision to transfer (by **DAY 11**) • Notify the parties of the Care Centre to which the proceedings are transferred and of the date and time of the Allocation Hearing/contested interim hearing • Direct the LA or the child's solicitor to prepare a **case synopsis (appendix B/1)** which shall be filed with the Care Centre and served within **2 days** of the First Hearing in the FPC (by **DAY 8**) • Except as to disclosure of documents, make only those **case management directions upon transfer** as are agreed with the Care Centre as set out in the CCP and the FPCP.	FPC on DAY 6
2.6	**Case Management in the FPC** In any case where the proceedings are **NOT** transferred to the care centre the **FPC** shall at the First Hearing: • Consider the **case management checklist (appendix A/3)** • Fix a date and time for a **Case Management Conference** (CMC) in the FPC within **54 days** of the First Hearing (between **DAYS 15 and 60**) unless all of the case management decisions set out at step 4.8 of this protocol can be taken at the First Hearing and the application can be listed for Final Hearing	FPC on DAY 6

	Action	Party and Timing
	• Fix a date for the **Final Hearing** or if it is not possible to do so fix a hearing window (either of which shall be not later than in the **3 week** period commencing the **37th WEEK** after the application was issued) • Consider whether a **Pre Hearing Review** (PHR) is necessary and if so fix a PHR not later than **2 weeks** and no earlier than **8 weeks** before the Final Hearing date/window • Give such **case management directions** as are necessary to ensure that all steps will have been taken prior to the CMC to enable it to be effective, in particular: • that a **statement of evidence** from each party (including the child where of sufficient age and understanding, but excluding the child's Guardian) is filed and served replying to the facts alleged and the proposals made by the LA in the initial social work statement • whether directions as to full and frank **disclosure** of all relevant documents need to be given and in any event give directions where necessary to ensure that the disclosure of relevant documents by the LA occurs within **20 days** of the First Hearing (by **DAY 26**) • whether a **core assessment (appendix F)** exists or should be directed to be undertaken by the LA before the CMC • Record on the **Standard Directions Form (SDF) (appendix A/1)** the Court's case management decisions and reasons and serve the directions given on the parties	
2.7	The **FPC** shall give a direction at the First Hearing that **no further documents** shall be filed without the Court's permission unless in support of a new application or in accordance with case management directions given at that hearing (the Court will consider directions relating to the filing of comprehensive evidence and documents at the CMC)	

STEP 3: Allocation Hearing & Directions

Objective — Target time: by DAY 11

To make provision for continuous and consistent judicial case management

	Action	Party and Timing	
3.1	Following Transfer Following transfer to the Care Centre or to the High Court all further hearings in the proceedings shall be conducted: • So as to ensure judicial continuity of case management in accordance with the protocol; • By one or not more than 2 judges who are identified as case management judges in the CCP (appendix E/1), one of whom may be and where possible should be the judge who will conduct the Final Hearing	Care Centre	from DAY 6
3.2	Allocation in the Care Centre Within 2 days of the order transferring proceedings to the Care Centre (normally by DAY 8) the court officer shall: • Allocate one and not more than two case management judges (one of whom may be and where possible should be the Judge who will conduct the Final Hearing) to case manage the proceedings in accordance with the protocol and the CCP • Where possible, identify the judge who is to be the Final Hearing judge • Upon receipt of the court file from the FPC, attach to the file the form C22 issued by the FPC, the case synopsis (appendix B/1) and a Standard Directions Form (SDF) (appendix A/1) and complete the SDF to the extent only of: • the names of the allocated and identified judges	Court Officer	by DAY 8

	Action	Party and Timing	
	• the proposed date of the CMC (which shall be within 54 days of the date of the First Hearing in the FPC ie between DAYS 15 and 60) • the proposed Final Hearing date or hearing window (which shall be not later than in the 3 week period commencing the 37th WEEK after the application was issued) • the proposed date of the PHR (which shall be not later than 2 weeks and no earlier than 8 weeks before the Final Hearing/trial window) • Inform the case management judge in writing: • of any other circumstances of urgency • of any contested interim hearing for an ICO • of any application to transfer to the High Court • of the date and time of the Allocation Hearing (which shall be between 3 and 5 days of the First Hearing in the FPC ie by DAY 11) • Notify the parties of the date, time and venue fixed for the Allocation Hearing, together with the identity of the allocated/nominated judges		
3.3	Section 37 Request for a Report and Transfer to a Care Centre Where in any family proceedings a Court decides to direct an appropriate LA to investigate a child's circumstances, the Court shall follow the guidance set out at appendix G. Where, following a section 37 request for a report, proceedings are transferred to the Care Centre:	Court Officer	within 2 days of the order of transfer

	Action	Party and Timing	
	• The transferring court shall make a record of the Court's reasons for the transfer on form C22 and the court officer of the transferring court shall send the court file, the order of transfer in form C49 and the record of reasons to the Care Centre within 1 day of the order • The court officer in the care centre shall within 2 days of the order transferring the proceedings take the steps set out at paragraph 3.2 and shall also: • inform the case management judge in writing of the transfer (and such circumstances as are known) • request the case management judge to consider giving directions as to the appointment of a Guardian and/or a solicitor for the child at or before the Allocation Hearing • notify all parties on form C47 of the names of the Guardian and/or the solicitor for the child when they are appointed • inform the LA solicitor or the child's solicitor of the requirement that a case synopsis (appendix B/1) be prepared which shall be filed with the care centre and served not later than 2 days before the date fixed for the Allocation Hearing.		
3.4	Allocation Hearing The Allocation Hearing in the Care Centre shall take place between 3 and 5 days of the First Hearing in the FPC (by DAY 11). At the Allocation Hearing the case management judge shall: • Consider whether the proceedings should be transferred to the High Court or re-transferred to the FPC • Determine any contested interim application for a care or supervision order • Where the proceedings have been transferred from a court following a section 37 request consider:	Case Management Judge	by DAY 11

Action	Party and Timing
• whether directions should be given to appoint a Guardian and/or a solicitor for the child in accordance with steps 1.2 to 1.4 of the protocol • whether any directions need to be given for the filing and service of LA documents in accordance with step 1.5 of the protocol • Consider the case management checklist (appendix A/3) • Fix a date and time for a CMC which shall be within 54 days of the First Hearing in the FPC (between DAYS 15 and 60) • Fix a date for the Final Hearing and confirm the identity of the Final Hearing judge or if it is not possible to do so fix a hearing window (either of which shall be not later than in the 3 week period commencing the 37th WEEK after the application was issued) • Fix a date and time for a PHR which shall be not later than 2 weeks and no earlier than 8 weeks before the Final Hearing date or window • Give such case management directions as are necessary to ensure that all steps will have been taken prior to the CMC to enable it to be effective, in particular: • that a statement of evidence from each party (including the child where of sufficient age and understanding, but excluding the child's Guardian) is filed and served replying to the facts alleged and the proposals made by the LA in the initial social work statement • whether directions as to full and frank disclosure of all relevant documents need to be given and in any event give directions where necessary to ensure that the disclosure of relevant documents by the LA occurs within 20 days of the First Hearing (by DAY 26)	

	Action	Party and Timing	
	• whether a core assessment (appendix F) exists or should be directed to be undertaken by the LA before the CMC • Having regard to the *Practice Direction* (*Family Proceedings: Court Bundles*) [2000] 1 FLR 536 (appendix D), if applicable, give directions to the LA setting out which of the following case management documents in addition to the case management questionnaire (appendix A/2) are to be filed and served for use at the CMC: • a schedule of findings of fact which the Court is invited to make (in particular so as to satisfy the threshold criteria) • any update to the social work chronology (appendix B/2) that may be required • the initial care plan (appendix F) • if there is a question of law; a skeleton argument with authorities • a summary of the background (only if necessary to supplement the case synopsis) • an advocate's chronology (only if necessary to supplement the social work chronology or the case synopsis) • Having regard to appendix D, give directions to the LA setting out the form of bundle or documents index that the Court requires • Complete the SDF (appendix A/1) to record the Court's case management decisions and reasons.		
3.5	Case Management Questionnaire Within 1 day of the Allocation Hearing (on DAY 12) the court officer shall serve on each party: • the completed SDF together with a • case management questionnaire (appendix A/2).	Court Officer	on DAY 12

	Action	Party and Timing
3.6	Allocation in the High Court Where an application is transferred to the High Court, the court officer shall within 1 day of the Allocation Hearing (on DAY 12): • In consultation with the Family Division Liaison Judge (or if the proceedings are transferred to the RCJ, the Clerk of the Rules) allocate a judge of the High Court who shall be the case management judge (and who may be the judge who will conduct the final hearing) to case manage the proceedings in accordance with the protocol and the CCP • If necessary to accord with the CCP, allocate a second case management judge in the Care Centre who shall be responsible to the allocated High Court judge for case management of the proceedings • Where possible, identify a judge of the High Court to be the Final Hearing judge • Attach to the court file the form C22 issued by the FPC, the case synopsis (appendix B/1) and a SDF (appendix A/1) and complete the SDF to the extent only of: • the names of the allocated judges • the date of the CMC (which shall be within 54 days of the date of the First Hearing in the FPC ie between DAYS 15 and 60) • the proposed Final Hearing date or window (which shall be not later than in the 3 week period commencing the 37th WEEK after the application was issued) Action • the proposed date of the PHR (which shall be not later than 2 weeks and no earlier than 8 weeks before the Final Hearing or window) • Inform the case management judge in writing of: • any other circumstance of urgency	Court Officer on DAY 12

	Action	Party and Timing	
	• any contested hearing for an ICO		
	• Within 1 day of receipt of the court file and completed SDF from the allocated High Court judge (by DAY 16), send to each party a copy of the completed SDF together with a case management questionnaire (appendix A/2)	Court Officer	on DAY 16
3.7	Allocation Directions in the High Court	Case Management Judge	by DAY 15
	Within 3 days of receipt of the court file (by DAY 15) the allocated case management judge shall:		
	• Consider the case management checklist (appendix A/3)		
	• Complete the SDF (appendix A/1) having regard to those matters set out at step 3.4		
	• Return the court file and the completed SDF to the court officer.		

STEP 4: The Case Management Conference

Objective	Target time: between DAYS 15 and 60

To consider what case management directions are necessary

- To ensure that a fair hearing of the proceedings takes place
- To timetable the proceedings so that the Final Hearing is completed within or before the recommended hearing window

	Action	Party and Timing	
4.1	**LA Case Management Documents** In every case the **LA** shall not later than **5 days** before the CMC prepare, paginate, index, file and serve: • The **case management documents** for the CMC that have been directed at the Allocation Hearing/Directions (step 3.4) and • A **case management questionnaire (appendix A/2)**	LA	**not later than 5 days before the CMC**
4.2	**The Court Bundle** Not later than **5 days** before the date fixed for the CMC, the **LA** shall: • For hearings to which the *Practice Direction* (*Family Proceedings: Court Bundles*) [2000] 1 FLR 536 (**appendix D**) applies or in accordance with any direction given at a First Hearing or Allocation Hearing, file with the Court a **bundle** • Serve on each of the represented parties an **index** to the bundle • Serve on any un-represented party a copy indexed bundle • For hearings to which **appendix D does not apply**, serve on all parties an **index** of the documents that have been filed	LA	**not later than 5 days before the CMC**
4.3	**Other Party's Case Management Documents** Not later than **2 days** before the date of the CMC **each party other than the LA** shall: • File with the court and serve on the parties the following **case management documents**	All Parties except the LA	**not later than 2 days before the CMC**

	Action	Party and Timing	
	• a **position statement** which sets out that party's response to the case management documents filed by the LA indicating the issues that are agreed and those that are not agreed. (A Guardian's position statement on behalf of the child should comment on the LA's arrangements and plans for the child) • a completed **case management questionnaire (appendix A/2)** • **Not** file any **other case management documents** without the prior direction of the Court		
4.4	**The Court's Preparation** Not later than 2 days before the CMC the court officer shall: • Place the **case management documents of all parties** at the front of the court file and at the front of any bundle that is filed by the LA • Deliver the court file and bundle to the case management judge who is to conduct the CMC • Ensure that any arrangements for video and telephone conferencing and with criminal and civil listing officers have been made	Court Officer	**not later than 2 days before the CMC**
4.5	**Advocates Meeting** Before **the day** fixed for the **CMC** or (where it has not been practicable to have an earlier meeting) not later than **1 hour** before the time fixed for the CMC, the **parties and/or their lawyers** shall: • Meet to **identify and narrow the issues** in the case • Consider the **case management checklist (appendix A/3)** • Consider the **case management questionnaires (appendix A/2)**	Advocates	**on or before the day of the CMC**

	Action	Party and Timing
	• Consider in accordance with the **experts code of guidance (appendix C)** whether and if so why any application is to be made to instruct an **expert** • Consider whether full and frank **disclosure** of all relevant documents has taken place • Draft a composite **schedule of issues (appendix B/4)** which identifies: • a summary of the issues in the case • a summary of issues for determination at the CMC by reference to the case management questionnaires/case management checklist • the timetable of legal and social work steps proposed • the estimated length of hearing of the PHR and of the Final Hearing • the order which the Court will be invited to make at the CMC	All Parties **on DAY 34**
4.6	**Availability** On **the day** of the CMC **the parties** shall complete and file with the Court: • **witness non-availability form (appendix A/4)** • A schedule (so far as it is known) of the names and contact details (professional address, telephone, fax, DX and e-mail) of: • the lead social worker and team manager • the Guardian • solicitors and counsel/advocates for each party • un-represented litigants • any experts upon whose evidence it is proposed to rely	

	Action	Party and Timing
4.7	**Conduct of the CMC** The CMC shall be conducted by one of the allocated case management judges or as directed by the FPC case management legal adviser in accordance with the protocol. It is the essence of the protocol that case management through to Final Hearing must be consistently provided by the same case management judges/legal advisers/FPCs. All advocates who are retained to have conduct of the final hearing shall: • Use their best endeavours to attend the CMC and must do so if directed by the Court • Bring to the CMC details of their own availability for the 12 month period following the CMC • Attend the advocates meeting before the CMC	
4.8	**The Hearing** At the CMC the **case management judge/court** shall: • Consider the parties' composite **schedule of issues (appendix B/4)** • Consider the **case management checklist (appendix A/3)** • Consider the parties' **case management questionnaires (appendix A/2)** and **case management documents** (steps 3.4 and 4.3) • If not already fixed at the First or Allocation Hearing, fix the date of the **Final Hearing** which shall be not later than in the **3 week** period commencing the **37th WEEK** after the application was issued	Case Management Judge

Action	Party and Timing
• If not already fixed, fix the date and time of the **PHR** which shall be not later than **2 weeks** before and no earlier than **8 weeks** before the Final Hearing • Give a **time estimate** for each hearing that has been fixed Consider whether any hearing can take place using video, telephone or other **electronic means** • Consider any outstanding application of which notice has been given to the Court and to the parties in accordance with the rules • Give all necessary **case management directions** to: • **timetable** all remaining legal and social work steps • ensure that full and frank **disclosure** of all relevant documents is complete • ensure that a **core assessment (appendix F)** or other appropriate assessments materials will be available to the Court • ensure that if any **expert** is to be instructed the expert and the parties will complete their work for the Court within the Court's timetable and in accordance with the **experts code of guidance (appendix C)** • provide for **regular monitoring** of the Court's case management directions to include certification of compliance at each ICO renewal and the notification to the Court by the Guardian and by each responsible party of any material non compliance • permit a **further directions hearing** before the allocated case management judge in the event of a change of circumstances or significant non compliance with the directions of the Court	

Action	Party and Timing
• update, file and serve such of the **existing case management documents** as are necessary • update, file and serve a **court bundle/index** for the PHR and for the final Hearing • ensure that the PHR and Final Hearing will be effective	

STEP 5: The Pre-Hearing Review

Objective

Target time: by WEEK 37

To identify and narrow the remaining issues between the parties and ensure that the Final Hearing is effective

	Action	Party and Timing	
5.1	**The Court's Preparation** The **court officer** shall: • In circumstances where **no PHR direction** has been given, send the court file/bundle to the case management judge during **WEEK 28** with a request for confirmation that no PHR is necessary or for a direction that a PHR be listed • **Notify** the parties of any **PHR direction** given by the case management judge • **List a PHR** where directions have been given by the case management judge (not earlier than **8 weeks** and not later than **2 weeks** before the Final Hearing ie between **WEEKS 29 and 37**) • Not later than **2 days** before the PHR: • place the **updated case management documents** directed at the CMC (if any) at the front of the court file and at the front of any bundle that is filed by the LA • deliver the court file/bundle to the judge/FPC nominated to conduct the PHR	Court Officer	**from WEEK 28**

	Action	Party and Timing	
	• ensure that any arrangements for video and telephone conferencing and with criminal and civil listing officers have been made		
5.2	**Advocates Meeting** In the **week** before the PHR **the advocates** who have conduct of the **Final Hearing** shall: • Communicate with each other and if necessary meet to **identify and narrow the issues** to be considered by the Court at the PHR and the Final Hearing • Consider the **pre-hearing review checklist (appendix A/5)** • **2 days** before the PHR file a composite **schedule of issues (appendix B/4)** which shall set out: • a summary of issues in the case • a summary of issues for determination at the PHR • a draft witness template • the revised estimated length of hearing of the Final Hearing • whether the proceedings are ready to be heard and if not, what steps need to be taken at the PHR to ensure that the proceedings can be heard on the date fixed for the Final Hearing • the order which the Court will be invited to make at the PHR	Advocates	**in the week before the PHR**
5.3	**Case Management Documents** **No case management documents** are to be filed for use at a PHR except: • Any **updated case management documents** directed by the case management judge at the CMC (step 4.8) • The composite **schedule of issues (appendix B/4)** • Documents in support of a **new application**.	Advocates	**between WEEKS 29 and 30**

	Action	Party and Timing	
5.4	**Conduct of the PHR** The **PHR** (or any directions hearing in the FPC which immediately precedes a Final Hearing) shall be listed before the judge/FPC nominated to conduct the Final Hearing. In exceptional circumstances the Court may in advance approve the release of the PHR but only to one of the allocated case management judges. The **advocates** who are retained to have conduct of the Final Hearing shall: • Use their best endeavours to secure their release from any other professional obligation to enable them to attend the PHR • Update the case management documents as directed at the CMC • Attend the advocates meeting.		
5.5	**The Hearing** At the PHR the **Court** shall: • Consider the **pre-hearing review checklist (appendix A/5)** • Consider the parties' composite **schedule of issues (appendix B/4)** • Confirm or give a **revised time estimate** for the Final Hearing • Confirm the **fixed dates, venues and the nominated judge** for the Final Hearing • Give such directions as are necessary to **update the existing case management documents** and the Court **bundle/index** having regard to the application of the *Practice Direction* (*Family Proceedings: Court Bundles*) [2000] 1 FLR 536 **(appendix D)** • Give such directions as are necessary to ensure that the Final Hearing will be effective	Court	**at the PHR**
5.6	**Dispensing with the PHR** Where the requirements of an advocates meeting have been complied with and all parties certify (in the composite **schedule of issues**) that:	All Parties	**before the PHR**

	Action	Party and Timing
	• The proceedings are ready to be heard • There has been compliance with the directions of the Court and • There is agreement by all parties to all of the directions proposed having regard to the **pre-hearing review checklist (appendix A/5)** The Court may decide to **dispense with the PHR** or deal with it on paper or by electronic means, including computer, video or telephone conferencing	

STEP 6: The Final Hearing

Objective — Target time: by WEEK 40

To determine the remaining issues between the parties

	Action	Party and Timing	
6.1	**The Hearing** • The judge or FPC identified in the allocation directions as confirmed at the PHR Where one of the allocated case management judges or an FPC has heard a substantial factual issue or there has been a 'preliminary hearing' to determine findings of fact it is necessary for the same judge/magistrates who conducted the preliminary hearing to conduct the Final Hearing.	Judge/FPC nominated for the Final Hearing	
6.2	**Case Management and Practice Direction Documents** Not later than **2 days** before the Final Hearing **the parties** shall: • Prepare, file and serve the **case management documents** for the Final Hearing as directed by the Court at the PHR • Prepare, file and serve the **court bundle or index of court documents** as directed by the Court at the PHR	All Parties	**not later than 2 days before the Final Hearing**

	Action	Party and Timing	
6.3	**The Court's Preparation** Not later than 2 days before the Final Hearing the Court officer shall: • Place any **case management documents** at the front of the court file and at the front of any bundle that is filed by the LA • Deliver the **court file/bundle** to the judge/FPC nominated to conduct the Final Hearing • Ensure that any arrangements for the reception of evidence by video link and telephone conferencing, interpreters, facilities for disabled persons and special measures for vulnerable or intimidated witnesses have been made	Court Officer	**not later than 2 days before the Final Hearing**
6.4	**Orders and Reasons** At the conclusion of the Final Hearing the **Court** shall: • Set out the basis/reasons for the orders made or applications refused in a **judgment** and where appropriate in the form of **recitals** to the order or in the case of an FPC in **form C22** • Annexe to the order the **agreed or approved documents** setting out the threshold criteria and the care plan for the child • Where the judgment is not in writing give consideration to whether there should be a **transcript** and if so who will obtain and pay for it	Court	**at the Final Hearing**
6.5	**Reserved judgment** In a complex case a judge (but not an FPC) may decide to reserve judgment and take time for consideration. Where judgment is reserved the Court will endeavour to fix a date for judgment to be given or handed down within **20 days** (4 weeks) of the conclusion of submissions. Advocates may be invited to make oral or written submissions as to consequential orders and directions at the conclusion of submissions or when the draft judgment is released.	Judge	**at the end of submissions**

	Action	Party and Timing	
6.6	**Disclosure** At the end of every Final Hearing the **Court** shall consider whether to give directions for **disclosure of documents**, for example: • In any case where it is proposed that the child should be placed for adoption and so that subsequent adoption proceedings are not delayed, to the LA adoption panel, specialist adoption agency and/or proposed adopters and their legal advisers for use in subsequent adoption proceedings • For any medical or therapeutic purpose • For a claim to be made to the CICA	Court	**at the end of the Final Hearing**

Appendix 6

FRAMEWORK FOR THE ASSESSMENT OF CHILDREN IN NEED AND THEIR FAMILIES

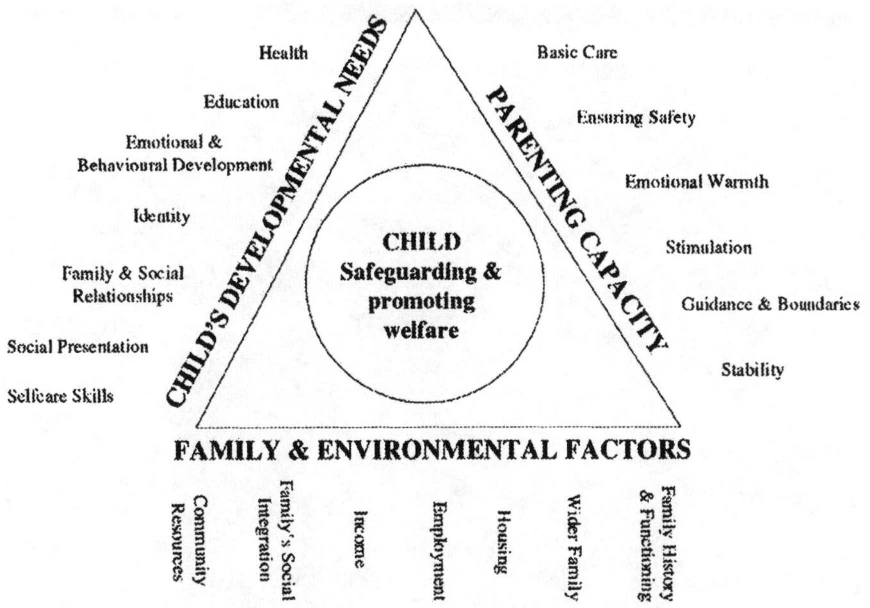

Appendix 7

SCHEDULE OF ITEMS IN RELATION TO THE EXERCISE OF PARENTAL RESPONSIBILITY

(1) Decisions that could be taken independently and without any consultation or notification to the other parent:

How the children are to spend their time during contact
Personal care for the children
Activities undertaken
Religious and spiritual pursuits
Continuance of medicine prescribed by GP.

(2) Decisions where one parent would always need to inform the other parent of the decision, but did not need to consult or take the other parent's views into account:

Medical treatment in an emergency
Booking holidays or to take the children abroad in contact time
Planned visits to the GP and the reasons for this.

(3) Decisions that you would need to both inform and consult the other parent prior to making the decision:

Schools the children are to attend, including admissions applications. With reference to which senior school C should attend this is to be decided taking into account C's own views and in consultation and with advice from her teachers
Contact rotas in school holidays
Planned medical and dental treatment
Stopping medication prescribed for the children
Attendance at school functions so they can be planned to avoid meetings wherever possible
Age that children should be able to watch videos, ie videos recommended for children over 12 and 18.

CHILD CARE AND ADOPTION LAW: INDEX